FAIR LENDING COMPLIANCE

T0271040

Wiley & SAS Business Series

The Wiley & SAS Business Series presents books that help senior-level managers with their critical management decisions.

Titles in the Wiley and SAS Business Series include:

Business Intelligence Competency Centers: A Team Approach to Maximizing Competitive Advantage, by Gloria J. Miller, Dagmar Brautigam, and Stefanie Gerlach

Case Studies in Performance Management: A Guide from the Experts, by Tony C. Adkins

CIO Best Practices: Enabling Strategic Value with Information Technology, by Joe Stenzel

Credit Risk Scorecards: Developing and Implementing Intelligent Credit Scoring, by Naeem Siddiqi

Customer Data Integration: Reaching a Single Version of the Truth, by Jill Dyche and Evan Levy

Information Revolution: Using the Information Evolution Model to Grow Your Business, by Jim Davis, Gloria J. Miller, and Allan Russell

Marketing Automation: Practical Steps to More Effective Direct Marketing, by Jeff LeSueur

Performance Management: Finding the Missing Pieces (to Close the Intelligence Gap), by Gary Cokins

For more information on any of the above titles, please visit **www.wiley.com**.

FAIR LENDING COMPLIANCE

INTELLIGENCE AND IMPLICATIONS FOR CREDIT RISK MANAGEMENT

CLARK R. ABRAHAMS
MINGYUAN ZHANG

BICENTENNIAL
BICENTENNIAL
1807
⊛WILEY
2007
BICENTENNIAL
BICENTENNIAL

JOHN WILEY & SONS, INC.

Library of Congress Cataloging-in-Publication Data:

Abrahams, Clark R., 1951—
        Fair lending compliance : intelligence and implications for credit risk management /
Clark R. Abrahams, Mingyuan Zhang.
             p. cm. —(Wiley & SAS business series)
        Includes index.
        ISBN 978-0-470-16776-2 (cloth)
        1. Credit—United States—Management. 2. Risk management—United States. 3. Bank
loans. I. Zhang, Mingyuan, 1960- II. Title.
        HG3754.5.U6A27 2008
        658.8′8—dc22

                                                              2007026259

Printed in the United States of America

10 9 8 7 6 5 4 3 2 1

CONTENTS

FOREWORD

Expanding economic opportunity to all segments has long been a policy objective in the American landscape. Its persistence over decades and across partisan lines speaks to the breadth and depth of support for this worthy goal. Currently, there are major shifts in how this objective can be achieved, largely as a result of the expansion of economic opportunities enabled by social and technological advances. What economic opportunity means today, with so many barriers lowered, is certainly different than how it was understood in earlier eras.

A crucial aspect of modern economic opportunity certainly has to be a person's ability to access mainstream finance. Despite the vast accomplishments of the American financial system, it has been estimated that approximately 35 million to 54 million people in the United States remain outside the credit mainstream. These failures of access for some speak as much to its importance as the remarkable improvements in access for countless more. For a variety of reasons, mainstream lenders have too little information on them to evaluate risk and thereby extend credit. These are the so-called "thin-file" and "no-file" Americans. Members of this group are disproportionately low-income earners, young, and ethnic minorities. Those in this group in need of credit often turn to check-cashing services, predatory lenders, and payday loan providers with effective interest rates as high as 500 percent.

The lack of reliable credit places them at a great disadvantage in building assets (such as homes, small businesses, loans for education, or auto loans) and thereby improving their lives. Mainstream lenders usually rely on credit history data found in credit files of the three major credit bureaus to determine whether and at what price credit should be extended. For millions of Americans who have not utilized mainstream credit, this creates a "credit catch-22"—you must have credit in order to get credit. The result of this dilemma is that many potentially credit-eligible borrowers are being denied credit owing to a lack of information, and not their actual credit profile.

A better solution may be to simply broaden the types of payment information reported to credit bureaus. Today, for instance, little utility and telecom payment data gets fully reported. And, although more difficult to collect, rental data also holds great promise. Such data cover a large portion of the population, including, and importantly, the segments of the population not covered well by traditional financial data already in credit files. And there are many other types of payments that are also likely to be valuable to some degree in assessing risk by demonstrating a degree of fiscal capacity and ability to make timely regular payments. Payments for cable, Internet, insurance, tuition, child care, remittances, and fixed payment cards represent just some of the more promising data sets.

Empirical research already conducted has confirmed the predictiveness of energy utility and telecom payment data with respect to future payment outcomes. And analysis has shown that the full reporting (positive and negative payment data) of nontraditional payment information to consumer reporting agencies (CRAs or credit bureaus) could help lift millions of Americans into the financial mainstream, essentially ensuring all telecom and utility customers are scoreable and have a credit file with a payment history. Since serious delinquencies in such payments are in many cases already reported to the bureaus either directly or indirectly, the challenge in these cases is really in having the on-time and moderately late payments also reported.

While bringing fully reported utility, telecom, and other alternative payment data online seems like a win-win-win scenario for all involved (the consumers, lenders, and the data furnisher's whose customers would have more of an incentive to pay on time), there are several obstacles.

One is a basic technological hurdle, collecting and standardizing the data to be furnished. For some industries, such as telecom and energy utilities, which are large, concentrated industries with relatively sophisticated billing systems, this is only a minor challenge. For other industries, such as apartment and house rentals or child care, this can be a significant challenge. Nonetheless, computing advances continue to reduce the cost of reporting.

Other hindrances to reporting are legislative and statutory prohibitions and uncertainties, particularly in the case of heavily regulated industries, like utilities and telecoms. Overcoming these requires getting out the message that the full reporting of customer payment data can greatly benefit underserved consumers without hurting other segments.

Another barrier deals with overcoming a lending culture that is comfortable with basing lending decisions on financial payment histories, but not as much with alternative payment histories. That is, financial institutions need to value this information and demand it from the bureaus. On the other side, the bureaus need to gather sufficient amounts of the alternative data to be able to demonstrate the value of the data to the financial institutions. This is a classic chicken-versus-egg problem.

It is absolutely crucial that financial institutions know what to do with alternative data and have the proper tools to optimally utilize this new information. These institutions are the end users of the alternative data and ultimately determine the data's value.

In the end, the potential benefits of alternative payment data that accrue to consumers, bureaus, data furnishers, and lenders is determined by how well the data are used. This is what makes Clark Abrahams and Mingyuan Zhang's work exciting and important for the many groups and organizations working to close the information gap for millions of Americans—and for the forward-thinking risk officers who are exploring how to maximize the value of emerging nontraditional data sets for their institution.

The scope of this book goes well beyond simply the creation of a tool for alternative payment data. It outlines a general and flexible framework for utilizing varying datasets, traditional and alternative, for assessing risk, pricing loans, accounting for information gaps, regulatory and internal policy compliance, model validation, segmentation analysis, and ensuring the appropriate information gets to the appropriate people in an organization. It emphasizes the overlap in these tasks and that all, optimally, require use of mostly the same underlying data, though to different degrees and in different combinations. Therefore, a single customizable framework, software, encompassing all the data can optimally perform each task and enable crucial linkages and analyses that involve multiple tasks. In other words, a single logical framework allows for analysis of and information on the big picture and to see how the various parts of problems and the organization work together.

The authors allow for sufficient flexibility, for instance, that lenders need not be forced to choose between flipping a switch and having a completely automated system decide loan approvals or making manual, judgmental decisions. Instead, a hybrid approach can be used in which a loan decision process is automated to some degree and manual to some degree. Such flexibility seems ideal in cases in which an organization is entering unfamiliar territory, either by entering new markets, expanding into underserved markets, or using new, alternative data.

At a larger level, the diffusion of these approaches—by lowering the hurdles to the use of new, alternative data and the construction of novel solutions—can help start a virtuous circle. Abrahams and Zhang's work allows for new experiments by enabling greater versatility to innovate, evaluate, and revise in easier, more creative, and more productive ways than ever before. Lenders, analytics experts, and policy makers will find in the pages that follow a promising start for a more financially inclusive society.

Michael A. Turner, PhD
President & Senior Scholar
The Political & Economic Research Council
Chapel Hill, North Carolina

PREFACE

There has been a growing emphasis in the banking compliance profession surrounding the convergence of risk management and compliance. Over the past decade, regulatory compliance examinations have adopted more of a risk-based examination approach, especially for larger and more complex enterprises. Our focus here is specific to fair lending compliance, and consumer and small business credit risk management. In this book we introduce some new applications of quantitative approaches for fair lending analysis, suggest an alternative credit approval model for all consumer and small business loans, and explore the interplay between the two areas using various segmentation schemes. In doing so, we want to help the reader make new connections between compliance and credit risk management and, as a result, see new possibilities for improving their current practices. We offer alternative loan underwriting models that we believe will support safe and sound lending while providing a more flexible process for qualifying creditworthy consumers, many of whom currently fall outside of the mainstream.

Lending has been around since the dawn of commerce. Initially, it was very localized and short term in nature. Early on, loans were often made based on a pledge of collateral (e.g., a loan for crop seed might be secured by livestock or a portion of land). Unsecured consumer and business loans were often made based on lender judgment, including factors such as overall wealth, social class, and the borrower's "good name." Over time, credit expanded as business franchises grew, and a better quality of life was possible via the acquisition of consumer goods that were affordable only via long-term financing. Today, the process for consumers, and to some extent businesses, to obtain financing to meet their needs is significantly driven by computerized statistical models. The practice of using credit scoring for consumer lending is widespread and well documented. Relative to small business lending, a recent survey[1] on the use of credit scoring found that nearly half of the respondents used credit scoring in loan underwriting. The consumer credit score of the owner(s) was the most prevalent one used. However, in nearly 20 percent of the cases where credit scoring was used, a business credit score was calculated and factored into the decision.

Looking to the future, there is increased pressure to further enhance the consumer and small business lending process for reasons of efficiency, and also compliance concerns around granting fair access to credit and the perceived objectivity afforded by the consistent application of empirically derived, statistically sound credit scoring models. Clearly, computer-based models represent a great advancement in many disciplines, including credit granting, loan portfolio management, and compliance testing. Among the many benefits that credit scoring has brought is the hastening of the development of the secondary market for consumer loans, which has provided needed liquidity to lenders who are able to risk-rate, price, and bundle loans for sale to investors in the capital market.

That said, in certain instances it may prove advantageous to exercise more control over the historically data-driven models, rather than letting those models dictate the outcome. Both judgmental and credit scoring approaches bear some weaknesses and strengths.[2] There is a bit of a conundrum here, namely "Would you rather (1) promote less efficient, more subjective, and less

---

1. Cowan, Charles D., and Adrian M. Cowan. *A Survey Based Assessment of Financial Institution Use of Credit Scoring for Small Business Lending*, United States Small Business Administration Office of Advocacy, November 2006.
2. See Exhibit 6.8 for strengths and weaknesses of all approaches.

consistent judgmental loan approval processes; or (2) rely entirely on data-driven scoring models? Fortunately, there is a way out of this conundrum, and we offer some solutions that can take advantage of the strengths associated with human judgment and computer models by means of a *hybrid approach*.

We assert that the motivation for considering, and ultimately embracing, these new approaches lies beyond process improvement for granting credit to *mainstream* consumers, although the business case is compelling enough to justify it. The real thrust for the timing of this technological change is the change in the consumer population itself, and the dynamics surrounding it, on which the standard current models may not fully capitalize. Consumer access to credit depends largely on point-scoring models that have evolved over the past several decades. A major premise of credit scoring models is that past performance determines future outcomes. Most credit models were developed based on samples that did not include unbanked population. This raises the question: "How can lenders qualify certain segments of the consumer population that have not historically been users of traditional credit, and hence do not have associated credit payment performance histories in credit bureau databases?" These models implicitly assume that unbanked people have no significant differences in credit characteristics from their mainstream counterparts. This assumption is not necessarily well founded and may hinder qualified consumers from accessing fair credit and meeting their financing needs. Credit market opportunities in emerging markets will be most heavily affected and this will further increase exposure to fair lending compliance violations.

A recent study conducted by the Political and Economic Research Council and the Brookings Institution Urban Markets Initiative confirmed that noncredit payment data can help predict credit risk.[3] Alternative data has always been around, but traditionally consumers have had to put themselves into debt and then make timely payments in order to demonstrate that they are creditworthy! Alternative data can be used to qualify consumers who pay their cash obligations as agreed, and its use represents the next logical step in the evolution of consumer credit models. Alternative data can help to speed the process of *mainstreaming* financially responsible cash-paying consumers whose dreams of a better life, including home ownership, continue to elude them. The propagation of new alternative credit models throughout the financial system will afford better and fairer chances for all borrowers and greater revenue for lenders, and deliver broader economic prosperity in communities across the nation. We recognize the importance of this work, and we share the enthusiasm and genuine excitement around this important development.

This book examines the connection between credit risk and fair lending compliance in order to allow a broader audience the opportunity to consider how prudent lending and fair and equal access to credit interrelate. Solutions are explored that enable lenders to profitably meet their regulatory and risk management guidelines. These solutions require a development methodology for achieving proper risk measurement and creating feedback mechanisms for continuous monitoring that will help to ensure fair banking compliance and accurate credit risk evaluation.

Advances in methodology can help lenders more effectively and efficiently manage credit and compliance risk while maximizing their shareholder returns. Key advances in this book include universal performance indicator (UPI), dynamic conditional process (DCP), risk evaluation/policy formulation system (REPFS),[4] multilayered segmentation (MLS), and the credit and compliance optimization process (CCOP). In particular, UPI provides a single measure of all risk exposures for easy, fast and thorough analysis, and deep understanding. DCP more closely captures business reality associated with lending to the unbanked, who lack sufficient amounts of credit history.

---

3. See Turner, Michael, S. Alyssa Lee, Ann Schnare, Robin Varghese, and Patrick D. Walker. "Give Credit Where Credit Is Due—Increasing Access to Affordable Mainstream Credit Using Alternative Data," Political and Economic Research Council and The Brookings Institution Urban Markets Initiative, ©2006.

4. REFPS is a particular instance, or form, within the general category of hybrid models. Hybrid models combine judgmental and quantitative approaches to decision making.

REPFS provides alternative underwriting and pricing models that can be used to quantify and monitor credit risk for consumer and small business markets. MLS provides critical context for compliance assessment and credit evaluation at various levels. CCOP seeks to balance dual objectives relating to risk-based fair lending. Collectively, these advances can help lending institutions strengthen their internal controls for identifying, measuring, evaluating, and monitoring risk.

PURPOSE OF THIS BOOK

This book attempts to bridge the gap between fair lending compliance and credit risk management by introducing several new methodologies and perspectives. The connection between fair lending compliance and credit risk management will be explored in new ways and sufficient detail to allow a broader audience the opportunity to consider how prudent lending and fair and equal access to credit "hang together." The end goal is to help a financial institution to develop a more effective risk management and compliance program so as to meet regulatory risk compliance requirements while growing revenue opportunities.

This objective can be addressed through the following ongoing initiatives:

- Thorough and simple monitoring, identification, and measurement of all relevant risks with particular emphasis on compliance and credit risks.
- Systematic analysis of risks to determine causality and develop mitigation strategies.
- Continuous improvement of lending practices and policies through adoption of risk evaluation processes that reflect economic, demographic, and market changes.
- Production of clear and consistent views of layers of outcomes, such as the individual consumer, household, neighborhood, and metropolitan area.
- Validation of risk evaluation processes to ensure that all elements of the credit risk management and loan compliance programs are maintained within appropriate tolerance levels.

ORGANIZATION OF TOPICS

The chapters in this book provide traditional approaches, coupled with several pioneering breakthroughs in methodology and technology, that can enable all stakeholders to gain a broader and deeper understanding of the subject matter and develop more effective, more efficient, and better-coordinated fair lending compliance self-assessment programs and credit risk management systems. Specifically, the following areas are covered:

Chapter 1 discusses how changes in America's demographic and economic trends create both regulatory challenges and market opportunities for lending institutions and how institutions can effectively respond to the changing environment and tap revenue potential. We try to establish why a change in thinking is particularly necessary now and explain how to make business cases for compliance risk management. It is important for a lending institution to develop a proactive compliance program and evaluate its maturity periodically in order to develop strategies to address any *compliance gaps* and improve return on compliance.

Chapter 2 includes overall fair lending compliance analysis methodology, components (including data, metadata, sampling, and business rules) and a strategy framework for approaching analysis. Included is a methodology and regulatory road map that specifies the appropriate approach for examining specific compliance areas that are covered in subsequent chapters. Similar coverage is provided relative to credit risk areas that can be addressed by quantitative approaches. Also emphasized is the need for information to be integrated from a variety of internal and external sources in order to build a complete and consistent view of the credit and compliance performance of the organization across customer groups, geographies, organizational entities, and so forth.

In Chapter 3, the analytic framework is initiated with a universal performance indicator approach. The goal is to obtain a comprehensive picture of overall compliance performance. This entails the exploration of a large amount of data and identification of risk focal points. This new methodology can help institutions evaluate overall business practices in any context with a standardized UPI that simultaneously rank-orders performance relative to all relevant factors.

If loan-pricing imbalances have surfaced and require further analysis, Chapter 4 provides a systematic approach for examining them and any contributing factors. The Federal Reserve's annual percentage rate spread tables and overage/underage analysis afford useful views along the path to understanding. Pitfalls to be avoided are revealed.

In case disparity persists, it is necessary to test for disparate treatment. While simple regression models can be used for this purpose, we introduce a new and powerful approach—the dynamic conditional process (DCP). This method is explained and illustrated in Chapter 5.

In Chapter 6, we introduce a hybrid model that affords qualitative benefits while preserving quantitative-based decision making. This approach has particular applicability to emerging markets. We address the compliance implications for credit risk management relative to consumer loan products, with examples drawn from mortgage, auto, credit card, and small business lending.

Proper segmentation is the key to getting good results, to validating those results, and to thoroughly and concisely explaining those results to all stakeholders. Chapter 7 integrates the key analysis methodologies discussed in the previous chapters into a critical unifying concept—the multilayered segmentation approach, which is used for risk and revenue evaluation and to formulate credit risk management strategies. This approach affords a complete and deep understanding of the driving forces behind outcomes and how those outcomes stack up against a variety of norms (historical, regulatory, market, industry, societal, economic) and both near-term and strategic goals (business, consumer, community, and local/state/federal government).

In Chapter 8, the topic of model validation is approached from both credit risk and compliance risk perspectives using an integrated analysis methodology. This integrated methodology uses the hybrid approach to perform a more comprehensive model validation in an intuitive way. Override analysis results are also integrated into this framework for compliance monitoring. A credit and compliance optimization process is offered for consideration as a unifying concept, and we describe how the UPI can play a role in model validation reporting.

WHO CAN BENEFIT FROM THIS BOOK

This book was written to address the needs of several audiences, from corporate executives to corporate and divisional compliance staff, loan officers, credit risk managers, and information technology (IT) professionals, as well as regulators, lawyers, legislators, and enforcement agencies at the federal and state government levels. In fact, this book can benefit all credit consumers, including entrepreneurs, because it provides them with the opportunity to develop a deeper understanding of loan evaluation processes and possible alternatives.

The book has sufficient technical material and references to be helpful to researchers and practitioners, but the concepts and methods are accessible to nontechnical readers who may wish to skip many of the details.

ACKNOWLEDGMENTS

We want to recognize Julie Platt, Jeff Hasmann, Jonathan Hornby, and Bob Tschudi for their assistance with the initial review of this book. We extend our deep appreciation to Robert Chu, Jeff Gilleland, Fiona McNeill, Naeem Siddiqi, John Talmage, Michael Turner, Robin Varghese, and Patrick Walker for their comments and suggestions based upon a detailed review of the manuscript. We are also indebted to John West for his guidance and coordination throughout on this effort.

Finally, we wish to thank Jim Goodnight for his unwavering support and encouragement of our research, and also for his direct input on some of the analytics.

FAIR LENDING COMPLIANCE

1

CREDIT ACCESS AND CREDIT RISK

Understanding the connection between credit access and credit risk is the key to developing a new generation of models and processes that preserve safe and sound lending while promoting inclusiveness in the credit market.[1] In this book, a chief goal is to explore the overlap between fair lending and credit risk in order for lenders to provide greater and more affordable access to credit while operating within acceptable risk/return thresholds. Specifically, we can describe each of these two credit-related areas and their connection as follows:

- *Credit access.* There are laws and regulations in place that are aimed at ensuring and monitoring fair access to credit.[2] Those laws and regulations spell out specific protected classes of consumers whose class membership cannot be considered as a factor in the lending process. Financial institutions have fair lending programs that are designed to help avoid any violations of those laws and regulations. The main thrust of a fair lending compliance program is to find and fix problems associated with credit access[3] and to effectively communicate performance to stakeholders in order to avoid or correct any misperceptions about the institution's lending performance.
- *Credit risk.* Regulators conduct periodic safety and soundness exams to review bank underwriting standards, among other things. Lenders have credit policies that spell out those standards, which reflect the institution's actual loan default experience and best judgment to ensure profitable, safe, and sound lending. When it comes to consumer and some small business lending, the criteria for loan approval, and possibly pricing, may be embedded in a custom credit scoring model that takes into account a predetermined sufficient set of relevant factors.[4] Often, the credit bureau score is a prominent factor in making a credit decision.
- *The connection.* Clearly, credit access for a protected class of consumers is driven by the credit risk profile of that group, relative to the institution's credit underwriting and pricing criteria, and by the lender's credit product marketing efforts and practices in different geographic areas within the franchise in general, and relative to the group in question. Factors such as decline rate disparities, and disparities associated with the rate of "above threshold"

---

1. Dugan, John C., OCC Comptroller, discussed the interplay between fair credit access and credit risk management. See Remarks for the OCC Workshop on Credit Scoring Model Validation in February 3, 2006, p. 7.
2. For example, Regulation B–Equal Credit Opportunity Act, the Fair Housing Act, Regulation C—Home Mortgage Disclosure Act, and Regulation BB—Community Reinvestment Act.
3. The term *credit access* is used in the broadest sense here to include pricing, marketing, steering, and redlining in addition to the actual granting of a loan (approve/decline decision).
4. The object of the credit granting exercise is to figure out the odds that someone is going to repay the debt as agreed and to decide accordingly on whether or not to grant the loan. Other details, such as pricing and terms associated with the transaction, are usually determined concurrently with the credit-granting decision. Credit can be tightened or loosened by adjusting the scorecard cutoff for credit approval.

1

loans, for protected versus nonprotected classes of consumers, are used to identify potential problems associated with credit risk evaluation. Factors such as disparities in market share and market penetration are indicators of potential problems associated with product marketing. Beneath the results layer, where problems surface, lies the proprietary decision layer. This is where risk is quantified and loan decision making is performed. It is also where consumer segmentation is performed and marketing strategies are developed and implemented. It is in this decision layer where art and science are used to address, in the most appropriate way, such things as incomplete information, missing data, new emerging populations, environmental socioeconomic changes, and changes in both the riskiness and prevalence of various distinct consumer and small business borrower profiles.

In the following sections, we describe the enterprise risk profile and the importance of an effective risk measurement system. Next, we review the evolution of some of the more relevant regulations, note some recent class action lawsuits for alleged consumer protection and fair lending violations, and share a brief outlook for future developments at the federal and state levels. We discuss how to prepare for the challenges created by changes in laws and regulations and markets with three fundamental principles that underpin corporate internal controls. Finally, we introduce return on compliance in terms of performance measurement and risk control, supported by a simple business case on fair lending technology investment.

ENTERPRISE RISK MANAGEMENT

Senior management and the board of directors of major financial institutions are charged with the following responsibilities relative to enterprise risk management (ERM) and compliance:

- Defining the risk management function itself and ensuring that the proper committee and organizational structures are in place to support ERM.
- Defining the corporation's risk preferences via risk policies and key risk measure tolerance specifications.
- Ensuring that staffing is adequate and appropriately skilled in risk management, and that the right incentives are in place.
- Making sure that adequate risk cushions exist to support both day-to-day operations and the firm's strategic business plan.
- Providing for employee training and development to foster organizational learning so as to lessen the likelihood of repeating past mistakes.
- Leading by example to mold the desired risk culture by effective communication and taking reinforcing actions.

The passage of the Sarbanes-Oxley Act in 2002 was brought about by serious concerns that resonated from regulators, stock exchanges, and institutional investors in the wake of corporate frauds and failures[5] (e.g., Barings Bank, Sumitomo, Enron, WorldCom, Adelphia) that saw billions of dollars in shareholder value vanish and threatened the stability of the equity markets. A resounding theme in these failures was ineffective management and board oversight of operations. Sarbanes-Oxley established new rules for corporate governance practices, and it has become increasingly important that corporations take notice and act to make any necessary improvements in their internal controls and external reporting. Consider the fact that interest rate risk on the balance sheets of consumers having adjustable rate mortgages is now translating to significant credit risk on lender balance sheets. By defining loan affordability and product suitability measures and

---

5. See *Testimony Concerning Implementation of the Sarbanes-Oxley Act of 2002*, William H. Donaldson, Chairman, U.S. Securities and Exchange Commission, September 9, 2003, www.sec.gov/news/testimony/090903tswhd.htm.

disparity indices, these risks could have been identified, monitored, and addressed prior to becoming a problem for the industry at large, and a concentration/asset quality issue for institutions in particular, who have seen their equity shares significantly decline in value.[6]

This book deals primarily with compliance and credit risk management, but we recognize that there is overlap between these two areas, and also spillover into other areas of risk. All financial institutions have internal controls in place that are designed to identify, measure, monitor, and control a variety of risks that fall into various broad categories.[7] An Office of the Comptroller of the Currency (OCC) handbook advises national banks that "Risk identification should be a continuing process, and should occur at both the transaction and portfolio level."[8] Risk identification is the main topic of Chapter 3 in this book, and we advocate a continuous, systematic process for examining lending patterns and loan performance in the aggregate (e.g., portfolio level). We also focus on loan decisioning, pricing, and marketing relative to both credit and compliance at the customer level. Measurement of risk is a demanding endeavor, and requires the use of statistical methods to help determine the significance and materiality of risk exposures. In the compliance realm, we devote several chapters to this topic. In the credit area, risk measurement sometimes requires the use of some fairly sophisticated mathematical algorithms to estimate the probability that a loan will default, or the extent to which the amount and timing of credit losses are likely caused by delinquency, or risk grade, migration. Concerning risk measurement, we cannot improve on the OCC's guidance:

> Accurate and timely measurement of risk is essential to effective risk management systems. A bank that does not have a risk measurement system has limited ability to control or monitor risk levels. Further, the more complex the risk, the more sophisticated should be the tools that measure it. A bank should periodically test to make sure that the measurement tools it uses are accurate.[9]

Risk monitoring should be performed regularly, with up-to-date information, and it should provide an accurate and consistent picture of risk exposures to all relevant stakeholders so that controls can be applied and so that any violations of policy, regulation, or law can be swiftly addressed. Some stakeholders may require less detail, but their higher-level picture should have the available dots behind it to connect to the more granular assessments and quantitative analyses.

At the enterprise, or highest, level, it is customary to periodically document the firm's risk profile as part of the capital plan. This corporate risk profile must have an accompanying explanation for the corporate capital plan's readership, namely the board of directors, regulators,[10] stock analysts, rating agencies,[11] and business partners. For example, Figure 1.1 depicts a sample risk profile.

While these categories of risk[12] are shown as distinct, they are interrelated. By recognizing their intersection points, their associated risks can be more effectively and efficiently managed. Operational risk is defined as the risk of failures, and losses, due to people, processes, or systems, and includes transaction risk. Compliance risk exposures can be measured relative to their associated business transactions and activities, for example, underwriting, loan pricing, marketing, and so forth. Compliance risk is interrelated with operational risk, and operational risk also can lead to market or credit risk.[13] This book focuses on major intersection points between credit risk and

6. Another crisis is unfolding in the subprime mortgage market for adjustable rate and option-priced loans that are repricing after a prolonged period of rising interest rates.
7. While there is no single categorization that has been adopted, the OCC's guidelines are used as a basis for the current discussion.
8. Administrator of National Banks, *Comptroller's Handbook for Large Bank Supervision*, United States of America Comptroller of the Currency, May 2001, pp. 5–6.
9. Ibid., p. 6. Chapters 4, 5, and 6 focus on risk measurement, with some elements on monitoring as well.
10. OCC, FDIC, Federal Reserve, OTS, SEC, State Banking Commissions, etc.
11. For example, Moody's, Standard & Poor's, Dun & Bradstreet.
12. For definitions of the risk categories, refer to Appendix 1A.
13. Jorion pointed that legal risk is often related to credit risk. See also Jorion, Philippe. *Value at Risk: The New Benchmark for Managing Financial Risk*, McGraw-Hill, 2007, pp. 22–27. Both Jorion and Duffie and Singleton,

Enterprise Risk Profile								
Risk Category	Quantity of Risk (Low, Moderate, High)		Quality of Risk Management (Weak, Satisfactory, Strong)		Aggregate Level of Risk (Low, Moderate, High)		Direction of Risk (Increasing, Stable, Decreasing)	
	OCC 6/30/07	Bank 6/30/07	OCC 6/30/07	Bank 6/30/07	OCC 6/30/07	Bank 6/30/07	OCC 6/30/07	Bank 6/30/07
Credit	Moderate	Moderate	Weak	Satisf.	High	Moderate	Increasing	Stable
Interest Rate	Moderate	Moderate	Satisf.	Satisf.	Moderate	Moderate	Stable	Stable
Liquidity	Low	Low	Strong	Strong	Low	Low	Stable	Stable
Price	Moderate	Moderate	Strong	Strong	Low	Low	Stable	Stable
Transaction	Moderate	Moderate	Satisf.	Satisf.	High	Moderate	Increasing	Stable
Compliance	High	High	Satisf.	Satisf.	High	High	Increasing	Increasing
Strategic					Moderate	Moderate	Increasing	Stable
Reputation					High	High	Increasing	Stable

FIGURE 1.1   CORPORATE RISK PROFILE

compliance risk and the opportunities they present for more integrated identification, measurement, monitoring, and control of associated risks. The outcome is stronger, more effective and more efficient internal controls for the enterprise.

LAWS AND REGULATIONS

Over the past 40 years, there have been many significant regulatory developments related to institutional lending practices and programs. During the period 1968–77, Congress enacted legislation designed to:

- Prohibit discrimination in the sale, rental, and financing of dwellings, and in other housing-related transactions.[14]
- Prohibit creditors from discriminating against credit applicants.[15]
- Increase lending to meet credit needs in underserved communities.[16]
- Collect data on loan applications[17] by census tract that, for the most part, are secured by residential real estate.[18]

---

categorized the risk faced by financial institutions into (1) market risk, (2) credit risk, (3) liquidity risk, and (4) operational risk (Duffie and Singleton also included systemic risk). They all considered regulatory and legal risk as part of operational risk. See Duffie and Singleton, *Credit Risk: Pricing, Measurement, and Management*, Princeton University Press, 2003, pp. 3–7.

14. Title VIII of the Civil Rights Act of 1968 (Fair Housing Act) Prohibited basis: race, color, national origin, religion, sex, familial status (including children under the age of 18 living with parents of legal custodians, pregnant women, and people securing custody of children under the age of 18), and handicap (disability).

15. Regulation B, the Equal Credit Opportunity Act (ECOA) of 1975. Prohibited basis: race, color, religion, national origin, sex, marital status, age, or because an applicant receives income from a public assistance program.

16. Regulation BB: Community Reinvestment Act (CRA) 1977.

17. Including actions taken on applications (i.e., origination, denial, incomplete, withdrawn, approved but not accepted, and loan purchased by institution).

18. Regulation C: Home Mortgage Disclosure Act (HMDA) 1975.

With the passage in 1980 of the Depository Institutions Deregulation and Monetary Control Act, state usury laws limiting rates lenders could charge on residential mortgage loans were preempted, which set the stage for a significantly broader pricing range for the subprime mortgage market. In 1989, Representative Joseph Kennedy (D-Massachusetts) obtained successful passage of an amendment to the Home Mortgage Disclosure Act (HMDA) that required reporting on loan applicant race and income. More recently, in 2002, HMDA was amended again to include loan pricing information for loans exceeding specific thresholds for spread over comparable-maturity treasury security yields.[19] The 2002 HMDA amendment took effect in 2004 for data reported in 2005 and thereafter. While the HMDA data do not represent a complete picture of lending practices, they are used by regulatory agencies as part of their screening activities for potential compliance violations, and the Federal Reserve Board issues an annual report on this data.[20]

Tom Miller, Attorney General of Iowa, in his keynote address at the 2007 Fair Lending Summit,[21] pointed to the convergence of consumer protection and fair lending/civil rights and he cited two issues driving the intersection. First, he pointed to the $295 million Ameriquest settlement.[22] While it is legal for lenders to charge what they want, selling tactics relative to representing costs to the borrower, and also cases where similarly situated borrowers in protected classes may appear to be charged more than their nonprotected class counterparts, can raise issues. Second, Attorney General Miller pointed to yield spread premiums (YSPs) for independent mortgage brokers, which are a source of compensation. If one to two points additional are charged to consumers and this practice is not evenly applied across the loan applicant base, especially if certain classes of applicants are more susceptible to accepting those costs, then this causes problems. The Ameriquest predatory lending practices case was not isolated. In fact, Attorney General Miller and his office led the national group that recently obtained the largest national consumer protection settlement ever with Household Finance, which totaled $484 million. Looking beyond the retrospective relief associated with these settlements, lenders are studying the injunctive relief that specifies going forward restrictions on business operations and practices, monitoring, and reporting requirements. Proactive lenders seize the opportunity to set the standard themselves, rather than waiting for injunctive relief on a future class action settlement to set the new standard.

Looking ahead, the prospect of Congress passing legislation on predatory lending appears to be strengthening, and as of March 2007, 27 states (including the District of Columbia) had already announced adoption or support[23] of the Conference of State Bank Supervisors/American Association of Residential Mortgage Regulators guidance on nontraditional mortgage product risks. These nontraditional mortgage products appear to present higher credit and compliance risk for both borrowers and lenders in subprime markets.

---

19. For first liens the trigger is three percent, while for subordinate liens the trigger is five percent. In 2002, the Board of Governors of the Federal Reserve System (FRB) issued several new regulatory changes, some of which became effective in 2004 (subject to 2005 filing), to improve the quality, consistency, and utility of the data reported under HMDA. The 2004 HMDA data, released to the public in the spring of 2005, was the first to reflect the new regulatory requirements and to include the pricing information.

20. Avery, Robert B., Glenn B. Canner, and Robert E. Cook. "New Information Reported under HMDA and Its Application in Fair Lending Enforcement," *Federal Reserve Bulletin*, 2005, pp. 344–394.

21. Miller, Tom. *The Emerging Nexus: Fair Lending Enforcement Issues and Enforcement with Consumer Protection Issues*, Keynote Address, Fair Lending Summit 2007, National Real Estate Development Center (NREDC), Washington, DC, March 26, 2007.

22. Attorney General Miller led the group of states bring action against the national lender.

23. Announcements ranged from "regulatory alerts" to "state guidance" to intent to "draft rules." Some states, including North Carolina (HB 1817), have passed predatory lending laws or amendments in 2007, and the Fair Mortgage Practices Act was introduced July 12, 2007 in the House of Representatives by House Financial Services Committee Ranking Member Spencer Bachus, and original cosponsors Reps. Paul Gillmor and Deborah Pryce. This particular piece of legislation aims to better protect homebuyers from predatory lending practices, with special focus to protecting the subprime market.

CHANGING MARKETS

The simple fact is that America's demographic, economic, and immigration trends over the past few decades have resulted in significant shifts in the pool of financial services consumers.[24] At the same time, gaps have persisted in such areas as home ownership. In 1949, when the Fair Housing Act was passed, there were approximately 43 million housing units and the national home ownership rate stood at 55 percent. Since that time, the number of housing units has more than tripled, while the home ownership rate has increased to 69 percent. Relative to race and ethnicity, the gap in rates is pronounced, and this is especially true for African-American and Hispanic consumers according to Figure 1.2 from the U.S. Census Bureau.

A fairly recent study indicated that Hispanic and Latino homeownership has been on the rise and could reach 60 percent by the year 2010.[25] In order for that to happen, the study points to the importance of continuing trends such as low interest rates and gains in education and income. It recommends creating a simpler and clearer home-buying and lending process and the adoption of more incentives for low-income and first-time home buyers. It also pointed out the importance of reducing the vulnerability of Hispanic consumers to predatory lending practices.[26] Measuring progress in the lending area requires the ability to properly interpret publicly reported information, such as the annual HMDA Peer Data made available by the Federal Reserve every year. Chapters 3 and 4 address approaches for analyzing HMDA data and combined data (internal, public, and third party). Detection of predatory lending patterns, and testing for potential fair lending compliance violations, are also covered in those chapters, as well as in Chapters 5, 6, and 8. Credit risk management and fair lending compliance go hand-in-hand, and lenders are increasingly required to communicate appropriately on both fronts to all stakeholders in a consistent, accurate, and timely manner.

	1996	1997	1998	1999	2000	2001	2002	2003	2004	2005
U.S. total	65.4	65.7	66.3	66.8	67.4	67.8	67.9	68.3	69.0	68.9
White	69.1	69.3	70.0	70.5	71.1	71.6	71.8	72.1	72.8	72.7
White non-Hispanic	71.7	72.0	72.6	73.2	73.8	74.3	74.5	75.4	76.0	75.8
Black	44.1	44.8	45.6	46.3	47.2	47.4	47.3	48.1	49.1	48.2
Other race	51.0	52.5	53.0	53.7	53.5	54.2	54.7	56.0	58.6	59.2
American Indian, Aleut, Eskimo	51.6	51.7	54.3	56.1	56.2	55.4	54.6	54.3	55.6	58.2
Asian, Pacific Islander	50.8	52.8	52.6	53.1	52.8	53.9	54.7	56.3	59.8	60.1
Hispanic	42.8	43.3	44.7	45.5	46.3	47.3	48.2	46.7	48.1	49.5
Non-Hispanic	67.4	67.8	68.3	68.9	69.5	69.9	70.0	70.8	71.5	71.2

FIGURE 1.2   HOME OWNERSHIP BY RACE AND ETHNICITY OF HOUSEHOLDER (1996–2005)[a]

[a]The home ownership rate is the percentage of home owning households in the given demographic group. Source is the U.S. Census Bureau Web: www.census.gov; Information Please ® Database © Pearson Education Inc.

---

24. According to the U.S. Census Bureau's Report on Minorities by County released August 9, 2007, approximately one in every 10 of the nation's 3,141 counties has a population that is greater than 50 percent minority.
25. Congressional Hispanic Caucus Institute HOGAR Initiative, *An Assessment of Hispanic Homeownership—Trends and Opportunities*, 2005, Section 1: Executive Summary, p. 3.
26. See Congressional Hispanic Caucus Institute, *National Housing Initiative Focus Group Findings: Cross-Site Report*, June 2004, findings from Atlanta, GA, Section IV Major Findings, Part B. Barriers to Homeownership, p. 36, for detailed supporting examples.

The number of consumers in the underserved market is in the tens of millions, with some portion falling into the underbanked or thin credit file category, and the rest is identified as unbanked.[27] By default, these consumers today may be denied credit or put into programs geared toward the subprime segment of the consumer credit pool. In the latter case, they are charged higher prices (rates, fees, margins) than those offered to "more established" consumers.[28]

Loan originators can significantly help provide fair access and pricing to individuals and households that fall outside of the more traditional credit-based financing model. In order to more rapidly assimilate the massive number of consumers who fall outside of the mainstream usage of credit, a key area is finding new ways to view and model their default risk. To do so, one must identify and tap alternative data sources that can provide significant information value relative to qualifying unbanked and underbanked consumers for financial products and services.[29] We recognize that some utility and other payment information has been available, and assessed to some degree, prior to this time. At least one of the major credit bureaus has maintained this type of information in some markets for over 20 years. In addition, a standard means for reporting alternative data has already been developed, for example, the Metro II format from the Service Bureau.[30] Over the past few years, the Information Policy Institute has conducted research on how underserved consumers can gain increased access to credit, especially in the area of nontraditional data.[31] Key findings of their latest study of 8 million credit files (including consumers with *thin files* or those that are *unscorable*) are that:

- There is similarity in risk profiles among traditional consumers and their nontraditional counterparts.
- Nontraditional data make extending credit easier.
- Minorities and the poor benefit more than expected from nontraditional data.
- Nontraditional data decrease credit risk and increase access.
- Nontraditional data has relatively little effect on the mainstream population.
- Scoring models can be improved with more comprehensive data.

---

27. "Lenders rely heavily on credit scores to make credit decisions. An estimated 32 million Americans, however, have credit files that do not have sufficient information to calculate standard credit scores. An additional 22 million have no files at all." See Afshar, Anna. "Use of Alternative Credit Data Offers Promise, Raises Issues," *New England Community Developments—Emerging Issues in Community Development and Consumer Affairs, Federal Reserve Bank of Boston*, Issue 1, Third Quarter 2005.

28. Studies have found that in case of "thin" or no credit history, minority applicants are more likely to be denied for a loan than nonminority applicants. For example, an analysis of the Boston Fed data (Han, Song, Learning and Statistical Discrimination in Lending, unpublished manuscript, 2002) found that, for the subsample with no credit history information, very large racial differences exist in underwriting outcomes, versus no racial differences for the subsample where information on credit history is available. This was termed as *statistical discrimination*. See also Ross, Stephen L. "What Is Known about Testing for Discrimination: Lessons Learned by Comparing across Different Markets," University of Connecticut Working Paper 2003-21, 2002, pp. 54–58. Another hypothesis that has been raised is that racial effects may be significant only for the financially disadvantaged subgroup. See Hunter, William C. and Mary Beth Walker. "The Cultural Affinity Hypothesis and Mortgage Lending Decisions," *Journal of Real Estate Finance and Economics*, Springer, vol. 13(1), 1996, pp. 57–70.

29. Afshar, 2005. Asfhar reports on alternative sources of payment data and that the "big three" national credit bureaus are beginning to investigate ways of expanding their own credit scoring models to include alternative data.

30. Using Metro II Credit Reporting Software, businesses report debtor and consumer accounts to the major credit reporting repositories. Supported industries include automobile dealers, finance companies, collection agencies, utilities, property management firms, banks, credit unions, mortgage companies, jewelry stores, government, law firms, educational institutions, medical billing agencies, and more.

31. See Turner, Michael, S. Alyssa Lee, Ann Schnare, Robin Varghese, and Patrick D. Walker. *Give Credit Where Credit Is Due: Increasing Access to Affordable Mainstream Credit Using Alternative Data*, Political and Economic Research Council and the Brookings Institution Urban Markets Initiative, December 2006; and Information Policy Institute, *Giving Underserved Consumers Better Access to the Credit System: The Promise of Non-Traditional Data*, July 2005.

Alternative information must be tapped that can be used to assess consumer riskiness; saving habits; employment stability; financial capacity; and breadth, depth, and history of relationships with providers of essentials (i.e., utilities, telecommunications, housing, transportation, etc.). Chapter 6 explores some new ways to develop models that can accommodate missing information and alternative data to help evaluate underserved and unbanked consumers for loans.

The foregoing discussion has touched on the "opportunity side" of compliance and risk management. Fair lending is no longer just a compliance issue. It has a significant impact on various aspects of an institution's business growth and operations. In particular, it will evolve to more directly affect an institution's marketing strategies and revenue-generating opportunities, largely through the evolution of a new generation of credit risk models and multilevel customer segmentation strategies.[32] These models and strategies will not only pertain to customers and the parameters of the financial transaction; they will span external factors in the macroeconomic, community-based, sociological, and cultural realms.

PREPARE FOR THE CHALLENGES

The foregoing discussion implies that institutions must effectively respond to the changing environment. Failure to do so can have serious consequences. From the view of the board of directors, the regulatory community, shareholders, and corporate management, the following are critical concerns that must be satisfied by any financial institution on a continual basis:

- Trust that financial performance results will be reported accurately and in a timely manner.
- Confidence in management's ability to swiftly detect and correct problems.
- Belief that the institution has processes and plans in place of sufficient quality to safeguard the operation, while providing a fair return to shareholders.
- Ability to achieve and maintain compliance with all applicable laws and regulations.
- Adequate internal control strength to ensure operational effectiveness and compliance with internal policies.
- Constantly strive for greater efficiency by identifying and eliminating redundant or unnecessary processes, people, and systems to ensure a streamlined organization.
- Mold a culture that is customer focused and results oriented, with individual accountability at all levels of the firm.

To ensure that these concerns are met, a financial institution's primary regulator will periodically conduct various exams to perform an independent verification. In order to avoid surprises in these exams, it is desirable to know ahead of time how well an institution is performing and complying with the laws and regulations in question. Financial performance is included, in addition to laws and regulations, because regulators worry a great deal about the financial strength of financial firms. They use the Uniform Financial Institutions Rating System[33] (commonly referred to as CAMELS), which focuses on capital adequacy, asset quality, management and administration, earnings, liquidity, and sensitivity to market risks.

Several problems confront most institutions that desire to institute a proactive versus reactive compliance program. First, it is very difficult to stay on top of the mountain of information that accumulates during each exam period (usually two or more years). Information emanates from a multitude of sources in a variety of databases on a mixture of platforms and operating systems.

---

32. As a result, the new OCC examination procedures emphasize evaluation of credit scoring in the context of fair lending. See OCC Fair Lending Examination Procedures: Comptroller's Handbook for Compliance, Appendix D, Fair Lending Sample Size Tables, April 2006, pp. 47, 95–97.

33. See Glantz, Morton, *Managing Bank Risk: An Introduction to Broad-Based Credit Engineering*. Academic Press, 2002, pp. 375–379.

Second, data is multidimensional and often must be compiled at the transaction or account level, then organized via segment, assessed, aggregated and compared, trended, and finally summarized. Compliance staff struggle in their attempts to make a multitude of meaningful comparisons relative to their past performance; to other lenders operating in the same market; and across geographies, legal entities, different types of loans, and different groups of loan applicants. Often, they are still in a risk investigation mode, rather than a risk mitigation mode, when the regulators begin to point out suspect patterns and potential issues. In short, they find themselves behind the curve with respect to business intelligence. Third, accessibility of information instills confidence in regulators, and it can be crucial in preparation for safety and soundness examinations. Often, internal analysis is not initiated until data is in the hands of the regulatory examiner or is triggered in quick-response situations, such as when a Community Reinvestment Act (CRA)-related protest is lodged, or when a problem surfaces as the result of a customer complaint, governmental inquiry, or discovery order related to a pending legal action is received, and so forth. In these situations, banks can exhaust the review period in a defensive mode while they attempt to gather data that would demonstrate satisfactory performance.

The question becomes: "How can financial institutions avoid surprise and the attendant reaction mode that accompanies it?"

The answer to this question is more easily stated than achieved. Specifically, institutions can achieve the desired result only after they have put effective processes in place to support an ongoing rigorous compliance self-assessment program. Lenders must maintain, improve, and validate existing credit risk evaluation models that are used to measure and price the risk of borrowers and their financial transactions. These processes must afford users with the confidence that comes with knowing that the business and analytic intelligence they provide is rooted in data, processes, and analytical engines that are transparent and that have undergone rigorous and comprehensive validation. Comprehensive, accurate, and timely business and analytic intelligence results in greater insight, leading to foresight and the ability to avoid surprises and costly missteps. Issues are surfaced early on and are dealt with appropriately before they pose problems and consume significant resources.

There are three regulatory concerns that have echoed across financial services over the past few years: (1) the need for process validation, (2) the necessity of having an issue surfacing culture, and (3) transparency.

Process Validation

With respect to any law, or regulation, or internal policy or guideline, how does an institution satisfy itself that it is *in compliance*? Often, compliance failures go undetected for some period of time, only to surface long after their occurrence during a formal regulatory exam, as the result of a customer or governmental agency complaint, or from inquiries from the news media. Enterprise compliance solutions must provide a window into the multilayered infrastructure of an organization. To accomplish this, information must be brought in from a variety of sources ranging from large central transaction systems, to process-owner business rule repositories, to individual departmental data stores. The information is interpreted, translated, and, if necessary, corrected before being stored. This information value chain is completed when an intelligent storage facility enables access that facilitates analysis, visualization, and subsequent reporting of results. What we have just described is an enterprise intelligence platform (EIP).[34]

Errors can originate in the data, or they can occur due to processing flaws. To the extent that processes can be automated, validation of computer programs is more sustainable and can be

---

34. For a more in-depth explanation and review of this kind technology and its components, see Schwenk, Helena, *SAS: SAS Enterprise Intelligence Platform*, Ovum Ltd., January 2006, www.ovum.com.

achieved and demonstrated far more easily than similar manual processing. Statistical sampling can be used to monitor data quality and collection process. For compliance testing and credit underwriting and pricing, it is important to evaluate loan policy, guidelines, and approval process.[35] Another source of errors is the misuse of models or the use of inaccurate models. We devote the last chapter of the book to the topic of model validation relatively to all aspects (i.e., input, processing, and output).

Issue Surfacing Culture

The cornerstone of this objective is clear communication that the messenger will not be shot and mistakes will happen, but attempts to conceal them will not be tolerated. Shareholder and regulator trust depends on the belief that the institution can effectively identify and manage risk exposures. It is important to quickly formulate and execute all necessary corrective measures and risk management strategies so as to lessen, or avoid, any negative consequences.

The hallmark of a chief executive officer (CEO), or C-level management, is leadership. Corporate leadership requires that executives set aside personal agendas and other conflicts of interest and do what is in the best interest of the firm and its reputation for high integrity, fairness in all business dealings, and transparency to regulator agencies, shareholders, and the public at large. Confidence that an institution knows what is going on, and quickly corrects problems before they become significant exposures is core to owning stakeholder trust and it is very difficult to recapture when major failures come to light or negative performance trends come into question. Major internal control failures that result in financial injury to customers can cause a financial institution to be put under close supervision by its primary regulatory agency. The resulting burden of greater regulatory oversight can approach an all-consuming exercise for executive management and the board audit and compliance committees. The military phrase "punishment will continue until attitude improves" may come to mind for an executive management team that finds that while they may have addressed most of the concerns that initially led to their problems, the closer oversight processes has managed to surface new and material internal control weaknesses in completely different areas, frequencies of corporate policy exceptions that are above tighter imposed regulatory thresholds, technical violations of regulations, or worse, clear violations of law.

Maintaining vigilance in this area is especially challenging in times where budgets are tight and focus is most often directed to revenue-generating activities in preference to rooting out rule-bending or rule-breaking behavior. Common reasons for not ensuring that sufficient early warning and intelligence-gathering systems are in place to detect violations of fair lending policy and law include:

- "If it doesn't appear to be broken, don't fix it."
- "We don't want to open a can of worms."
- "We don't want to waste resources checking out false warnings."
- "It is more defensible to not know about a problem than to surface possible warning signs and do nothing about them."
- "We don't want to create evidence that can be discovered by a plaintiff or government oversight/enforcement agency and used against us in court."

The path commonly referred to as the *ostrich approach* is sometimes promoted by one or more of these lines of reasoning.

Unfortunately, this sort of defensive strategy may save money in the short run, but it exposes the institution to potentially much higher future costs associated with consequences of preventable

---

35. This is one of the principles for credit risk management. See Basel Committee on Banking Supervision, "Principles for the Management of Credit Risk," July 1999, p. 15, paragraph 43.

and undetected regulatory violations. Those consequences include direct losses stemming from immediate financial losses on transactions, or across a portfolio or customer segment. Losses may continue over time, with lawsuits, business interruption, restitution, write-downs on asset values, regulatory and taxation penalties, higher insurance premiums, lower debt ratings, distraction of company senior management from normal priority of responsibilities, loss of shareholder value, damaged employee morale, and reputation/brand damage. A recent Wharton Business School study[36] reported that operational loss events have a significant negative impact on stock price (market value) on the institution for both the banking and insurance industries. The size of the market value loss for an institution was found to be several times (i.e., four to five times) the operational loss reported by the institution.[37]

A strategy of "not wanting the power to know what is going wrong" exposes the board of directors to civil money penalties and fines that potentially could surpass director and officer (D&O) issuance coverage. The simple truth is: What you don't know *can* hurt you, your firm, and your corporate board. Hence, it would seem that there should be ample justification for investments in time and resources on strengthening internal controls, and leveraging technology so as to lessen the likelihood that serious problems will go undetected. Putting together a business case for compliance technology investment is an exercise that must be specific to each institution. This is because risk exposures and control strength vary by institution. For example, relative to HMDA and fair lending, two institutions may have identical volume and a similar geographic footprint, but different odds ratios and disparity indices. With respect to controls, one lending institution may be using old technology or manually intensive processes that are error-prone versus another institution that has a state-of-the-art compliance solution in place. In most cases, analysis will show that the cost of such an investment is small in comparison with the expected market value erosion. As we will see in the next major section, you need to estimate expected losses by taking into account both the likelihood and impact of various sorts of problems, or outcomes, under different scenarios and adjust for market value erosion as a final step (i.e., the four to five times factor mentioned earlier).

As a key strategy, financial institutions need to *signal* their effectiveness in compliance risk management and control. Public disclosure of your ERM program is an example of one such signal. The delivery mechanism could be a supplemental section in the corporate annual report or a stand-alone report issued periodically to shareholders, stock analysts, and rating agencies. This can serve to minimize potential market value erosion when an operational event ends up happening by chance even when compliance risk management and effectiveness of controls in the institution are of high quality. Certainly, if an institution that is not subject to Basel II compliance[38] were to voluntarily raise the bar on itself and qualify for the advanced measurement approach under Basel II for credit or operational risk management, that would also be a signal.

Another Wharton Study[39] showed that there is spillover effect (in terms of stock price drop) on other institutions in the industry when large loss events occur. That is, investors perceive the report of a large operational event as symptomatic of poor operational risk management and controls throughout the industry. An industry effect generally makes sense for certain environmental factors (e.g., movements in interest rates, where compression of spreads occurs when rates rise and widening of spreads occurs when rates fall). Still balance sheet structure can amplify, or mute, the industry average affect. The market does have access to a fair amount of financial information.

---

36. See Cummins, J. David, Christopher M. Lewis, and Ran Wei. "The Market Value Impact of Operational Loss Events for US banks and insurers," *Journal of Banking & Finance*, Vol. 30, Issue 10, October 2006, pp. 2605–2634.
37. Recent settlements in compliance areas such as predatory and subprime lending practices that have been in the multi-hundred-million-dollar range represent huge operational losses stemming from thousands of individual transactions.
38. For example, insurance companies, nonbank financial companies, medium-sized banks in the United States.
39. Cummins, Lewis, and Wei, 2006.

In the case of operational failures, this result falls more into the category of "guilt by association." Markets do not have access to control strength information to gauge vulnerability to the same type of event across firms. The spillover impact is scary because it is not rooted in demonstrable linkages, but rather market perception. Thus, a financial institution can suffer market value erosion due to poor compliance risk management in other institutions—something completely beyond its control. Of course, the average effect is much smaller than the average market value erosion of the institution in which the event happened.

All the more reasons for good financial institutions to signal their effectiveness in compliance risk management and control to the market. Signaling is needed because, in the foreseeable future, investors and rating agencies will not be in a position to determine after the fact whether one institution is better than another in compliance risk management.

Transparency

Transparency refers to the ability of any interested party to view the operation and all of its parts in such a manner as to make it readily apparent to the observer what is being performed and how it is being performed. This not only facilitates third-party review (e.g., internal audit or primary regulator), but it also facilitates end-to-end process validation. For starters, transparency begins with compliance solution design and standards that:

- Foster self-documenting procedures and system-generated reports and analysis.
- Require internal program comments by developers.
- Produce external functional documentation that provides linkage to specific regulatory requirements.
- Afford extensive solution operational documentation that specifies exactly how the application operates, its source inputs, data translations, data and metadata management, algorithms, analysis methodology, and how outputs are derived.

Cryptic annotations understood only by the original developers will not suffice. Solution development and application documentation are very different skills—rarely found in the same individuals, particularly for complex, large-scale solutions.

You will need to have documentation expertise available not only for the development stage and ongoing change management of the automated portions of your self-assessment program, but also to document the manual procedures followed by staff as they perform tasks throughout the self-examination cycle. This becomes even more important during a regulatory examination, where examiners expect full disclosure of the entire process. In-house compliance staff must be prepared and capable of convincing corporate executives, the board of directors, external auditors, and regulatory examiners that compliance program verification is achieved on an ongoing basis. That can become a daunting task, especially with large and complicated in-house systems. Point solutions, which are not end to end, become fragmented, and process validation must be made transparent at every control point where a separate application boundary is crossed, such as import/export to a spreadsheet or a proprietary reporting package. Transparency is elusive when dealing with a multivendor, multicomponent fair lending solution strategy.

If public attention is drawn to your lending practices, it will be hard to defend your position if the compliance system lacks auditability. Simply put, your self-assessment solution must provide the ability to trace a logical line from origination systems to aggregate reports. Preliminary adverse findings and trends should be subjected to statistical analysis and significant and material results must be traceable to root causes and supporting information.

Determine Compliance Strategies

The previous section discussed fundamental principles for lending institutions to prepare for challenges posed by changes in markets and regulations. Now we discuss how to develop strategies to put these principles into action. These strategies will not only require new and improved policies and procedures, but also the means to measure and monitor performance of compliance programs. It is important to evaluate your current position in terms of program maturity in order to design appropriate compliance strategies.

Compliance program evolution is intertwined with corporate information evolution. Davis, Miller, and Russell (2006) present an information evolution model. The model classifies companies based on their maturity in "managing information as a strategic asset as a function of infrastructure, people, process and culture." The model entails five stages relative to information capabilities.[40] Compliance programs also fall into one of five different stages of maturity, and Figure 1.3 shows the stages in order of increasing maturity, effectiveness, efficiency, and control strength.[41]

At Stage 1, governance is in place (e.g., committees meet regularly with written charters, and a basic program is in place that is board approved). Processes are largely manual and unreliable. Standards lack consistency and controls are poor.

In Stage 2, previously mastered tasks can be repeated. This stage is characterized by the existence of some business unit–level standards, policies, and procedures, especially relative to

	Maturity				
Characteristics	**Stage 1 Initial**	**Stage 2 Repeatable**	**Stage 3 Defined**	**Stage 4 Managed**	**Stage 5 Optimizing**
Governance in place: committees with BOD-approved charters meet regularly	X	X	X	X	X
Departmental policy and procedures in place for at least the most risky activities		X	X	X	X
Technology deployed and compliance testing performed but not risk based or effective		X			
Compliance testing performed effectively			X	X	X
Technology effectively utilized			X	X	X
Enterprise policy and procedures and metrics in place				X	X
High-level enterprise risk assessment				X	X
Detail-level enterprise risk assessment					X
Consistent continuous testing and self-evolving standards and policies					X

FIGURE 1.3 COMPLIANCE PROGRAM MATURITY MODEL

---

40. The five stages are (1) Operate, (2) Consolidate, (3) Integrate, (4) Optimize, and (5) Innovate, as described by Davis, Jim, Gloria J. Miller, and Allan Russell. *Information Revolution: Using the Information Evolution Model to Grow Your Business.* John Wiley & Sons, 2006.
41. Brickman, Joel, and Paul Kurgan, "New Challenges for Enhancing Regulatory Risk Management on an Enterprise Level," Regulatory Compliance Risk Management Conference, American Conference Institute, November 29–30, 2006, slides 19–20.

the more risky activities undertaken through the normal course of business. Technology is in place, but is not effectively implemented. Compliance testing is performed but is not risk based or effective in many instances.

In Stage 3 the key compliance processes are characterized and fairly well understood, and where risk assessments are performed for all business units. Standards, policies, and procedures are adequate to address risks at the business unit level. Technology and testing are effectively implemented, but enterprise reporting is still hampered by inability to aggregate information and the existence of silo inconsistencies.

By Stage 4, the compliance processes are measured and controlled. This stage is where enterprise risk metrics are defined, and tolerances are board approved in policies and enforced through documented procedures and assigned responsibilities. Effective surfacing and proper escalation of issues and accountability for timely resolution is commonplace. High-level assessment is performed at the enterprise level. Standards, policies, and procedures are consistent throughout, and technology and compliance testing are aligned. There is more focus on developing integrated information and technology that will support cross-functional needs and initiatives. Stage 4 builds on the achievements of Stage 3 via continuous process improvement of ways to better identify, measure, monitor, and control compliance risk and strengthen internal controls. Strategies are formulated from more powerful risk evaluations of current and potential exposures that, in turn, are fueled by more complete and meaningful information. The insight gained results in greater foresight.

At Stage 5, the focus is on process improvement. This stage is where a firm realizes a sustainable advantage in the compliance risk management arena. Detail-level enterprise assessments are performed. Standards, policies, and procedures self-evolve. There is consistent, continuous testing performed and consistent reporting performed at all levels. Repeatability and adaptability of analytical processes is routine.

Clearly, an institution would benefit from attaining stage 5, the highest compliance maturity level. The general consensus is that most firms are at stage 3 of compliance program maturity. Therefore, most companies need to make the case for stronger, more mature programs. However, it is challenging to make the case to invest in the areas that will safeguard as opposed to generating revenue. It is more difficult for a CEO to (1) justify to Wall Street investors his decision to spend money on preventative measures such as strengthening internal controls and the corporate compliance self-assessment program that reduce shareholder return, than it is to (2) justify to the board of directors spending four times as much (or more) to mount a legal defense and gather supporting data and analysis in the wake of a class-action lawsuit alleging lending discrimination. The reason is that in the first instance, capital spending is voluntary, whereas in the second instance there is no choice in the matter and spending even greater sums of money has become a necessity. The reason for emphasizing the foregoing points is to make the case for a proactive compliance program that anticipates and heads off trouble, rather than reacting after the fact and mounting a defensive strategy. The next section discusses the tangible returns associated with a solid compliance program, and Appendix 1B frames the business case for a significant compliance risk management technology upgrade in a simple and intuitive manner.

RETURN ON COMPLIANCE

Historically, there has not been much attention given to making business cases for compliance risk management. This is primarily due to a couple of factors. First, compliance solutions tended to cover the bare minimum to meet the legal or regulatory requirement. Second, the requirement had to be met, so there could be little debate over whether to spend money to avoid a violation of law.

Today, the landscape has changed. It is no longer enough to be "compliant" at a point in time. It is now important to anticipate, and indeed head off, future violations. A recent survey of 175 executives at global financial firms revealed that compliance is the number two profit concern, with globalization capturing the top spot, and risk in the number three spot.[42] The same study found that advanced compliance capabilities can be a competitive advantage. It also noted that noncompliance is more costly than just penalties, that costs of piecemeal approaches are escalating, and that lack of coordination among initiatives is a common problem.

Fortunately, on a parallel track, we have seen great strides in technology, especially with the advent of business intelligence that can deliver compliance and risk solutions for an ever widening area of regulations, including credit risk management and fair lending. One of the impediments to any modeling exercise is getting the required data. The source of the data consists of a combination of quantitative modeling results for disparate impact and disparate treatment testing, and various other sources of compliance intelligence that we point to in the nonquantitative realm in Figure 2.10, such as mystery shopping results, policy assessments, and so on. With additional choices now available, management is confronted with the question: "What is it worth to have the power to know the institution's potential compliance exposures, so that appropriate action can be taken to fix current problems and head off future ones?"

A simplified framework for constructing a business case for elevating the institution's compliance program to the next level of maturity, or for maintaining a mature program in the wake of constant changes and challenges, appears in Appendix 1B.[43] Most companies budget for expenses and capital expenditures on an annual basis. Constructing a business case is usually a prerequisite for obtaining approval to add resources, upgrading technology, and so forth. This high-level business case for a compliance technology upgrade points out examples of the sorts of things that need quantification. In developing this simple business case, we have tapped the examination guidelines to identify four primary areas of key risk factors; exam focal points typically will drive off of these, and they vary by institution based on a number of criteria (e.g., past examination findings, HMDA data, prevailing customer complaints, etc.). Business intelligence solutions can help trace events to their root cause in order to find and fix problems. By benchmarking performance and setting thresholds on key indicators, you can identify performance that is out of the norm or trending negatively, and set priorities and focus accordingly. This presumes the following questions have been answered. How should performance be measured, and what level of compliance performance is desired? Who decides and who sets the standards? How often should the standards be reviewed and changed? Should reviews be performance triggered?

In addition to making a business case for improving regulatory compliance risk management, we see a solid case to be made for adopting a more integrated approach toward compliance risk management and ERM in general. At the highest level, the board of directors has responsibility for gauging the risk-bearing capacity of the firm and setting risk tolerances accordingly. The board, however, can only know based on what management provides to them, the opinions of independent auditors, and possibly external legal counsel and consultants retained by it or management. It is vital that critical information on risk exposures be appropriately quantified and surfaced to the board in a timely manner. This requires solid risk management and rigorous control assessment. All forms of internal and environmental changes must be monitored. The process should be efficient to ensure complete coverage, while avoiding redundancy. We assert that a more fully integrated approach strengthens the capability to account for, indeed exploit, natural dependencies that exist across compliance areas so as to avoid over/underestimating risk exposures. An example would

---

42. Ribeiro, Jack. "Global Services Industry Outlook—Shaping Your Strategy in a Changing World." Deloitte & Touche USA LLP, 2006 and Brickman and Kurgan, 2006, slides 2–4.

43. Model assumptions concerning the probability distributions of various categories of compliance exposures and the impact of compliance controls may be based on experience in the field, and also on data and test results from the institution's fair lending self-examination program. The impact of fair lending exposures can be estimated from both past internal information, and also external sources such as public disclosures of the terms of settlements of lawsuits brought for violations of related laws and regulations.

be credit risk management and fair lending compliance, because credit scoring impacts access to credit in addition to controlling credit default risk. Another would be incorporating CRA goal setting with effective tapping of emerging markets using alternative credit underwriting models for nontraditional users of credit, while simultaneously satisfying strategic plan goals aimed at improving the lender's annual HMDA peer fair lending results. In Chapter 8, we explore ways to address these multiple objectives using a credit and compliance optimization process (CCOP).

Appendix 1A
TAXONOMY OF ENTERPRISE RISKS

Credit risk   Risk arising from an obligor's failure to meet the terms of any contract with the bank or otherwise failing to perform as agreed. Arises anytime bank funds are extended, committed, or otherwise exposed through actual or implied contractual agreements.

Interest rate risk   Risk arising from movements in interest rates. The economic perspective focuses on the value of the bank in today's interest rate environment and the sensitivity of that value to changes in interest rates.

Liquidity risk   Risk arising from an inability to meet obligations when they come due, possibly incurring unacceptable losses. Includes the inability to manage unplanned decreases or changes in funding sources or address changes in market conditions.

Price risk   Risk to earnings or capital arising from changes in the value of portfolios of financial instruments. This risk arises from market-making, dealing, and position-taking activities in interest rate, foreign exchange, equity, and commodities markets.

Transaction risk   The current and prospective risk to earnings and capital arising from fraud, error, and the inability to deliver products and services, maintain a competitive position, and manage information. Risk is inherent in efforts to gain strategic advantage and in the failure to keep pace with changes in the financial services marketplace. Transaction risk is evident in each product and service offered. Transaction risk encompasses product development and delivery, transaction processing, systems development, computing systems, complexity of products and services, and the internal control environment.

Compliance risk   Risk arising from violations or nonconformance with laws, rules, regulations, prescribed practices, or ethical standards.

Strategy risk   Risk arising from adverse business decisions or improper implementation of those decisions. A function of the compatibility of an organization's strategic goals, strategies developed to achieve those goals, and the quality of implementation.

Reputation risk   Risk arising from negative public opinion. Affects the ability to establish new relationships or services, or to continue servicing existing relationships. Can expose the bank to litigation, financial loss, or damage to its reputation.

Appendix 1B
MAKING THE BUSINESS CASE

This appendix presents a simplified numerical example to illustrate return on compliance program investment. The modeling technique used is Monte Carlo simulation. Model assumptions concerning the probability distributions of various categories of compliance exposures and the impact of compliance controls can be estimated. The basic idea is that we have risks, controls designed to deal with risks, and a gap that exists when dollar risk exposures are netted against controls over dollar exposures. The gap may be positive, negative, or zero. A positive gap says that there is some residual risk of loss. A negative gap says that there is a surplus of capacity to deal with risks that exceed those considered to fall within assumed ranges for the modeling exercise. A zero gap means that according to the model assumptions and current business environment, the risk exposure is covered.

For the purposes of illustration we adopt a simplified view of quantifying fair lending regulatory risk. There are several other areas of fair lending exposure; here, we consider just four, namely underwriting, pricing, steering, and redlining. We will not go through all four areas in detail, but we do want to drill down a bit further into one of them, namely, pricing, to examine how one can quantify exposures and then postulate a model that can be used to construct a range of possible outcomes.

Consider pricing risk from a fair lending perspective, which we cover in greater detail in Chapter 4. Actual damages are authorized by the Equal Credit Opportunity Act (ECOA), Fair Housing Act (FHA), Unfair and Deceptive Acts and Practices (UDAP), and state statutes (predatory lending laws), and pertain to economic injury. For punitive damages, a plaintiff must show intent (e.g., predatory lending where minorities are targeted, etc.). The general idea is that pricing exposures are a function of monetary damages, the cost of policy and procedure changes, staff training, regulatory fines and greater oversight burden, direct legal defense and court costs, consequences of damaged reputation, and so forth.

Isolating compensatory monetary damages, we find that these expenses are a function of the injured class definition, and the loss definition. The injured class and loss definitions are based on the allegation that entails the amount of points and interest differential and the incidence by product type, geographic area, and time period. Measurement of damages requires a definition of what level of statistical significance is material[44] and scenario testing where assumptions are varied to gauge the effect on damages. The damage measurement can be done on a group average differences basis or on actual differences by borrower. For example, if the method is average differences, we might have 5,000 class members with a protected class average loan rate of 9 percent, a nonprotected class average loan rate of 6 percent, for a difference of 3 percent. If the average loan amount is $100,000 and the average actual loan term is 60 months, then the average

---

44. This may be determined by the court, negotiated based on statistical significance, the Reasonable Person Rule, etc.

settlement for a single loan would be in the neighborhood of $15,000, and for the entire class the damages would be in the neighborhood of $75 million!

So far, we have only quantified compensatory monetary damages. The injured class can request a jury trial. Publicity and potential damages are very significant, and agreeing to a settlement to avoid that scenario can be very costly. Increased regulatory oversight can consume management and open cans of worms everywhere—not just around the cause of the action. The question becomes: "What else is wrong with the institution's internal controls that pose a serious risk that remains undetected?" With heightened scrutiny, problems can snowball. The other categories of risk exposures can be estimated in a similar fashion. To recap, the process consists of identifying how many instances of a potential violation exist, estimating the likelihood that an issue will be raised, and gauging the impact per instance and then multiplying probabilities times the impact to estimate total exposure.

Turning to controls, quantification can be done relative to each exposure individually to net out to a residual risk exposure, or it can be done at a high level. For the sake of illustration we use a collective, high-level range—best/worst case ($16/$10.5 million) and most likely ($12 million) estimate. This assumes an average $12 million risk reduction with the current level of staffing and costs associated with fair lending compliance areas. Realistically, you can only throw so many bodies at a problem, and we assume in this particular case that $16 million is the limit without changing the technical environment. The other levers that are available would be the parameters around your internal control structure, such as:

- *Underwriting.* Regression 95 percent confidence level by channel, by loan purpose, by region.
- *Pricing.* Overage/underage incidence 0.5 percent; amount $= 15$ basis points (bp).
- *Pricing.* HMDA peer data average spread $= 25$ bp over/75 bp under threshold.
- *Steering.* Percent subprime qualified for prime less than 5 percent.
- *Redlining.* HMDA peer data market penetration disparity index less than 1.5x.

Tightening your control structure by incrementally performing more rigorous monitoring as problems surface, by adding metrics and lowering policy thresholds to reduce false negatives, is the most commonly encountered strategy. A compliance intelligence solution upgrade represents another option that requires a larger initial investment, but can afford significant reduction in exposures to costly compliance failures. The compliance solution upgrade can also include technology that can test with models having a closer fit to the business reality, so that problems can be better surfaced without dramatically increasing the number of false positives, as would be the case by simply tightening down the parameters described above. Analogous to the operational risk paradigm, the expected compliance exposure (cost) is the average annual aggregate financial impact, and unexpected compliance exposure represents the volatility above this average at a specified confidence level.

Figure 1.4 provides the estimated exposures by compliance area for our business case. For pricing, we are assuming that there is a minimum exposure of zero dollars, maximum of $18 million, and most likely exposure of $2 million. These estimates are based on the institution's pricing disparity ratios in the HMDA data, on compliance testing results relative to underages and overages, both amount and incidence, and so on. Similarly for the other areas, the estimates would be based on key risk indicators and also specific compliance testing results for those respective areas. (We describe these tests in Chapters 3, 4, and 5.)

We do not go into the derivation of the distributions, and emphasis here is not on the specific form of the distributions, but rather the idea of using standard distributions to model risk. By specifying risk distributions, the volatility is captured to incorporate unexpected outcomes in the business case. The dollar exposures are estimated by running 6,000 trials using these distributions.

Compliance Examination Area	Assumed Distribution and Parameters	Estimated Dollar Exposure
Underwriting	Truncated normal distribution $\mu = 1$; $\sigma = 2$; Min = 0; Max = $6MM	$2,008,919
Pricing	Triangular distribution Min = 0; Max = $18MM; Most likely = $2MM	$6,559,755
Redlining	Truncated normal distribution $\mu = 1.5$; $\sigma = 3$; Min = 0; Max = $12MM	$3,009,435
Steering	Lognormal distribution $\mu = 2$; $\sigma = 1.5$	$1,986,977
Total	Exposure composite distribution	$13,565,086

FIGURE 1.4   EXPOSURE DISTRIBUTIONS BY COMPLIANCE EXAMINATION AREAS

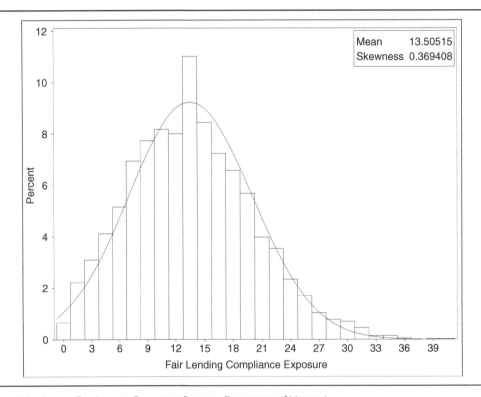

FIGURE 1.5   ANNUAL FAIR LENDING COMPLIANCE EXPOSURE DISTRIBUTION ($MILLIONS)

The combination of these outcomes represents the $13.5 million total exposure to fair lending risk in a single year as depicted in Figure 1.5.

In the beginning of this appendix we introduced the concept of the gap, and this result, coupled with a simulated $12,750,000 risk reduction from current control structures (based on the triangular distribution assumptions stated earlier), leaves a quantified gap for the business case that amounts to an average of $750,000 in year one. The simulation model in this example also tells us that if our goal is a zero gap over each of the next five years, the likelihood of meeting goal with a *status quo strategy* in each of years 1 through 5 is approximately 73, 19, 43, 56, and 63 percent, respectively.

Using the prevailing five-year cost of funds rate as a conservative discounting factor, and discounting beginning in year two, we find that the exposure over five years is $7.5 million, in today's dollars, in order to maintain the status quo. As an alternate strategy, we consider the impact of a technology upgrade. Suppose that the compliance department, in partnership with the Mortgage Subsidiary and Community Development Bank, purchases a new integrated compliance solution that spans Fair Lending/HMDA/CRA at a cost of $5.0 million over five years. The result is a lowering or risk of operational losses associated with potential violations of various laws and regulations. Under the Basel II Advanced Measurement Approach, the institution will have an updated control self-assessment relative to operational risk. We consider the case where the impact on capital is to lower requirements by $10 million due to reduced likelihood of violations either occurring or going undetected relative to the following regulations and areas:

- Regulation C—HMDA
- Regulation BB—CRA
- Fair Lending—FHA/ECOA
- Regulation Z—TILA/HOEPA
- Sales practices: Regulation AA—UDAP
- External broker/dealer
- Marketing diversity
- Systems and technology infrastructure

If we assume a hurdle rate of 15 percent, then there is an annual pretax benefit of $1.5 million associated with the $10 million in capital that has been more profitably deployed. Over five years, discounting again at 7 percent per year (beginning in year one), the accumulated savings in present day's dollars is $6.15 million pretax.[45]

We see in this example that a $5 million investment in new technology can substantially strengthen internal controls and achieve a gap of zero over the next five years. Capital reserve reduction associated with the new technology results in an additional $10 million of capital being productively deployed at the hurdle rate. The benefit from this alone can pay for a significant portion of the cost of a new solution.

---

45. Some cash flows in this example are discounted over time, while others are not, such as the capital reserve reduction. This is not material to the overall result.

2

METHODOLOGY AND ELEMENTS OF RISK AND COMPLIANCE INTELLIGENCE

This chapter provides building blocks for all subsequent chapters, namely data, policy and business rules, statistical methods, and process. Ensuring the accuracy and timeliness of the data is an important and necessary step for meaningful analysis. We describe the compliance data by source, and how to prepare the data for analysis. Next, we introduce typical sampling methodologies and process that are used to develop *unbiased* and *efficient* data collection procedures for compliance analysis. The importance of capturing associated lending policy business rules is underscored and illustrated. We then discuss types of statistical analysis and provide a case for a systematic analysis approach. The scope of fair lending for regulatory examination has been defined by the Federal Financial Examination Interagency Council (FFIEC), and consists of 49 factors.[1] The strategy matrix appearing at the end of the chapter maps the most appropriate statistical methods to those 49 factors.

ROLE OF DATA IN FAIR LENDING COMPLIANCE INTELLIGENCE

Fair lending analysis, like all other analysis, begins with the data. This section addresses the primary areas from which data must be integrated for subsequent analysis.

Categories of Data and Sources

There are three main sources of data for analysis. We consider these sources in no particular order. While it is undeniable that the public data report end results, and not what caused those results, these data are useful indicators of potential risk exposure, and merit further attention. This view is consistent with the Federal Reserve Board's position that "Home Mortgage Disclosure Act (HMDA) data may help lenders analyze and monitor their lending patterns."[2] Clearly, the initial HMDA filing information will create perceptions in both the regulator and the public's minds, relative to an institution's fair lending performance. As a result, bank regulators will do screening based on it and the public will form opinions based on it. Hence, it is important that lenders connect the dots between the HMDA data and their true compliance performance. In order to do so, they must source and append their own internal data. This entails first planning the analysis, deciding how to segment data for the analysis and what data to include. Finally, there are additional sources of information that are both external and nonpublic that are usually acquired. These data

---

1. See Appendix 2A for details.
2. See Avery, Robert B., and Glenn B. Canner, *New Information Reported under HMDA and Its Application in Fair Lending Enforcement*, Federal Reserve Board Publication, September 2005, p. 393.

are highlighted in the following sections. The intent here is to provide illustrative examples with broad coverage. Later on, in the appropriate sections of the book, a complete inventory of required data elements is provided for each major analytic approach that is presented to address a specific compliance concern.

Public Data

These data include annual HMDA raw peer data that is available from the FFIEC and provide a detailed record for every mortgage application filed by every reporting lending institution. In addition, the FFIEC provides census data spanning demographics, housing, and income by geographic area. The FFIEC HMDA respondent holding company hierarchy is required to build enterprise views of institutions with multiple legal entities filing HMDA data. Treasury yields for various maturities of bills, notes, and bonds are obtained monthly from the FFIEC Web site and are used to calculate the annual percentage rate (APR) spread for each loan application per the 2002 Amendment to Regulation C.

A complete specification of the data elements making up the HMDA Loan Application Register (LAR) for the current year can be found at the FFIEC Web site.[3] This is uniform for every institution, which is particularly advantageous in situations where institutions are interested in sharing information. For example, in the case of a proposed merger or acquisition, it is desirable to examine fair lending profiles for the combined entity. For the HMDA-based view, HMDA LARs for the respective institutions can simply be merged and input to the standard analysis and reporting process.

Company Internal Data

These data relate primarily to borrower credit application–based qualification factors such as income, net worth, current monthly housing payment, years on job, years at current address, and so on. In addition, information on borrower credit history is obtained from as many as three different bureaus and merged into a single performance record that tracks delinquent behavior across revolving, installment, and mortgage trade lines by frequency and age and also captures foreclosures, repossessions, judgments, liens, and bankruptcy occurrences over time. In addition, information can be obtained for other relationships and products the customer has with the institution, such as nonsufficient funds (NSF), balance, and account vintage for deposit products; overlimit, slow payment, delinquency, and charge-off performance on loan products; balances and account age relative to brokerage accounts that span money-market accounts, investment holdings, and retirement accounts. Another important source is the official HMDA file that is scrubbed, passed through the federal edits, and accepted by the company's primary regulator as the official HMDA filing data. This includes certain information that is not made available to the public, such as credit score, net worth, loan-to-value ratio, and debt-to-income ratio.

Third-Party Supplied Data

These data include small business and farm data, geocodes at a census tract level and latitude/longitude global positioning information, property appraisal and value appreciation information by geographic area, credit bureau trend information at varying geographic levels, consumer life-cycle, psychographic/demographic profiling information, and a host of additional economic, household, and business indicators at varying geographic levels.

---

3. www.ffiec.gov/hmda/doc/spec2006.doc.

Compliance Self-Testing Data Model

The data model that supports a self-testing program is somewhat institution specific. It depends on the organizational complexity; the array of products and programs offered; the uniformity of loan policy across lending divisions and subsidiaries; the nature and number of retail channels; the number of geographic markets in the institution's Community Reinvestment Act assessment areas and overall marketing footprint; the mix of conventional and government program originations; the mix of bulk, flow, and broker-based applications in the wholesale side of the business; the degree of centralization of credit policy governing underwriting and pricing; and so on. Generally speaking, Figure 2.1 gives a flavor for the span of data required to perform various fair lending analyses.

This information is drawn from numerous sources, including, but not limited to, lender loan origination systems, lender underwriting and pricing guidelines and policies, credit bureau files, the Census Bureau metropolitan statistical area, counties and census tract demographic data, a quarterly geocoding database, the FFIEC Web site for monthly treasury yields and annual peer data, the Federal Reserve Board annual corporate parenting hierarchy for HMDA respondents, and the Department of Housing and Urban Development (HUD) annual metropolitan median income data.

Group	Description/Example	Group	Description/Example
APL	APPLICANT	INS	INSURANCE
	Customer type (individual/joint)		Insurance flag
BAL	BALANCE	INT	INTEREST
	Loan face amount		APR spread
COA	CO-APPLICANT	MAT	MATURITY
	Co-applicant race		Loan origination date
COL	COLLATERAL	ORG	ORGANIZATIONAL
	Appraisal amount		Legal entity
CRD	CREDIT TRADELINES	PAY	PAYMENT
	Number of times 30DPD - mortgage		Payment shock
DSN	DECISION	PRD	PRODUCT CLASSIFICATION
	Action taken		HMDA loan purpose
CMP	COMPLIANCE	PUB	PUBLIC RECORD
	HOEPA flag		Bankruptcy indicator
FEE	FEE	RSK	RISK
	Overage/underage amount		Credit bureau score
ALT	ALTERNATIVE DATA	REL	RELATIONSHIP
	Number of times 30DPD - utilities		Customer profitability tier
GEO	GEOGRAPHIC	SYS	SYSTEM
	FIPS state code		Application ID

FIGURE 2.1 EXAMPLE OF SOME SELF-TESTING DATA MODEL VARIABLE CATEGORIES

Data Preprocessing Considerations

A great deal of time and effort go into the sourcing, extraction, verification, correction, translation, and preparation of data for the analysis step. This activity is commonly referred to as *preprocessing* and some data mining books devote several chapters to various aspects of it. Much of the preprocessing has to do with defining model variables that are derived from raw, atomic-level data and the adoption of a standard variable coding scheme for the modeling phase. An example of a standard variable coding scheme might be that all indicator variables that can take on two values (i.e., binary), are defined so that a value of 1 always means yes and 0 always is interpreted to be no. Standardization makes model development and interpretation easier and less complicated.

Depending on the type of statistical analysis that is being performed, data preparation may include mathematical transformations. This is largely driven by the properties of the data, either collectively or individually. For individual observation properties, a method called trimming can be used to deal with outliers that may skew results. Take, for example, months of reserves in a mortgage lending application. It may be the case that having more than 24 months of reserves for meeting a house payment obligation is not of an incremental information value to a model. In this case, any observations that have greater than 24 for the number of months of reserves would be set equal to 24. For collective properties, an examination of the distribution of outcomes in several populations of interest may reveal unequal variances, non-normality, truncation, censoring, and so forth. In these circumstances, adjustments may be made to the observations themselves, to summary observation variables, or to the options associated with the statistical procedures that will be used for the analysis.

The following section provides some examples of the derivation of model variables used in a typical mortgage underwriting regression model that tests for disparate impact relative to a protected class of loan applicants.[4]

Creating Model Variables

Model variable definition is a vital step in constructing models to capture business reality. In later chapters it becomes apparent how important the variable definitions and derivations are to risk and compliance analysis. Figure 2.2 provides examples of regression model variables that were specified based on loan policy and actual practice in the field. Our focus is on the preprocessing aspects and not on listing the most relevant variables in the model. The target code structure is the domain of values that creates the variable from the source information.

An understanding of where the data comes from and underlying assumptions is critical. Specifically, legacy system content expertise is absolutely essential. The next section addresses this topic.

Importance of Metadata Management

Metadata essentially is "the data that describes how data are derived, used, and managed."[5] Each data element is associated with a source. Each source has associated information, such as name and contact information pertaining to the owner/provider of the information, the name of the program that creates the information or the data file/warehouse where the information resides, frequency of distribution/refreshing of the information, the file structure, the format of the information,

---

4. For a more in-depth discussion of data preparation, refer to Pyle, Dorian. *Data Preparation for Data Mining*, Morgan Kaufmann, 1999, pp. 141–140.
5. See Davis, Jim, Gloria J. Miller, and Allan Russell. *Information Revolution: Using the Information Evolution Model to Grow Your Business*, John Wiley & Sons, 2006, p. 89.

Variable Name	Target Code Structure	Derivation Business Rule
Credit history	0 - good, 1 - bad, 2 - insufficient	If (Sufficiency = 1 and Performance = 0) then 0; if (Sufficiency = 1 and Performance = 1) then 1; else 2
Sufficiency	1 - yes; 0 - no	If CSI < 2, then 1; else 0
Performance	0 - good; 1 - bad;	If (MDCI = 1 or bankruptcy = 1), then 1; else 0
CSI (credit score indicator)	0 - below 661; 1 - 661+; 2 - missing	If (Score LE 660) then 0; if (Score > 660), then 1; else 2
MDCI (major derogatory credit indicator)	0 - none; 1 - 1 or more	If (Number of times 60 DPD + Number of times 90 DPD + Number of major derogatory trades) > 0, then 1; else 0
Bank deposit relationship indicator	1 - yes; 0 - no	If Relationship type in ('01','02','33', '44','57') or (Savings = 1 or (DDA = 1 and (DDA_Balance > 6500 or DDA_Balance Average > 3000) and DDA_Account Term > 24)), then 1; else 0

FIGURE 2.2   REGRESSION MODEL VARIABLES

and the access mechanism for obtaining the information.[6] For example, in a mortgage lending system there may be as many as four applicants on the loan file. It is critical to understand how to determine how many applicants are associated with a particular loan application, which information pertains to individual versus summary-level items, and how to calculate compliance fields such as race/ethnicity when joint applications are involved.

Data element metadata includes the name of the source field, its location on the source file or table, the length of the field, the type of the field, a business description of the field, a list of valid values for categorical fields, a range of valid values for numeric valued fields, the default value used in the event the field is not populated due to missing data, or if the data is not applicable for a particular observation (e.g., co-applicant gender field in the case where there is a single loan applicant).[7] In addition to sourced data, there is the need to maintain metadata on generated fields of information that are required, such as applicant race/ethnicity. It is important to maintain a chronology of metadata definitions to capture and apply the correct derivation rule in an environment where regulatory requirements change. For example, prior to 2004, primary and co-applicant applicant race were captured as single fields in order to derive joint applicant protected and nonprotected classes. From 2004 going forward, primary applicant and co-applicant ethnicity also needed to be included in order to define the protected classes and nonprotected class in question.

Metadata management is important to ensure consistency when pulling information from many different platforms and environments, such as the public, internal, and third-party sources previously noted. It also enables analysts to locate and correct data problems early on before they creep into the analysis. These problems run the gamut from duplicate records to the incidence of values that fall outside the allowable domain of values for a particular field in one or more records, or

---

6. For a discussion on data collection process for fair lending analysis, see Collins, M. Cary, and Frank M. Guess. "Improving Information Quality in Loan Approval Processes for Fair Lending and Fair Pricing," presented at the Massachusetts Institute of Technology's Information Quality Conference, October 20–22, 2000.
7. For a more in-depth treatment, see Pyle, 1999, Chapter 4, pp. 125–135.

to values that fall in a suspect range (e.g., applicant birth year prior to 1900), or to default values that are at variance with what is expected.

Data may be consistent and valid for a given element and may still be inaccurate. An example would be where combinations of values for related data elements raise doubts on accuracy, such as a mortgage applicant flagged as having insufficient cash at closing, but at the same time four months of cash reserves and monthly discretionary income of $2,500. Similarly, an HMDA filing record that indicates a loan purpose code of 2, signifying home improvement, that also has a loan origination system code of 89, signifying a mobile home without land, would be viewed as being collectively inaccurate without saying which item of information is in error. Collateral codes represent a rich example of metadata and the importance of consistency because they so often combine several other data elements, such as lien status (primary, secondary) and dwelling type (single-family residence, condo, townhouse, business office, farm, condotel, mobile home with/without land, raw land) which requires that they be internally consistent with other data elements in the database, such as loan purpose, property type, and lien status. The shaded values in Figure 2.3 highlight potential data problems.[8]

A different example of inaccuracy is a property address that conforms to all edit checks and geocodes properly, but is simply the wrong address for a particular mortgage loan application, based on the hardcopy credit file. The latter example may elude metadata management–based controls, but can be addressed via regular quality control sampling.

The main point is that solid metadata management can play a significant role in reducing the persistence of errors in data that will be used for analysis. Metadata is vital to the data

Collateral Information		HMDA Filing Information		
Code	Description	Purpose	Property Type	Lien Status
1	Detached home, 1st mortgage	1	2	1
2	Detached home, 2nd mortgage	1	3	2
3	Multifamily condo, 1st mortgage	1	3	3
4	Mobile home w/land, 2nd mortgage	3	1	2
5	Church	1	1	4
6	Farm or ranch, 1st mortgage	3	1	3
7	Business office 1st mortgage	1	1	2
8	Raw land	1	1	4

FIGURE 2.3   FAIR LENDING DATA PROBLEMS

8. Interpretation of the values of the HMDA codes is available from the FFIEC Web site and is found in the Loan/Application Register Code Sheet. In this instance the values for loan purpose are: (1) home purchase, (2) home improvement, (3) refinancing; for property type they are: (1) one-to-four family (other than manufactured housing), (2) manufactured housing, (3) multifamily; for lien status they are: (1) first lien, (2) subordinate lien, (3) not secured by a lien, (4) not applicable (purchased loans).

processing validation exercise that is required by internal auditors and regulatory examiners. Effective metadata management ensures the level of transparency that is now expected for safe and sound controls associated with compliance programs in general, and fair lending statistical analysis in particular.

While data and metadata play a critical role in successful statistical modeling and analysis, the next section addresses the importance of determining how much data is required in the statistical testing and modeling process to ensure that the final results will be valid and effectively capture what is needed to form conclusions and make recommendations on courses of action to mitigate unacceptable levels of compliance risk.

SAMPLING

The objective of sampling is to provide unbiased information that will be useful to develop statistical models that meet government agencies' sampling guidelines.[9] In fair lending analysis, we need to explore whether discrimination on a protected basis played into the decision to grant credit, or how to price the loan. A proper sampling method can ensure an *unbiased* and *efficient* procedure for collecting data to be used for various kinds of analyses. In this section, we review some sampling considerations, process, schemes, and practical applications.

General Considerations

A sampling scheme is said to be *unbiased* if the expected disparity measured for the sample is equal to that of the entire applicant population. Sampling bias can be avoided by adopting a scheme that results in a representative sample of loan applications for a protected group processed within a specific time frame, market, loan program, income range, and loan amount. An *efficient* sample, however, would exhibit the lowest standard error of the measured minority/nonminority disparity for a given sample size. A complete discussion of bias and efficiency is beyond the scope of this section. There is a wealth of material available on statistical sampling methodology in general, and sampling methods specific to modeling fair lending compliance.[10]

Consider the following simple example of sampling selection criteria, where applications are gathered over some fixed time period (e.g., third through fourth quarter of 2007. Figure 2.4 displays the selection criteria for a typical sampling exercise.

It is important to determine what course of action will be taken if one or more items included in the selection criteria turn up missing in an observation. Based on the criteria above, missing data would fall out of the allowable ranges and would be excluded. However, typically in main-effects regressions,[11] elimination of observations having one or more items of missing or invalid data can

---

9. The OCC's fair lending program follows general guidelines that specify: (1) a minimum requirement of 50 observations for denials and approvals in each race group; (2) sampling may be *choice-based* depending on how the lender decisions loan applications; and (3) for stratified schemes, how to allocate sample size within sampling strata. The OCC has an examiner's handbook on sampling methodology, available from their Web site. It also provides a good overview and also many specific details on application. In the simplest case, where lenders want to pick a random number of LAR records to check for accuracy against paper records. More complex cases involving multiple conditional criteria require data partitioning, sampling without replacement, and maintenance of minimum sampling quotas.

10. For general discussion on sampling, see Cochran, W. G. *Sampling Techniques*, 3rd ed. John Wiley & Sons, 1977. For sampling on fair lending analysis, see for example, Clarke, Judith A., and Marsha J. Courchane. "Implications of Stratified Sampling for Fair Lending Binary Logit Models," *Journal of Real Estate Finance and Economics*, Vol. 30, No. 1, February 2005, pp. 5–31.

11. *Main effects* refers the effects of single, individual independent factors on the regression response variable. Interaction effects refers to the effects of combinations of factors on the response variable.

Selection Criteria	Applications Included
Race/ethnic groups	African-American, white Hispanic, white non-Hispanic
Decision date	7/1/2007–12/31/2007
Type	Conventional
Purpose	Home purchase or refinance
Occupancy	Owner occupied
Action	Originated, approved but not accepted, or declined
State	OH, KY, PA, VA, MD
LTV	> 0% and ≤ 150%
DTI	> 0% and ≤ 125%
Loan amount	> $0
Income	> $0

FIGURE 2.4   SELECTION CRITERIA

result in the loss of a significant portion of the population being sampled. Alternatives to throwing out observations include:

- Inclusion of the observations in the analysis with the objective of finding important patterns relating to the missing data.
- Researching and providing values for items having missing information.
- Substituting an estimate for the missing values.
- Exploiting the structure of the business problem, which can render the missing information unimportant.
- Collapse the analysis on the missing field(s) in question and produce a high-level analysis from which more detailed analysis can be conducted.

To illustrate these options, we provide the following examples:

- The most immediate example of the first option would be to calculate the incidence of missing data relative to the selection criteria variables (e.g., for nonprotected class versus protected class applicants, by state, in the third versus fourth quarter 2007, by action type, or by combinations of variables, e.g., home purchase originated in the District of Columbia for protected class applications versus the identical combination for nonprotected class applications).
- The second option will be constrained by time and cost considerations, but affords the most reliable answer to the problem.
- The third alternative may be appropriate in situations where there is a fairly reliable proxy for the missing item and an exact answer is not as important as being in "the neighborhood" of the true value.
- The fourth option is explained in more depth in Chapter 7, but essentially it associates each observation with a unique segment of the population and determines if the missing data is relevant to that segment. If not, then the observation may be excluded with *zero impact* on the analysis.
- To illustrate the fifth option, suppose a significant number of observations did not have values for state. In this case, those observations could be included and a total market analysis performed that ignored geographic location. Next, individual analyses could be conducted by state. If the results showed little variation between the individual state and

the total market analyses, then the conclusion would be that the missing information was not of consequence for the specific purpose of the study.

Sampling Process

Sampling requires preprocessing in order to facilitate the observation selection process. This preprocessing includes importing external data (e.g., HMDA, census data), decision policy data, and credit data. Exclusion logic is then applied to restrict observations as may be required. Key fields are validated and any additional variables needed are created. Next, the number of available observations for each segment to be sampled is determined. Based on that information, sampling quotas for each test and control cell[12] are determined.

Suppose the goal of the sampling is to develop models to test underwriting compliance relative to white Hispanic applicants for a particular business line, say a mortgage company, in two metropolitan statistical areas (MSAs), for owner-occupied properties that were decisioned during the first six months of 2007. The immediate question that arises is how many models are needed? Some considerations include:

- Owner-occupancy status is an important split because the intended use of the property for investment versus residence has a bearing on the default risk.
- Loan purpose is another important split because there are different policies that govern underwriting and pricing for home purchase versus refinance versus home improvement loans:
  - Within loan purpose, there may be a need to distinguish refinancings where the current mortgage is with the lender in question versus with a competitor.
  - For home improvement loans, there may be a distinction made between the value of the property being financed before versus after improvements.
- Geographic markets define another key sampling variable, and in this instance we are looking for two particular MSAs. In general, however, distinction would need to be made relative to granularity, that is, a separate model by MSA, by state, by region, by assessment area, or by total franchise. If insufficient data exists at the MSA level, then summarization may need to be done at the state or perhaps regional level.
- Action taken is another important variable. Approvals would include both originations and approved-not-accepted. Declines would be counted separately. Incomplete and withdrawn applications would be excluded if the analysis is focused on decline disparity, but may be included if the analysis is to assess lender assistance in the application process.
- Date action taken is another field that will be used to exclude applications falling outside of the required time frame.

Figure 2.5 provides the report that would display the sample counts for the ten models[13] in question. In this case, the same observations may be selected for both home improvement categories, since they differ only by the definition of the property value. While this may impact other information items, such as the loan-to-value ratio, it will not impact the specific observations selected. It will, however, require some "post sampling" preprocessing to generate the proper information relating to the property value scenarios.

The counts captured in Figure 2.5 can be examined to ensure sufficient data is available for the model development and validation. Once this is done, the actual sampling may be performed according to one of the methods discussed in the following section.[14]

---

12. Sample size determination is addressed in Appendix 4E.
13. The number of MSAs multiplied by the number of loan purpose categories gives the number of models.
14. Within each sample segment, there will often be some deliberate oversampling to cover not only model development but also a holdout sample for subsequent model validation.

MSA	DC Metro	DC Metro	Atlanta Metro	Atlanta Metro
Applicant race/ethnicity	White Hispanic	White non-Hispanic	White Hispanic	White non-Hispanic
Home purchase	Approved ____ Declined ____	Approved ____ Declined ____	Approved ____ Declined ____	Approved ____ Declined ____
Refinance—with lender	Approved ____ Declined ____	Approved ____ Declined ____	Approved ____ Declined ____	Approved ____ Declined ____
Refinance—with competitor	Approved ____ Declined ____	Approved ____ Declined ____	Approved ____ Declined ____	Approved ____ Declined ____
Home improvement— value as is	Approved ____ Declined ____	Approved ____ Declined ____	Approved ____ Declined ____	Approved ____ Declined ____
Home improvement— value post-improvement	Approved ____ Declined ____	Approved ____ Declined ____	Approved ____ Declined ____	Approved ____ Declined ____

FIGURE 2.5   NUMBER OF OBSERVATIONS AVAILABLE TO DRAW SAMPLES FOR TEN MODELS

Statistical Sampling Schemes

Compliance examinations may require judgmental, statistical, or combined sampling.[15] Most of the statistical sampling methods can be performed using commercially available statistical procedures.[16] With statistical sampling, each unit in the survey population has a known, positive probability of selection. This property of statistical sampling avoids selection bias and enables you to use statistical theory to make valid inferences from the sample to the survey population. There are two primary types of statistical sampling schemes available. One is called *equal probability* sampling methods, which include simple random sampling, unrestricted random sampling (with replacement), systematic random sampling, and sequential random sampling. The other is called *probability proportional to size* (PPS) methods, which include sampling with or without replacement, systematic sampling, algorithms for selecting two units per stratum, and sequential sampling with minimum replacement.

In practice, statistical sampling often needs to be combined with judgmental sampling. For example, the Office of the Comptroller of the Currency (OCC) often uses choice-based sampling for statistically modeled fair lending exams.[17] In choice-based or case-control stratified sampling methods, a predetermined number of denied and approved loan applications are obtained and then recorded. In some cases, a further level of stratification is undertaken, with the sampling stratified also by race, that is, the subjects for collection of additional data are stratified jointly by outcome (loan approved/denied) and protected class variable (race). Such a sampling procedure is sometimes called two-phase stratified sampling, stratified case-control sampling, or stratified choice-based sampling, and it is very common in many fields including epidemiology and accountancy. By selecting a sample of a suitable size from each stratum, it is possible to produce

---

15. See OCC *Sampling Methodologies: Comptroller's Handbook*, August 1998. See also OCC *Fair Lending Examination Procedures—Comptroller's Handbook for Compliance*, Appendix D, Fair Lending Sample Size Tables, April 2006, pp. 47, 95–97.
16. For example, SAS/STAT software's SURVEYSELECT procedure provides a variety of methods for selecting probability-based random samples. The procedure can select a simple random sample or can sample according to a complex multistage sample design that includes stratification, clustering, and unequal probabilities of selection.
17. Dietrich, Jason. "The Effects of Choice-Based Sampling and Small Sample Bias on Past Fair-Lending Exams." Mimeo. Office of the Comptroller of the Currency, 2001, p. 3.

parameter estimates that are considerably more precise than that given by a simple random sample from the population. This also can be performed based on the distribution of *handle cells*.[18]

While data, metadata, and sampling play a critical role in successful statistical modeling and analysis, the next section addresses the importance of developing an in-depth familiarity with credit policy, procedures, and practices in the field.

Role of Policy Business Rules in Statistical Analysis

Just as data must be sourced to fuel the analytical process supporting compliance testing and investigation, policy business rules must also be sourced to ensure that models are framed properly and include the relevant factors that have a bearing on the question the model is attempting to address. This holds true for all analyses discussed in subsequent chapters.

In fact, sourcing of policy rules precedes sourcing of data for almost all fair lending analysis. The reason is simple. Until the business rules for the process that is being evaluated are known, the data requirements are impossible to specify. In-depth examples are provided later in the individual chapters that delineate the analytical processes and compliance testing methodologies.

Categories of Business Rules

Policy

The first category of policies and sources relates to translation of the policies themselves into detailed processing rules. The main thrust of these rules is to ensure that an acceptable level of credit quality is maintained and that credit risk is appropriately priced and passed on to the consumer in the terms and pricing of the product for all loans originated. Here we are speaking of policy rules for a particular business activity, such as loan underwriting, pricing, or marketing. For example, underwriting policy rules specify conditions that are required to approve a loan. In capturing a business rule, it is imperative to also capture the business definition and detailed specification of every component of the business rule. The source of this information is usually the Corporate Credit Policy area, or, in a more decentralized environment, the credit administration group in each line of business. Loan operations and the information technology areas are also potential sources for this information. Note that there may be regional processing centers in large lending institutions that may apply additional criteria, or modify general policy rules, to better conform to their specific regional experience.

What is written in the credit policy manuals is not always what gets executed in the day-to-day operational trenches and deal-doing. The author has interviewed dozens of loan underwriters separately in a multichannel, multiregional, multi-line-of-business setting where the necessity of conducting business differently in various settings is apparent due to differing business mix, business practices, and geographic emphasis. As a consequence, the data and policies gathered to perform fair lending analysis must be distinguished within the prevailing business paradigm that is distinctive to each lending institution. In order to specify a model that captures how each line of business uses data to make lending decisions, a model consensus session (MCS)[19] with lead underwriters from each major delivery channel for each line of business may need to be conducted. For example, this might translate to a separate MCS for retail, telephone, Internet, and broker channels within the mortgage company, general banking, and consumer finance businesses.

Consider the case where a policy rule says that an applicant falling into a certain risk segment based on credit bureau score, credit history, debt-to-income ratio, and loan-to-value range may

---

18. The handle concept is defined in Chapter 5.
19. This will be defined later in Chapter 5.

be approved provided that they have an *established* relationship with the institution. Assuming the prerequisite information relating to the customer risk segment is completely specified, the definition of what constitutes an established relationship is critical. This might pertain to the customer's deposit relationship in terms of the number of years they have been a customer and also the average balance in dollars that they have maintained over that period of time. It might also translate to the institution's lending experience with the customer, both in terms of past loans (were they paid on time and were they comparable in amount, term, and program/product) or in terms of current aggregate exposure (credit card, lines of credit, installment loans, other mortgage loans, etc.).

Next, suppose that the policy rule had said that an applicant falling into the identical circumstances may be approved provided they have a *strong* relationship with the institution. In that case, the criteria for loan and deposit relationship might be combined and considered relative to one another with some dollar floor applied (e.g., the customer must maintain a deposit balance that constitutes 20 percent of their combined credit exposure across the institution, and, in any event, no less than $15,000 at any point in time).

Exceptions

Another category of policy rules pertains to policy exceptions. In general, management wants to hold policy exceptions to a minimum threshold level. For example, in the case of credit scoring underwriting models, the policy exceptions are specified in the form of high-side and low-side override review rules. Management may decide that they want to have no more than 3 percent low-side overrides (granting a loan when the scoring system fails to qualify the applicant) and no more than 8 percent high-side overrides (declining a loan that is score qualified). Often, more than one rule may apply to a particular credit applicant. It is therefore important to capture the priority of review rules that are applied to determine high- or low-side overrides in the event only a single reason is retained for the final approve/decline decision. Otherwise, the override reasons captured will not maintain consistency on a case-by-case basis. Ideally, all relevant information associated with override rules should be captured for those applicants that fall into the override population. Specific examples will be provided later in the book for home equity lending and credit card products. The main point to remember is that a proper analysis of scoring system overrides for possible fair lending violations must consider, and control for, the policy override rules in order to arrive at an unbiased comparison of override rates for protected and nonprotected class credit applicants. Failure to source all of the relevant policy rules will render the analyst unable to discern similarly situated protected and nonprotected class overrides, and unable to perform comparisons of their respective population segments associated override rates.

Concentrations

Yet another category of policy rules pertains to concentrations. This is generally applied at a portfolio-level and would be sourced from the chief credit officer or corporate credit administration. Examples include situations where an institution wants to limit its subprime exposure to preset levels based on the ratio of exposure to the institution's tier 1 capital, or there may be a regional exposure cap based on business growth targets, or a cap on the percentage of loans to convenience stores, sole proprietorships, etcetera. This type of information may be particularly useful when performing HMDA trend analysis and peer comparisons relative to market penetration and origination rates in particular geographic areas or on a corporate level relative to protected classes in general. The timing of any directives to limit business during the evaluation period is important. In addition, any decisions to add, emphasize, deemphasize, or sunset loan products or loan programs would be important information to source from the lines of business affected. This type of information will not be explored in further depth in subsequent chapters, but it was important to make the point early on that these types of policies can have an impact when thresholds are reached or surpassed in the retail book of business.

TYPES OF STATISTICAL ANALYSIS

Statistical analysis is concerned with scientific methods for collecting, organizing, summarizing, analyzing, and presenting data, as well as with drawing valid conclusions and making reasonable decisions based on statistical methodologies. Statistics can be used to describe data or make inferences from data. Fair lending deals primarily with inferential statistics,[20] which focuses on the conditions under which inferences are valid. Inferential statistics involves everything from simple hypothesis testing to sophisticated multivariate modeling. Simple hypothesis testing examples include ones using t-test or Fisher's exact chi-square test.[21] Examples of multivariate models used are logistic regressions, linear regressions, and tree models.[22] Inferential statistics seeks to confirm or refute a particular hypothesis about a population of interest, and it can take a simple or more complex form, as illustrated in the examples below.

- *Simple hypothesis testing.* "Is the incidence of a particular credit practice significantly different for a protected class versus nonprotected class of customers?" If overages were assessed for female borrowers at a rate of 50 percent, and male borrowers at a rate of 45 percent, hypothesis testing would seek to determine if the difference of 5 percent in proportions is statistically significant.
- *Multivariate analysis.* "Can the difference in the home improvement loan approval experience for minority and nonminority mortgage applicants be fully explained via generally accepted credit underwriting practices?" A regression model can be developed for the purpose of predicting the probability of denial for different groups of applicants. After the model is developed, a variable representing the race/ethnicity of the applicants is allowed to enter into the model for consideration. If the race/ethnicity variable is found to be significant, then a preliminary finding of possible disparate treatment is rendered and an in-depth manual file review is undertaken to determine the causes and any corrective action.

Descriptive statistics involves analysis, which seeks only to describe a given group, without drawing any conclusions or inferences of a more general nature. An example of descriptive statistical application would be to examine different groups of credit applicants (over a given time horizon) by gender, to learn their characteristics with respect to critical underwriting success factors (e.g., debt-to-income ratio, loan-to-value ratio, credit score, credit history, income, etc.). Examples of descriptive measures derived from the data include the minimum, average, maximum, range, variance, and so on.

Early on in an investigation, statistical analysis is more effective than other methods such as reviewing files. This is because statistical methods provide the ability to look at, or make inferences about, all of the data, rather than isolated instances. Hence, broad, general statements can be made as a result of analysis versus an in-depth explanation of specific cases. It is highly inefficient and

---

20. For an overview of statistical analysis to fair lending compliance, see Yezer, Anthony M., Lawrence B. Lindsey, and William M. Isaac. *Fair Lending Analysis: A Compendium of Essays on the Use of Statistics.* American Bankers Association, 1995.
21. These tests can be easily performed with SAS procedures. For example, FREQ procedure can be used to perform Fisher's exact test. For details, see *SAS/STAT 9.1 User's Guide.* SAS Institute, 2003. See also Stokes, Maura E., Charles S. Davis, and Gary G. Koch. *Categorical Data Analysis Using the SAS System.* SAS Institute Inc., 1995, pp. 23–26.
22. Such as Classification and Regression Trees (CART), chi-square automatic interaction detection (CHAID), and so forth. For details about selecting appropriate testing methods, and multivariate models, see Agresti, Alan. *Categorical Data Analysis.* John Wiley & Sons, 2002.

less reliable to perform manually intensive, time-consuming file reviews as a primary assessment tool. That said, when the statistical findings are significant, compliance staff rely on in-depth file reviews to determine the detailed causes of the significant finding via specific examples of disparate treatment for similarly situated loan applicants or borrowers.

COMPLIANCE SELF-TESTING STRATEGY MATRIX

A thorough, effective, and efficient fair lending compliance self-examination program must consider two primary dimensions. The first dimension is the scope of the self-examination program. The other dimension is the approaches used to identify, measure, monitor, and control the risks that are in scope for the program. This second dimension splits into qualitative and quantitative areas. Later in this section we delineate several specific approaches that fall into each area.

Consider that fair lending risks can stem from failure to execute appropriately in the following broad categories:

- *Advertising/marketing/sales*. Attract a diverse customer base, provide equal access, consistent assistance, avoidance of steering, avoidance of redlining, avoidance of reverse redlining, avoidance of loan flipping, and so on.
- *Underwriting*. Apply fair and consistent decision criteria; ensure fair referral process is in place for all customers
- *Pricing*. Should be fair, avoid fee packing, ensure fee waivers are performed equitably, and ensure that frequency and amount of discretionary price adjustments are balanced across protected class and nonprotected class consumers.
- *Operational*. Technical compliance with laws, maintenance of fair lending data, and ensure processes are error-free.
- *Outreach*. Development of programs to access a broad customer base and develop/maintain strategic alliances with governmental agencies, community groups, specialized lenders, and so on.
- *Advocacy*. Acknowledge/track written discrimination complaints in a timely fashion and perform analysis to identify any potential patterns of discrimination.
- *Education*. Ensuring that the sales force, underwriters, and all others connected with the lending process are well versed in the principles and practical application of fair lending in their respective areas.

The fundamental question is: "How do you test for failures in any/all of these areas?" Fortunately, we did not have to "reinvent the wheel" as the FFIEC developed Fair Lending Examination Guidelines over five years ago. Hence, we have adopted the list of 49 specific examination factors, which fall into seven broad categories, and are used to assess a lending institution's fair lending performance by their primary regulator. The broad categories of factors are:[23]

1. [C] Compliance Program Discrimination Factors
2. [O] Overt Indicators of Discrimination
3. [U] Indicators of Potential Disparate Treatment in Underwriting
4. [P] Indicators of Potential Disparate Treatment in Pricing
5. [S] Indicators of Potential Disparate Treatment by Steering
6. [R] Indicators of Potential Discriminatory Redlining
7. [M] Indicators of Potential Disparate Treatment in Marketing

---

23. See (Appendix 2A) for the definitions of each FFIEC fair lending examination factor, and the respective identifier for each factor.

It can be very useful to array these examination factors as rows in a matrix and then define columns to cross-reference them relative to the approach(es) used to address potential exposures. The columns may be institution specific. For the purposes of this discussion, we consider 11 general approaches, falling into two broad categories that are used to assess a lending institution's fair lending exposures. They are displayed in Figure 2.6.

The approaches listed in Figure 2.6 may be briefly described as follows:

(L1) Policy assessments consist of a thorough evaluation of credit policy guidelines, standards, forms, procedures, and practices for all business lines that pertain to the loan application process, loan underwriting, pricing, marketing, and account management in order to determine the degree to which consistent treatment is afforded to all credit applicants and customers and all applicable laws, regulations, and internal policies are followed. This is a rather sweeping definition. In order to provide more concreteness, the following are examples of types of questions that policy assessments attempt to address:

Do the corporation's credit underwriting policies conform to fair lending laws and regulations and are they being maintained to ensure that policy threshold values for all applicable business rules are appropriate, if not optimal, for all pertinent classes of applications processed?

Do credit policies promote outreach by giving appropriate flexibility in product and program design to better accommodate underserved consumers and communities?

Do credit pricing policies conform to fair lending laws and regulations and are they being maintained to ensure that policy threshold values for all applicable business rules are appropriate, if not optimal, for all pertinent classes of loans being priced?

Do compensation policies for staff that are rewarded for loan production, in addition to, or in place of, a predetermined salary disadvantage customers who are members of a protected class or cause them to be treated differently from other customers?

Are marketing and advertising campaigns geared toward attainment of a diverse customer base?

Have programs and partnerships been formed with community groups, community-based lenders, and government agencies to foster referrals of protected class applicants to the institution?

Does customer-facing staff provide comparable level of assistance to all customers and prospective customers?

ID	Approach	ID	Approach
[L]	Qualitative approaches	[N]	Quantitative approaches
L1	Policy assessments	N1	Universal performance indicator ranking CRA/HMDA analysis
L2	Mystery shopping	N2	Statistical testing/modeling
L3	Customer advocacy	N3	Review of scorecards and overrides
L4	Operational risk control self-assessment	N4	Matched pair file reviews
		N5	Geographical information and mapping
		N6	MIS reporting
		N7	Operational risk KRIs

FIGURE 2.6 TYPES OF ANALYTICAL APPROACHES

(L2) Mystery shopping seeks to evaluate the "preapplication" process for fair and equal treatment of applicants falling into Federal Housing Authority (FHA) or Equal Credit Opportunity Act (ECOA) defined protected classes and it is associated with direct channel consumer business lines. It is normally conducted by an independent consultant.

(L3) Customer advocacy addresses complaints of discrimination, including: (a) timely written acknowledgement to the parties involved; (b) investigation into potential patterns of practice that directly cause, or increase chances of, discrimination; and (c) reporting findings and recommendations to management, and tracking of complaints through final resolution.

(L4) Operational risk control self-assessment provides for a periodic evaluation of internal controls to gauge their effectiveness in reducing risk of violations of laws and regulations and limiting exceptions to policy within an acceptable range. While qualitative in nature (usually a questionnaire completed by process owners and business managers), the responses may be based on the results of rigorous testing and detailed audits in addition to subjective opinions supplied by operations and field staff and seasoned managers.

(N1–N6) These quantitative approaches will be explored in further depth in subsequent chapters, and are fairly self-explanatory.

(N7) Operational risk key risk indicators represent measures of various types of risk that pose the threat of future losses to the enterprise. Again, this is a rather sweeping definition. In order to provide more concreteness, the following examples of fair lending key risk indicators are offered:

   o Percentage of consumer complaints alleging discrimination for a protected class.
   o Scoring system override rate disparity for a protected class versus nonprotected class.
   o Inflated real estate appraisal disparity for a protected class versus nonprotected class.

Given the row and column definitions, we can now construct a strategy matrix that maps approaches for addressing each examination factor. Figure 2.7 presents the results using only the row and column identifiers to allow for a more compact display of the mapping. It also tallies the rows, and provides a grand total of instances of approaches across the 49 exam factors.

A quick check indicates that there is at least one approach (usually many more) that is associated with each exam factor. On average, there are three approaches for each exam factor, and a 1-to-2 split between qualitative and quantitative approaches. Since the focus of this book is on quantitative approaches, the qualitative methods will not be covered in any detail. FFIEC definitions of the 49 exam factors appear in (Appendix 2A). While we have attempted to cover the most common applications, we do not have an example of every approach for each exam factor, such as regression analysis applied to redlining.[24]

CREDIT RISK MANAGEMENT SELF-TESTING STRATEGY MATRIX

Analogous to fair lending compliance, credit risk management safety and soundness self-exami-nation requires consideration of two primary dimensions. The first dimension is the scope of the self-examination program, and the second dimension is the identification of approaches to address the identification, measurement, monitoring, and control of the "in-scope" risks that the program is designed to address.

---

24. E.g., for the R2, N2 combination in Figure 2.7, see Avery, Robert B. and Buynak, Thomas M., "Mortgage Redlining: Some New Evidence," Economic Review, Federal Reserve Bank of Cleveland, Summer 1981, ISSN 0013–0281, pp. 18–32.

#	Qualitative (L)				Quantitative (N)						
	L1	L2	L3	L4	N1	N2	N3	N4	N5	N6	N7
C1											1
C2				1							
C3				1							1
C4											1
C5				1							
C6				1							1
O1	1			1			1				
O2	1	1		1			1	1			
O3							1				
O4		1	1	1							
O5	1	1	1	1							
U1					1	1		1			1
U2					1					1	
U3					1						1
U4	1			1							
U5	1			1			1				
U6				1			1	1			
U7					1		1			1	1
U8	1								1		
U9			1		1					1	1
P1	1					1			1		
P2	1			1					1		
P3	1			1		1	1	1	1		
P4		1		1	1	1		1	1		1
P5			1		1				1	1	
S1					1						
S2	1	1		1		1		1		1	1
S3					1	1		1			
S4					1	1		1	1	1	1
S5			1							1	1
S6	1	1		1		1		1		1	
S7	1	1		1							
S8					1				1		
R1					1				1		1
R2					1	1			1		1
R3					1				1		
R4									1		1

FIGURE 2.7   COMPLIANCE STRATEGY MATRIX

#	Qualitative (L)				Quantitative (N)						
	L1	L2	L3	L4	N1	N2	N3	N4	N5	N6	N7
R5	1				1				1		
R6	1				1				1	1	
R7		1		1							
R8			1						1		1
R9					1				1		
M1	1			1							
M2	1			1							
M3	1									1	
M4	1				1				1		
M5	1								1	1	
M6					1				1		
M7	1		1							1	1
Tot	20	8	7	20	19	9	7	9	15	16	17

FIGURE 2.7   (continued)

Our focus here is on credit risk specific to consumer and small business lending and on those categories of exam factors that can be addressed by quantitative approaches. Hence, this is a more narrow coverage than that afforded to fair lending compliance.

The first dimension of the self-examination program for credit risk management includes:

- *RE—risk evaluation for underwriting/pricing.* Scoring model variables and attribute point values, model factor information value, factor importance ranking, factor interactions (pairwise and multiway), factor conditional structures, and default probabilities associated with score or hybrid risk index.
- *PM—portfolio monitoring.* Composition relative to underwriting factors, volume, growth, shifts in composition, risk rating and trend, delinquency and trend, exception tracking,[25] loss forecasting, reserve management, and stress testing.
- *CC—credit concentration.* Borrower-level, geographic, product-type, maturity, collateral, industry, risk tier (e.g., subprime, A, B, C, D paper), highly leveraged loans, self-employed, start-up company, out of market area, policy exceptions, loans not guaranteed by principals, and other segmentation criteria.
- *PF—policy formulation and credit control.* Changes in key risk indicators, overall diversification, underwriting/pricing factor thresholds, credit limit, exception thresholds, concentration limits, and weighing risk/reward trade-offs.
- *MM—model management.* Ongoing performance monitoring, periodic validation.

Figure 2.8 summarizes the types of analytical approaches that can be used to address each of these broad examination areas. We cover all but two of the methods in later chapters, and we defer further explanation of them. For those two methods, namely vintage cohort[26] and Monte

---

25. Includes exceptions relative to underwriting, policy, or documentation.
26. See Glenn, Norval D. *Cohort Analysis.* Sage Publications, 1977, for an explanation of the general method, and Siddiqi, Naeem, *Credit Risk Scorecards.* John Wiley & Sons, 2006, pp. 181–183.

ID	Approach
SR	Standard reporting
DR	Drilldown (OLAP) reporting
GC	Graphing/charting
CS	Credit scoring
BSM	Behavioral simulation method
UPI	Universal performance indicator
DCP	Dynamic conditional process
REPF	Risk evaluation and policy formulation (*hybrid* system)
VCA	Vintage cohort analysis
OER	Ordinary least square (OLS) with econometric behavior variables regression
MCM	Monte Carlo methods

FIGURE 2.8 TYPES OF ANALYTICAL APPROACHES

Carlo,[27] we cite references that explain the method and describe how it is used. It is important to note that in many instances (e.g., loss forecasting), there may not be a single best approach. In these instances, several different approaches can be used and their results averaged in order to obtain at the most reliable estimate.[28]

The columns may be institution specific. For the purposes of this discussion, we consider 11 general approaches that are used to help assess a lending institution's credit risk exposures.

This list is not meant to be complete. It provides some of the more commonly encountered approaches. Just as was the case for fair lending compliance, it can be very useful to array these self-examination factors as rows in a matrix and then define columns to cross-reference them relative to the approach(es) used to address potential exposures. We do so in Figure 2.9.

Self-Examination Program	Quantitative Method											Total Methods
	SR	DR	GC	CS	BSM	UP1	DCP	REPF	VCA	ORE	MCM	
RE				1			1	1		1		4
PM	1	1	1	1	1	1	1	1	1	1	1	11
CC	1	1	1			1		1	1		1	7
PF	1	1	1	1	1	1		1				7
MM	1	1				1						3
Total	4	4	3	3	2	4	2	4	2	2	2	32

FIGURE 2.9 CREDIT RISK STRATEGY MATRIX

---

27. See Ross, Sheldon. *Simulation*, Harcourt/Academic Press, 1997, pp. 218–243 for a more rigorous treatment of the subject; and Hull, J. C. *Options, Futures, and Other Derivatives*, 4th ed. Englewood Cliffs, NJ, 2000, pp. 406–411, for a simpler application.
28. This technique is often referred to as *ensemble modeling*.

RE deals with estimating and pricing risk at individual loan level and appropriate methods are covered in Chapters 5 and 6. PC and CC deal with portfolio-level risk assessment. CC can be a big contributor to unexpected losses and is a large cause of bank failures and forced mergers that is controlled by setting and enforcing exposure limits. RE, PM, and CC all provide input to PF, where credit policy is managed for all levels of lending activity. MM is an integral part of the credit risk management process, and it ensures that risk measurement is sufficiently accurate.

MATCHING APPROPRIATE STATISTICAL METHODS TO REGULATORY EXAMINATION FACTORS

Choice of statistical methods depends on the objectives of testing, the available data, and the nature of the relevant policies and business rules governing the area of interest. Generally speaking, underwriting evaluations associated with credit scoring system–based decisioning are most often conducted using a variety of methods falling into the category *override analysis*. For underwriting evaluations associated with multifactor decisioning, regression is preferred. For pricing analysis involving the incidence of high-cost loans, logistic regression is appropriate. If the target variable in a pricing regression is the APR spread, or loan rate, then ordinary least squares regression is appropriate. For pricing evaluations involving the average fee or interest amounts, the *t*-test is commonly used, but analysis of variance (ANOVA) and/or nonparametric analysis may be most appropriate, depending on the distributional properties of the data. For pricing evaluations involving the incidence of fees or discounts, the Fisher's exact chi-square test is the best technique for determining if differing rates of incidence are statistically significant.

At a higher level, there is a need to view the experience of the enterprise at varying: organizational entities, geographic market levels, product access channels, prohibited basis and control groups, loan products, decision centers, and time frames. The ability to view and hone in on combinations of these dimensions to surface potential exposures is critical. In the parlance of regulators, combinations of these elements are referred to as *examination focal points*. Once these focal points are identified, they must be prioritized based on a number of factors, including degree of measurable potential risk exposure they represent, relation to any areas of needed improvement that were cited in prior examinations, regulatory priorities, current areas of class-action litigation, current areas of heightened regulatory or community activist scrutiny, and recent changes in any of the following areas that have an impact on the combination of elements in question during the examination period in question:

- Changes in lines of business, in products and services offered, or in organizational structure.
- Changes in loan origination, data warehousing, or other pertinent application (information technology) systems.
- Changes in brokers, dealers, correspondents, counterparties, or third-party service providers.
- Changes in markets serviced, in application or loan volume, significant turnover, or vacancies.
- Any new or significantly revised policies and procedures.

There is also a need at a higher level to assess performance relative to peers, and the industry as a whole, within the appropriate business context. Fortunately, a useful body of information for this purpose is compiled by the government annually under the Regulation C, the Home Mortgage Disclosure Act. It is vital that lenders of HMDA-reportable loans must be capable of connecting the dots from the HMDA raw data to their true fair lending performance, so as to synchronize external stakeholder perceptions with reality.

In general, there are very legitimate reasons for pursuing analyses on "limited sets of information," and we see several clear drawbacks to deploying an exhaustive, brute-force strategy toward compliance testing. Cost and efficiency are primary. A well-designed systematic approach can quickly and efficiently identify and prioritize the largest risk exposures, allowing the institution to focus on the items that exhibit the most pronounced risk potential.

CASE FOR A SYSTEMATIC APPROACH

There are many paths to understanding. There are also many different starting points. For example, there may be a customer complaint, an official external inquiry, a story in the newspaper, a spike in quarterly HMDA reported results, an audit finding, a mystery shopping result, or an inquiry from a community group. Often, these types of starting points are accompanied by surprise, which many agree is a manager's worst enemy. What you do not know can hurt you and your organization. But how does one go about making it their business to know what is going on so as to avoid surprise and achieve a truly proactive compliance management mode of operation? The authors believe that it is of fundamental importance to craft a self-examination program that is rooted in a systematic approach. Subsequent chapters of this book explain exactly what that approach entails. The purpose here is to provide an overview of the fair lending analytic process. Figure 2.10 illustrates the main idea surrounding the systematic approach.

The first step is to identify the examination factors that define the purpose of the analysis. In the absence of specific known compliance issues, the universal performance indicator can quickly and thoroughly provide an assessment of most critical areas needing attention. The second step is to identify any segments exhibiting disparate levels above policy thresholds. The third step is to test for disparate treatment within the segments identified in Step 2. Step 4 is to construct examples for any significant findings in Step 3 to support model conclusions. The final step is to summarize the findings and make recommendations. Note that as the analysis deepens, we have increasing number of variables within an expanded set of segments, which results in fewer observations. Models on more homogenous segments, made possible by various new analysis methodologies, exhibit better test power and performance, and we describe them in subsequent chapters.

Once data are available, the systematic approach can begin at the highest level with public information that may include the annual HMDA peer data. Just as regulatory agencies may use this HMDA data for screening purposes, to identify areas within institutions where greater scrutiny of lending practices is warranted, lending institutions can leverage it to compare themselves with peers, peer groups, or the industry at large. Moreover, this data can help institutions be more efficient, by using it to determine where the greatest potential risk exposures are and, conversely, areas where they are not, thereby prioritizing budget and resource expense.

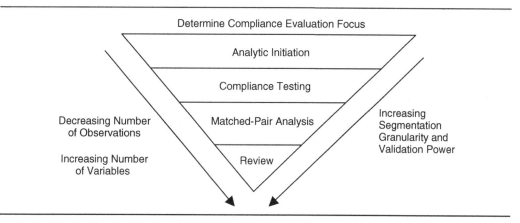

FIGURE 2.10 SYSTEMATIC APPROACH

Chapter 3 provides an in-depth treatment on how to immediately convey the HMDA-based "fair lending exposure picture" using a universal performance indicator. We will also discuss how this indicator decomposes into different perspectives on lending activities, drawing on examples from the FFIEC 2005 peer HMDA detail data. Moreover, we illustrate how this methodology for fair lending analysis can readily be extended to include nonpublic data that spans borrower risk, channel, transaction, market, and collateral information.

As one moves deeper into the inverted triangle in Figure 2.10, the complexity of statistical testing increases from simple univariate analysis and comparison tests of summary statistics to multivariate models and multiway comparisons. If significant and material results persist, matched-pair comparisons will be produced and comparative file reviews conducted to either refute or validate findings with case-by-case examples. The process just described is covered in detail in Chapters 4 and 5. We have carefully constructed examples along the way that illustrate pitfalls and trip-wires that one encounters when they attempt to perform even routine, seemingly straightforward analyses. Essentially, the compliance analyst must be careful not to assume away key requirements of the method they are using or misapply the method itself. Some examples covered include implications of performing a one- versus two-tailed test;[29] ensuring key data assumptions hold (e.g., equal variance, normally distributed data); and handling the analysis if assumptions are violated. For example, unequal variance, non-normality, truncated, doubly truncated, or censored distribution can occur.

Essentially, the idea behind the systematic approach is to avoid overkill and time wasted checking what is correct. It also avoids the syndrome of generating hundreds of reports on the off chance they may be used someday. It has been said that the only thing worse than not knowing about a problem is to possess the information pertaining to it, and doing nothing about it. We contend that any reports you are going to produce should be reports that you are going to review in some depth; otherwise, do not produce them.[30]

SUMMARY

This chapter described the relevant inputs to fair lending and credit risk analysis, that is, data and policy rules. It highlighted some of the key areas of compliance and risk exposure that need to be addressed by a compliance and credit risk management program, together with the kinds of quantitative approaches that are often used to perform analysis of those exposures. Finally, we proposed a systematic process that can help to both strengthen, and shorten, the path to achieving the organization's desired level of regulatory compliance performance. Some key points are:

- Complete, accurate, and timely data are required for success.
- Sampling should be conducted using proper statistical methods.
- Policy and operational business rules must be captured and reflected in the analysis.
- Self-testing strategies for fair lending compliance, and credit risk should match assessment areas (e.g., regulatory examination factors) with appropriate methods for testing and analysis.

To assist the reader in navigating the remainder of the text, a chapter-by-chapter cross-reference to the key areas and approaches is provided in Figure 2.11. Readers interested in a particular exam risk areas, or in particular compliance risk management approaches, may find this especially useful.

---

29. As we will discuss in Chapter 4, two-tailed test can cause significance level to be only half of the desired value, since two-tailed test of $\alpha = 0.05$ is equivalent to one-tailed test with $\alpha = 0.025$.

30. A complete discussion of this topic is beyond the scope of the book, but see McGuire, Matthew P., Frank A. Hirsch, Jr., Wesley D. Few, and Clark R. Abrahams. "The HMDA Internal Analysis Conundrum: How to Avoid the Creation of Evidence to be Used Against You," *Real Estate Finance Journal*, Spring 2006.

#	Chapter Title/Subsection (Where Applicable)	FFIEC Factor	Approach
3	Universal Performance Indicator/Peer Analysis and Compliance Risk Monitoring	U1–U3,U7,U9; P4–P5; S1,S3–S4,S8; R1–R3,R5–R6; M4,M6	N1,N5–N6
4	Loan Pricing Analysis	P1,P3–P4	N1–N2
4	Overage/Underage Analysis	P3–P4	N2
4	Loan Pricing Analysis/Matched-Pair Analysis	U1; P4; S4	N4
5	Regression Analysis for Compliance Testing	U1; S2–S4,S6; R2	N2,N4
5	Regression Analysis for Compliance Testing/Matched-Pair Analysis	O2; U6; P3–P4; S2–S4,S6	N4
6	Alternative Credit Risk Models	U1; P3	N1–N2
6	Hybrid Models and Override Analysis	O1–O3; U5–U7; P3	N3
7	Multilayered Segmentation	U1; P3	N2–N3
8	Model Validation	U1; P3	N1–N3
#	Chapter Title/Subsection (Where Applicable)	Credit Risk Factor	Approach
3	Universal Performance Indicator	PM, CC	DR, UPI
4	Loan Pricing Analysis	RE	SR, CS
6	Alternative Credit Risk Models	RE, PF	CS, REPF
7	Multilayered Segmentation	RE, PM, CC, PF	BSM, UPI, DCP, REPF
8	Model Validation	MM	CS, DCP, REPF

FIGURE 2.11 COVERAGE OF RISKS AND APPROACHES BY CHAPTER

Appendix 2A
FFIEC FAIR LENDING EXAMINATION FACTORS WITHIN SEVEN BROAD CATEGORIES

	Compliance Program Discrimination Factors		Indicators of Potential Disparate Treatment by Steering
C1	Overall institution compliance record is weak.	S1	For an institution that has one or more subprime mortgage subsidiaries or affiliates, any significant differences, by loan product, in the percentage of prohibited basis applicants of the institution compared with the percentage of prohibited basis applicants of the subsidiary(ies) or affiliate(s).
C2	Prohibited basis monitoring information is incomplete.	S2	Lack of clear, objective standards for (i) referring applicants to subsidiaries or affiliates, (ii) classifying applicants as "prime" or "subprime" borrowers, or (iii) deciding what kinds of alternative loan products should be offered or recommended to applicants.
C3	Data and/or recordkeeping problems compromised reliability of previous examination reviews.	S3	For an institution that makes both conventional and FHA mortgages, any significant differences in the percentage of prohibited basis group applicants in each of these two loan products, particularly with respect to loan amounts of $100,000 or more.
C4	Fair lending problems were previously found in one or more bank products.	S4	For an institution that makes both prime and subprime loans for the same purpose, any significant differences in percentages of prohibited basis group borrowers in each of the alternative loan product categories.
C5	The size, scope, and quality of the compliance management program, including senior management's involvement, is materially inferior to programs customarily found in institutions of similar size, market demographics, and credit complexity.	S5	Consumer complaints alleging discrimination in residential loan pricing.
C6	The institution has not updated compliance guidelines to reflect changes in law or in agency policy.	S6	A lender with a subprime mortgage company subsidiary or affiliate integrates loan application processing for both entities, such that steering between the prime and subprime products can occur almost seamlessly: that is, a single loan processor could simultaneously attempt to qualify any applicant, whether to the bank or the mortgage company, under either the bank's prime criteria or the mortgage company's subprime criteria.

			Indicators of Potential Disparate Treatment by Steering
	Overt Indicators of Discrimination	S7	Loan officers have broad discretion regarding whether to promote conventional or FHA loans, or both, to applicants and the lender has not issued guidelines regarding the exercise of this discretion.
O1	Including explicit prohibited basis identifiers in underwriting criteria or pricing standards.	S8	A lender has most of its branches in predominantly white neighborhoods. The lender's subprime mortgage subsidiary has branches that are located primarily in predominantly minority neighborhoods.
O2	Collecting information, conducting inquiries, or imposing conditions contrary to express requirements of Regulation B.		**Indicators of Potential Discriminatory Redlining**
O3	Including variables in a credit scoring system that constitute a basis or factor prohibited by Regulation B or, for residential loan scoring systems, the Fair Housing Act.	R1	Significant differences, as revealed by HMDA data, in the number of loans originated in those areas in the lender's market that have relatively high concentrations of minority group residents compared with areas with relatively low concentrations of minority residents.
O4	Statements made by the institution's officers, employees, or agents which constitute an express or implicit indication that one or more such persons have engaged or do engage in discrimination on a prohibited basis in any aspect of a credit transaction.	R2	Significant differences between approval/denial rates for all applicants (minority and nonminority) in areas with relatively low concentrations of minority residents.
O5	Employee or institutional statements that evidence attitudes based on prohibited basis prejudices or stereotypes.	R3	Significant differences between denial rates based on insufficient collateral for applicants from relatively high concentrations of minority residents and those areas with relatively low concentrations of minority residents.
	Indicators of Potential Disparate Treatment in Underwriting	R4	Other patterns of lending identified during the most recent CRA examination that differ by the concentration of minority residents.
U1	Substantial disparities among the approval/denial rates for applicants by monitored prohibited basis characteristic (especially within income categories).	R5	Explicit demarcation of credit product markets that excludes MSAs, political subdivisions, census tracts, or other geographic areas within the institution's lending market and having relatively high concentrations of minority residents.
U2	Substantial disparities among the application processing times for applications by monitored prohibited basis characteristic (especially within denial reason groups).	R6	Policies on receipt and processing of applications, pricing, conditions, or appraisals and valuation, or on any other aspect of providing residential credit that vary between areas with relatively high concentrations of minority residents and those areas with relatively low concentrations of minority residents.
U3	Substantially higher proportion of withdrawn/incomplete applications from prohibited basis applicants than from other applicants.	R7	Employee statements that reflect an aversion to doing business in areas with relatively high concentrations of minority residents.

	Indicators of Potential Disparate Treatment in Underwriting		Indicators of Potential Discriminatory Redlining
U4	Vague or unduly subjective underwriting criteria.	R8	Complaints or other allegations by consumers or community representatives that the lender excludes or restricts access to credit for areas with relatively high concentrations of minority residents. Examiners should review complaints against the lender filed with their agency; the CRA public comment file; community contact forms; and the responses to questions about redlining, discrimination, and discouragement of applications, and about meeting the needs of racial or national origin minorities, asked as part of "obtaining local perspectives on the performance of financial lenders" during prior CRA examinations.
U5	Lack of clear guidance on making exceptions to underwriting criteria, including credit score overrides.	R9	A lender that has most of its branches in predominantly white neighborhoods at the same time that the lender's subprime mortgage subsidiary has branches which are located primarily in predominantly minority neighborhoods.
U6	Lack of clear loan file documentation regarding reasons for any exceptions to normal underwriting standards, including credit scoring overrides.		**Indicators of Potential Disparate Treatment in Marketing**
U7	Relatively high percentages of either exceptions to underwriting criteria or overrides of credit score cutoffs.	M1	Advertising patterns or practices that a reasonable person would believe indicate prohibited basis customers are less desirable.
U8	Loan officer or broker compensation based on loan volume (especially loans approved per period of time).	M2	Advertising only in media serving nonminority areas of the market.
U9	Consumer complaints alleging discrimination in loan processing or in approving/denying residential loans.	M3	Marketing through brokers or other agents that the lender knows (or has reason to now) would serve only one racial or ethnic group in the market.
	Indicators of Potential Disparate Treatment in Pricing	M4	Use of marketing programs or procedures for residential loan products that exclude one or more regions or geographies within the lender's assessment or marketing area that have significantly higher percentages of minority group residents than does the remainder of the assessment or marketing area.
P1	Relationship between loan pricing and compensation of loan officers or brokers.	M5	Using mailings or other distribution lists or other marketing techniques for prescreened or other offerings of residential loan products that explicitly exclude groups of prospective borrowers on a prohibited basis; or exclude geographies (e.g., census tracts, ZIP codes, etc.) within the institution's marketing area that have significantly higher percentages of minority group residents than does the remainder of the marketing area.
P2	Presence of broad discretion in pricing or other transaction costs.	M6	Proportion of monitored prohibited basis applicants is significantly lower than the group's representation in the total population of the market area.

	Indicators of Potential Disparate Treatment in Pricing		Indicators of Potential Disparate Treatment in Marketing
P3	Use of a system of risk-based pricing that is not empirically based and statistically sound.	M7	Consumer complaints alleging discrimination in advertising or marketing loans.
P4	Substantial disparities among prices being quoted or charged to applicants who differ as to their monitored prohibited basis characteristics.		
P5	Consumer complaints alleging discrimination in residential loan pricing.		

Source: FFIEC Fair Lending Examination Factors within Seven Broad Categories.

3

ANALYTIC PROCESS INITIATION

As described in Chapter 2, compliance analysis begins at the highest level with public information that portrays loan underwriting and pricing results relative to differing loan purposes, dwelling types, lien status, owner occupancy, geographies, and so on. A universal source is the annual Home Mortgage Disclosure Act (HMDA) peer data. Other data that are acquired by lending institutions are also required for a complete view. Because there are many factors to consider, it can be difficult to put these results in an organized and meaningful way that is both simple, and thorough. The universal performance indicator (UPI) methodology described in this chapter offers a solution to this problem.

UPI can find geographic areas or other segments that have the greatest combined risk exposures to potential compliance violations, through the ability to simultaneously consider all relevant factors versus looking at individual factors. These factors include denial disparities, fallout disparities, origination disparities, pricing disparities, market penetration disparities, affordability disparities, and foreclosure disparities. In terms of broad categories of information, relevant factors in fair lending analysis fall into the following headings: macroeconomic influences, geographic influences, borrower credit history, borrower wealth and financial capacity, borrower noncredit payment history, borrower insurance profile, borrower relationship with lender, borrower education and length of time in profession and with current employer, borrower negotiation skills, collateralized property characteristics, product and loan program features and requirements, transaction terms and conditions, lender-specific factors, market influences, and channel effects. Each of these categories can be further expanded into subcategories. For example, the property characteristics category is comprised of many subcategories, including: appraisal/value, appreciation trend, occupancy status, age, type of construction, and location—especially income area. UPI accommodates a large number of variables with a handful of factors that can capture sufficient information to determine areas for further analysis.

In the following sections, we first describe the overall analysis framework of the UPI methodology. We then describe how to use this methodology to define, measure, and monitor fair lending compliance risk. We provide some specific examples to show how to enhance a lender's ability to effectively monitor their fair lending practices and meet regulatory challenges.

UNIVERSAL PERFORMANCE INDICATOR

In recent years, federal enforcement agencies have expanded both the standards and scope of fair lending regulations. In addition to expanding the HMDA reporting requirements, regulatory agencies have also extended enforcement programs defined to curb predatory lending and racial redlining. For example, the Office of the Comptroller of the Currency (OCC) issued antipredatory lending guidelines[1] that defined certain loan terms, conditions, and features as "susceptible" to abusive, predatory, unfair or deceptive lending practices. Such programs aid regulatory agencies in their ongoing monitoring of the lending activities of national banks and their operating subsidiaries. Banks that fail to adequately comply with these requirements may be subject to substantial counterproductive consequences, including monetary penalties and even unrecoverable reputation damage.

These new standards and regulations will continue to increase a mortgage lender's regulatory burden, fair lending scrutiny and compliance risk exposure. This requires the establishment of a simple, flexible, and thorough process for ongoing monitoring and evaluation of performance relative to both regulations and examination guidance, and corporate policies and goals. This process can become a competitive advantage in a dual sense: (1) those institutions that do not perform effectively and efficiently in this area can suffer consequences serious enough to threaten their market share and brand; and (2) with some simple adjustment of metrics, a UPI can be transformed into a revenue indicator that can be used to spot opportunities for profitable expansion into new geographic markets and customer segments. Such a systematic process becomes the core of an institution's fair lending risk management system that ties to internal controls and monitors transactional activities. Naturally, this risk management process addresses all aspects of potential lending disparities, including loan denial/approval, pricing, credit assessment, channel selection, program/product steering, and market territory emphasis (redlining and reverse redlining). An efficient monitoring system, with integrated data and well-designed statistical models, can vastly reduce time and resource requirements. This permits proactive initiatives for reducing risk, helping avoid more detailed examination preparation and lowering the organization's total cost of compliance, while ensuring that all of the bases are covered.

Traditionally, this compliance risk management process has been, and continues to be, very complicated and time consuming, with numerous evaluation standards, controls, criteria, and perspectives. In addition, subcategories of analysis performed in isolation have characterized what amounts to a somewhat fragmented and inefficient approach. For example, a denial disparity analysis is often performed across markets for purchase versus refinance or home improvement loans for government versus conventional loans, first versus subordinate lien status, protected versus nonprotected classes of applicants, and so on. Separately, an analysis of loan pricing, especially above-threshold loans, is performed for different channels, geographies, for fixed versus variable rate loans, by loan purpose for different protected classes, and so forth. Similarly, redlining, steering, and potential predatory lending analyses are also conducted, not to mention time to decision, fallout, appraisal to loan amount requested and appraisal to final sales price, and many other analyses. After all of the analyses are performed, they must be compiled and summarized and a top-level view constructed to "tell the story" in an executive summary, complete with an identification of where the largest risks reside, their order of priority, and their interrelationships.

The last point is important, because it is possible that in the process of compiling results, some important patterns and connections may be missed. For example, a metropolitan area may exhibit a pattern such as favorable disparity for protected-class loan originations, unfavorable disparity for above-trigger loan incidence, and highly favorable disparity for market penetration. An individual analysis may capture unfavorable performance only relative to pricing. However, the combination of disparities should be interpreted as a pattern of potential reverse redlining, or targeting specific protected classes for higher-priced loans.

UPI can help monitor and evaluate overall lending practices, prioritize areas with extreme disparity (or combinations of disparities), and benchmark overall disparity risk for purposes of comparison and ranking. Specifically, this methodology can be used to examine risk and compliance

---

1. OCC Guidelines Establishing Standards for Residential Mortgage Lending Practices, *Federal Register*, Vol. 70, No. 24, February 7, 2005, Rules and Regulations, pp. 6329–6332.

performance from a variety of perspectives across various groups of loan applicants defined by such factors as race, gender, age, income level, and thin-credit file consumers. UPI accomplishes this with a set of disparity indices that depict a particular group's performance relative to a control group and can include underwriting, pricing, marketing, and product steering factors. The totality of performance is examined from a number of critical fair lending compliance perspectives. The UPI is then calculated from a "risk-free" vantage that can be viewed relative to its component disparity indices, while measuring the overall risk. Various references can also be created to calibrate and examine this indicator from different aspects of the business.

OVERALL FRAMEWORK

The overall compliance analysis framework for UPI is described in Figure 3.1. The first step of the process is to define disparities based on business and regulatory requirements to capture risk exposures from different lending perspectives. This involves choosing the indices, identifying needed data elements, defining treatment and control groups, and specifying index calculation. The next step is to ensure that the appropriate records are selected, outliers are trimmed, and defaults are set and optimized so that the error rate can be minimized. The third step is to calculate the universal performance indicator. In this step, indices are represented with singular indicators relative to predefined reference points. Then, these singular indicators are combined into a UPI. Lending performance can then be monitored using these disparity indices and indicators at various levels within an institution or across different institutions, competitors, or industry composite(s). For those segments with high valued indicators, further analysis can be conducted to trace for root causes.

DEFINE DISPARITY

Before we can derive indices, we must define disparities. In fair lending analysis, a *disparity* is defined in terms of a treatment group results (e.g., protected group) relative to that of the control group (e.g., nonprotected group). This is designed so that the more unfavorable the result is to the treatment group, the larger is the disparity. So from a fair lending compliance perspective, the larger the disparity, the greater the exposure.

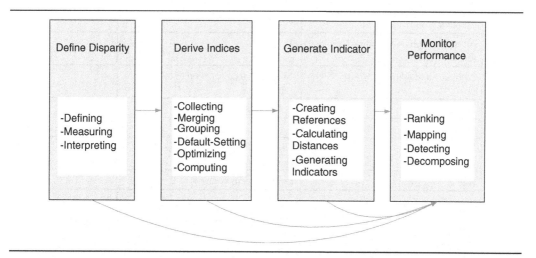

FIGURE 3.1 HIGH-LEVEL DESCRIPTION OF UPI DEVELOPMENT PROCESS

Defining Protected (Treatment) and Nonprotected (Control) Groups

To define a disparity index, one first needs to define which groups of borrowers are in one or more treatment (protected) classes, and which borrowers are in one or more control groups (nonprotected). While this may sound straightforward, the situation becomes complicated when you consider joint applications, or more expansive definitions of the control group. For example, if testing for race/ethnicity effects, then the control group is white non-Hispanic for individual borrower applications, and both primary and secondary borrowers are white non-Hispanic in the case of joint applications. For illustration purposes, Figures 3.2 and 3.3 list the control groups for individual borrowers and joint borrowers, respectively. Actual definitions may vary depending on business requirements and regulatory guidance.

Group	Protected	Control
Race and Ethnicity		
White non-Hispanic		X
All other	X	
Either N/A	Not protected, but need to test for significance	Do not Include, even if white w/Ethnicity N/A
Gender	Female	Male
Age	62 and over	Under 62

FIGURE 3.2   INDIVIDUAL BORROWER

Group	Protected	Control
Race and Ethnicity		
Both white non-Hispanic		X
All other groups—both same	X	
All other groups—Mixed incl. either race or ethnicity N/A	X	
Both race and ethnicity N/A	Not protected, but need to test for significance	
Gender	Both female	
Other comb		X
Both N/A	Not protected, but need to test for significance	
Age	Primary borrower 62+	
Other Comb		X
Both N/A	Not protected, but need to test for significance	

FIGURE 3.3   JOINT BORROWER

Types of Disparity Indices

A disparity index can be either results based or decision based. In fair lending, results-based indices are based on lending results such as loan originations, denials, fallouts, market penetration, loan pricing, or loan product. Decision-based indices reflect attributes or factors that contribute to the lending decision, such as applicant income, loan-to-value (LTV) ratio, debt-to-income (DTI) ratio, credit bureau score, or other risk factors. For example, for race/ethnicity the protected groups include Native American, Pacific Islanders, Asian, African-American, Hispanic, or other/mixed, while the control group can be white non-Hispanics. Disparity indices can be generated for any population segment and compared to a control group.

In the following examples, we define the protected group based on race/ethnicity as *treatment group* and the nonprotected group (e.g., white non-Hispanic) as *control group*. However, indices can be derived for income, age, gender, credit assessment, and many other factors.

Results-Based Indices

Results-based indices are indices that convey how particular groups of consumers were treated relative to a control group of consumers with respect to approval of a loan, pricing of a loan, type of product sold (e.g., nontraditional mortgages), marketing emphasis and ability to attract their business, level of assistance provided, length of time to decision, loan amount granted versus loan amount requested, ratio of appraisal amount of property to selling price, percentage of loans with prepayment penalties, percentage of adjustable rate mortgages (ARMs) having prepayment penalties that extend beyond the initial price reset anniversary, incidence of refinancing within the last two years, net tangible benefit ratio,[2] and suitability ratio.[3] Following are definitions of several of the more typical ones:

Denial disparity index (DDI) is the rate of denials of a specific protected class, or treatment group (TG), relative to the rate of denials for the nonprotected class or control group (CG). The protected class denial rate enters the numerator in the DDI. When the control group has a relatively low denial rate, and the protected class group has a relatively high denial rate, the DDI will take on a value greater than one and show some disparity.

Givens: Numerator % TG denials = # TG denials / # TG Apps

Denominator % CG denials = # CG denials / # CG Apps

Formula: DDI = % TG denials /% CG denials

Example: Native American denials in MSA 39580;

Native American denials = 3; CG denials = 119

Total Native American Apps = 10; Total CG Apps = 595

FDI = (3/10)/(119/595) = 1.5

Origination disparity index (ODI) is the rate of origination of the control group relative to the origination rate for a specific protected class group. For this index, and with the other indices, large values indicate a certain level of disparity and thus potential disparity relative to the control

---

2. Applicable in the case of loan refinancing, an unfavorable disparity would signal that a protected class was subjected to refinancing transactions exhibiting a low net tangible benefit more at a higher rate relative to their non-protected class counterparts. In addition to possibly signaling loan flipping, a form of predatory lending, a disparity might indicate targeting of a particular group with this practice, which would also have fair lending implications.

3. The notion of suitability involves not only qualifying an applicant for the loan, but determining if it is the best loan for the consumer. An important consideration in the case of adjustable rate, or nontraditional, mortgage is the consumer's ability to service debt in the future if interest rates rise and the monthly payment amount increases significantly.

group. Therefore, the control group origination rate enters the numerator in the ODI. When the control group has a relatively high origination rate, and the protected class group has a relatively low origination rate, the ODI will show some level of disparity.

Givens: Numerator   % CG orig = # CG orig / # CG Apps

Denominator   % TG orig = # TG orig / # TG Apps

Formula: ODI = % CG/% TG

Example: Asian-Americans in MSA 39580;

Asian Orig = 4; CG orig = 201

Total Asian Apps = 10; Total CG Apps = 595

ODI = (201/595)/(4/10) = .844

Fallout disparity index (FDI) is the rate of fallout of a specific protected class group relative to the fallout rate of the control group. The protected class rate enters the numerator in the FDI. When the control group has a relatively low fallout rate and the protected class group has relatively high fallout rate, the FDI will show some relative level of disparity.

Givens: Numerator   % TG fallout = # TG fallout / # TG Apps

Denominator   % CG fallout = # CG fallout/ # CG Apps...

Formula: FDI = % TG / % CG

Example: Asian in MSA 39580; Asian Fallout = 4; CG fallout = 90

Total Asian Apps = 10; Total CG Apps = 595

FDI = (4/10)/(90/595) = 2.67

Market penetration index (MPI) is the population size of a specific protected class group relative to their application rate within a particular geographically defined area (e.g., census tract, metropolitan statistical area [MSA], assessment area, etc.). This index captures the degree to which various lines of business are penetrating the protected class applicant pool. The formula is:

Givens: Numerator   % TG population = # TGPop./Total MSA Pop.

Denominator   % TG apps = # TGApps. / Total MSA Apps

Formula: MPI = % TG population / % TG Apps

Example: Asian in MSA 39580;

Asian Pop. = 49,574; Total Pop. = 2,959,950

Asian Apps = 10; Total Apps = 1,732

MPI = (49,574/2,959,950)/(10/1,732) = 2.89

Depending on data availability, other results-based indices can be created. The following are some additional examples:

Product disparity index (PDI) is the rate of a high-priced loan product (i.e., loans with a spread > 3%) of a specific protected class group relative to the high-priced loan product of the control group.

Subprime product application mix disparity index (SPAMDI) is the proportion of subprime loan applications for a specific protected-class group relative to their total applications, divided by the same ratio associated with control group applicants. This index captures the degree to which subprime products are marketed to protected classes relative to their control group (i.e., nonprotected class) counterparts.

Subprime product origination mix disparity index (SPOMDI) is the proportion of subprime loans for a specific protected class group relative to their total originations, divided by the same ratio associated with control group borrowers. This index captures the degree to which subprime products are sold to protected classes relative to their non-protected class counterparts.

Decision-Based Indices

Decision-based indices help identify and quantify the relative proportion of control group applicants, relative to the protected class group, that exhibit higher risk among the more critical credit risk and application decision factors. Examples include factors that characterize a borrower's character, capacity, capital, and collateral. Corresponding indices include credit bureau score, debt ratio, net worth, liquid assets, months of reserves, payment shock ratio, current affordability ratio, and LTV. In each case, a value greater than one indicates that control group applicants are less qualified than their protected-class counterparts. As in the prior section, we provide some examples.

Debt-to-income disparity index (DTIDI) is the proportion of control group applicants with high DTI (i.e., > 0.4) relative to the proportion of minority applicants with high DTI.

> Givens: Numerator % TG with DTI > 0.4 = # TG
> DTI > 0.4/# TG Apps
> Denominator % CG with DTI > 0.4 = # CG DTI > 0.4/# CG Apps
> Formula: DTIDI = % CG with DTI > 0.4/% TG with DTI > 0.4

Loan-to-value disparity index (LTVDI) is the proportion of control group applicants with high LTV (i.e., > 80) relative to the proportion of protected class applicants with high LTV measures.

Bureau score disparity index (BDI) is the ratio of the percentage of control group low bureau score applicants relative to that of the protected class low bureau score applicants.

Income disparity index (IDI) is the proportion of control group low-income applicants to protected-class low-income applicants.

Interpreting the Disparities

As discussed in the foregoing examples, the disparity indices are defined so as to provide a consistent interpretation in all cases and we provide a recap now of those contextual interpretations.

- For results-based disparities, a disparity value less than one indicates the treatment group (such as a protected-class group) is favored, while any value greater than one indicates nonparity and disfavor of the treatment group. An index of one indicates neither group is favored.

- For decision-based disparities, a disparity value less than one indicates the treatment group (such as a protected-class group) is less qualified. Conversely, any value greater than one indicates the treatment group is more qualified than the control group. An index of one indicates neither group is more qualified.

Experience using this approach will be necessary in order to determine appropriate threshold values for the disparity indices relative to initial fair lending performance screening. Based on analysis of results-based indicators sourced from public data, and also limited trial-and-error with decision-based data, we have found values greater than 1.5 are indicative of the need for more detailed examination. We recommend that a lender set different thresholds to capture disparities in a cost-effective way, depending on data availability, prevailing regulatory requirements and specific business needs. In general, segments or areas with insufficient data, or a small number of observations, should have relatively higher thresholds. Based on other input, such as past problems, customer complaints, or adverse trends, a stricter (lower) threshold should be set. In summary, threshold values may be adjusted to fit varying sets of circumstances.

Indices are grouped according to their business context. For example, the outcome of a mortgage application is captured by the individual indices associated with the results-based indicator. Similarly, the factors associated with borrower risk are reflected in the indices associated with the decision-based indicator. Furthermore, this concept extends to the other dimensions of mortgage underwriting, pricing, and marketing activities that may be broken down within segments that are defined by other classification variables, such as channel, quarter application was decisioned, loan purpose, loan type, single-family-dwelling indicator, property type, lien status, owner occupancy status, agency, loan amount tier, borrower income tier, income classification of census tract where property is located, and so forth.

DERIVE INDICES

After defining each individual disparity index, the next step is to apply those definitions to available data sources and derive the indices. This involves data collection, record selection, data aggregation, default setting and optimization, and index calculation. The overall process is described in Figure 3.4.

Disparity indices can be calculated for each protected-class group relative to the control group at various geographically or institutionally defined levels. For example, at the MSA level, all low-income, all moderate-income, all middle-income, and all high-income census tracts could be summed within each MSA, respectively; alternatively census tract, state, congressional districts, assessment areas, organization, entities, and other levels could also be defined. Calculations can be based on rates derived from numbers associated with the index being measured or their associated dollar amounts. They can also be derived relative to the classification variables mentioned in the last section.

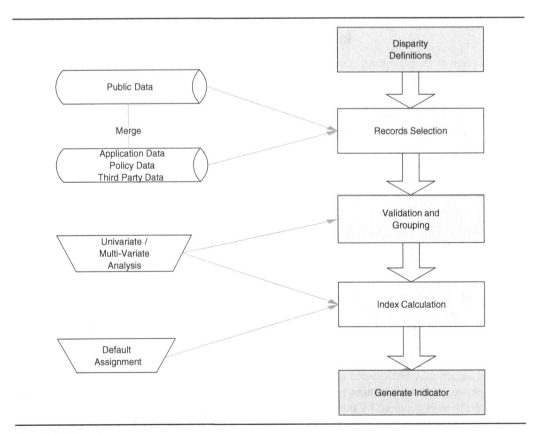

FIGURE 3.4   DERIVE INDICES

Data Collection

In this step, data from various sources are prepared for index generation. The types of disparity indices that can be calculated depend on both data availability and examination objectives. At a minimum, UPI-based fair lending analysis for both individual lender, and peer comparison, requires HMDA Loan Application Register (LAR) data and census data. Figures 3.5 and 3.6 show some sample input data that are typically used for these purposes.

This data is required for the calculation of the market penetration disparity index, which compares the percentage of households in a particular geographic area relative to the percentage of credit applications for that same protected class. For example, the fourth entry of Figure 3.5 shows that for census tract 201.01 in county 253 the percentage of protected-class households is 50 percent. That means that we would expect half of the credit applications in that census tract to come from protected-class applicants. The market penetration index tests for this result, and will have a value of 1.0 when this is true, and a value greater than 1.0 when there are relatively fewer protected-class applications in the application pool than there are protected-class households in the census tract. Hence, this census data provides the information needed to calculate the percentage of protected-class households in a geographic area for the entire United States and U.S. territories, which amounts to over 68,000 census tracts.

The sources for credit history information include the three major credit bureaus, and the lender's internal loan performance information. Figure 3.6 shows an example in which hypothetical credit history data is merged with the HMDA data and loan application data.

Consider the last entry in the figure, which provides merged information for loan application number 10. We see that this is an application taken in Abilene, Texas, for the purpose of home purchase, and that it is a first-lien, conventional mortgage loan in the amount of $180,000. The applicant, who is a Native American, has a credit bureau score of 776, an LTV of 43 percent, and a DTI of 38 percent. The application was approved.

Record Selection

Record selection can be based on previous data analysis such as a chi-square test, as shown in Figure 3.7. In this example, we test for significance in loan application decision results across minority status.

Census Year	MA	State Code	County Code	Census Tract	Population	Protected Class Population	% Protected Class Population
2005	10180	48	59	301	8673	675	7.78
2005	10180	48	59	302	4232	408	9.64
2005	10180	48	59	9999.99	12905	1083	8.39
2005	10180	48	253	201.01	6268	3134	50.00
2005	10180	48	253	201.02	1	1	100
2005	10180	48	253	202	2876	1023	35.57
2005	10180	48	253	203	2541	681	26.8
2005	10180	48	253	204	4118	1439	34.94
2005	10180	48	253	205	4982	481	9.65
2005	10180	48	253	9999.99	20785	7033	33.84

FIGURE 3.5   U.S. CENSUS DATA

Loan Number	MSA	Loan Purpose	Lien Status	Loan Type	Loan Amount	FICO Score	Loan-to-Value Ratio	Debt-to-Income Ratio	Joint Race	Action Result
1	10180 - ABILENE, TX	Home purchase	FIRST LIEN	CONVEN-TIONAL	469,730	777	0.2978	0.1042	ASIAN or NATIVE HAWAIIAN (ANH)	Origi-nated
2	10180 - ABILENE, TX	Home improve-ment	FIRST LIEN	CONVEN-TIONAL	163,900	566	0.6269	0.3433	NON-HISPANIC WHITE (NHW)	Origi-nated
3	10180 - ABILENE, TX	Refinance	JUNIOR LIEN	GOVERN-MENT BACKED	149,347	689	0.5937	0.4742	HISPANIC WHITE (HW)	Approved but not accepted
4	10180 - ABILENE, TX	Home improve-ment	FIRST LIEN	CONVEN-TIONAL	198,606	686	0.9452	0.3028	NON-HISPANIC WHITE (NHW)	Origi-nated
5	10180 - ABILENE, TX	Home improve-ment	FIRST LIEN	CONVEN-TIONAL	122,335	625	0.5513	0.202	NON-HISPANIC WHITE (NHW)	Declined
6	10180 - ABILENE, TX	Home improve-ment	FIRST LIEN	CONVEN-TIONAL	172,330	548	0.716	0.2906	NON-HISPANIC WHITE (NHW)	Declined
7	10180 - ABILENE, TX	Home purchase	FIRST LIEN	CONVEN-TIONAL	160,822	526	0.6807	0.3571	BLACK OR AFRICAN AMERICAN (AA)	Incom-plete
8	10180 - ABILENE, TX	Refinance	JUNIOR LIEN	GOVERN-MENT BACKED	177,684	820	0.5274	0.3731	2 OR MORE NON-WHITE RACES (TNW)	Origi-nated
9	10180 - ABILENE, TX	Home purchase	FIRST LIEN	CONVEN-TIONAL	182,795	820	0.7638	0.3017	NATIVE AMERICAN (NA)	With-drawn
10	10180 - ABILENE, TX	Home purchase	FIRST LIEN	CONVEN-TIONAL	180,000	776	0.4308	0.3800	NATIVE AMERICAN (NA)	Origi-nated

FIGURE 3.6   SAMPLE INPUT DATA

Minority Status	Statistic	Action Taken (Type)			Total
		DENIED	ORIGINATED	FALLOUT	
ALL OTHERS, INCLUDING HISPANIC	Frequency	2168	1664	926	4758
	Expected	1799.1	2040.6	918.29	
	Cell chi-square	75.633	69.499	0.0647	
	Percent	27.1	20.8	11.58	59.48
	Row pct	45.57	34.97	19.46	
	Col pct	71.67	48.5	59.97	
WHITE NON-HISPANIC	Frequency	857	1767	618	3242
	Expected	1225.9	1390.4	625.71	
	Cell chi-square	111	102	0.0949	
	Percent	10.71	22.09	7.73	40.53
	Row pct	26.43	54.5	19.06	
	Col pct	28.33	51.5	40.03	
		3025	3431	1544	8000
	Total	37.81	42.89	19.3	100

Statistic	DF	Value	Prob
Chi-square	2	358.289	<.0001
Likelihood ratio chi-square	2	363.368	<.0001
Mantel-Haenszel chi-square	1	126.002	<.0001
Phi coefficient		0.2116	
Contingency coefficient		0.207	
Cramer's V		0.2116	

FIGURE 3.7 OVERALL DATA EVALUATION FOR RECORD SELECTION (HYPOTHETICAL DATA)

The chi-square test shows that, overall, the minority group has a higher denial rate than the nonminority group (45.57 percent versus 26.43 percent), and the difference is statistically significant at $\alpha = 0.01$ percent level.[4] In this case, the chi-square test indicates that there is a significant disparity between minority group and nonprotected-class groups across loan underwriting decisions for a specific loan purpose and lien status combination. This particular segment may be selected for further analysis.

Record selection is also impacted in situations where:

- *Information is not reportable.* For example, purchase loans may be excluded from the analysis. Other examples could be product specific for inclusion or exclusion, such as home equity lines of credit.

4. For specific explanation of chi-square testing results, see the FREQ procedure in SAS/STAT 9.1 User's Guide, SAS Institute Inc., 2003.

- *Special market segments are to be considered.* For example, military bases or foreign territory may be excluded.
- *Information is incomplete.* This can occur when information is missing because the applicant failed to supply it or the lender was unable to infer it or capture it from another source.

Data Aggregation

Since a disparity index is defined at specified aggregated level, data needs to be grouped by business, geography, or other classification criteria. Typically, for fair lending analysis, data are aggregated by MSA, census trace, state, channel, branch, and so on. In this example, data are grouped by MSA to calculate disparity indices.

In this step, distribution of calculated indices is analyzed to ensure outliers are replaced with defaults. For example, indices with extreme values are analyzed with distribution plots. These plots are similar to those that appear later in the chapter (Figures 3.22 and 3.23). Depending on results, a determination is made regarding the need to use alternative values. The following sections describe circumstances requiring the use of alternative values and some methods for deriving them.

Insufficient Data Issues

Since fair lending disparity indices are expressed in ratios of lending results for a treatment group relative to a control group, it is important to have valid underwriting or pricing results at various aggregated levels. Unfortunately, this is not always possible at some levels (e.g., county or census tract). For example, in some census tracts, there may not be any particular application results (approvals, denials, withdrawals, etc.). So these fields associated with those census tracts must be treated as a special missing value. In these cases, the consequences of eliminating a census tract not only cause the loss of valuable and pertinent information, but it also increases the risk of overlooking areas representing significant exposure. Consider the case where a particular census tract possesses no data for originations, but where there are many denials or fallout applications. Clearly, it will be important to retain this census tract. This situation is different from typical missing data issues[5] and requires a different resolution. The key distinction here is that some default values should be set at aggregate levels, and values of data are not manipulated at the detail level.

Remedy for Insufficient Data

Setting default values for calculating disparity indices when data are insufficient is the recommended approach. How this is accomplished can significantly impact the results. If default values are assigned to represent the worst possible scenarios, then the number of false-negative errors will be minimized. However, other considerations must be taken into account. Assignment of default values needs to reflect the severity of data issues, the desired level of disparity testing power (false negative versus false positive), stability of class ranking to defaults, or combination of defaults, and other criteria as dictated by business needs and legal/regulatory requirements.

---

5. There are a host of alternatives for imputing missing values, depending on the nature of the data (see Little, R. J. A., and D. B. Rubin. *Statistical Analysis with Missing Data*. John Wiley & Sons, 2002). Missing value imputation can be done at the detailed record level, prior to index calculation or for the index itself, again, depending on the nature of the missing data and what other information is available.

It is also important to examine how sensitive the indicator ranking is to the default values. The main concern here is ranking stability. For example, if there are no loan originations for a protected class in a particular census tract but there are some for the nonprotected class, the default for the origination disparity index could be assigned to penalize for the lack of protected-class originations. The possible default value can be any value greater than parity (i.e., 1.0), and a value should be selected to ensure that the associated risk exposures are not overstated. In the extreme case, the census tracts having defaulted values would have vastly disproportionately high UPI.

As a starting point, we can assign default values as follows: (1) a value of 1.0 represents a parity point or no sufficient data for both a protected class (treatment group) and the nonprotected class (control group); (2) a value of 0.5 represents favorable performance relative to the protected classes when there is no data for the nonprotected class but there is data for the protected class; and (3) a value of 1.5 represents unfavorable performance relative to a protected class when there is data for the nonprotected class but there is no data for the protected class.

Figure 3.8 shows an example of scenario table used to select sets of defaults with minimum required number of observations (i.e., five in this case). This figure illustrates the usefulness of a scenario simulation table for enumerating all combinations of favorable default values within a prescribed range (i.e., zero to one), while holding other defaults constant (i.e., unfavorable missing data default of 1.5 and parity value of 1.0) for the first ten iterations. The process involves iterating through a full range of different scenarios, specified by the combinations of possible default values. Default setting usually involves some trial iterations or alternatively, some type of optimization process. In the case of simulation, sensitivity of outcomes to assigned default values can be observed by recalculating the UPI after each iteration and comparing rank orderings.

Calculating Indices

After records are selected, grouped, validated, imputed, and summarized to the desired level, they can be easily used to calculate indices based on definitions as described in the previous section. Each observation (e.g., MSA, state, institution) will then have one record that contains all calculated indices for the analysis. Indices are calculated by type of disparity (decision based and

Scenario Number	Favor	Disfavor	Neutral	Minimum # of Obs
1	0.9	1.5	1	5
2	0.8	1.5	1	5
3	0.7	1.5	1	5
4	0.6	1.5	1	5
5	0.5	1.5	1	5
6	0.4	1.5	1	5
7	0.3	1.5	1	5
8	0.2	1.5	1	5
9	0.1	1.5	1	5
10	0	1.5	1	5

FIGURE 3.8 SIMULATED SCENARIOS FOR DEFAULT SETTING

results based, and protected-class designation). To ensure accuracy, indices at different levels of aggregation can be recalculated as needed. However, if there are sufficient data at the lowest level, the calculated indices can also be aggregated to a higher level. To calculate indices, all available data including the census data, the loan application, credit data, and any other data relevant to the loan decision process (such as property, channel, etc.) should be merged so that each observation (e.g., MSA, state, institution, etc.) will then have one record that contains all calculated indices for the analysis. Indices are calculated by type of disparity (decision based and results based, and race). To ensure accuracy, indices at different levels of aggregation can be recalculated as needed. However, if there are sufficient data at the lowest level, the calculated indices can also be aggregated to a higher level.

The tabular view in Figure 3.9 gives more specific examples that illustrate the basic interpretation of these calculated disparity indices.

Recall that disparity values greater than 1.0 are an indication that the protected class has been disfavored relative to the nonprotected class of credit applicants. In this example we note that the fourth entry in the table indicates that for Abilene, Texas, the white non-Hispanics have a loan origination rate that is three and a half times higher than their Hispanic white counterparts. Disparity values less than 1.0 are an indication that the protected class has been favored relative to the nonprotected class of credit applicants. In this example we note that the ninth entry in the table indicates that for Akron, Ohio, the Asian group of applicants has a rate of application fallout (i.e., incomplete, withdrawn, or approved but not accepted results) that is only half of the fallout rate for the white non-Hispanic group. Finally, the sixth row in the table shows that the rate of above-threshold priced loans for African-American in Aguadilla-Isabella-San Sebastián, Puerto Rico, was identical to that for white non-Hispanic borrowers. In that instance, there is no disparity existing between the protected and nonprotected classes.

Once calculated, these indices can be examined in a number of ways, from ranking reports, thematic maps, and statistical graphics. Figure 3.10 illustrates one such report, representing lending disparities by race group and disparity type at the MSA level.

Metropolitan Area	Race	Disparity	Type
10180 - ABILENE, TX	ASIAN	0.068	Loan origination
10180 - ABILENE, TX	BLACK OR AFRICAN-AMERICAN	0.742	Loan origination
10180 - ABILENE, TX	NATIVE HAWAIIAN/OTHER PACIFIC ISLND	0.005	Loan origination
10180 - ABILENE, TX	HISPANIC WHITE	3.500	Loan origination
10380 - AGUADILLA-ISABELA-SAN SEBASTIÁN, PR	ASIAN	0.006	Loan pricing
10380 - AGUADILLA-ISABELA-SAN SEBASTIÁN, PR	BLACK OR AFRICAN-AMERICAN	1.000	Loan pricing
10380 - AGUADILLA-ISABELA-SAN SEBASTIÁN, PR	NATIVE HAWAIIAN/OTHER PACIFIC ISLND	0.001	Loan pricing
10380 - AGUADILLA-ISABELA-SAN SEBASTIÁN, PR	HISPANIC WHITE	3.149	Loan pricing
10420 - AKRON, OH	ASIAN	0.500	Application fallout
10420 - AKRON, OH	BLACK OR AFRICAN-AMERICAN	0.621	Application fallout

FIGURE 3.9 DISPARITY MEASURES

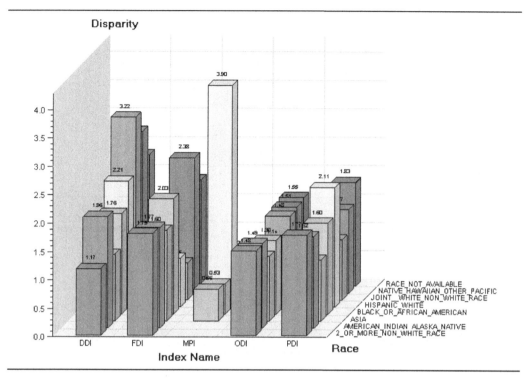

FIGURE 3.10 MSA LEVEL DISPARITY INDICES BY INDEX TYPE

The tallest bar in the figure corresponds to a market penetration disparity that approaches a value of four for white Hispanic applicants. This result indicates that, based on the population census, one would expect almost four times as many mortgage applications for white Hispanics in the particular MSA than were actually taken. The highest denial disparity is for joint applications where one of the applicants is white and the other applicant is nonwhite. That group had a denial rate that was over three and a half times higher than the control group, which consists of purely white non-Hispanic applicants.

GENERATE UNIVERSAL PERFORMANCE INDICATOR

Each disparity index measures performance from a unique business perspective. Since there can be many types of disparity indices, it can be increasingly difficult to evaluate the overall performance relative to fair lending compliance for an entire organization. Furthermore, possible correlations between indices can make it difficult to differentiate high- versus low-risk areas, and to compare and rank large numbers of potentially correlated disparity indices across geographic regions, lines of business, or institutions. In this section, we describe how we can use the UPI to address these concerns, simply and thoroughly. In this process, indices are transformed into a set of uncorrelated coefficients. Then an appropriate distance formula is selected to calculate their distance from a predefined reference point (or risk-neutral point). This can be used as a singular indicator to capture the performance from a specific dimension or aspect. Figure 3.11 provides a pictorial representation of the process flow for generating the UPI.

A UPI can be derived based on a set of singular composites (or indicators) that measure the risk from a specific perspective, such as lending decision, results, property, or market. Moreover,

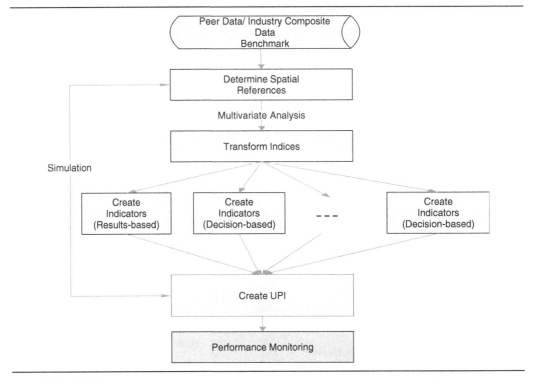

FIGURE 3.11   UPI GENERATION

UPI provides a comprehensive (i.e., overarching) of the entire lending process by combining all available indices and their associated composites. UPI can be used to rank-order and categorize risk to prioritize further analysis and related investigations. There are various methods available for combining singular indicators into a universal indicator. A weighted average approach can be used to approximate the universal indicator. The advantage of this approach is that lending disparity and risk disparity can have different weights, which may be determined based on different factors. For example, the risk disparity indicator can be assigned a smaller weight if it contains fewer factors or indices, or the data quality is less dependable.

Different options or considerations are compared and evaluated in order to determine the most appropriate method. Selection of the optimal approach should include evaluation criteria such as error rate, potential cost, and data quality. In addition, the sensitivity of the UPI to false-positive and false-negative results is impacted, and may be controlled, by the appropriate choice of factors, including:

- Specification of the minimum allowable sample size for component index calculation, which is based on requirements of the statistical methods used, actual experience with production data, and guidance from legal counsel or regulators.
- Setting of reward/penalty/neutral default values in instances where there is insufficient data, as discussed in a previous section.
- Collapsing observation unit variables (e.g., forming collections of geographically contiguous census tracts, within the same income tier, from individual tracts having too few observations).
- Collapsing protected class categories (e.g., constructing a minority classification, or collapsing certain classifications having too few observations into and "other" classification).

- Combining observation unit variables with protected-class variables (e.g., income grouping at the census tract level to create purely low-income portion of MSAs, purely moderate-income portion of MSAs, etc.).

A more detailed examination of these topics is beyond the scope of this chapter.

Distance Calculation Methodology

To calculate the distance from a risk-free point, we need to compute a set of linear coefficients based on principal component analysis (PCA) of the disparity indices. PCA has been widely used in a variety of business applications in order to reduce dimensionality. It can simplify the computation process while maintaining relatively accurate risk measurement by capturing the variances associated with key variables.[6] PCA is a decomposition technique that produces a set of expression patterns known as principal components. Principal components are uncorrelated, linear combinations of the original input variables (such as disparity indices) and can be computed as:

$$Y = X^*W \tag{3.1}$$

where Y is the n-by-p linear combination indicators; X is the n-by-p centered data matrix; W is the p-by-p matrix of weights (coefficients), obtained from an eigenvector-eigenvalue decomposition of the covariance matrix of the data.[7]

There are exactly p principal components, and each is a linear combination of the observed variables. Principal components are all mutually orthogonal. The first principal component (i.e., PC) is the linear combination of the observed variables with maximum variance. The second PC is the linear combination of the observed variables, out of all linear combinations orthogonal to the first, with maximum variance. Given this decreasing variance property, much of the variance (information) in the original sets of principal components (normally two or three) is captured. In other words, variance of the p variables concealed in the original data set can be revealed on the first few principal components, since principal components provide maximal separation between the classes (or groups) with substantial indices. This interesting feature allows us to often detect the observations with extreme values (outliers) in a space defined by only one, two, or three principal components. After performing PCA, a scatter plot can display the first and second principal components (representing the largest fraction of the overall variability) on the vertical axis and horizontal axis, respectively.

Distance is one of the important elements in measuring and analyzing spatial objects. There are a number of methods that can be used to calculate a standardized distance from a base or a reference point.[8] One of the most popular distances is the Mahalanobis distance. Mahalanobis distance (MD) is a normalized distance (i.e., in the normal distribution from the center (M) to a point (X)). It is based on correlations between the variables and which different patterns could be identified and analyzed with respect to base or reference point.[9] The distance between two N-dimensional points is scaled by the statistical variation in each component of the point.

---

6. For examples of PCA applications in risk measurement, see Jorion, Philippe. *Value at Risk: The New Benchmark for Managing Financial Risk*, McGraw-Hill, 2007, pp. 211–215; and Hull, John. *Options, Futures, and Other Derivatives*, 4th ed. Prentice Hall, 2000, pp. 357–361.

7. The computation can be performed with SAS procedures, such as PRINCOMP, FACTOR, or IML. For details, see SAS/STAT 9.1 User's Guide, and SAS/IML User's Guide, SAS Institute Inc., 2003. For details on using SAS/IML software to perform PCA analysis, see Srivastava, M. S. *Methods of Multivariate Statistics*, John Wiley & Sons, 2002, pp. 397–427. For a more general discussion on PCA computation, see Tabachnick, B. G., and L. S. Fidell. *Using Multivariate Statistics*. Allyn & Bacon, 2001, pp. 582–620.

8. Typically, they include Euclidean Distance, Manhattan Distance, Great Circle Distance, Mahalanobis distance, and so on.

9. See Taguchi, G., and R. Jugulum. *The Mahalanobis-Taguchi Strategy: A Pattern Technology System*. John Wiley & Sons, 2002, pp. 21–31; Tabachnick, and Fidell, 2001, pp. 68–70; Kaufman, L. and P. J. Rousseeuw. *Finding*

The MD has the advantage of utilizing group means and variances for each variable, as well as the correlations and covariance between measures. The squared MD from x to group t can be calculated as

$$M - (x - m_t)'S_t^{-1}(x - m_t) \qquad (3.2)$$

where M is the generalized squared distance; S_t represents the within-group covariance matrix or pooled covariance matrix; m_t is the p-dimensional vector containing variable means in group t; x is a p-dimensional vector containing the quantitative variables of an observation. With a k-nearest-neighbor method, the pooled covariance matrix is used to calculate the MDs. With a kernel method, either the individual within-group covariance matrices or the pooled covariance matrix can be used to calculate the MDs.[10]

MD essentially addresses the question of whether a particular case would be considered an outlier relative to a particular set of group data. In general, this risk exposure estimation methodology can involve the following steps:

Step 1. Measure risk from a risk-free point. Simulated values are assigned to risk-free points[11] and other references.[12]

Step 2. Calculate principal components to represent all actual disparity indices and simulated reference indices.

Step 3. Estimate MDs from partial or all principal components, for both actual indices and simulated indices.

Step 4. Group risk exposure indicators into classes. For example, there can be three risk groups: (1) high risk, to capture the classes with one or more extreme high disparity indices (greater than or 3); (2) medium risk, to capture the classes with most indices around 1.5 to 2; and (3) low risk, to capture the classes with most indices less than 1.5.

This process can be applied independently or simultaneously to results-based, decision-based, and other types of indices, as shown in Figure 3.11. Since the MD is a standardized continuous value with a minimum value of zero, a relatively higher value of MD represents a potentially more severe lending disparity or risk. Furthermore, the notion of results-based and decision-based indices can be extended to include all aspects of a particular family of financial transactions. For example, the decision-based index involves borrower considerations but can be expanded to include collateral, product, channel, market, and other factors.

Index Transformation

Distance formulas such as Mahalanobis are, in general, not directly applied to the disparity indices. Instead, they use coefficients (e.g., principal components) calculated from a set of indices. By default, the PCA approach is used.[13] This is due to the fact that indices are highly correlated, while principal components are orthogonal and can provide maximum separation of class variance using just the first few principal components. In general, we need to generate principal components, eigenvectors, and their eigenvalues, which measure the contribution of a principal component to the explained variance. We then need to determine number of principal components based on the

---

Groups in Data. John Wiley & Sons, 1990; and Srivastava, M. S., *Methods of Multivariate Statistics*, John Wiley & Sons, 2002, pp. 19, 58–59.

10. See the DISCRIM procedure in the SAS/STAT User's Guide.

11. The simulated risk neutral point for the case where there are six indices would have the following disparity input values: 1.0, 1.0, 1.0, 1.0, 1.0, 1.0.

12. The simulated reference point corresponding to the situation where the first disparity index corresponded to a denial rate for protected groups that was double that of the control group, while all of the other, say five, indices were held at parity would have the following disparity input values: 2.0, 1.0, 1.0, 1.0, 1.0, 1.0.

13. Alternative approaches include factor analysis, canonical discriminant analysis, and others.

# Principal Components (PCs)	Eigenvalue	Difference from Next Eigenvalue	Proportion of Variance Explained	Cumulative Proportion of Variance Explained
1	13.508445	3.240611	0.3752	0.3752
2	10.267834	2.634282	0.2852	0.6605
3	7.6335521	3.043384	0.212	0.8725
4	4.5901685	4.590169	0.1275	1

FIGURE 3.12   DETERMINE NUMBER OF PCS TO USE FOR INDICATOR CALCULATION

MSA	PC 1	PC 2	PC 3	Distance
Ref_1 (all 0.5s)	−1.78775	−1.53241	0.00123	2.45224
Ref_2 (neutral point or 1s)	−1.03499	−0.42695	0.01238	0
Ref_3 (all 1.5s)	−0.28223	0.67851	0.02353	2.45224
Ref_4 (all 2s)	0.47054	1.78397	0.03468	3.468
10180 – ABILENE, TX	−0.30675	4.2216	0.13204	5.66679
10380 – AGUADILLA-ISABELA-SAN SEBASTIÁN, PR	1.92348	−0.37272	−2.49321	7.47961
10420 – AKRON, OH	1.59693	2.14787	−1.9556	5.05871
10500 – ALBANY, GA	−2.11402	5.84954	3.90217	7.43522
10580 – ALBANY-SCHENECTADY-TROY, NY	−0.7193	−1.48208	−0.9322	3.49375
10740 – ALBUQUERQUE, NM	−0.34375	−0.14451	−2.06444	4.75447

FIGURE 3.13   PRINCIPAL COMPONENTS AND DISTANCES FOR ACTUAL MSAS AND FOUR GENERIC REFERENCE POINTS

required minimum cumulative variance explained by the first "n" principal components (e.g., it may be that the first three principal components capture 90 percent of the observed variation in the data). Figure 3.12 shows the first three principal components represented more than 85 percent variation and so they can be selected for indicator calculation.

Since reference points are merged together with the actual indices to calculate principal components, the principal components for the same reference points can be different depending on the actual index data they are merged with. Principal components are calculated from these simulated indices and are combined with the principal components calculated from the actual indices. Figure 3.13 shows principal components and distances for four scenarios, along with those from actual indices, for the "results-based" indicator.[14]

14. There is no business interpretation of the principal component values, because they represent linear contrasts of the input disparity indices. Still, the values are useful for plotting observations, together with reference points, that can show how or where any particular observation, or group of observations, falls relative to combinations of threshold values for the disparity indices that have direct business and compliance interpretation.

Create References

Potential fair lending risk exposure can be defined as the deviance of disparity indices (DIs) for a particular class from the center, *risk-free* reference point. This reference location is determined when all indices are set to one (i.e., no disparities). This deviance can be best measured with a standardized distance.

A simulation approach can be used to generate indices for reference points. For example, 0, minimum point; 1, the risk-free point; 1.5, medium-risk point; or 2, the high-risk point. An example is shown in Figure 3.14.

In practice, reference point values must be specified for every disparity index for every protected-class and nonprotected-class grouping. For example, consider that a reference point for Asian applicants may have as inputs values of 1.0 for market penetration, decline, origination, fallout, credit score, high DTI, and low LTV disparity indices to indicate parity for all of those factors and a value of 2.0 for above threshold pricing disparity. The number of defaults that are set is a function of the number of protected classes and nonprotected classes being modeled, and the number of disparity indices making up the results-based and decision-based components[15] of the universal performance indicator. Typically, a large number of classes are simulated with index values from 0 to a specified upper threshold. For example, if the threshold is set at 3, then the simulated area represents a collection of all classes that have indices less 3.0. The thresholds used to create this area can be set at different values to reflect specific business needs or compliance requirements.

Categorize Singular Indicators

There can be many kinds of index-based indicators (distances). For simplicity, we use two different kinds of disparities (results based and decision based). Disparity needs to be calculated for each type index separately. In order to represent the degree of potential disparity with a singular indicator, the two distances need to be combined. To do so, one first needs to establish a relationship between the two disparities. Figure 3.15 shows that the coordinates of the distances can be divided into four quadrants based on their combination of results-based indices and decision-based indices, as listed below:

Ref. Pt.	Low LTV DI Value for Native American	Low LTV DI Value for Hispanic Non-White	Low LTV DI Value for African-American	Low LTV DI Value for Asian	Low LTV DI Value for Hispanic White	Low LTV DI Value for Two+ N-H White	Low LTV DI Value for Two+ N-H White
Ref_1	0.5	0.5	0.5	0.5	0.5	0.5	0.5
Ref_2	1	1	1	1	1	1	1
Ref_3	1.5	1.5	1.5	1.5	1.5	1.5	1.5
Ref_4	2	2	2	2	2	2	2

FIGURE 3.14   DETERMINE REFERENCE POINTS: SPECIFYING LOW LTV DISPARITY INDEX VALUES FOR RACE/ETHNICITY CATEGORIES

---

15. Results-based indices typically reflect outcomes such as the HMDA action result categories of origination, decline, fallout (i.e., any of: approved but not accepted, withdrawn, incomplete), whereas the decision-based indices relate to the qualification of the borrower (i.e., high credit score, high debt-to-income ratio, low loan-to-value ratio) or some other consideration due to the collateral, terms and conditions of the loan product, channels with different cost structures, or other factors that can help to explain outcomes.

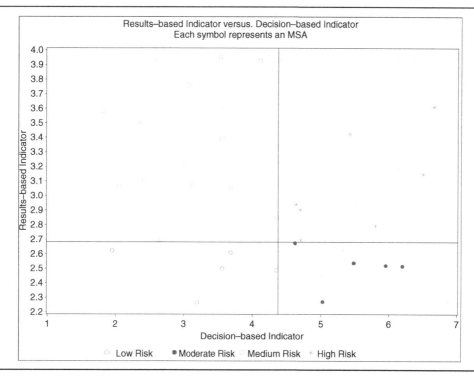

FIGURE 3.15 CATEGORIZING INDICATORS: RESULTS VS. DECISION BASED

1. *High-risk quadrant.* High/high disparity: This quadrant captures the classes (e.g., MSAs, states, etc.) with both high decision-based indices and high results-based indices. For example, this may indicate that a minority applicant has a lower default risk relative to the nonprotected-class group (the control) but is charged with a high rate spread or is more likely to be denied for a loan. Therefore, this quadrant represents the highest fair lending risk disparities and should be the main focus of the analysis.
2. *Medium-risk quadrant.* High/low disparity: This quadrant captures the classes (e.g., MSAs, states, etc.) with high results-based indices and medium to low decision-based indices. For example, this may represent the classes in which a minority applicant has an equal default risk relative to the nonprotected-class group (the control) but is charged with a higher rate or is more likely to be denied for a loan. Therefore, this quadrant contains the classes/groups with medium fair lending risk.
3. *Moderate-risk quadrant.* Low/high disparity: This quadrant captures the classes (e.g., MSAs, states) with low results-based indices and medium to low decision-based indices. For example, this may represent the classes in which a minority applicant has a lower default risk relatively to the nonprotected-class group (the control) and is charged with a similar or lower rate or is less likely to be denied for a loan. Therefore, this quadrant contains the classes/groups with moderate or low fair lending risk.
4. *Low-risk quadrant.* Low/low disparity: This quadrant captures the classes (e.g., MSAs, states) with low results-based indices and medium to low decision-based indices. For example, this may represent the classes in which a minority applicant has a higher or equal default risk relative to the nonprotected-class group (the control) and is charged with a similar rate or is equally likely to be denied for a loan. Therefore, this quadrant contains the classes/groups with low or no fair lending risk.

Note that the horizontal and vertical reference lines in Figure 3.15 represent distances calculated based on simulated indices. In this figure, they are based on index = 1.5, a predefined acceptable disparity.

Since the size of each of the quadrants and distances from each observation to the simulated risk-neutral point are influenced by the choice of thresholds, the classification errors and required resources to analyze them can vary accordingly. Therefore, it is important to select thresholds that proportionately capture the fair lending risk, while minimizing the false-positive error costs as much as possible. In general, one may use the following approaches to determine the appropriate thresholds:

- *Clustering.* This method classifies the classes/groups based on the squared distances calculated from both results-based disparity indices and decision-based disparity indices so that the sum of the within-quadrant variation can be minimized. Typically, clustering methods also involve the calculation of Euclidean distance (see Equation 3.3 for a definition).
- *Error rate and cost matrix approach.* This involves the analysis of the costs resulting from false positive error (type I) rate and false negative error (type II) rate, respectively. The objective is to minimize the total cost due to errors. To do so, a matrix that associates costs with error types needs to be constructed, and a scenario analysis with different thresholds needs to be performed.

Recognizing that it is the combination of statistical analysis and business knowledge that affect the selection of the performance thresholds, the following factors need to be considered when the methods described above are applied:

- *Stage of fair lending examination and analysis.* For example, in the early stage of the examination, it may be more important to reduce "false-negative" errors, as they can be hard to detect in a later stage.[16] Therefore, thresholds that result in a high false-positive error rate and lower false-negative error rate may be preferred.
- *Data availability and quality.* For example, if the data contains a lot of missing values and insufficient observations to calculate disparity indices, a high false-positive error rate may be more likely. Therefore, the thresholds may be set to capture the groups with extreme disparity that are less likely to be a result of false positives. As mentioned previously, another method would be to rethink the operating unit that one is measuring at and consider pooling observations where possible to achieve sufficient sample counts (e.g., consolidating contiguous census tracts that fall into the same income tier). This problem does not generally occur at the MSA level, except possibly for certain protected classes. In those instances, a coarser classification scheme can be adopted such as consolidating protected class groupings having sparse data into an "other" classification.

Selecting Distance Calculation Methods

Different approaches are used to create a single risk indicator from a set of disparity indices. In some instances, it is preferable to employ weighted average techniques and determine the weights associated with various indices. However, a weighted average approach can be time consuming, and may result in an unwieldy number of weighted combinations. An alternative approach is to simply use average or maximum values associated with indices. However, this simplified approach may not capture extreme index values since averaging can smooth out outliers. The result is a

---

16. See Avery, Robert B., Patricia E. Beeson, and Paul S. Calem, "Using HMDA Data as a Regulatory Screen for Fair Lending Compliance," *Journal of Financial Services Research*, Vol. 11, February/April 1997, p. 9.

muting of the severity of risk exposure. The Euclidean distance offers yet another measure of overall risk, but it also suffers from similar drawbacks.

As noted earlier, one way to compute a singular indicator is to use MD measure, which considers the deviation from a "risk-free" point to specific reference point. This risk-free reference point is conceptually a neutral, no-risk location, and can be defined from the principal component dimensions, from which distances to all calculated disparities are measured. The main advantage of this approach is that the distance can be calculated at different scales, and measured from various reference points. Furthermore, distance is a standardized value, serving as a single evaluation metric for measuring overall risk exposure, that can be efficiently calculated, readily communicated (e.g., in reports or maps) and is also a valid input parameter for other analytical investigations.

The following examples illustrate why the proposed singular indicator method provides superior risk ranking capability. Figure 3.16 lists fair lending indices for selected lenders and references representing different risk levels.

There are several options for ranking the banks by fair lending risk. For comparative purposes, risk ranking is determined by using the singular indicator, Euclidean distance formula and arithmetic sum. Clearly, the risk indicator values calculated with the UPI approach represent the most effective way to capture extreme disparities and risk, while considering variances across both lenders and disparity indices. Figure 3.17 illustrates that when the Euclidean distance formula is

Lender/ Reference Point	Origination Disparity Index	Denial Disparity Index	Fallout Disparity Index	Product Disparity Index	Market Penetration Disparity Index	Universal Performance Indicator	Composite Distance	Euclidean Distance
Very High Risk Ref.	3	3	3	3	3	4.30385	15	4.47214
High Risk Ref.	2.5	2.5	2.5	2.5	2.5	3.72724	12.5	3.3541
Medium Risk Ref.	2	2	2	2	2	3.04328	10	2.23607
Lender 6	1.77	1.1	1.64	1.1	1.37	2.5563	6.98	1.07675
Lender 4	1.06	0.87	1.09	1.73	1.73	2.21947	6.48	1.04614
Lender 3	1.2	1.65	1.36	1.73	1.1	2.19401	7.04	1.06536
Low Risk Ref.	0.5	0.5	0.5	0.5	0.5	2.15192	2.5	1.11803
Moderate Risk Ref.	1.5	1.5	1.5	1.5	1.5	2.15192	7.5	1.11803
Lender 7	1.34	1.07	1.43	1.19	0.85	2.14567	5.88	0.60332
Lender 8	1.33	1.49	1.39	1.27	0.94	2.00153	6.42	0.76
Lender 1	0.98	1.62	1.49	1.53	0.97	1.95734	6.59	0.95221
Lender 5	1.72	1.76	1.28	1.39	1.7	1.77021	7.85	1.34778
Lender_2	1.77	1.32	1.21	1.31	1.67	1.7386	7.28	1.13331
Lender 9	0.85	1.78	1.38	1.48	1.31	1.40057	6.8	1.04967
Lender 10	0.87	1.03	1.18	0.97	1.23	1.39099	5.28	0.32249
Parity Ref.	1	1	1	1	1	0	5	0

FIGURE 3.16 MEASURING RISK WITH DIFFERENT DISTANCE FORMULATIONS

Lender/ Reference Point	Orig. Disparity Index	Denial Disparity Index	Fallout Disparity Index	Product Disparity Index	Market Penetration Disparity Index	UPI	Euclidean Distance
Lender 6	1.77	1.1	1.64	1.1	1.37	2.5563	**1.07675**
Low Risk Ref.	0.5	0.5	0.5	0.5	0.5	2.15192	**1.11803**

FIGURE 3.17   EUCLIDEAN DISTANCE VERSUS UPI

Lender/ Reference Point	Orig. Disparity Index	Denial Disparity Index	Fallout Disparity Index	Product Disparity Index	Market Penetration Disparity Index	UPI	Composite Distance
Lender 4	1.06	0.87	1.09	1.73	1.73	2.21947	**6.48**
Moderate Risk Ref.	1.5	1.5	1.5	1.5	1.5	2.15192	**7.5**

FIGURE 3.18   COMPOSITE DISTANCE VERSUS UPI

used to rank risk, Lender 6 has a lower risk ranking than the low-risk reference. In fact, Lender 6 has greater disparity and risk as captured by UPI.

Figure 3.18 shows what happens when a simple composite arithmetic approach is used to rank risk. In this case, Lender 4 ranks lower than the moderate-risk reference, when, in fact, Lender 4 contains higher disparities and should be ranked higher as captured by UPI.

Note that distances and principal components are different for the same simulated scenario number in different cases. The distance values can be affected by number of indices, number of principal components retained, and number of classes. Because distances and principal components are calculated relative to different actual indices, different numbers of indices in a class also produce different distances, even where index values are the same.

Create the UPI

The UPI can be calculated based on the following Euclidean distance formula[17]:

$$D = \left[\sum (x_i - x_0)^2\right]_j^{1/2} \qquad (3.3)$$

It is the squared root of sum of distance between a class x_i and the reference point x_0 over all j classes. In a special case of two classes, it is simply the distance between the x-y coordinates of each point and the origin (0, 0).

Figure 3.19 shows an example that ranks MSAs by a singular indicator that is based on the Euclidean distances. This can also be calculated using weighted average approach. Different approaches are compared and evaluated. Selection criteria include:

---

17. There are other approaches available. For example, one can use the weighted average approach and its advantage is that lending disparity and risk disparity can have different weights, which may be determined based on different factors. The risk disparity indicator can be assigned with a smaller weight if it contains fewer factors or indices, or the data quality is less dependable, vice versa.

MSA	Results-based	Decision-based	UPI
10380 – AGUADILLA-ISABELA-SAN SEBASTIÁN, PR	7.47961	5.21761	9.11965
10500 – ALBANY, GA	7.43522	5.01633	8.96917
13020 – BAY CITY, MI	5.5966	6.80429	8.81024
12620 – BANGOR, ME	7.43478	4.69898	8.79525
11020 – ALTOONA, PA	6.58965	5.67914	8.6992
10780 – ALEXANDRIA, LA	6.54906	5.36183	8.46401
11100 – AMARILLO, TX	7.15369	3.89709	8.14633
15180 – BROWNSVILLE-HARLINGEN, TX	7.16412	3.87118	8.14314
11500 – ANNISTON-OXFORD, AL	5.7571	5.64698	8.06428
10180 – ABILENE, TX	5.66679	5.70906	8.04399

FIGURE 3.19   RANK MSAS BY UPI

- *Error rate.* The one that has the lowest error rate (false positive versus false negative) is selected.
- *Potential cost.* If a false-positive error is more expensive, then more weigh is put on so that a false-positive error can be captured.
- *Data quality.* The method used minimizes the effects of data quality issues and generates more stable ranking of classes.

In viewing Figure 3.19, it is helpful to visualize the quadrant plot appearing earlier in Figure 3.15. These metropolitan areas would fall in the upper rightmost quadrant, indicating that the protected class of applicants residing in them were not only treated unfavorably relative to their nonprotected counterparts, but they are actually more qualified based on various credit qualification variables. This "disconnect" for the geographic areas in question would tend to indicate the need for further analysis, and perhaps disparate treatment testing, which is described in Chapter 5.

PERFORMANCE MONITORING

One of the major advantages of using UPI methodology is that it can facilitate compliance risk monitoring when it is integrated with various kinds of visualization techniques that are commonplace in risk reporting. Figure 3.20 illustrates how visualization can be implemented. For example, universal performance indicators can be decomposed to a set of coefficients first where multidimensional plots can readily detect outliers. The following step is to further decompose results into disparity indices for tracing root causes and identification of the protected groups involved in a particular geographic area. Persistent imbalances indicating a disparate impact for one or more protected classes of credit applicants may require more in-depth analysis, which we cover in Chapters 4 and 5. Naturally, any combination of individual indices can be reaggregated to singular or universal performance indicators for various ranking purposes.

This process may include one or more of the following steps:

Step 1.   Assess universal measures of risk exposure.
Step 2.   Prioritize high-risk exposures for further investigation.
Step 3.   Evaluate risk from alternative perspectives, introducing additional dimensions when necessary.

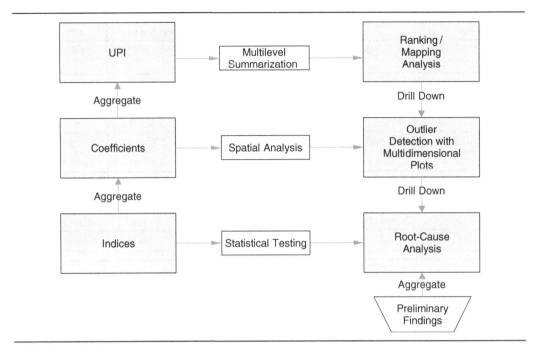

FIGURE 3.20   MONITORING FAIR LENDING RISK

Step 4. Filter risk exposure to limit investigations and avoid wasting time and resources.
Step 5. Locate and examine outliers to determine their nature and causes.
Step 6. Identify contributing risk factors for more common high-risk exposures.
Step 7. Assess individual disparities.
Step 8. Isolate specific cases for more detailed analysis.

Ranking

Lending institutions need to identify and evaluate fair lending risk exposure across all lending activities, and at different levels of granularity. This can be accomplished, in part, by monitoring and managing fair lending risk exposure with the UPI. Reports and data visualizations are also useful vehicles to explore key drivers of risk, and their interactions, for all calculated measures. Multiway effects associated with performance metrics such as origination, decline, and fallout rates can also be viewed and subjected to further multidimensional "drill-downs." With these key fair lending performance drivers and their combined effect on a variety of target variables, lenders can detect the riskiest compliance areas (or aspects of their business), prioritize them, identify contributing factors, and design actionable strategies to manage and mitigate fair lending practice violations. Figure 3.21 is one such example ranking MSAs from high risk to low, as well as the associated singular indicators.

Once the highest exposure, or riskiest, areas are identified, one can explore the data to examine the factors that contribute to the exposure magnitude as shown in Figure 3.21. It shows that Aguadilla-Isabella-San Sebastián, Puerto Rico, is the highest-ranked MSA, and appears in the first row of the figure. An examination of the disparity indices shows that the market penetration disparity index has a value of 10.891, which says that the pool of loan applications in that MSA reflects less than a tenth of the percentage of applications from one or more protected classes than one would expect, given the representation of the protected class households in the general

MSA	Income Disparity Index	DTI Disparity Index	LTV Disparity Index	Bureau Score	Origination Disparity Index	Denial Disparity Index	Fallout Disparity Index	Market Penetration Disparity Index	Price Disparity Index	Global Indicator
10380 – AGUADILLA-ISABELA-SAN SEBASTIÁN, PR	1.161	0.91	0.864	1.639	1.225	1.616	1.156	10.891	0.534	9.11965
10500 – ALBANY, GA	0.913	0.868	1.256	1.3	1.229	0.875	2.7	0.772	2.563	8.96917
13020 – BAY CITY, MI	1.708	0.538	0.661	0.826	1.275	3.146	0.91	0.096	0.646	8.81024
12620 – BANGOR, ME	1.303	0.77	0.933	1.06	1.024	1.04	1.288	0.089	4.503	8.79525
11020 – ALTOONA, PA	0.931	0.813	1.188	1.625	0.871	0.938	1.375	0.056	2.5	8.6992
10780 – ALEXANDRIA, LA	1.652	0.969	0.73	0.979	1.396	3.416	0.733	0.223	0.665	8.46401
11100 – AMARILLO, TX	1.048	0.668	0.517	1.384	2.071	2.167	1.366	0.787	0.58	8.14633
15180 – BROWNSVILLE-HARLINGEN, TX	0.581	1.005	0.702	1.09	1.6	2.947	1.478	6.073	0.53	8.14314
11500 – ANNISTON-OXFORD, AL	0.996	0.939	0.892	1.393	1.155	1.366	1.308	0.603	1.313	8.06428
10180 – ABILENE, TX	0.745	0.72	1.284	1.741	1.301	0.878	2.994	0.811	1.039	8.04399

FIGURE 3.21 RANKED MSAS AND THEIR CONTRIBUTING INDICES

MSA population. Moreover, the BDI indicates that the protected-class applicants have a lower incidence of low credit scores than their nonprotected-class counterparts, and somewhat favorable results relative to income. This MSA would fall into the upper rightmost quadrant in Figure 3.15, and deserves further investigation.

Within each MSA, one can also examine exposure relative to loan purpose, property type, race/ethnicity, gender, age, line of business, channel, and so on. These segmentation criteria are usually applied after the UPI is computed, but there is no reason why they cannot be applied beforehand. For example, loan purpose could be used to separate home purchase loans from refinancings and home improvement loans. The analysis previously described could be conducted within these broad loan purpose categories, so that loan applications for loans having different purposes are not commingled.

Alternate Reference Contexts for Examining Exposure

As mentioned, potential fair lending risk exposure is measured by the deviation of disparity indices from a neutral point for both minority and nonprotected classes.[18] MD is a continuous, interval measure with a minimum value of zero. The greater the distance, the more severe the disparity, and the greater the risk exposure relative to a given class.

By default, MDs are calculated based on this risk-free reference point. However, they can also be calculated relative to other references, such as the lower bound risk point or an average/benchmark risk point. These different references can then be used to measure disparity severity from a number of different perspectives and standards.

In order to intuitively and effectively measure and compare fair lending risk exposure, principal components and MD are calculated from a risk-free (or central) basis, and then compared with a set of artificial references. Various references can be created from different criteria for comparison purposes. Typically, the following references can be considered:

- Lower bound risk point, determined by assuming a value of 0 for each of the indices.
- Average risk point, calculated by using an average value for all indices.
- Benchmark risk point, obtained by using average indices across all institutions.
- Upper bound risk point, calculated by assigning a maximum allowed value for each index, for example, a value of 2 or 3 can be used to create this point.

Various graphical plots can be generated from multiple reference point examinations in order to separate high-risk classes from low- or medium-risk classes. Figure 3.22 provides an example of using a three-dimensional graph to identify classes with high fair lending risk. This plot uses the first three principal components decomposed from their corresponding UPI. Reference points with neutral or low risk are created with predetermined disparity index values. The ten MSAs having the greatest UPI are represented by the pyramids, versus all other MSAs represented by cubes. In this way, one can visualize the proximity of observed MSAs to these reference points.

Furthermore, a surface contour can be created to better separate the high-risk classes from the low-risk classes.[19] As shown in Figure 3.23, one can use simulations to create a surface depicting fair lending risk (identified in the grey area), based on the combinations of all predetermined reference values. The classes that are outside of the surface area are identified as outliers (e.g., those having a pyramid shape) and they are subjected to further analysis to determine the contributing factors.

18. This is created by assuming a value of one for each of the indices.
19. This type of contour can be created using scenario or Monte Carlo simulation techniques based on a set of predesigned reference points and can also be done as an interpolated surface with SAS/STAT procedures (e.g., KRIGE2D).

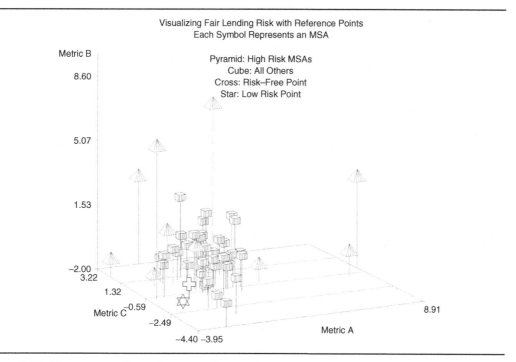

FIGURE 3.22 VISUALIZATION OF EXTREME INDICES WITH REFERENCE POINTS

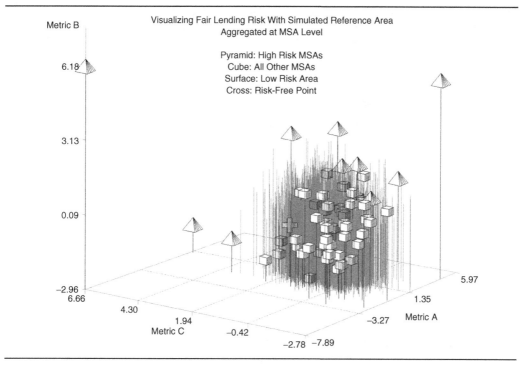

FIGURE 3.23 VISUALIZATION OF EXTREME INDICES WITH A SIMULATED REFERENCE AREA

Alternatively, individual disparity indices also can be perturbed in an incremental fashion to measure the impact on their contribution to overall fair lending exposure (i.e., UPI).

Examples of Other Visual Analyses

UPI can be powerful when used in conjunction with maps in fair lending analysis. Geographical regions, such as MSAs, states, counties, neighborhoods, voting districts, and census tracts, are color-coded based on the calculated UPI to signal the degree of fair lending risk produced for quickly and easily communicating key areas for further analysis and investigation. Figure 3.24 shows such as example, in which states are color-coded by UPI based on 2006 released HMDA peer data. In this example, the dark areas represent high risk, medium shading represent medium risk, and the light shade or no shade represent low risk areas. Further preliminary review of Washington, D.C., one of the high-UPI areas, reveals that the denial disparity is double, and price disparity is quadruple, for protected-class applicants defined by joint race/ethnicity. Similar coloration schemes also can be used for comparisons against competitors. Such representations can be particularly helpful in detecting exposure associated with redlining and predatory lending.

Trend analysis can also be easily conducted when UPIs are calculated over time (e.g., by month, quarter, or year). Figure 3.25 shows such an example when multiple MSA are compared by UPI from 2005–2006 released HMDA data. It shows which MSAs have a greater compliance risk exposure compared with the previous year.

SUMMARY

This chapter has described a UPI approach for defining, measuring, monitoring, and managing compliance risk. This is a general modeling framework that can be applied to different risk

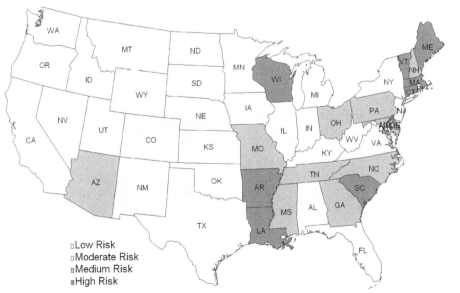

Universal Performance Indicator by State
Based on 2006 Released HMDA Peer Data

☐ Low Risk
☐ Moderate Risk
▨ Medium Risk
■ High Risk

FIGURE 3.24   STATE-LEVEL UPI RANKING ON A MAP

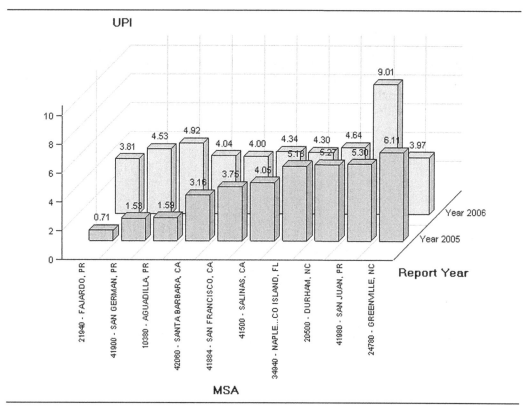

FIGURE 3.25 RISK INDICATOR BY MSA AND REPORTING YEAR BASED ON 2005–06 RELEASED HMDA PEER DATA

management areas or to revenue-generating initiatives. In order to further describe the systematic approach toward fair lending compliance analysis, we made a conscious decision to emphasize how UPI is used as a starting point for compliance risk management. There are many paths to understanding. The primary contribution of UPI is to immediately point the compliance analyst to the largest areas of exposure so that efforts can be prioritized appropriately and so that time is not wasted generating needless reports or in "checking what is right." The application of the UPI framework readily extends to all other areas of enterprise risk management (ERM). To illustrate this, we provide an example for liquidity risk management in Appendix 3A.

Relative to the opportunity side, by simply substituting "consumers having a thin, or no, credit bureau file" everywhere that "protected class" or "treatment group" appears, and by also substituting "mainstream credit consumers" everywhere that "nonprotected class" or "control group" appears, the identical methodology applies for assessing performance in serving the underbanked and/or emerging markets.[20] As we will see in Chapter 7, the ability to distinguish opportunities in different market segments and geographies represents a competitive advantage. Orienting UPI toward emerging markets enables an enterprise to rank-order segments and geographies by revenue potential. This includes, but is not limited to, consumer and business lending; community investment; location of retail outlets; public, private, and joint real estate development projects; public transportation projects; and so on. The analysis methodology described leverages well-established

---

20. Appropriate indicators need to be defined and included in order to capture opportunities.

and robust technology to perform the required computations and surface findings in an intuitive and highly actionable manner.[21]

In the next several chapters, we will discuss how to further analyze results obtained from UPI, such as pricing analysis, ovcragc/undcragc analysis, disparatc trcatmcnt tcsting, override analysis, and matched-pair analysis. Like a fair lending compass, UPI points the way to further stages of analysis by identifying those segments of business that require deeper investigation and prioritization.

---

21. For example, top ten super-neighborhoods having greatest untapped spending power, top ten branch locations having highest revenue potential, quadrant analysis of census tracts where market penetration is lowest yet revenue potential for nonmainstream consumers is high, and so on.

Appendix 3A
UPI APPLICATION EXAMPLE: LIQUIDITY RISK MANAGEMENT[22]

Financial institutions wage a constant battle between achieving a high-net-interest margin and maintaining the ability to raise sufficient funds at an acceptable cost within a set period of time. Their investment decisions relative to the money they receive, together with other funding they have secured, must reflect their commitment to repay customers on demand. Furthermore, federal and state regulators require liquidity because they recognize the volatility associated with many transaction accounts. Depositors require liquidity sufficient to meet their maturing contracts according to the terms of their agreements, and borrowers require liquidity so they can make full use of their lines of credit and, when necessary, extend their borrowed funds. Liquidity is therefore typically measured with respect to funding, asset quality, and potential demand.

To apply a UPI approach, we define liquidity management disparity indices based on funding, asset quality, concentrations, and demand metrics for the enterprise.

- A funding disparity index can be represented as the firm's funding ratio[23] divided by that of a comparable industry composite (e.g., similarly situated financial institutions with respect to asset size, funding scale, access to global markets, etc.). High index values indicate a greater funding risk relative to peer institutions. Similar funding disparity indices can also be created to measure disparities relative to market funding composition, and key underlying ratios (such as net borrowed funds as a percent of total assets, net borrowed funds to equity, core deposits as a percent of total deposits, total loans and leases as a percent of total deposits, etc.).

- An asset quality disparity index can be defined relative to any of a number of key ratios, such as nonperforming assets as a percent of Tier 1 capital plus ALLL (allowance for loan and lease losses), nonperforming assets as a percentage of loans and leases, net charge-offs as a percentage of loans and leases, provision expense as a percentage of loans and leases, reserve for credit losses as a percentage of loans and leases, past due loans as a percentage of loans, subprime exposure as a percentage of loans, loans to developing countries as a percentage of total loans, and so on. High index values indicate a greater asset quality risk relative to peer institutions.

---

22. This brief example may be expanded to include liquidity management for alternative enterprises, such as hedge funds, which exhibit a heterogeneous set of risks that include credit and liquidity among the systematic factors. Liquidity risk is commonly modeled in this context by analyzing autocorrelation of historical returns, whereby serial correlation typically falls out as a proxy for liquidity risk.

23. This measures the proportion of nonliquid assets funded by market-based funds. A higher value implies a greater reliance on market-based, short-term funds. Funding ratio = market-based funds less liquid assets divided by total assets less liquid assets, where market-based funds = negotiable CDs + borrowed funds + foreign time deposits; liquid assets = funds sold + trading accounts + time deposits placed + U.S. Treasury and agency securities.

- A concentration disparity index can be defined relative to any of a number of key ratios that capture potential overexposure relative to individual companies, counterparties, industry segments, countries, geographic regions, brokers/dealers, highly leveraged transactions, subprime credits, fixed-income securities possessing long durations, and so on. High index values indicate a greater concentration risk relative to peer institutions.
- A demand disparity index can be defined as the utilization of outstanding commitments divided by the average utilization ratio across peer institutions, or the ratio of the dollar amount of standby letters of credit to Tier 1 capital divided by the average ratio across peer institutions, or the ratio of estimated daily net cash flows over the next 30-day period relative to the past 30-day cycle across peer institutions.[24] These disparity ratios all capture different aspects of demand risk relative to a historical norm for the institution. High index values indicate an overall greater market demand risk.

Different thresholds are determined for each distinct metric to indicate the risk level associated with funding, asset quality, concentrations, and demand metrics for the enterprise. The use of a peer composite represents one possibility. Another would be historical norms, simulated values from scenario-based stress testing, targets from the institution's three-year strategic plan, or regulatory guidelines (e.g., OCC Canary Report).

Once funding, asset quality, concentration, and market demand disparity indices are defined and measured, one can calculate principal components, singular and universal performance indicators as described in the previous sections. Thus, institutions can be ranked by a single liquidity risk indicator. This will help financial executives develop more effective balance sheet strategy that will enable them to maximize their net interest margin by benefiting from changes in interest rates and customer demands while protecting liquidity.

---

24. Obviously, there are limitations on external data availability, but considerable financial information and key ratios may be obtained from the Uniform Bank Performance Reports (UBPR) available from the FFIEC, and other bank performance data available from oversight agencies such as the Federal Reserve Board and the Federal Deposit Insurance Corporation (FDIC). For a practical discussion on the use of this data see Gardner, Mona J., Dixie L. Mills, and Elizabeth S. Cooperman, *Managing Financial Institutions: An Asset/Liability Approach*, Dryden Press, 2000, pp. 199–248.

4

LOAN PRICING ANALYSIS

The universal performance indicator (UPI) methodology described in Chapter 3 incorporates metrics for a host of factors, including pricing that can be calculated relative to any segment at any level.[1] While the regulatory oversight agencies have made it abundantly clear that they will not take their eye off of loan denials, redlining, and fallout disparities for protected classes, a stronger focus has been given to loan-pricing analysis in recent years.[2] Predatory lending concerns, in general, have also risen over the same period of time and many states have enacted laws to combat such practices as charging and financing excessive points[3] and fees, requiring large prepayment penalties coupled with high interest rates, and loan flipping.[4] One state attorney general, Thomas J. Miller from Iowa, testified in 2003 before a House subcommittee that problems and practices in the subprime market in particular were not limited to marginal players, citing the prevailing two largest subprime lenders as being the target of actions by either state or federal agencies. One of those lenders paid a record $484 million to affected borrowers.[5]

Concerning borrower race and ethnicity, African-American and Hispanic borrowers are disproportionately more highly represented in the subprime market at all income levels.[6] One particular study found that for most types of subprime home loans, African-American and Latino borrowers are more likely to receive higher-rate loans than white borrowers, even after controlling for applicable risk factors. The pricing disparities between minority and nonminority groups are large and statistically significant.[7] Another study found that disparities actually increase as income

1. Examples of segments are geographic or organizational, and examples of levels are channel, product, loan purpose, loan type, or property type.
2. For example, "the incidence of higher-priced lending for conventional first-lien home-purchase loans on owner-occupied, one- to four-family, site-built homes rose from 11.5 percent in 2004 to 24.6 percent in 2005." Much effort has been focused on explaining the possible underlying contributing factors. See Avery, Robert B., and Glenn B. Canner, "Higher-Priced Home Lending and the 2005 HMDA Data," *Federal Reserve Bulletin*, September 18, 2006, pp. 123–166.
3. *Points* refers to discount and loan origination fees. One point equals 1 percent of the principal amount of the mortgage.
4. At least 31 states have predatory lending statutes, including Arkansas, California, Colorado, Connecticut, the District of Columbia, Florida, Georgia, Illinois, Indiana, Kansas, Kentucky, Maine, Maryland, Massachusetts, Michigan, Mississippi, Nebraska, Nevada, New Jersey, New Mexico, New York, North Carolina, Oklahoma, Pennsylvania, South Carolina, Texas, Utah, Virginia, West Virginia, Wisconsin, and Wyoming.
5. Miller, Thomas J. "Protecting Homeowners: Preventing Abusive Lending While Preserving Access to Credit," Testimony before the Subcommittee on Financial Institutions and Consumer Credit and the Subcommittee on Housing and Community Opportunity United States House of Representatives," November 5, 2003, pp.4–5.
6. Renuart, Elizabeth, National Consumer Law Center. "An Overview of the Predatory Mortgage Lending Process," Fannie Mae Foundation Publication, Housing Policy Debate, 2004, p. 477.
7. See Gruenstein B. D., Keith S. Ernst, and Wei Li. "Unfair Lending: The Effect of Race and Ethnicity on the Price of Subprime Mortgages", p. 5, Center for Responsible Lending, www.responsiblelending.org, 2006.

increases.[8] Recently, there have been a number of class-action lawsuits relating to pricing discrimination where plaintiffs are seeking injunctive relief, disgorgement and restitution of money obtained as a result of alleged discretionary pricing policy differences in points, fees, and interest rates. On July 11, 2007 the NAACP filed a Federal class action lawsuit against fourteen of the country's largest subprime mortgage lenders that alleges racial discrimination in lending practices.

Both government agencies and lending institutions have recognized the importance of monitoring and analyzing loan-pricing information. With the release of the 2006 Home Mortgage Disclosure Act (HMDA) peer data, observers had an opportunity to interpret trends associated with the new HMDA pricing data and it has raised many questions.[9] As a result, there has been increasing focus on exactly how loans are priced and concerns about the fairness of the models used to calibrate and price risk. To all related constituencies, this requires the ability to effectively screen the large amount of HMDA data and quickly identify disparity areas to focus on.[10]

This requirement presents a lending institution with both the opportunity and challenge to successfully demonstrate its delivery on the commitment to fair pricing of loans. Lending institutions need the ability to effectively monitor, manage, and improve their loan-pricing practices, quickly identify any "regulatory risk" areas, and be prepared to satisfactorily explain any significant pricing disparities between the protected and nonprotected groups. As a by-product of conducting such an analysis, a risk-based pricing relationship can be defined and then used to validate the observed pricing disparities.[11] Hence, an institution can view and contrast how risk is allocated across a multitude of pricing dimensions, and then explore by drilling down from aggregate values to the detail, by geography (from national level to census tract detail), or by organizational entity (from total enterprise to individual loan officer within a branch).

In this chapter, we describe how to use a systematic loan-pricing analysis method to detect statistically significant pricing disparities among protected/nonprotected groups. The structure of this chapter is designed to first provide a basic understanding of complexity of loan-pricing models, factors, and governance. Then we describe pricing analysis using HMDA data. Next, we present a systematic analytical methodology to identify possible pricing patterns and examine them to determine the magnitude and pervasiveness across protected groups and geographies within an overall context for the lender's fair lending practices. We then discuss overage and underage analysis, which is geared toward monitoring discretionary pricing where it is exercised and controlled (i.e., at the loan officer and branch levels). In this case, statistical testing for disparate impact can be directly applied to either frequency or average amount of the overage or underage. Finally, we describe how to create case-based examples to support statistical findings. Overage/underage analysis data requirements and sample size determination are included in Appendices 4C and 4E, respectively.

---

8. For example, low-income African-Americans receive 2.3 times as many subprime loans as their white counterparts, while for upper-income African-Americans the factor was 3.0 times. For Hispanics the corresponding factors were 1.4 and 2.2. See Bradford, Calvin. "Risk or Race? Racial Disparities and the Subprime Refinance Market," Washington, DC: Center for Community Change, 2002.

9. Abrahams, Clark R., "Interpreting the New HMDA Pricing Data," June 14, 2006, ABA Regulatory Compliance Conference (SAS Institute Publication posted on ABA Compliance Post-Conference Web site).

10. In 2005, there were approximately 34.26 million loan records for calendar year (CY) 2004 reported by 8,121 financial institutions. In 2006, there were about 30.17 million home loan records for calendar year 2005 by about 8,848 lenders. See Avery and Canner, 2006, p. 129.

11. The process would involve using logistic regression results to score each loan applicant and rank them by risk based on their denial/default probability. Higher probability will imply higher risk. Only those applications whose loans were actually approved and originated will be selected and divided into different risk groups (high, medium, or low, etc.) according to the score. The score range is then compared with the actual pricing range (rate spread class) to determine if the level of risk for a loan applicant is consistent with the rate they are charged. This can be done by comparing their distributions or nonparametric analysis of variance (ANOVA).

UNDERSTANDING LOAN PRICING MODELS

Before we describe our loan-pricing analysis methodology, we cover some of the basics concerning how lenders price their loans at the total portfolio, portfolio segment, and account levels.

Governance

Pricing policy is typically governed by a pricing committee. This committee compares the institution's internal pricing, product mix, refinance share, and other factors with those of major lenders on a market-by-market basis. In the case of mortgage lending, the Loan Pricing Committee pricing input typically includes an overview of the national mortgage market; application/origination volumes by product and channel/region; competitive rate/point information, routinely gathered by line organizations; independent surveys conducted by external firms (for major markets on a weekly basis); Internet Web site searches for pricing information; portfolio product pricing results; and secondary product pricing.

A loan base rate[12] is set at the product level, and it must take into account loan amount, loan term, origination costs, servicing costs, prepayment expectation, and expected net-loss rate. Base rates are adjusted at the market and portfolio level and reflect market conditions, marginal funding costs, return-on-capital requirements, competitive positions, and financial leverage, proportional to risk, tax rate, collection costs, and recovery costs.

In practice, marginal funding costs are obtained from the corporate funds transfer pricing (FTP) system. Capital allocation reports are produced for different products and credit segments. Activity-based costing can be used to provide greater accuracy, and can consider the varying cost structure by channel. For net-credit loss estimates, a variety of different forecasting models (account-level score based, economic regression based, Markov behavior based, vintage based) are used to predict performance of segments defined by product, cohort, portfolio risk segment, and so on. For acquisition cost, separate estimates are developed for each channel.

Figure 4.1 provides an example of a pricing spread derivation for a prime versus a subprime loan. The pricing spread formula is calculated as: [(return on capital/financial leverage)/(1 − tax rate)] + expected net loss rate + collection and recovery cost. For a prime loan, we can substitute the values and evaluate the expression as follows: [(15%/20:1)/(1 − 0.35)] + 0.32% + 0 = 147 basis points (bp). Similarly for a subprime loan, which has higher return and associated loss and cost components, the expression becomes: [(20%/10:1)/(1 − 0.35)] + 1% + 0.11% = 418 bp.

As risk increases, financial leverage for a firm decreases, while targeted return on capital (ROC) grows. It is important to establish objectives for ROC and portfolio growth, recognizing that competition is a constraining factor.

The pricing committee publishes prices on fixed rate loans (daily) and variable rate loans (weekly) based on market movement/volatility, the shape of the yield curve, and the internal portfolio rate distributions. Line organizations seek to maximize ancillary fee income, subject to competitive pressures. Fair lending requires a consistent fee structure across channels, units, and locations that is in compliance with laws and regulations. Pool eligibility for mortgage-back securities (MBSs)[13] depends on the various risk factors and pricing caps that are also imposed. For example, for adjustable rate mortgages (ARMs), a 250-bp limit on the initial period rate and a 350-bp cap on the margin may be imposed, with the added requirement that no more X percent of aggregate balances of loans in the pool represents margin pricing between 250 bp and 350 bp.

12. Examples of base rates are 6-month Treasury bill average, 6-month LIBOR (London Interbank Offered Rate), 6-month CD (certificate of deposit) index, one-year Treasury note average, or spot, 3-, 5-, 7-, and 10-year Treasury bonds, etc.
13. For a detailed review of MBS, see Fabozzi, Frank J. and Pollack, Irving M. *The Handbook of Fixed Income Securities*. Dow Jones-Irwin, 1987, Chapters 15–18, pp. 352–449.

For a bank quoted rate:	600 bp
Cost of funds:	−250 bp
	350 bp
Operation/overhead:	−125 bp
	225 bp
Losses:	−75 bp
	150 bp
Income Taxes (35%):	−55 bp
Net Spread:	**95 bp**

FIGURE 4.1   DERIVATION OF NET SPREAD GIVEN A QUOTED RATE

To ensure transparency and consistency, the line organization needs to document all pricing considerations, and organizations need uniform procedures for approval of fee waivers. A best practice is to institute systems that support fee assessment and waiver tracking within standard business procedures that are owned by the line organization. Furthermore, balance sheet management policy may require a set minimum percentage for originated loans that meets conforming standards, for securitization or sale in the secondary market.

In a more general vein, this same pricing methodology is applied within loan portfolio segments. That is why credit card issuers are able to offer low fixed rates (e.g., 6 percent) to particular segments of customers, even though the overall portfolio net credit loss rate may be 5 percent, the cost of operation/overhead 4 percent, the cost of funds 3 percent which would imply a 12 percent rate at a minimum would be required to break even. This is not an irrational pricing strategy because it is not offered to all customers. Consider Figure 4.2, which shows an automobile lending pricing spread example where the portfolio segments are defined by credit bureau score bands.

In this example, a lower credit score range has a higher risk-adjusted return on capital (RAROC), lower leverage, a higher expected net credit loss (NCL), a higher recovery and collection cost, and a higher net spread associated with it than any higher credit score range. In practice, there is usually an additional nominal accommodation made to the dealer in the form of a program discount, say 25 to 30 bp, that comes out of the bank's net spread. In Chapter 7, we explore the use and implications of segmentation schemes for portfolios, consumers, geographies, and markets that are helpful in defining homogenous groups with respect to profitability, risk, and untapped potential.

Custom Score	RAROC	Leverage	Pretax Ratio (bp)	Exp NCL (bp)	Collection/ Recovery Cost (bp)	Net Spread (bp)
260 < x < 281	10%	100:1	10	20	1	31
240 < x < 261	12%	80:1	15	30	2	47
220 < x < 241	15%	15:1	100	45	4	149
200 < x < 221	17%	10:1	170	70	8	248

FIGURE 4.2   AUTOMOBILE LENDING PRICING SPREAD EXAMPLE

Taxonomy of Pricing Factors

We now briefly examine categories of loan pricing factors, in no particular order.

- *Borrower credit risk.* Factors include credit history, income, debt-to-income ratio, credit score, payment shock, months of reserves, loan-to-value ratio (LTV), liquidity, and net worth. These factors are considered in combination with other credit risk–related factors and price adjustments are derived to ensure the lender will cover costs related to any net credit losses, including collection and possible foreclosure costs, over the life of the loan. In addition, a risk-adjusted spread is sometimes factored into the pricing adjustments to meet the lender's financial objectives for the business line.
- *Product interest rate risk and credit terms/conditions.* Factors vary by product and include contractual maturity, fixed versus variable versus interest-only rate, base rate, repricing frequency, payment terms (down payment, balloon, etc.), prepayment restrictions/penalties, and reamortization restrictions. Prepayment restriction and penalties are more prevalent in subprime lending. For example, according to Fannie Mae and estimates from the Department of Housing and Urban Development (HUD), the percentage of mortgages having prepayment penalties is 43 to 80 percent for subprime loans and only 2 to 11 percent for prime loans.[14] Furthermore, as pointed out in a Federal Reserve Board (FRB) report, "Lenders compensate for the [prepayment] risk, either by including prepayment penalties in their loan contracts, or by pricing the risk in their calculation of the interest rate on the loan."[15] The penalty can be as much as 4 to 5 percent of the outstanding loan amount.[16]
- *Program subsidies and special accommodations.* Factors include community development lending initiatives, introductory rate, special terms on standard products for a limited period and specific target market, special promotion, program-specific features associated with FHA/VA/Fannie Mae/Freddie Mac, such as fee waivers, rate lock options, down payment assistance, no closing costs, and so forth. Examples of program subsidies and accommodations would be a set limit of broker fees, a cap on the current rate +3/8 percent, ability to lock up to 15 days prior to closing, or a waiver of all lender and third-party service fees, including points and origination fees.
- *Transaction and collateral aspects.* This includes the following:
  - ○ *LTV.* In the case of a home improvement loan, the value may be determined based on either the value of the property as is, or the estimated market value after improvements have been made.
  - ○ *Lien status.* The first lien, and any other claims on the property, would be taken into account with a combined ratio (CLTV).
  - ○ *Loan amount.* The relative cost to the borrower of smaller loan amounts is often higher due to fixed processing costs and the fact that loan officers tend to be compensated on volume more than the number of deals. Because the effort to book a half dozen $50,000 mortgages is far greater than that to book a single $300,000 mortgage, the loan officer may charge an additional amount to compensate himself for his time based on the larger deals he would otherwise be doing.
  - ○ *Financial securities pledged as collateral.* For example, 401 K assets pledged for 10 percent of purchase price of property being financed results in only a 10 percent

---

14. See Immergluck, Dan. *Credit to the Community: Community Reinvestment and Fair Lending Policy in the United States.* M. E. Sharpe, 2004, p. 122.

15. Avery, Robert B., Glenn B. Canner, and Robert E. Cook. "New Information Reported under HMDA and Its Application in Fair Lending Enforcement," *Federal Reserve Bulletin,* Summer 2005, p. 369.

16. See Hecht, B. L. *Developing Affordable Housing; A Practical Guide for Non-Profit Organizations.* John Wiley & Sons, 1999, p. 76.

cash down payment with no private mortgage insurance (PMI) required, while affording lower financing cost due to income and possible capital gain associated with the pledged assets.

○ *Appraisal fraud.* Inflated appraisals, when identified, should have the corresponding LTV ratio adjusted as needed or excluded from the analysis.

- *Borrower/product options.* Factors include mortgage life insurance (may be required depending on down payment and pledged collateral if applicable), buy-down points, lock period, escrow (hazard insurance, taxes, etc.), rate caps, and prepayment capability.
- *Borrower negotiation skills.* Borrower expertise and negotiation skills definitely play a role in the process of mortgage loan pricing.[17]
- *Processing cost.* Factors include administrative costs relative to marketing, underwriting, and processing through closing that can be captured in the form of an origination fee.
- *Market/price risk.* Factors include the level, shape, and direction of market yield curves, anticipated and actual price movements occurring between lock date and actual funding date, and actual widening or compression of spread quarter-to-quarter over the Federal Financial Examination Interagency Council (FFIEC) benchmark treasury notes/bonds. When there is a lot of volatility or upward pressure on interest rates, then the borrower will have to pay more for certain features relating to lock period, float-down, and so on, or for imbedded options in the mortgage product itself. Obviously, if there is less liquidity in the market, that can also cause demand to exceed supply, with the obvious result on prices.
- *Competitive influences.* In order to achieve volume targets, lenders may vary prices from market to market over time, and when there is a new entrant in a market with aggressive, below-market pricing campaign, this can have a pronounced effect, in the short run, on lender pricing. Hence, when fees do not match the quoted price, at least a part of the reason may be that a fee was partially or entirely waived to meet the competition's pricing.
- *Channel.* On the retail side, there are often pricing differentials due to costs associated with the source of the transaction (e.g., bank branch, mortgage sales office, call center, subprime sales office, direct mail, Internet, and private banking). Some Internet lenders promise to waive the origination fee altogether, saving the borrower one point on the loan amount (which can be substantial). In the wholesale channel, brokers pay fees to third parties that they pass along as part of their fee. The origination fee goes to the broker, who may also charge separate processing and administration fees, not to mention appraisal, credit report, and property inspection. Relative to the wholesale channel, there is also a yield spread premium that is customarily passed on to the borrower via points or a higher rate. On the retail side, pricing concessions are common for private banking customers. This can have a pronounced effect on the urban/rural or inner city/suburban results for a given assessment area. Finally, loan officers in call centers may not earn any commissions on overages.

The annual percentage rate (APR) does not capture all fees, and since it is a summary measure, it is advisable to monitor how individual fees are assessed across the borrowing population. Rate sheets and fee schedules are maintained on a continual basis and distributed to all loan officers and brokers. Originators are responsible for using current rate sheets and fee schedules. Disparities need to be analyzed to ensure that pricing is not

---

17. Research conducted jointly by faculty at the University of Tennessee and the Federal Reserve Bank of Atlanta, supports this conclusion. See Black, Harold, Thomas P. Boehm, and Ramon P. Degennero, "Is Discretionary Pricing Discriminatory? The Case of Mortgage Overages," *Review of Black Political Economy*, Vol. 31, No. 4, Fall 2004, pp. 59–68.

being set in a discriminatory manner. To accomplish this, variances from the fee schedules should be flagged for control and protected class groups. Both the amount and frequency of deviations from the fee schedules should be calculated and compared for appraisal fees, application fees, and other fees listed in Figures 4.41 and 4.42. The same should be done for fee waivers (listed in Figure 4.40). Furthermore, a geographic analysis, splitting on low-, moderate-, middle-, and upper-income census tracts in place of protected-class segmentation, can also be performed to provide strength to fair lending monitoring and risk exposure identification, as well as providing information for stakeholder communication on loan pricing concerns.

Points charged by third parties (broker and correspondent channels) also need to be monitored. There should be guidelines provided to all brokers that articulate policy with respect to the maximum number of points that can be charged for origination-related items as well as points charged for rate discounts. Analysis should be similar to that previously described, and disparities should be reported by protected class, census tract income groups, and by broker on at sufficient frequency to allow for early detection of any adverse trends.

SYSTEMATIC PRICING ANALYSIS PROCESS

In this section we describe a systematic testing methodology for fair pricing of loans. This entails a sequential, well-defined process of examining disparities and suspect pricing patterns between protected and nonprotected groups. At each sequential stage, the statistical significance, and the necessity for further analysis, are determined.

Overall Analysis Process

The basic systematic methodology involves the following steps as shown in Figure 4.3:

Step 1. **Perform prescreening.** This is to identify the data segments that may have significant compliance risk exposures. Initial identification of pricing compliance exposures may begin with review of the data using the universal performance indicator (with particular emphasis on pricing-related, or multifactor patterns that combine market penetration, origination, and other disparities).[18] Another important source of information for initial screening is the Federal Reserve Board's HMDA rate spread tables.[19] These sources are used as preliminary screening to provide initial insights and guidance for more detailed analysis. Customer complaints can also provide an indication of potential problem areas.

Step 2. **Perform chi-square test.** This is to test for the significance of the incidence of high priced loans on selected segments.

---

18. For example, at the American Conference Institute's Eighth National Forum on Anti-Predatory Lending Compliance (held November 17–18, 2005) Steven Rosenbaum, Chief of Housing and Civil Enforcement Section of the U.S. Department of Justice Civil Rights Division provided the following example of several HMDA-based disparity indicators that combine to form a pattern of potential racial targeting for high priced loans: (1) an unfavorable high priced loan disparity for a protected class, coupled with (2) a high market penetration relative to the same protected class, combined with (3) a highly favorable value for the origination disparity ratio relative to the protected class. The interpretation in the case of race/ethnicity would be that this represents a pattern where minorities are sought out and charged significantly higher rates on their loans than their nonminority counterparts and also where nonminorities are originating loans at a much lower rate than their minority counterparts in the particular geographic market in question.

19. See Figure 4.30 for a listing of these tables and Figure 4.31 for an example of one of the tables for a specific geographic area (Washington, D.C., metropolitan area).

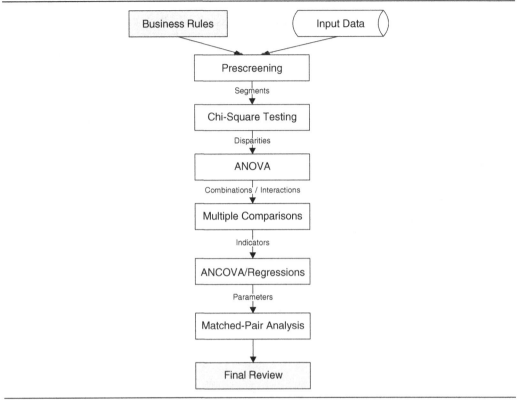

FIGURE 4.3   SYSTEMATIC ANALYSIS PROCESS

Step 3.   **ANOVA (analysis of variance) test.** This is to identify the combinations and interactions of the categorical variables (risk factors) that have significant impact on pricing for the selected segments.

Step 4.   **Multiple comparisons.** Perform pairwise comparisons across and between protected groups and the control group. The results can be used to create indicator variables for regressions.

Step 5.   **ANCOVA (analysis of covariance)/regression analysis.** This requires including additional continuous variables based on the results based on the previous analysis results.

Step 6.   **Matched-pair analysis.** The predicted parameters together with all previous findings will be used for constructing matched pairs for detailed comparisons between individual loan applicants falling into different groups relative to protected/nonprotected status coupled with the application action result, credit score qualification, or other system loan recommendation or loan decision (including pricing, counteroffers, product/program referral, etc.).

Step 7.   **Final review.** Selected loans will be subject to detailed manual comparative file reviews when significant and material results persist.

This is a general process and can start from any step as dictated by business needs and available information. For example, if it is already known that there is a significant pricing disparity between two race groups for the home purpose and conventional loans in a particular metropolitan statistical area (MSA), then we can directly start from Step 5 for regressions analysis by including more borrower characteristic variables (such as bureau score, LTV, and debt-to-income [DTI] ratio).

Chi-square testing is performed to determine if there is a statistically significant price disparity between a treatment (protected) group and the control group (nonprotected).[20] The next step is to identify one dependent variable (DV) such as rate spread and one or more categorical independent variables (IVs) for ANOVA testing. The main goal here is to examine pricing disparities across all protected and nonprotected groups and test if those disparities are statistically significant across one or more categorical variables. ANCOVA extends ANOVA by supplement IVs with continuous variables or covariates. Here, ANCOVA is to test whether a protected group is treated the same as a nonprotected group by including and comparing interactions or intercepts.[21]

Next, lending policy rules are used together with the results from ANOVA/ANCOVA testing to conduct a full regression analysis. The chief aim of regression modeling is to examine whether protected class membership contributes to pricing disparities, when all relevant factors are present.

ANOVA testing is a fundamental component in this systematic pricing analysis.[22] It provides inputs to the regression analysis, which, in turn, also provides feedback to validate or modify the previous ANOVA testing. The ANOVA testing process and its relationship to ANCOVA, regression analysis, and matched pair analysis are represented in Figure 4.4. The process depicted is continuous and iterative. ANOVA testing is performed on various combinations of segments to minimize false negative errors. For example, even when ANOVA testing shows no significant pricing disparities across race groups by metropolitan statistical area, loan type, owner occupancy, and lien status, further segmentation by income or loan amount, coupled with testing may be still required. For each segment, it is also important to test for data sufficiency and violations of assumptions. This will be discussed in detail in later sections of this chapter.

Detailed Description of Pricing Analysis Process

Input Data Collection

Performing pricing analysis can involve data from various sources, which were described in detail in Chapter 2. The following data are typically required for pricing analysis:

- *Public data.* The FFIEC HMDA peer data released in the fall of each year on CD-ROM. The FRB produces HMDA APR spread tables.[23] The census bureau also provides tables that can be merged with the public HMDA data to allow for city and county level reporting and to create additional analysis variables or indices.
- *Third-party data.* Geocoding vendors provide data packs that can be used to perform rooftop geocoding and perform CASS[24] certified address verification. Dun & Bradstreet and other business information suppliers provide small business and farm data at census tract levels for use in analysis of lending patterns, market share, and peer analysis. Credit bureaus provide borrower payment histories for all reported credit, and some noncredit, tradelines and credit scores.
- *Internal lender data.* This consists of company-specific data, or policy data, such as bank branch/ATM locations, bank Community Reinvestment Act performance evaluation (P/E) data by MSA/census tract, bank detailed HMDA data not reported publicly, bank loan

---

20. This analysis may be performed at varying levels of pricing thresholds, such as appear on the FRB rate spread tables (e.g., for first lien home purchase loans, the threshold values might be 3 to 3.99 percent, 4 to 4.99 percent, 5 to 5.99 percent, 6 to 6.99 percent, 7 to 7.99 percent, and 8.00 percent or more).
21. For detailed discussion on Analysis of Covariance, see Tabachnick, B. G., and L. S. Fidell, *Experimental Design Using ANOVA*, Thomson Higher Education, 2007, pp. 379–473.
22. We are indebted to Dr. Jim Goodnight for suggesting in October 2005 that we use the ANOVA method for HMDA pricing analysis.
23. See Figure 4.30 for a list of these tables.
24. CASS is a U.S. Postal Service acronym for Coding Accuracy Support System.

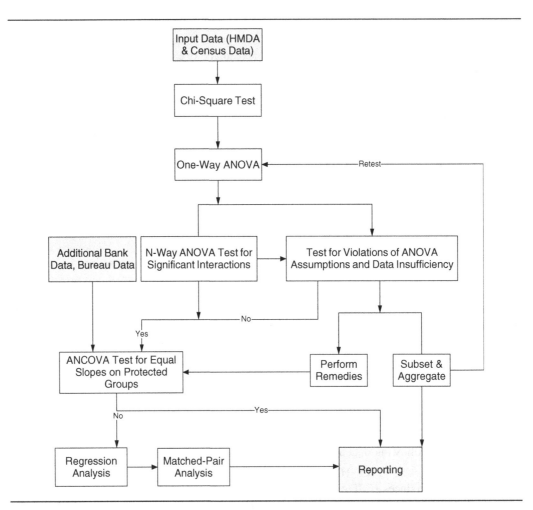

Figure 4.4   Anova Testing Flow Process

application data beyond the realm of HMDA (e.g., credit score, debt ratio, LTV), some of which can be used as covariates for regression analysis or matched-pair analysis.

Preliminary Screening

A preliminary statistical testing process can quickly examine large numbers of loan subsets and identify possible pricing disparities that require further analysis. Some preliminary pricing analysis can be performed using HDMA rate spread tables, as shown in Appendix 4A, and, within a metropolitan area, regulators can use this information to spot potentially discriminatory pricing patterns, and pricing outliers, by comparing individual lenders with their peer group.

Chi-Square Testing

The chi-square goodness-of-fit test can be applied to a univariate distribution of binned data (i.e., continuous data, or very granular discrete data, that has been put into a manageable set of distinct classes or ranges of values). This test is very easy to perform, yet powerful, for detecting significant differences by segment across protected classes. Figure 4.5 illustrates chi-square test

Race	Observed Above-Threshold Loans	Expected Above-Threshold Loans	Chi-Square	Percent of Above-Threshold Loans	Total Loans	Average Rate Spread (Above-Threshold)	Price Disparity Index	Significant
Native Hawaiian/Other Pacific Island	72	67.64	0.281	12.654	569	2.202	1.01	No
Hispanic White	51	45.529	0.657	13.316	383	2.623	1.063	No
American Indian/Alaska Native	99	100.687	0.028	11.688	847	2.03	0.933	No
Non-Hispanic White	408	387.176	1.12	12.527	3257	2.186	1	
Race not Availalbe	45	46.837	0.072	11.421	394	2.273	0.912	No
Asian	64	72.752	1.053	10.458	612	2.148	0.835	Yes
Joint (White/non-white race)	52	48.977	0.187	12.621	412	2.158	1.008	No
Black or African American	111	137.895	5.246	9.569	1160	2.075	0.764	Yes
2 or more non-white races	49	43.508	0.693	13.388	366	2.385	1.069	No

FIGURE 4.5   CHI-SQUARE TEST RESULTS EXAMPLE

results for a two-way frequency table (race groups versus loan price range).[25] These results contain the names of race groups, number of above-threshold loans, number of total loans, chi-square test statistics, and price disparity index. In this example, the chi-square test indicates that there is a strong relationship between joint race and loan price range. Specifically, the observed number of above-threshold loans for black or African-American is significantly higher than expected, although their associated mean spread for above-threshold loans is not significantly above the overall mean. A similar test can be applied to a three-way frequency table that is stratified by an additional analysis variable, such as gender.

Overview of ANOVA Testing

ANOVA is a technique for analyzing experimental data in which one or more *response* (or *dependent*) variables are measured under various conditions identified by one or more classification variables. In an ANOVA, the variation in the response is separated into variation attributable to the classification variables, and variation attributable to random error. An ANOVA constructs tests to determine the significance of the classification effects. A typical goal in an ANOVA is to compare means of the response variable for various combinations of the classification variables.

An ANOVA may be written as a general linear model (GLM). Analysis of variance procedures use the model to predict the response for each observation.[26] The difference between the actual and predicted response is the *residual error*. Most of the procedures fit model parameters that minimize the sum of squares of residual errors. Thus, the method is called *least squares regression*. The variance due to the random error, σ^2, is estimated by the mean squared error (MSE or s^2). The F-value is the ratio of mean square for model (MSM) divided by mean square for error (MSE).[27] The F-value and corresponding P-value are reported in the ANOVA table.

---

25. For simplicity, this table contains only the above-threshold loans.
26. See Tabachnick, B. G., and Fidell, L. S., op. cit., 2007, pp. 70–71,
27. For details, see PROC GLM, *SAS/STAT 9.1 User's Guide* (2003), SAS Institute Inc., Cary, NC.

One-Way ANOVA Testing

For loan-pricing analysis, the one-way ANOVA can be used to test if rate spread varies significantly across protected classes. This can be performed on the data aggregated by loan product, marketing channels, or regions for all lending institutions. Through subsetting, or aggregating, the data by specified analysis variables, we attempt to control for most, if not all, of the effects of the analysis variables so that the protected variable can explain as much of the remaining variation in rate spread as possible. The F-statistic and corresponding P-value are used to determine the significance level. In general, if the reported P-value is less than or equal to 5 percent, we can conclude that there is a statistical difference between the means of the protected and nonprotected groups.

The simplest ANOVA model can be written as:

$$Y_{ij} = \mu + \alpha_i + \varepsilon_{ij} \tag{4.1}$$

Y_{ij} is the jth value of the response variable for the ith group. It is a continuous dependent variable, such as rate spread. μ is the overall population mean of the dependent variable, α_i referred as the effect of group i, is the difference between the population mean of the ith group and the overall mean, μ. This is associated with the independent variables, also called predictor or explanatory variables, usually include race, gender, ethnicity status, or minority status. ε_{ij} is the difference between each observed value of response and the mean for that group.[28]

In general, the main results from the ANOVA testing can point to factors that show a statistically significant difference between group means. It can also identify significant interactions between two categorical factors, and provide the F-statistic, P-value, and degrees of freedom. One-way ANOVA tests can be used for high-level screening to select the seemingly "risky" areas for further analysis. For example, Figure 4.6 displays one-way ANOVA testing results by specified protected variables and MSA segment. It also flags violations of ANOVA assumptions including normal distribution and equal variance.

Based on the preliminary one-way testing results, we can perform additional tests for significance of interactions between a protected variable and a segment variable. For example, Figure 4.7 shows that variable called Joint Race has a significant effect on rate spread, and it also has a significant interaction with variable MSA. This lends itself to further analysis to identify the MSAs where the race groups have significant effects on rate spread.

MSA Segment	Response Variable	Interest Variable	Normality Flag	Equal Variance Flag	ANOVA Test Significance Flag
1	rate_spread	joint_race2	0	0	1
1	rate_spread	joint_ethnicity	0	0	1
2	rate_spread	joint_race2	0	0	1
2	rate_spread	joint_ethnicity	0	0	1
3	rate_spread	joint_race2	0	0	0
3	rate_spread	joint_ethnicity	0	0	0
4	rate_spread	joint_ethnicity	0	0	1
4	rate_spread	joint_race2	0	0	1

FIGURE 4.6   ANOVA TEST FOR SIGNIFICANT INTERACTION

28. For detailed discussion on the forms of ANOVA models, see also Miller, Ruppert, G. Jr., *Beyond ANOVA*, Chapman & Hall, 1997, pp. 67–71.

Analysis Variables	Significance	Dependent Variables	Degree of Freedom	F-value	P-value
joint_ethnicity	1	rate_spread	3	73.56842	1.84E-47
joint_race	1	rate_spread	6	45.18184	1.88E-55
minority_status	1	rate_spread	1	19.6834	9.16E-06
joint_ethnicity*ma	1	rate_spread	727	1.196236	0.000227
minority_status*ma	1	rate_spread	353	1.162753	0.019193
joint_race*ma	1	rate_spread	1037	1.096437	0.017107

FIGURE 4.7   ANOVA TEST FOR SIGNIFICANT INTERACTION

Two-Way/N-Way ANOVA

The one-way ANOVA test is especially powerful in instances where all analysis variables can be controlled. In such cases, higher-order ANOVAs can be simplified into a one-way ANOVA. However, in many cases it can be difficult to control some of the analysis variables. Furthermore, we may want to know if the interactions between two categorical variables impact the dependent variable. When "n" categorical predictor variables are present, an "n-way" ANOVA is needed. The simplest n-way ANOVA is a two-way ANOVA, which includes two independent categorical variables (hence the name *two-way*):[29]

$$Y_{ij} = \mu + \alpha_i + \beta_j + (\alpha_i\beta_j) + \varepsilon_{ij} \qquad (4.2)$$

An n-way ANOVA can also be used to validate if the one-way ANOVA testing is appropriate. For example, if testing shows there is no significant interaction between the race and gender or income level, then one-way ANOVA testing without the income factor can be considered appropriate. In the absence of this higher-order result, the one-way testing could be misleading.

In general, a two-way ANOVA test can be used to determine:

- The presence of a significant interaction between the risk variable (e.g., race) and the analysis variable (e.g., income). For example, if both minority and low-income applicants are charged a higher rate, and if an interaction is significant at 5 percent level, then the interaction will be flagged in the output table (and used in subsequent regression analysis).
- The persistence of significance of the effects if one attempts to control for an analysis variable. Consider the analysis variable income, and suppose that for all applications in the same low-income group, significant variation by race in average rate spread persists. In such a case, the two-way model cannot be reduced to a one-way model.
- The income groups where the difference in rate spread is significant if you subset the data by income.
- Whether further subsetting by additional analysis variables is required (e.g., in cases where no significant effects were found).

Two-way ANOVA test results can be used to determine the significance of two different analysis variables, and their interaction, provided the following conditions are met: (1) the group variances of each analysis variable are equal, (2) the analysis variable is normally distributed, and (3) the sample has sufficient number of observations. ANOVA results can provide important inputs for the regression analysis in later steps.

---

29. See Miller, 1997, pp. 117–128.

Obs	Joint Race	Income Indicator	Rate Spread	FICO Score
1	Non-Hispanic white	Upper income	3.65572	628
2	Black or African American	Upper income	2.44417	712
3	Non-Hispanic white	Upper income	4.2616	621
4	Non-Hispanic white	Upper income	3.72423	751
5	Non-Hispanic white	Upper income	2.78589	532
6	Non-Hispanic white	Upper income	1.1401	599
7	Non-Hispanic white	Upper income	1.52044	525
8	Non-Hispanic white	Upper income	4.67034	612
9	Black or African American	Upper income	3.01372	651
10	Non-Hispanic white	Upper income	2.04179	642
11	Non-Hispanic white	Low income	3.27736	652
12	Non-Hispanic white	Low income	3.51337	785
13	Black or African American	Low income	5.46129	596
14	Non-Hispanic white	Low income	2.62509	566
15	Black or African American	Low income	4.982	641
16	Non-Hispanic white	Low income	3.54803	658
17	Non-Hispanic white	Low income	3.30989	753
18	Non-Hispanic white	Low income	1.48711	664
19	Non-Hispanic white	Low income	3.36781	597
20	Black or African American	Low income	4.70904	506

FIGURE 4.8   INPUT DATA FOR ANOVA TESTING BY RACE GROUP AND INCOME

Source	DF	Sum of Squares	Mean Square	F Value	Pr > F
Model	1	4.76123917	4.7612392	3.87	0.0649
Error	18	22.171025	1.2317236		
Corrected Total	19	26.9322641			

FIGURE 4.9   ONE-WAY ANOVA TESTING RESULTS IN INSIGNIFICANT RACIAL IMPACT

Figure 4.8 lists the data used in the following illustrative example. As shown in Figure 4.9, if a one-way ANOVA test is used without considering the interaction of income and race, the test fails to reject the null hypothesis at 5 percent significance level. The conclusion is that the race effect is not significant.

Continuing with this example, if a two-way ANOVA test is performed by including income level as an analysis/segmentation variable, then the test results show that the race effect is significant (i.e., the P-value is less than 5 percent). Figure 4.10 shows the rate spread data subset by race and income, and we notice that the rate spread is affected by the interaction of income level and race when data are subset by race and income level. In other words, rate spread is higher if the applicant is both a minority and in a low-income group.

joint_race2	income_indicator	rate_spread LSMEAN
Black or African American	Low Income	5.05077844
Black or African American	Upper Income	2.72894113
Non-Hispanic white	Low Income	3.01837835
Non-Hispanic white	Upper Income	2.97501257

FIGURE 4.10   RATE SPREAD SUBSET BY RACE AND INCOME

Source	DF	Sum of Squares	Mean Square	F Value	Pr > F
Model	3	11.2373742	3.7457914	3.82	0.0308
Error	16	15.6948899	0.9809306		
Corrected Total	19	26.9322641			

FIGURE 4.11   TWO-WAY ANOVA TESTING BY RACE AND INCOME RESULTS IN SIGNIFICANT RACIAL IMPACT—OVERALL MODEL

Source	DF	Type I SS	Mean Square	F Value	Pr > F
joint_race	1	4.7612392	4.7612392	4.85	0.0426
income_indicator	1	1.7617531	1.7617531	1.8	0.1989
joint_race*income_ind	1	4.714382	4.714382	4.81	0.0435

FIGURE 4.12   TWO-WAY ANOVA TESTING BY RACE AND INCOME RESULTS IN SIGNIFICANT RACIAL IMPACT

Figure 4.11 provides outputs that indicate the overall model fits the data well.

Figure 4.12 shows significant racial effect. The interaction of income level and race is also statistically significant.

ANOVA versus *t*-Test

Both the ANOVA and the *t*-test are based on similar assumptions. They both assume data or residuals are normally distributed, have equal variances, and observations are independent. The one-sample *t*-test compares the mean of the sample to a given number. The two-sample *t*-test compares the mean of the first sample, minus the mean of the second sample, to a given number. The paired-observations *t*-test compares the mean of the differences in the observations to a given number.[30]

When there are only two groups in the population, the *t*-test is a special case of ANOVA. Thus, either test will always yield similar results. However, the ANOVA technique is much more powerful, efficient, and flexible. This is especially true for the cases where there are more than two groups, more than one categorical variable, and when there are interactions among multiple categorical variables, as is common in loan pricing analysis. If the *t*-test is used, when ANOVA would be better suited, one must perform all possible *t*-tests, called multiple *t*-tests. For example, if there are four race groups, then each of the race groups will

---

30. The TTEST procedure in SAS performs *t*-tests for one sample, two samples, and paired observations.

be individually compared with the other three race groups, and so on. Using this procedure, there would be 10 different t-tests performed. In this case, there are two issues associated with such multiple t-tests. First, because the number of t-tests increases geometrically as a function of the number of groups, analysis becomes cognitively difficult when the number of tests reaches seven or more comparisons. An ANOVA organizes and directs the analysis, allowing easier interpretation of results. Second, by doing a greater number of analyses, the probability of committing at least one Type I error somewhere in the analysis increases. The ANOVA procedures can perform a fewer number of hypothesis tests in order to reduce Type I error rate. Compared with the t-test, ANOVA can also be more robust when one or more assumptions are violated, and various remedies are available to reduce the effects caused by assumption violations.

Validating Analysis Assumptions

This section describes the assumptions of ANOVA testing, the possible effects of assumption violations, how to validate the assumptions, and the remedies if one or more assumptions are violated.[31]

- *Normality.* This means normally distributed data for each group. In general, ANOVA performs robustly when departures from normality occur, provided that the sample size is large enough. When this assumption is violated, the test may not be able to capture true difference across sample groups (true positive decreases). In other words, a "true difference" is more likely to be misclassified as "no difference," or a false-negative error. As noted in Chapter 3, this should be especially avoided in early stage of compliance testing. There are various tests and plots that can be used to check normality. A comparison of the observed distribution with normal distribution may be performed, and if the P-value associated with the test statistic is less than, say, $\alpha = 0.05$, then there may be a significant departure from the normal distribution. This can be diagnosed by plotting residuals to check for a normal probability pattern or by examining a histogram of the residuals. For example, we can plot residuals (x-axis) versus the fitted values from the ANOVA model.[32] A random scatter pattern around the zero reference line for each of the fitted values would suggest a normal distribution. Any patterns or trends on the plot may indicate model assumption violations.[33] Figure 4.13 shows an example in which rate spread residuals by joint race group category exhibit a significant departure from the normal distribution. In this case, variable transformation is an option. Typically, logarithmic or square root transformations are sufficient.[34] When data is highly skewed or there are extreme outliers, nonparametric methods or robust estimation may be more appropriate.[35]
- *Equal variances.* ANOVA is robust when sample sizes are equal, and the test suffers power when variances are unequal. However, when sample sizes are unequal, this problem is even more pronounced. If the variance for the more sizable group is larger, the ANOVA loses power. If the variance for the smaller group is larger, type 1 error increases (false positive). For example, minority and nonminority groups may have an identical average rate spread, but the dispersion for the minority group could be twice as much as that of another group.

31. For a general discussion on ANOVA assumptions, see also Tabachnick and Fidell, 2007, pp. 86–90.
32. For detailed discussion on this graphical analysis, see Cook, R. D. *Regression Graphics.* John Wiley & Sons, 1998, pp. 4–9.
33. For example, the UNIVARIATE procedure, one of the basic statistical procedures in SAS, provides easy testing and plotting for the purpose of normality check.
34. See Tabachnick and Fidell, 2007, pp. 94–96, for choice of data transformations.
35. See Miller, 1997, pp. 16–32, for detailed discussion on variable transformations, nonparametric techniques, and robust estimation.

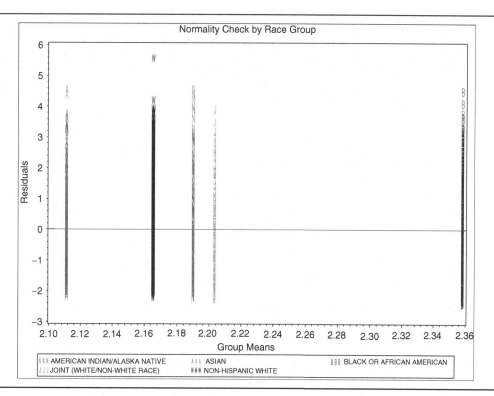

FIGURE 4.13 NORMALITY CHECK WITH RESIDUAL PLOT

We can guard against the type I error by using Levene's squared residuals test for variance homogeneity.[36] Several other methods are available to handle unequal variances including a Welch ANOVA,[37] and a nonparametric ANOVA.

- *Data independence.* Data dependence is a commonly encountered issue that is often associated with data collection and sampling process. The effects of data dependence effects depend on the nature of the relationship. If the observations are positively correlated, type 1 error (false positive) increases. If they are negatively correlated, the test power can suffer (true positive decreases). For example, if the rate spread for ARMs is less than that for longer maturity fixed rate loans, then a difference in rate spread between protected and nonprotected applicants may be correlated to a difference in frequency of ARMs and fixed rate loans. In this case, protected class applicants may have a higher rate spread if they choose fixed rate contracts more frequently than their nonprotected counterparts. This dependence can be lessened or eliminated if sampling is stratified by loan product. Several methods are available to test if observations are independent. For example, one can use the Durbin-Watson test on the data sorted by loan action date to detect if residuals of the data

---

36. In general, if the p-value of Levene's test is less than 5 percent, then you can say the variances are not equal. Levene's test offers a more robust alternative to Bartlett's procedure. That means it will be less likely to reject a true hypothesis of equality of variances just because the distributions of the sampled populations are not normal. Furthermore, when non-normality is suspected, Levene's procedure is a better choice than Bartlett's. See the GLM procedure in *SAS/STAT User's Guide*.

37. Welch's ANOVA is variance weighted one-way ANOVA and it is also available within the GLM procedure in SAS/STAT.

are independent.[38] If data dependency involves both rows and columns, the contingency table can be a convenient way to examine and measure the type and level of dependency.[39]

- *Data sufficiency.* The ability of the ANOVA test to detect differences in class averages that lead to rejection of the null hypothesis depends on the sample size (the number of observations used in analysis). For a particularly large sample, the test may reject the null hypothesis that two process means are equivalent. However, in practice the difference between the two means may be relatively small, to the point of having no real practical significance. Similarly, if the sample size is small, a difference that is large in practical terms may not lead to rejection of the null hypothesis. The number of observations required to analyze the behavior of an unknown population mean will be influenced by the P-value, (the risk of rejecting a true hypothesis), β (the risk of accepting a false null hypothesis when a particular value of the alternative hypothesis is true), and value of the population standard deviation. In Appendix 4E we include an example sample size calculation for ANOVA testing.

Nonparametric ANOVA

The parametric ANOVA test is relatively robust relative to violations of the normal distribution and homogeneity of variance assumptions due to its available remedies. However, when those basic assumptions are seriously violated, a nonparametric ANOVA testing may be more appropriate.[40] Unlike parametric ANOVA, which compares specific parameters of two or more samples, the nonparametric test compares the probability distributions of samples. It tests whether two sampled distributions have identical shape and location. In instances where tests indicate that the distribution is significantly skewed, and variances of race groups are significantly different, we can use a nonparametric ANOVA approach to test whether rate spread for two race groups have similar distribution and means.

While nonparametric tests make fewer assumptions regarding the nature of distributions, they are usually less powerful than their parametric counterparts. However, nonparametric tests are more appropriate, and they can also be more powerful in cases where assumptions are violated and interval data is treated as ordinal.

For example, ANOVA tests can be used to detect whether there is a significant difference in rate spread among four race groups, as shown in Figure 4.14. In this case, there are only seven observations in each group, the data are not normally distributed, and variances are not equal. ANOVA assumptions are therefore violated. A parametric ANOVA test shows the F-value is 2.36 and P-value is 0.1. Therefore, at the 5 percent significance level, ANOVA fails to reject the null hypothesis. The conclusion is that there is no significant difference in mean rate spreads.

However, if one uses a nonparametric ANOVA, as illustrated in Figure 4.15, the P-value is 0.046 and, appropriately, the null hypothesis is rejected. The conclusion is that a significant mean rate spread exists among the four race groups.

---

38. See the SAS REG procedure in the *SAS/STAT User's Guide*.
39. See Agresti, Alan. *Categorical Data Analysis*. John Wiley & Sons, 2002, pp. 78–80; Christensen, Ronald. *Log-Linear Methods and Logistic Regression*. Springer, 1997, pp. 30–32, for a discussion on testing data dependence with two-way contingency tables, and Conover, W. J. *Practical Nonparametric Statistics*. John Wiley & Sons, 1999, pp. 227–237, for detailed examples on how to use the contingency table for examining data dependency.
40. Nonparametric methods are superior to parametric methods particularly when data contains outliers and heavy-tailed distributions. See Conover, 1999, pp. 116–119.

Analysis Variable: Rate Spread						
Race/Ethnicity	N Obs	Mean	Std Dev	Minimum	Maximum	N
African-American/Black	7	4.2285714	0.4191829	3.7	4.8	7
American Indian/Alaska Native	7	4.4857143	0.9940298	2.7	5.7	7
Asian	7	3.7	0.7047458	2.5	4.5	7
White non-Hispanic	7	3.7714286	0.095119	3.6	3.9	7

Source	DF	Sum of Squares	Mean Square	F Value	Pr > F
Model	3	2.9525	0.9841667	2.36	0.0969
Error	24	10.0171429	0.417381		
Corrected Total	27	12.9696429			

FIGURE 4.14 STATISTICAL TESTING: VALIDATING ASSUMPTIONS—ANOVA TESTING EXAMPLE

Median Scores (Number of Points Above Median) for Variable Rate					
Classified by Variable Joint_race					
Joint Race	N	Sum of Scores	Expected Under H0	Std Dev Under H0	Mean Score
African American/Black	7	5	3.5	1.124228	0.714286
American Indian/Alaska Native	7	5	3.5	1.124228	0.714286
Asian	7	3.5	3.5	1.124228	0.5
White non-Hispanic	7	0.5	3.5	1.124228	0.071429

Average scores were used for ties.

Median One-Way Analysis	
Chi-square	8.011
DF	3
Pr > Chi-square	0.0458

FIGURE 4.15 STATISTICAL TESTING: VALIDATING ASSUMPTIONS—NONPARAMETRIC ANOVA TESTING EXAMPLE

Here, the sums of the median scores are used to conduct the Brown-Mood test for more than two race groups.[41] The mean score is always less than 1, and can be used to measure the proportion of applicants that are priced above the 50th percentile. In this example, 71 percent of the African

41. This test can be performed with the SAS NPAR1WAY procedure using the MEDIAN option. Here median scores equal to "1" for observations greater than the median, and "0" otherwise. Other score and test types are also available. See *SAS/STAT User's Guide*.

American applicants are priced above the medium, or 50th percentile, versus only 7 percent for the white non-Hispanic applicants.

Interpreting ANOVA Testing Results

When pricing data contains only limited information about borrower's characteristics and credit history, omitted variables may cause the estimate for the protected class indicator variable to carry a portion of the true effects of those variables.[42] In other words, the effects for the protected class variable may be overestimated given borrower characteristics and payment behaviors are unknown. Accordingly, an ANOVA may indicate there are statistically significant differences in group means, when in fact, there are not. This is known as a "false positive" and can be caused by various factors such as insufficient number of observations, outliers, and missing values, in addition to the omitted variable effect.[43]

When data are not properly segmented, an ANOVA may not be able to detect the true race effects in pricing disparities. Therefore, when the testing shows no significance in the rate-spread difference across different groups, it also can be a "false negative." This can also be caused by violations of ANOVA assumptions explained in the next section.

To reduce Type I and improve ANOVA testing power, the ANOVA testing process will be performed on rate spread for a set of key analysis variables. Multiple comparisons will also be performed in each of the test designs whenever the protected variables have more than two groups. The testing results will be sorted (i.e., listed) by factor variables or their combination, according to their significant level or differences for further analysis.

Multiple Comparisons

For more than two means, an ANOVA F-test indicates whether the means are significantly different from each other, but it does not tell you how the individual means differ from one another. Multiple-comparison procedures (MCPs), also called *mean separation tests*, give you more detailed information about the differences among the means. MCPs are used to control for the family-wise error (FWE) rate. For example, suppose that we have four groups and we want to carry out all pairwise comparisons of the group means. There are six such comparisons: 1 with 2, 1 with 3, 1 with 4, 2 with 3, 2 with 4, and 3 with 4. Taken together, the set of comparisons is called a family. If we use, for example, a t-test to compare each pair at a certain significance level α, then the probability of Type I error (incorrect rejection of the null hypothesis of equality of means) can be guaranteed not to exceed α, only individually, for each individual pairwise comparison, but not for the whole family. To ensure that the probability of incorrectly rejecting the null hypothesis for any of the pair-wise comparisons in the family does not exceed α, multiple comparisons methods that control the family-wise error rate need to be used. FWE is the probability of making a false claim when the entire family of inferences is considered. We can compare the average effects of three or more "groups" to decide which groups are priced higher/lower, and by how much, while controlling the probability of making an incorrect decision at the family level.[44]

To test if loan-pricing disparities between minority groups and nonminority groups are significant, Dunnett's two-tailed multiple test is performed, testing if mean rate spread for any minority

---

42. Bias associated with omitting explanatory variables has been a concern for many mortgage lending discrimination analyses. See Ross, Stephen L., and John Yinger. *The Color of Credit: Mortgage Discrimination, Research Methodology, and Fair-Lending Enforcement*. MIT Press, 2002, pp. 96–110, for a review on this topic.

43. This issue was also discussed by Calem, P. S., and S.D. Longhofer. "Anatomy of a Fair-Lending Exam: The Uses and Limitations of Statistics," 2000, FRB Working Paper.

44. A variety of multiple comparison methods are available with the MEANS and LSMEANS statements in the GLM procedure found in Base SAS and SAS/STAT software, respectively.

group is significantly different from a single control (non-Hispanic white) for all main effects means. Dunnett's test is best used when the only pairwise comparisons of interest are comparisons with a control after a significant result has been obtained in an ANOVA. The procedure allows for comparisons to be made between the experimental groups and the control group, but does not allow experimental groups to be compared to each other. It is an exact test (its family-wise error rate is exactly equal to α) and can be used for both balanced and unbalanced one-way designs.[45]

For example, in loan-pricing analysis we can have eight different race groups. If we use white non-Hispanic as the control, we will have seven comparisons with the control group. Tukey's honestly significant difference (HSD) comparison procedure, or a Bonferroni correction, can jointly control pairwise comparisons to provide more powerful inference, and tighter intervals, than otherwise would be the case. These techniques allow you to reduce the likelihood of false-positive results.[46]

In theory, pairwise comparisons can be performed for all possible combinations of any two groups (protected versus nonprotected) with the Tukey method. However, since we are usually only interested in a particular set of the comparisons, such as the means between a nonprotected group and protected groups, we use the Bonferroni method to contrast the difference between a treatment group and the controlled group. For example, non-Hispanic white can be used as the control group to contrast with each of the minority groups. Similar comparisons can also be done by income class, gender, bureau score, LTV class, debt-ratio class, among others.

Figure 4.16 is an example of Dunnett's two-tailed multiple comparisons. It shows which pairs of race groups have significant pricing disparities, given the ANOVA testing has found that at least one race group has a mean rate spread that is significantly different from the others. This figure also shows lower and upper confidence levels for the difference between means. The pairs can be ranked by the value of the difference between means to address the severity of the pricing disparities.

ANCOVA and Regression Analysis

When the input data contains very limited variables and bank-specific information, no conclusions can ever be drawn based solely on the ANOVA testing. Often, contextual factors are required for further understanding. Given the limited variables available in this stage, an ANCOVA and regressions with protected variable indicator present a natural extensions to further analyze the role of protected variables in pricing disparities which are identified though preliminary ANOVA testing.[47] In this step, additional variables not available in the public HMDA data are included, such as LTV, debt ratio, credit bureau score, and loan amount. A typical ANCOVA with a two-level indicator model can be expressed as follows:

$$Y_i = \beta_0 + \beta_1 X_i + \beta_2 X_i T + \beta_3 X_i T + \varepsilon_j \qquad (4.3)$$

Here, T is an indicator variable, which can be race, minority status, or gender, and can have two or more levels depending on how many classes are in a categorical variable.

---

45. For a detail discussion of multiple comparisons using the SAS System, please see Westfall, P.H., R.D. Tobias, D. Rom, R. D.Wolfinger, and Y. Hockberg, *Multiple Comparisons and Multiple Tests Using the SAS Systems*, 1999, SAS Institute Inc., pp. 54–57, 135–148. For a theoretical discussion on use of Dunnett's method for multiple comparisons with a control group, see Hsu, Jason C. *Multiple Comparisons: Theory and Methods*, 1996, Chapman & Hall, pp. 43–64.

46. In addition to using SAS procedures which contain over twenty different methods for multiple comparisons, one also can easily use JMP for this purpose. For details, see *JMP Statistics and Graphics Guide*, Release 6, 2005, SAS Institute Inc., Cary, NC, USA, pp. 116–121.

47. When more variables are available, a full regression analysis can be performed to further investigate the impact of the protected variables on loan underwriting or pricing decision.

Multiple Comparison by Race and State

Subset by Loan Purpose, Loan Type, Property Type, and Lien Status

Effect	Dependent	Method	Comparison	LowerCL	Difference	UpperCL	Significance	State
joint_race	rate_spread	Dunnett	Black or African American–Non-Hispanic white	1.04534	1.30401	1.56268	1	UT
joint_race	rate_spread	Dunnett	American Indian/Alaska Native–Non-Hispanic white	0.31049	0.64299	0.97548	1	CK
joint_race	rate_spread	Dunnett	Race not availalbe–non-Hispanic white	0.13692	0.53778	0.93864	1	AL
joint_race	rate_spread	Dunnett	Asian–Non-Hispanic white	0.04557	0.35319	0.6608	1	AL
joint_race	rate_spread	Dunnett	Native Hawaiian/Other Pacific Island–Non-Hispanic white	−0.03638	0.27783	0.59204	0	SC
joint_race	rate_spread	Dunnett	Joint (white/non-white race)–Non-Hispanic white	−0.3908	0.01447	0.41975	0	MI
joint_race	rate_spread	Dunnett	2 or more non-white races–non-Hispanic white	−0.39811	−0.02052	0.35707	0	MI

FIGURE **4.16**   TESTING FOR RACE EFFECTS AT THE STATE LEVEL

The ANCOVA and regressions with indicators can perform the following tasks:

- Testing whether the pricing disparities between different groups can be explained by including additional variables and the interrelationships between explanatory factors.
- Determining whether a variable indicating protected-class membership is still statistically significant after including additional explanatory variables.
- Testing whether the slopes for the treatment and control groups on rate spread are equal. For example, one can use this to test if minority/nonminority groups are treated equally.
- Validating results and providing feedback for ANOVA testing.
- Determining whether further analysis with additional variables is required. This can include matched-pair analysis, full regression analysis, and risk-based pricing analysis.

An interaction plot can be used to visualize the interaction between a protected variable and other continuous predictors. For example, Figure 4.17 shows how the bureau score affects rate spread differently for a minority group and a nonminority group.

Matched-Pair Analysis

Matched-pair analysis is a fundamental fair lending analysis technique.[48] The purpose of constructing matched pairs is to examine in greater detail, on a case-by-case basis, results that are statistically

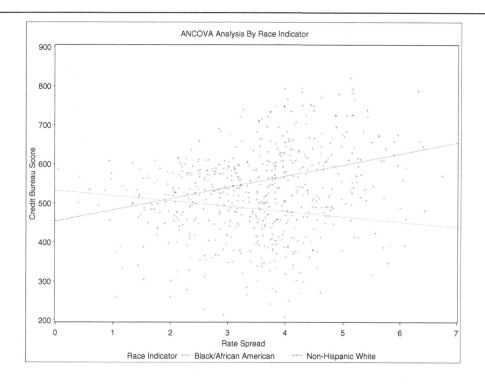

FIGURE 4.17 INTERACTION PLOT

---

48. See Calem, Paul S., and Glenn Canner. "Integrating Statistical Analysis into Fair Lending Exams: The Fed's Approach," in Anthony M. Yezer (ed.), *Fair Lending Analysis: A Compendium of Essays on the Use of Statistics.* American Bankers Association, 1995, pp. 118–119.

Type of Analysis	Universe of Protected Class Observations Requiring Matches
Pricing	
• Loan annual percentage rate (includes finance charges but not other fees)[1]	Minority applicants corresponding to an applicant population segment whose corresponding model results were found to be statistically significant, indicating a higher pricing of comparable loans (OLS Regression Model), or a higher probability of receiving an "above threshold" loan (Logistic Regression Model).
• Overages/underages	This presents a special case for identifying matched pairs because the presumption is that the discretionary factors are other than ones you can match on for comparative purposes.[2] The segments where either the amount, or incidence, or overage or underage is statistically significant across protected and nonprotected classes would be targeted. The segment in that case would be further restricted to a particular branch office or loan officer. The matching criteria should exclude the factors that have already been considered in discretionary pricing.[3]
Mortgage Underwriting	
• Sampling performed in advance of model	Selection based on sampling quota within segment where protected class applicants are randomly selected and non-minority applicants are matched to each minority observation.
• Sampling performed on model results	Declined minority applicants corresponding to an applicant population segment whose corresponding model where results were found to be statistically significant
Override[4]	
• Highside	Score-qualified minority applicants that were declined in a segment found to be significant (e.g., an end-node of a tree-based model or a result set of a regression-based model)
• Lowside	Score-unqualified non-minority applicants that were approved (e.g. an end-node of a tree-based model or a result set of a regression-based model)

FIGURE 4.18   TYPES OF ANALYSIS

[1] See Appendix 4B for lists of finance and non-finance charge fees for mortgages.
[2] This is because the standard factors appear on pricing sheets and the pricing adjustments associated with them are completely specified by policy. In practice, analysis centers more on the magnitude of the overages/underages, which is usually restricted via a cap, and the number of overages and proportionate lack of underages in the protected class groups. Also, patterns of practice from one reporting period to another are examined.
[3] Because practices vary by lender, the matching criteria will also vary, for example, loan amount may be used for matching if it is not formerly part of the loan pricing process.
[4] Override analysis will be detailed in Chapter 6.

significant in an attempt to determine root causes. No model will contain every scrap of information. The rationale for using statistical analysis is to efficiently and effectively isolate instances of persistent and unexplained differences in outcomes between protected and nonprotected classes of consumers. Hence, the starting point for identifying which observations of possibly disadvantaged protected-class applicants is to examine the output from a statistical model, as opposed to, say, including every declined protected-class applicant for a mortgage loan. The output we are referring to comes in different forms, depending on the type of analysis being performed, as shown in Figure 4.18.

We will consider the different forms of matched-pair analysis in the respective chapters where the different types of analyses referred to in the figure are covered.[49] Finding files that are a close match can be difficult. Two mortgage applications may be similar in credit qualifications, but the properties being purchased may have different features and different market values. Thus, from a statistical perspective, it is hard to determine whether differences detected are the result of randomness.[50]

In the foregoing discussion of pricing analysis, matched-pair analysis follows after the ANOVA, ANCOVA, and regressions wherein the protected variable indicator has revealed some areas in which pricing disparities are statistically significant, and thus further analysis is required. Some important considerations have been mentioned in the literature on what needs to be controlled when creating matched pairs.[51] For example, if the pricing analysis shows that some variables such as bureau score, LTV, DTI, income, and loan amount have significant impact on dependent variable rate spread, then we may use the following specific rules to create matched-pair tables:[52]

- The rate spread for the minority application is higher than that of the nonminority application.
- The absolute value of (minority credit bureau score) − (white non-Hispanic credit bureau score) is $\leq$ X. When X = 5, the minority applicant score must be within 5 points of the nonminority applicant score.
- The absolute value (white non-Hispanic LTV) − (the minority LTV) is $\leq$ X%. When X = 10, the minority applicant's LTV must be within 10 percent of the nonminority applicant's LTV.
- The absolute value of (white non-Hispanic DTI) − (minority DTI) is $\leq$ X%. When X = 10, the minority applicant's DTI must be within 10 percent of the nonminority applicant's DTI.
- The absolute value of (white non-Hispanic income) − (minority income) is $\leq$ Y%. When Y = 8, the minority applicant's income must be within 8 percent of the nonminority applicant's income.
- The absolute value of (white non-Hispanic loan amount) − (minority loan amount) is $\leq$ Y%. When Y = 8, the minority applicant's income must be within 8 percent of the nonminority applicant's income.

In practice, choices of values for X or Y can range from 5 to 15 percent, depending on data quality and availability. Also, regulatory guidance should be taken into account (e.g., the 8 percent rule of thumb for borrower income and loan amount).

Additional matching rules can be created based on the bank policy data and the statistics of the data.

---

49. For mortgage underwriting see Chapter 5, and for overrides see Chapter 8.
50. See Calem and Canner, 1995, for limitations of traditional matched-pair approach.
51. See Avery, Robert B., Patricia C. Beeson, and Paul S. Calem, "Using HMDA Data as a Regulatory Screen for Fair Lending Compliance," *Journal of Financial Services Research*, Vol. 11, February/April 1997, pp. 9–42. Some examples of matching criteria cited are product, market, same quarter of action date, within 8 percent absolute difference of loan amount, and within 8 percent absolute difference of income.
52. The thresholds may vary by business requirements, regulatory needs, and/or data availability. The variable X may take on different values for LTV than for DTI, etc. For factors like credit score, LTV and DTI, it may be necessary to vary the values of X to regulate how many matched pairs are to be considered. If X for one or more factors is set too low, there may not be any matches. Conversely, if X is set too high, then too many matched pairs will be generated and the degree of similarity may be too relaxed.

Segment			White Non-Hispanic Applicants							African-American Applicants							
Quarter Booked	Term in Months of Loans	MSA	Loan Number	Rate Spread	Loan Amount	Bureau Score	Loan-to-Value Ratio	Income	Debt-to-Income Ratio	Loan Number	Rate Spread	Loan Amount	Bureau Score	Loan-to-Value	Income	Debt-to-Income Ratio	Price Difference
4	360	99999	6473	0.74	434939	820	0.2543	300948	0.1637	6455	3.547	460642	820	0.3141	280167	0.1173	2.807
3	360	12580	2886	1.978	184949	679	0.8641	95574	0.3416	2816	3.716	182779	672	0.8915	101835	0.2773	1.738
4	360	16974	5959	1.107	416452	820	0.2615	251514	0.1698	6053	2.769	443869	820	0.3085	266248	0.1285	1.662
4	360	12060	7757	1.205	568772	820	0.2567	274740	0.079	7776	2.704	565003	818	0.2973	289483	0.1717	1.499
4	360	12060	2021	2.585	209149	544	0.6062	109092	0.2036	1801	3.879	200394	535	0.6224	118517	0.2654	1.294
2	360	22744	4309	0.676	252639	740	0.6949	88369	0.1984	4233	1.859	274086	739	0.7157	85203	0.1514	1.183
3	360	99999	4126	0.459	407714	778	0.343	279760	0.1597	4141	1.527	421478	772	0.2649	280677	0.1421	1.068
4	360	12060	1949	2.14	216290	674	0.6874	78834	0.2604	1515	3.196	225037	659	0.6807	83948	0.2098	1.056

FIGURE 4.19 MATCHED-PAIR REPORT RANKED BY PRICING DIFFERENTIAL

110

The steps for matched pair analysis are:

Step 1. Determine the variables and rules to create matched pairs for protected-class and nonprotected-class groups.

Step 2. Apply the rules to create the datasets for protected-class matched applicants and nonprotected-class matched applicants.

Step 3. Merge the selected protected-class matched applicants with nonprotected-class matched applicants based on the specified criteria.

Step 4. Select the top five control group matched pairs for each treatment group applicants for reporting and further analysis.

Figure 4.19 provides an example of matched-pairs ranked by pricing difference. The reader should note that year-to-year, even quarter-to-quarter, matched-pair comparisons can be tricky due to changing market conditions. For results to be meaningful, these effects must be taken into consideration.

In 2005, HMDA filing data contained more threshold loans than the prior year. While 30-year fixed rate mortgage loan spreads are reported for regulatory purposes based on the 20-year Treasury yield, they are actually priced from much shorter maturities. In Figure 4.20, one can immediately see that over the 27-month period through March 2006, the yield curve flattened to a zero spread between the six-month T-bill and 20-year T-bond rates—the bill/bond (BB) spread dropped 400 basis points (bp) from January 2004 to zero in March 2005. When the yield curve is relatively flat (as was the case in 2005, which witnessed a 120-bp average monthly differential from the 6-month T-bill to the 20-year bond), more loans will be reported as above threshold than when the yield curve has a more normal shape (2004 saw a 350-bp average monthly differential from the 6-month T-bill to the 20-year bond). This distortion makes period-to-period comparisons difficult. For matched-pairs, the effect can be very significant when viewing a borrower whose loan was

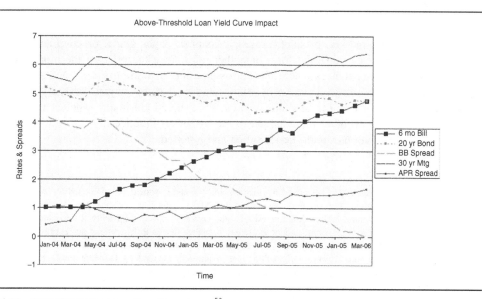

FIGURE 4.20　ABOVE-THRESHOLD LOAN YIELD CURVE IMPACT[53]

---

53. Source: Treasure Yields—http://www.ustreas.gov/offices/domestic-finance/debt-management/interest-rate/yield .shtml, and Mortgage Rates—http://www.mbaa.org/marketdata/data/01/mba30yr_rates.htm.

originated in January with a "matched-pair" selected from December loan closings. In order to make these sorts of comparisons, an adjustment to the yield must be made. Because loans vary by loan maturity and pricing mechanisms, the adjustment must be made on a loan-by-loan basis.

OVERAGE/UNDERAGE ANALYSIS

The systematic approach described up to this point is geared toward identifying, and controlling for, factors that can help explain differences in pricing between protected and nonprotected groups of borrowers. In the case where purely the discretionary component of pricing is available (e.g., the actual amount of adjustment up or down), then a comparative analysis can be performed directly on the amount of adjustment for protected and nonprotected classes of applicants without having to control for any other factors. Typically, this analysis examines both amount and incidence of overages and underages separately, and is performed at the branch and loan officer levels. Overages and underages represent the difference between the lender's market quote, and the price the borrower pays for the financing of the loan. If the borrower pays more, the difference in price is termed an overage.[54] If the reverse is true, the difference is an underage. From a lender's perspective, authorization of the use of overages and underages is necessary in order to be competitive in the marketplace, provide flexibility in pricing, and retain and attract superior talent for their retail sales force.

Overage fees, or underage discounts, vary in amount and frequency of application. They are often split between the loan officer and the lending institution, with some exceptions.[55] How fees are split does not directly impact the consumer and the practice differs by line of business, channel, and product within a given lending institution. That being said, compensation systems are designed to influence behavior, and any imbalances across protected classes that relate to purely discretionary items should bear very close examination (e.g., statistical testing for significance and legal and management action where findings are judged to be material and in violation of policy).

Typically, lender guidelines put a cap on additional fees to ensure that the maximum price adjustments, plus a customary 1 percent origination fee, do not exceed the 3 percent threshold. The cap can vary by market, product, program, channel, paper grade, or combination thereof. Furthermore, overages can take the form of higher rates since the price of the mortgage can be adjusted down in circumstances where the borrower wants to minimize cash necessary to close the transaction. Regulation Z, Truth in Lending, requires that the annual percentage rate (APR) disclosure to the customer takes this into account, so it should not matter whether the overage is obtained via points or a higher rate charged to the borrower. Practice may, at times, differ from policy and those exceptions should be identified and reported.

---

54. The overage, expressed as a percent of the loan amount (points) is sometimes calculated as Overage = Quoted Loan points − Required Origination fee − Required Rate Sheet points. The rate sheet considers many factors, such as loan product/program, lock period, interest rate, etc. Overages can be the results of negotiated extra discount points, or an over par interest rate, and are expressed in points. One point equals one percent of the loan amount. The overage calculation formula may also include adjustments for other costs absorbed by the lender, e.g., Overage = Total points charged borrower − Origination points required by the lender − Discount points stated on rate sheet − Closing costs paid by the lender. See Longhofer, Stanley, D., "Measuring Pricing Bias in Mortgages," Federal Reserve Bank of Cleveland, August 1998, page 2.

55. For example, some lenders do not share any fees with loan officers for the call center channel, employee loans, or relocation programs. In addition, any portion of an overage that exceeds a preset policy cap is usually not split with the loan officer. The policy cap for overages is generally larger than the cap for underages. Loan officers may have their authority to charge overages revoked, with forfeiture of any related compensation if they have persistent trends for either exceeding the caps or for statistically significantly charging protected classes either a higher volume or amount of overages, or a lower volume or amount of underages, relative to the corresponding nonprotected class of borrowers.

In order to ensure the guidelines are being met, it is important to monitor results at appropriate operating unit level. Usually, the operating unit is defined to be comparable and controllable such as a branch office, or loan officer. This monitoring should capture violations of policy in order for corrective action to be taken. For the retail channel, if a particular branch or loan officer exhibits a certain number of violations over consecutive reporting periods, then various kinds of remedial actions are instituted by the lender's legal department. This may take the form of warning letters, forfeiture of commission, and possible termination of employment.

On the wholesale side, brokers and their agents should be monitored for pricing practices, but overage and underage analysis per se is not applicable. This is primarily due to two factors. First, there is no available universal baseline spanning brokers that can be used to separate discretionary from nondiscretionary components of their pricing, and even if addressed on a broker-by-broker basis, individual brokers may be reluctant to specify this level of pricing detail. Second, any single lending institution typically only receives a portion of the broker's business, and an evaluation of the broker practices would need to include data from all of the lenders that the broker does business with to form a complete picture and there is no consolidated source for this data. That said, brokers should be monitored, and if a particular broker or agent exhibits a certain number of violations over consecutive reporting periods, then various kinds of remedial actions are instituted by the lender's management. This may take the forms of warning letters, more stringent pricing guidelines, and possible termination of contract.

Failure to deal with this level of detail can lead to unwanted surprise at best and disaster at worst. Consequences can include:

- Damaged employee morale due to inaccurate coaching discussions and possible incorrect disciplinary actions.
- The need to rerun production monitoring systems for past reporting periods.
- Dealing with a backlog of issues of fallout to the previous bullet.
- Regulatory loss of confidence and greater oversight and process validation requirements.
- Wasted effort tracking down false-positive results.
- Additional injury to customer base as false-negative results fail to surface significant problems.
- Reputation damage caused by management statements that ultimately are proven to be in error due to unanticipated circumstances, faulty assumptions or definitions, misapplication of statistics, or misinterpretation of models and results.

The remainder of the chapter describes how to perform overage/underage analysis to examine whether or not a bank's discretionary pricing is executed fairly across all customer groups. In particular, this analysis will help identify loan officers and branches that may be engaging in unfair discretionary pricing. The analysis addresses the following questions:

- Do protected classes have a higher incidence of overage than nonprotected classes? This can be done by comparing loans with an overage to all other loans (no adjustment or underage). More branches and loan officers will be flagged if overages are only compared to loans with no adjustment.
- Do protected classes have a lower incidence of underage than nonminorities do? This can be done by comparing loans with an underage to all other loans (no adjustment or overage). More branches and loan officers will be flagged if underages are only compared to loans with no adjustment.
- For loans with an overage, do protected classes pay more overage points than nonminorities do?
- For loans with an underage, do protected classes receive smaller discounts than nonminorities do?

- Any other components of discretionary pricing should be addressed in addition to overage and underage?
- Are protected classes charged higher discretionary fees than the nonprotected? Are they subject to more variability in discretionary pricing than the nonprotected?

To understand discretionary pricing, it is important to review what risk-based pricing consists of and how its components contribute to loan pricing.

Risk-Based Pricing Considerations

Recall the discussion and examples relative to pricing governance, which introduced risk-based pricing. Essentially, risk-based pricing is the practice in the financial services industry to charge different interest rates on the same loan to different people based on their credit risk (potential probability of default).[56]

It allows lenders to make loans that otherwise they would be compelled to turn down because, collectively, those loans would exhibit default rates that would render the entire pool to be unprofitable at a fixed price. Put another way, loan applications are risk rated and assigned to a particular grade, or pool, of similarly risk-rated transactions. That risk rating relates to the probability that the loan will not be satisfactorily repaid, that is, it will result in a default. The additional rate spread on loans in a higher than average risk class is the extra premium lenders require to cover their anticipated incremental losses for that pool of loans. Note that lending institutions pay mortgage brokers yield spread premiums (YSPs) based upon the difference between the rate of interest charged on a borrower's loan and rate of interest required by the lender. In these cases, the broker decides how much, if any, of the YSP to pass along to the borrower.[57]

The public HMDA results have raised questions and concerns among many stakeholders, and the following sequence of questions is fairly typical:

- If the racial makeup of the risk pools of rated loans is skewed, what conclusions can be drawn?
- Would this imply that there is some bias in the risk-rating system?
- If not, would that imply that loans associated with certain racial groups are inherently riskier?
- If so, is the incremental risk due to the borrower's choice of loan terms and conditions, or the potential for appreciation in value and liquidity of the collateral, etc.?

It is important for lenders to explain results relative to their performance record that reside in the public domain so that misunderstandings and false conclusions can be minimized. Proper conclusions can be formed only after in-depth analysis is performed on all of the relevant data. A series of contexts is usually required in order to illustrate how observed disparate impact connects to the ultimate finding of the presence, or absence, of a disparate treatment of a particular group.[58] Each context is supported by a series of well-reasoned, clear, and concise facts that can span multiple layers of aggregation and segmentation in support of the ultimate finding. Cascading through multiple layers of segmentation, the most relevant components driving results, which were

---

56. Risk-based pricing practices have been used to justify the risk premiums associated with the risk of late payments or bankruptcy. See Edelberg, Wendy. "Risk-Based Pricing of Interest Rates in Household Loan Markets," Federal Reserve Board working papers in the Finance and Economics Discussion Series (FEDS), 2003.

57. For in-depth discussion of YSPs, see Jackson, Howell E., and Burlingame, Laurie, "Kickbacks or Compensation: The Case of Yield Spread Premiums," *Stanford Journal of Law, Business and Finance*, Volume 12, Number 2, pages 289–361, Spring 2007 (specifically, Section C, Part 2).

58. For detailed discussion and examples on disparate impact and disparate treatment, and their connections, please see Ross, Stephen L. and John Yinger, *The Color of Credit: Mortgage Discrimination, Research Methodology, and Fair-Lending Enforcement*, MIT Press, 2002, pp. 273–312.

outlined in the first part of this chapter, can be highlighted in general terms without compromising proprietary underwriting business rules. In this fashion, it is possible to insert a performance context around headlines alleging unfair pricing and present a progression of borrower segment views that effectively synchronizes public perception with reality. The UPI, discussed in Chapter 3, can help build those fair lending/pricing performance storylines.

While inconsistencies, or exceptions to policy, usually contribute to disparate impact on a particular group, the pricing function itself may actually have a disproportional effect on certain protected classes when consistently applied. Furthermore, when loans are priced off a rate sheet that specifies separate adjustments for factors, or limited factor combinations, then the accuracy of the estimated default probability due to the credit risk components of the loan price may be in question. This is especially true when one, or more, of the credit risk pricing adjustment factors were developed without consideration of all other pricing adjustment factors that are associated with credit risk and the adjustment factors are not jointly independent. The result is that the risk may be overstated, or understated, depending on the nature of the correlations that exist between the factors. In short, if many positive adjustments (additional points or rate increments) are made, the resulting price may overprice the actual risk of the transaction. Validity of the pricing adjustment depends on how the data are collected, and the sophistication of the risk-based pricing method. It is uncommon for a single price adjustment to be based on more than a three-factor combination (e.g., LTV, score band, and DTI). One possible remedy would be to use a scoring approach where factor dependencies could be measured and a single score-based risk adjustment could be made for specific score ranges, in order to arrive at a final risk-based rate and points quote. Another approach would be to consider the pricing factors simultaneously using a hybrid model, which is described in detail in Chapter 6. The key point is that rate sheets should be reviewed to determine the extent to which the implicit assumption of "independence" is justified from both credit risk and fair lending compliance perspectives. The worst scenario is that a lender is both mispricing the risk and magnifying their fair lending exposure.

It is important that messaging on HMDA should address the fact that pricing involves many factors, and that *in many instances it is the particulars of the transaction, and not factors associated with the borrower*, that can cause a loan to be priced higher. Lenders need to be prepared to provide summary level data on the nature of transactions that are prevalent for different protected classes of applicants and borrowers versus the associated control group, to explain the influence of the type of mortgage transaction, and associated options, played into the final result. This requires that lenders define codes that uniquely identify reasons for pricing adjustments, and also exceptions to policy. These codes should enable the lender to identify the adjustment or exception category. A helpful tip is not to have an "other" category because this will end up with 40 to 60 percent of the cases. Also, it is helpful to capture the associated exception reason(s) in order of importance, and who authorized the adjustment or exception.

In summary, the ability to disaggregate pricing components into the various categories discussed previously, including any final yield premiums or price reductions, is necessary in order to make the pricing mechanism transparent. Monitoring of practices should be taken down to the most basic operating-unit levels (e.g., loan officer, broker agent, branch, sales office, and broker). Policies should identify key risk indicators, statistical testing parameters, tolerance levels, corrective actions and circumstances requiring escalation of performance trends. Several practical issues that are important to monitoring pricing adjustments are:

- Communicate the justification for overages and yield spread premiums, their relationship to credit tiers, any caps or limitations on their application and how those limitations are enforced, how line management ensures that they are being applied consistently and fairly, and finally what sort of monitoring procedures and reporting mechanisms are in place to ensure accurate performance assessments can be made by management, while affording ease of validation by internal audit.

- Having comprehensive and reliable data and processes in place, as described, will enable the lender to explain to stakeholders how the organization ensures that pricing, underwriting, and marketing are performed in accordance with corporate policies and all applicable laws and regulations. Issue surfacing, transparency, and process validation are essential for a successful compliance program—and all three should be integrated into the day-to-day business operations of the line organization.

- The wholesale channel presents additional challenges. To control the pricing process, lenders can opt to provide guidelines and caps on fees to brokers and agents, and require that they be met before a deal is closed. Another approach is to allow for greater flexibility, with minimal guidelines, but very thorough monitoring to ensure that patterns of practice that are not acceptable result in proper notification back to the broker, and if necessary, termination of the relationship.

- Another concern arises when a borrower with "A" credit status shops for financing with a lending affiliate that caters to subprime lending. In these instances, if the borrower is not made aware that they qualify for less costly credit, then a higher-priced loan may not be due to any lack of consistency of treatment, but rather the borrower's "choice" of a particular business entity to deal with, or with product selection. This situation may also arise in cases where the customer is referred to a subprime lending operation from another business unit, such as the mortgage bank or general bank, for reasons other than the borrower's credit standing, such as the type of terms and conditions, loan amount tier, and so on, that are being requested. It would be helpful to include a code on the application file to indicate whether the applicant is a "walk-in," referral, shopping for a specific product or program feature, or other reasons.

At this point it is helpful to consider a simple example of mortgage pricing. Suppose a mortgage holder with units in a multiunit high-rise property wanted to refinance their loan to take advantage of lower rates and free up some equity for other uses. Further assume that the borrower is a nonresident of the United States, but has established a good credit history with a credit bureau score in a neutral range. He is not interested in buying down his rate, because he wants to minimize up-front fees. Further assume that the following options are desired: Extension of rate lock for an additional 60 days and waiver of all escrows. It turns out that the property is 4 units in a 10 story high-rise. The borrower deals in real estate for his primary business, and so he has a higher-than-normal debt ratio of 54 percent. The prior loan amount was $450,000 and the new desired loan amount, with cash out, is $550,000. Let us suppose that the current rate on a 30-year fixed rate loan is 5.75 percent. The loan officer would typically pull up a screen on the lending institution's loan origination system and enter any/all adjustments to the price using published rate sheets that are issued from the pricing desk on a daily basis for fixed rate loans. Figure 4.21 illustrates this simple case.

As previously mentioned, a problem associated with having a lot of adjustments for individual factors is that the factors may not be independent, which can result in the consumer's being overcharged.

Pricing Concessions

Concessions occur when there is any deviation from loan policy or any change favorable to the borrower is made to the rates, fees, margins, or ceilings published on the rate sheet. Pricing desk policies for both approving and gauging the degree of pricing concessions, are usually controlled by the secondary marketing department. Any costs associated with making rate concessions are charged to the loan originating unit and some associated processing costs may, or may not, be charged back to the borrower. Concessions are usually reported in the aggregate by segments defined by product code, lock period, prepayment penalty, loan purpose, loan amount, occupancy:

ABC NATIONAL BANK ORIGINATION SYSTEM
LOAN NUMBER _xxxxxxxx___

PRODUCT: CONV/1ST LIEN/30 YR FIXED/REFINANCE

BASE RATE: 5.75%
LOAN AMOUNT: $550,000
PRICE

DELTA	FACTOR/REASON	OPTION CHOICE	RATE	POINTS
1	EXTEND LOCK	60 DAYS		+1/2
2	CASH OUT	80 < LTV < 90	+3/4	
3	WAIVE ESCAROWS	TAX/INS		+1/4
4	MULT FAM DWEL	3–4 UNITS	+3/8	
5	HIGH RISE	10-STORIES	+3/8	
6	US RESIDENCE	NON-PERM ALIEN		+1/4
7	LOAN AMT TIER	500 M–600 M	+1/2	
8	DEBT RATIO	50 < DTI < 55	+1/2	
9	ORIGINATION	STANDARD		1

TOTAL ADJUSTMENTS: 2.50%   2.00%

ALL-IN RATE + POINTS: 8.25%   +$11,000

APR (Assumes no other fees at closing)   8.463%
30-Year Treasury Bond Yield: 4.663%
HMDA APR Spread: 3.800%

Other Nonfinance Fees Adjustments

PRICE

DELTA	FACTOR/REASON	OPTION CHOICE	RATE	POINTS	$$$
1	Title insurance	Search Fee (on B/S)			−150
2	Inspection fee	Off Beaten Path			+200
3	Appraisal review	Comm. Appraisal Req'd			+450

Post-APR ADJUSTMENTS: 0.0   0.0%   +500
                                                        RATE%   PTS.% $FEES

TOTAL COST TO BORROWER: 8.25%   2.00% $11,500
Total cost of transaction   8.473%

Assume actual term of 5 yrs

                                                        RATE%   PTS.% $FEES
TOTAL COST TO BORROWER: 8.25%   2.00% $11,500
Total cost of transaction   9.132%

FIGURE 4.21   SIMPLIFIED MORTGAGE PRICING EXAMPLE

primary, second home, investment, LTV range, property type, or number of units (one to four). For a list of concession types and fee waiver types, see Figures 4.39 and 4.40. Reports should include the following important components:

Rate Concession Reason

- Extension (number of days), renegotiation, other.
- Other factors: Prior concession(s) granted to the borrower (requiring the need to indicate specific loan numbers, maintaining action chronology).

Discretionary/Subjective Process

- Frequency/nature of requests may vary by protected class.
- Should have guidelines in place—overrides should require management approval/ documentation.
- Customer service concessions can adversely impact fair lending goals.
- One must track the quality of concessions and details by protected classes.
- One must track exceptions to policy guidelines and the loan officer's attention to obtaining proper authorization.

Concessions made at the loan level are influenced by many factors such as competition or the overall economy. Loan officers sometimes find themselves under significant additional pressure to achieve lending volume targets. Sometimes, guidelines are tighter than other times. Due to these fluctuations, a chronology of guideline changes needs to be maintained to view results in a proper historical context.

Finally, pricing concessions should be monitored separately from overages and underages. This ensures that circumstances where a lender waives a fee and then charges an overage to make up the difference are doubly captured and not "netted out." It would be appropriate to allow offsetting calculations to determine the total cost to the borrower.[59]

Analysis Process

Some lenders examine overage/underage results at an aggregate level, and only perform more detailed analysis when indicated. For management reporting and macro trending, a summary by loan purpose and loan type, for both numbers and percentages of overages and underages, can be performed. This could be done at the enterprise level in total, and for each borrower group. In this way, preliminary indications of possible problems may surface. Additionally, further drill-down analysis by state, MSA, legal entity, and so on may be performed.

Other lenders take a different approach, because overages and underages are directly attributable to individual lender discretion. This is an area where the application of more in-depth testing may conducted on a predetermined basis. This type of statistical testing can be used to determine whether the incidence, or amount, of overages and underages differs significantly for various protected classes of borrowers, when compared with the control group. In the retail channel, these tests may be performed for individual branches or loan officers, or both.

The flow diagram in Figure 4.22 describes the overall analytical process and steps. This figure shows that chi-square test and ANOVA test are two major methods used to test overage/underage disparity in pricing. In practice, regressions also can be used to identify any possible significant contributors on overage/underage as described in the previous sections.

---

59. A discussion of total borrower costs in mortgage lending may be found in Jackson and Burlingame (2007), op. cit.

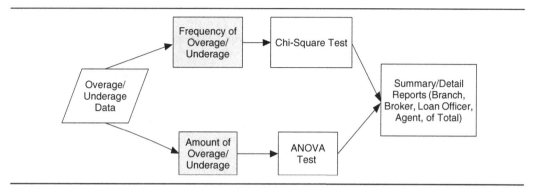

FIGURE 4.22 OVERALL ANALYSIS PROCESS

Data Collection

The first step in data collection is to gather the required inputs for the analysis. A "bare-bones data model" is provided for this purpose in Appendix 4C. The second step is to define which groups of borrowers are in one or more protected classes[60] and which ones are in one or more control groups that you want to analyze and monitor. While this may sound straightforward, the situation becomes complicated when you consider joint applications. For the definition of the control groups for individual borrowers and joint borrowers, see Chapter 3. It should be noted that borrowers may fall into multiple protected groups. The standard practice is to test for each protected group individually (e.g., African-American, white Hispanic, non-white Hispanic, Asian-American, female, applicants over 62 years of age, etc.). An example would be an African-American female over 62 years old. The question becomes: "What would be the control group in this case?" While the theoretical answer might be white non-Hispanic males under 62 years old, in practice, lenders usually test individually for race, gender, and age. That said, there may be value to testing using combined criteria, and some lenders may opt to do so.

The reporting window should be sufficiently long to ensure adequate sample sizes, but not so long as to mask more current trends. Some lenders will use a rolling six-to-nine-month observation window, but report quarterly or monthly. Only loans eligible for an overage or an underage are included in the extract for analysis. This means that all types, purposes, and occupancies that meet the eligibility conditions are reported. Statistical testing is completed for control and test groups. In the retail channel, all branches and loan officers on record for the period would be included in the database for the reports.

The significance of any differences found, in either frequency or amount, can be determined by appropriate statistical testing. Usually, the pricing analysis methods, described earlier in this chapter, can be readily applied for this purpose. It is customary for lenders to monitor and assess the overages and underages, both in frequency and amount, over a given reporting period (typically rolling six months reviewed quarterly). This is can be handled by creating a corporate committee to oversee discretionary mortgage pricing. All protected classed are compared with their appropriate control group. The following several sections describe fully the type of tests performed, some pitfalls to watch out for, generation of matched pairs, how to set up a monitoring process, and a detailed description of reporting.

---

60. Prohibited factors include race, color, sex, religion, national origin, marital status, disability, familial status, age, or receipt of public assistance income.

Testing the Overage/Underage Amount for Significance

Various methods can be used for testing the overage/underage amount for significance. Typical analysis that can be performed are

- *Data summary statistics.* These include the number of protected-class and nonprotected-class loans, the number of occurrences of overages and underages, and the average overage/underage for protected classes and nonprotected classes, by loan officer and by branch office. Additional summary statistics are produced for those loan officers and branches having at least two protected-class and two nonprotected-class overages/underages, respectively. Those summary statistics include the number of protected-class overages/underages, the number of nonprotected-class overages/underages, the average protected-class overage/underage amount, the average nonprotected-class overage/underage amount, the standard deviation of protected-class overage/underage amount, and the standard deviation of nonprotected-class overage/underage amount. A chi-square test similar to the one shown in Figure 4.15 can be produced to describe which protected groups are disfavored. Other summary table examples appear in Figures 4.24 and 4.25.
- *Paired comparisons.* These are performed and results are produced after appropriate data assumptions are validated (e.g., testing for equality of variances at loan officer and branch levels).[61]
- *Multiway analysis.* A three-way cross tabulation and comparison of branch, by multiple protected classes, by overage/underage classification can be performed.

Since fair lending analysis does not consider reverse discrimination, the test is only relevant when a protected class is disadvantaged. This requires one-tailed test at proscribed level of significance (e.g., $\alpha = 0.05$). If a two-tailed test is used, false-negative errors may result. Figure 4.23 shows that for loan officers Smith and White there is, on average, a 25-bp higher overage assessed to Native Americans than for their white non-Hispanic counterparts. It is up to the lender's legal counsel to determine whether this significant difference is material and warranting action.

It is important to interpret missing values and to include them in calculation of percentages and other statistics. The P-values for the appropriate one-tailed tests are computed, depending on whether the discretionary pricing is an overage (right tail) or an underage (left tail). Additional

Segment			# of Overages		Mean Overage		Test of Mean Underage Difference		
Branch	Office	Loan Officer	Protected	Non-protected	Protected	Non-protected	Mean Underage Difference	P-Value	Significance
101	10110	Smith	18	94	0.375	0.125	0.25	0.001	Yes
101	10111	Hughes	19	78	0.375	0.525	−0.15	0.001	No
102	10113	White	49	238	0.375	0.125	0.25	0.001	Yes
103	10115	Stewart	86	422	0.375	0.525	−0.15	0.001	No

FIGURE 4.23 OVERAGE AMOUNT ANALYSIS: OFFICER-LEVEL REPORTING WITHIN BRANCH FOR NATIVE AMERICAN GROUP

---

61. One example is to use the SAS TTEST procedure (*SAS/STAT User's Guide*, 2003), which produces the t-statistic value for equal variance, degrees of freedom for equal variance test, two-tail p-value for equal variance test, t-statistic value for unequal variance, degrees of freedom for unequal variance test, two-tail p-value for unequal variance test.

Loan Officer	Nonprotected Class			Protected Class			Statistical Testing Results		
	Frequency	%Expected	%Actual	Frequency	%Expected	%Actual	%Difference	P-value for Chi-Square	Significance
Hughes	70	80.856	42.683	36	25.144	70.588	27.905	0.0004989	Yes
Smith	87	95.95	50.289	45	36.05	69.231	18.942	0.0088012	Yes
Stewart	378	421.12	44.681	182	138.88	65.233	20.552	3.00E-09	Yes
White	214	238.78	43.673	93	68.222	66.429	22.755	2.03E-06	Yes

FIGURE 4.24   OVERAGE ANALYSIS: SUMMARY OF AMOUNT AND FREQUENCY ANALYSIS

variables created for the incidence of overage/underage analysis include the inferred number of protected-class overages/underages, the difference between the actual number of protected-class overages/underages and the number of inferred protected-class overages/underages, and a flag that signifies whether or not the aforementioned differences are significant. Figure 4.24 shows an example of this. Summary variables, by protected class, for these results are then compiled by loan officer and branch for comprehensive reporting and trend analysis. For example, loan policy may consider three exceptions defined as significant differences in either amount or frequency of either overages or underages across race/ethnicity or gender-based protected classes over two reporting periods as requiring a warning or possibly some disciplinary action.

When testing the overage/underage frequency for significance, the way in which the ratios are constructed can make a big difference in findings. A primary consideration is which loan originations are included, or excluded. In some cases, underage analysis excludes overages and vice versa. If the object is to detect a difference in average price, then all loans should be included.

Figure 4.25 shows that all loan officers have a higher than expected overage frequency associated with Native-Americans. Based on the Chi-square test, these results are all significant. Again, it is up to the lender's legal counsel to determine whether or not this significant difference is material and warranting action.

Loan Inclusion Consideration

Another important aspect is to test for the significance in amounts across different groups, or between treatment group and control group. When testing the overage/underage frequency for significance, how the ratios are constructed can make a big difference in findings. A primary

Loan Officer	Total Number of Loans	Number of Protected-Class Loans	Total Number of Overages	Number of Overages Protected-Class	Predicted Number of Overages Protected	Overage Difference	P-Value for Chi-Square	Flag
Hughes	215	51	116	38	27.516	10.484	0.000746	Yes
Smith	238	65	142	48	38.782	9.218	0.006261	Yes
Stewart	1125	279	625	203	155	48	2.58E-11	Yes
White	630	140	337	99	74.889	24.111	3.61E-06	Yes

FIGURE 4.25   OVERAGE ANALYSIS: OFFICER-LEVEL NATIVE AMERICAN VERSUS WHITE NON-HISPANIC GROUPS

consideration is which loan originations are included or excluded. In some cases, underage analysis excludes overages and vice versa. If the object is to detect a difference in average price, then all loans should be included.

Suppose in a particular branch, loan prices are adjusted for both the control group and the minority group.Say in a particular branch, loan prices are adjusted for both the control group and the minority group. The following cases show how it can be different whether or not all loans are included:

- A branch is identified as an exception if not all loans are included. In Figure 4.26, if underages are excluded when calculating the average overage (Frequency 1), the branch will be identified as an exception to policy. If all loans are included when calculating the average overage (Frequency 2), the branch will not be identified as an exception to policy.
- A branch is identified as an exception if all loans are included. In Figure 4.27, if underages are excluded in the denominator of the frequency calculation, there is a *lower* difference detected for the treatment group. If all loans are included, there is a higher difference detected for the treatment group.
- A branch is okay whether or not all loans are included. Figure 4.28 shows that if underages are excluded, there is a lower difference. If all loans are included, there is *no* difference detected between treatment and control.
- A branch is identified as an exception whether or not all loans are included. In the example in Figure 4.29, there is a higher difference detected in either case.

These examples demonstrate the importance of transparency relating to how measures are calculated and suspect patterns are surfaced.

In the case of combined race and ethnicity, the control group is white non-Hispanic and there are 10 protected classes. In the case of gender, the control group is male and there is one protected class. In total, for any particular reporting period, there could be as many as 44 exceptions (11 protected groups times 4 types of violations).

Group	# Overage	# Par	# Underage	Frequency 1: No Underages	Frequency 2: All In
Minority	10	0	90	100.00% **EXCEPTION**	10.00%
Control	25	50	25	33.33%	25.00%
Total	35	50	115	41.18%	17.50%

FIGURE 4.26   BRANCH IDENTIFIED AS AN EXCEPTION IF NOT ALL LOANS INCLUDED

Group	# Overage	# Par	# Underage	Frequency 1: No Underages	Frequency 2: All In
Minority	30	60	10	33%	30% **EXCEPTION**
Control	25	25	50	50%	25%
Total	55	85	60	39%	27.5%

FIGURE 4.27   BRANCH IDENTIFIED AS AN EXCEPTION IF ALL LOANS INCLUDED

Group	# Overage	# Par	# Underage	Frequency 1: No Underages	Frequency 2: All In
Minority	30	60	10	33%	30%
Control	30	30	40	50%	30%
Total	60	90	50	40%	30%

FIGURE 4.28   BRANCH IS OKAY WHETHER OR NOT ALL LOANS ARE INCLUDED

Group	# Overage	# Par	# Underage	Frequency 1: No Underages	Frequency 2: All In
Minority	30	70	0	30% **EXCEPTION**	30% **EXCEPTION**
Control	20	60	20	25%	20%
Total	50	130	20	27.7%	25%

FIGURE 4.29   BRANCH IDENTIFIED AS AN EXCEPTION WHETHER OR NOT ALL LOANS ARE INCLUDED

Materiality

A legal opinion should be sought for cases where there is a statistically significant finding, but the amount is very small (e.g., a one-basis-point difference in average overage or underage amount, and only a few observations to support frequency comparisons).[62] The root cause should be determined for a particular finding. For example, suppose there is a high incidence of underages in excess of a threshold. The root cause may be operational in nature (e.g., processing delays for rate locks). In these cases, the customer may have been quoted a particular rate, but a delay in registration and lock may have caused an apparent rate change. As such, the lender would stand by the quoted rate, holding the customer harmless. In theory this should happen with equal frequency across protected groups. These and other operational-related underage issues should be analyzed separately, and not included in discretionary pricing monitoring reports.

Data integrity, or lack of it, can also play a role. What gets reported in overages or underages may be masked by certain practices or business rules in other areas. Suppose tracking is performed using a database in the compensation area to determine what loan officers are actually paid in additional commissions. This may not agree with HMDA analysis or detailed fee and waiver monitoring described previously. Inconsistent numbers are the enemy of an effective communication program.

OVERAGE/UNDERAGE MONITORING OVERVIEW

The purpose of the overage/underage monitoring process is to identify and mitigate the risk associated with disparate pricing of loans to consumers who are members of protected classes. Periodic exception and summary trend reports track policy violations. These reports are typically

---

62. The sample size required to analyze the behavior of an unknown population mean will be influenced by the p-value, or α; the risk of rejecting a true hypothesis, value of β; the risk of accepting a false null hypothesis when a particular value of the alternative hypothesis is true; and value of the population standard deviation. See Appendix 4E for some examples of determining required sample size.

produced for presentation and review at a mortgage pricing steering committee. Supporting these reports are supplemental analytical results described in this section.

A typical process for determining the appropriate actions to be undertaken to address violations would be as follows:

Step 1.   Line management and the committee review Web-accessible reports to identify specific branches and/or loan officers flagged as having originated loans that violate pricing policy. Types of violations include overages above a cap, underages above a cap, frequency of overages charged to one or more a protected classes is statistically significantly higher than that for the nonprotected group, frequency of underages charged to one or more a protected classes is statistically significantly lower than that for the nonprotected group, average amount of overages charged to one or more a protected classes is statistically significantly higher than that for the nonprotected group, and average amount of underages charged to one or more a protected classes is statistically significantly lower than that for the nonprotected group.

Step 2.   Line management contacts the appropriate branch office manager, who informs the loan officers who were flagged as exceptions. Typically, loan officers do not receive compensation for any overage amounts exceeding the established cap amount.

Step 3.   A root-cause analysis of the reasons behind the statistically significant results is normally required. If reason codes are made available to the solution, this information can be surfaced in the supporting analytical information and detailed reports. This is very important, because exceptions due to operational causes should not be counted from a fair lending view, nor should loan officers be held responsible for them. In those instances where a branch office is in violation, but no loan officers in the branch, many explanations are possible and further analysis may be required.

Step 4.   The organization implements corrective actions based on current information and trend information obtained from the solution.

It is customary for lenders to monitor and assess the overages and underages, both in frequency and amount, on a rolling six-month period, reviewed on a quarterly basis. As shown in the previous section, for the retail channel, if a particular branch, or loan officer, exhibits a certain number of violations over consecutive reporting periods, then various kinds of remedial actions are instituted by the lender's legal department. This may take the forms of warning letters, forfeiture of commission and possible termination of employment. For the wholesale channel, if a particular broker or agent exhibits a certain number of violations over consecutive reporting periods, then various kinds of remedial actions are instituted by the lender's management. This may take the forms of warning letters, more stringent pricing guidelines, and possible termination of contract.

A legal opinion should be sought for materiality in cases where there is a statistically significant finding, but the amount is very small (e.g., a one-basis-point difference in average overage or underage amount), and only a few observations to support frequency comparisons.[63]

Finally, it is important that the root cause is determined for each particular finding, as discussed in the following examples:

- Suppose there is a high incidence of underages in excess of a threshold. The root cause may be operational in nature (e.g., processing delays for rate locks). In these cases, the customer may have been quoted a particular rate, but a delay in registration and lock may

---

63. The sample size required to analyze the behavior of an unknown population mean will be influenced by the p-value, or; the risk of rejecting a true hypothesis, value of β; the risk of accepting a false null hypothesis when a particular value of the alternative hypothesis is true; and value of the population standard deviation. Selection of $= 0.05$, and $\beta = 0.1$ implies that the minimum required sample size will be 11. See Appendix 4E for more examples.

have caused an apparent rate change. As such, the lender would stand by the quoted rate, holding the customer harmless. In theory, this should happen with equal frequency across protected groups. These and other operational-related underage issues should be analyzed separately and not included in discretionary pricing monitoring reports.

- Data integrity, or lack of it, can also play a role. What gets reported in overages or underages may be masked by certain practices or business rules in other areas. For instance, suppose that tracking is performed using a database in the compensation area to determine what loan officers are actually paid in additional commissions. This may not agree with HMDA analysis or detailed fee and waiver monitoring performed by corporate compliance staff. Inconsistent numbers are the enemy of an effective monitoring overage/underage program.

SUMMARY

This chapter described how to conduct a loan-pricing analysis using a systematic statistical analysis approach. This approach started with some simple and fundamental statistical methods such as the ANOVA/ANCOVA testing methods. The analytical process deepened so long as significant findings persist that involve more analysis variables but fewer observations. When circumstances warrant, more complicated statistical methods are required. This chapter also covered the topic of discretionary pricing for mortgages, specifically overages and underages. This is an area where statistical analyses can be performed immediately on the discretionary component to test for disparate treatment, rather than having to control for multiple factors.[64] Typically, the analysis pinpoints the root causes at a branch, or even loan officer level, where corrective action can be taken. Overage and underage analysis at higher levels can be important to spot trends or identify broad areas, such as geographic regions or business channels, where business practices differ or different organizational influences may be present. However, the typical focus is more granular and closer to where discretion in pricing actually occurs.

Findings from this and Chapter 3 provide critical input to compliance testing, which is covered in the next chapter. This is in alignment with the systematic approach described at the end of Chapter 2. In Chapter 5, we introduce a methodology called dynamic conditional process (DCP) that we view as an advance over the standard regression approach. Advantages of the approach, such as its ability to better accommodate missing data, are discussed, and examples are provided to help illustrate the method. We also revisit the subject of matched pair analysis, which is an important part of disparate treatment assessment. We show how DCP can help to locate the most extreme cases of disparity among potential matched pairs.

---

64. Given overage or underage in amount or incidence, one can immediately test the hypothesis that two groups have different average amounts or frequencies with standard statistical methods, such as Fisher's exact chi-square, Student's t-test, and ANOVA.

Appendix 4A
PRICING ANALYSIS FOR HMDA DATA

HMDA data is widely used by consumer groups to determine where they will target complaints. The general availability of this information, not to mention the new Federal Reserve APR spread tables, poses a significant need to fully understand the implications, and alternative interpretations, of what amounts to an incomplete body of information on lender compliance performance. Inclusion of rate spread in the HMDA LAR filing makes the information more readily accessible and increases the scope of fair lending analysis. Despite some limitations, the HMDA data does provide regulators and lending institutions with an initial screening as to whether or not to proceed with a more detailed (and possibly costly) statistical review aimed at investigating any apparent disparities revealed from HMDA data alone.[65] As a result, regulatory screening on pricing data will help identify institutions showing potentially discriminatory patterns in their pricing practices for minority mortgage applicants.

Federal Rate Spread Tables

Federal rate spread tables can be used to compare historical results for peers and the industry as a whole, or by markets and other geographies (states, congressional districts, regions, total United States—benchmark). The analysis can be performed separately by legal entity, total corporation, channel, and organizational units (processing center, branch, loan officer, broker, and agent). It can be helpful to include detailed drills with high-level aggregates (e.g., where disparities persist, to derive benchmarks for historical and cross-sectional comparisons). This bridges the "headlines" with the "final results." Additional statistical testing for significance may be conducted. We now examine some examples taken from the 2004 HMDA data. Figure 4.30 provides a list of some of the standard tables for pricing analysis.

For example, Figure 4.31 is a specific example of pricing for conventional, owner occupancy, purchase, first-lien mortgage applications taken in the Washington, D.C., metropolitan area.

Pricing Disparity Analysis

High cost-disparity ratios should be based on *all* loans, not just the number of loans above thresholds. In Figure 4.31, the ratio for higher-priced loans in the 3 to 4 percent category for whites is equal to 94 (column D) divided by 1403 (column C), that is, 6.7 percent. Similarly for African-Americans, the calculation is identical, which equates to 8.9 percent. Finally, the disparity

---

65. For example, even with no evidence of violations, the FDIC examines pricing outliers that list preliminary scoping information based on HMDA data, and when an institution on the list changes its charter, the FDIC will offer its preliminary information to the federal regulator with enforcement jurisdiction. See FDIC, Examiner Use of Home Mortgage Disclosure Act Data to Identify Potential Discrimination, Audit Report, September 2006, www.fdicoig.gov/reports06/06-023-508.shtml.

Table Number	Description
11-3	Pricing for Conventional Home Purchase, 1st Lien, Owner-Occupied
11-4	Pricing for Conventional Home Purchase, Junior Lien, Owner-Occupied
11-7	Pricing for Conventional Refinance, 1st Lien, Owner-Occupied
12-1	Disposition of Applications for Pricing for Conventional Manufactured Home Purchase, 1st Lien, Owner-Occupied
12-2	Pricing for Conventional Manufactured Home- Purchase, 1st Lien, Owner-Occupied
A4	Disposition of Preapprovals for Conventional Home Purchase, 1st Lien, 1- to 4- Family Dwelling
Summary B	Loan Pricing Information for Conventional Loans

FIGURE 4.30 SELECTED FEDERAL PRICING TABLES

ratio is the ratio of the previous two ratios, where the numerator equals the minority ratio (8.9 percent) and the denominator equals the white ratio (6.7 percent). The disparity ratio is 1.33 percent.

The disparity ratios are stable (relatively constant) in the example in Figure 4.32.

PRICING INFORMATION FOR CONVENTIONAL HOME-PURCHASE LOANS, FIRST LIEN, 1- TO 4-FAMILY OWNER-OCCUPIED DWELLING (EXCLUDES MANUFACTURED HOMES), BY BORROWER OR CENSUS TRACT CHARACTERISTICS, 2004

MSA/MD = 47894 – WASHINGTON – ARLINGTON – ALEXANDRIA, DC – VA – MD – WV

BORROWER OR CENSUS TRACT CHARACTERISTICS	NO REPORTED PRICING DATA#	REPORTED PRICING DATA#	PERCENTAGE POINTS ABOVE TREASURY-ONLY INCL. LOANS WITH APR ABOVE THE THRESHOLD						MEAN	MEDIAN
			3 – 3.99 #	4 – 4.99 #	5 – 5.99 #	6 – 6.99 #	7 – 7.99 #	8 OR MORE #		
BORROWER CHARACTERISTICS										
RACE										
AMERICAN INDIAN/ALASKA NATIVE	12	2	2						3.44	3.44
ASIAN	63	3	3						3.34	3.35
BLACK OR AFRICAN AMERICAN	249	31	25	6					3.56	3.45
NATIVE HAWAIIAN/OTHER PACIFIC ISLAND	3									
WHITE	1284	119	94	22	2	1			3.64	3.49
2 OR MORE NON-WHITE RACES	24									
RACE NOT AVAILABLE	508	54	47	7					3.50	3.41
ETHNICITY										
HISPANIC OR LATINO	244	22	22						3.30	3.28
NOT HISPANIC OR LATINO	1067	95	73	21		1			3.66	3.50
JOINT (HISPANIC OR LATINO/NOT HISPANIC)	25	2	1	1					3.80	3.80
ETHNICITY NOT AVAILABLE	807	90	75	13	2				3.57	3.47
MINORITY STATUS										
WHITE NON-HISPANIC	1284	119	94	22	2	1			3.64	3.49
ALL OTHERS, INCLUDING HISPANIC	859	90	77	13	2				3.52	3.41
INCOME										
NA	258	27	23	4					3.54	3.38
LOW INCOME	247	24	19	5					3.61	3.68
MODERATE INCOME	385	34	28	6					3.57	3.46
MIDDLE INCOME	528	49	42	7					3.51	3.42
UPPER INCOME	725	75	59	13	2	1			3.64	3.54

FIGURE 4.31 Pricing Example: Washington, DC for Conventional, Owner Occupancy, Purchase, First Lien

47894 - WASHINGTON- ARLINGTON- ALEXANDRIA, DC-VA-MD-WV	A	B	C	D	D/C
Race	Not Reported	Reported	Total Loans	3–4% Count	3–4%
White	1284	119	1403	94	6.7%
AfAm	249	31	280	25	8.9%
				Ratio:	1.33%

FIGURE 4.32   WASHINGTON, DC, MSA RACE EXAMPLE

47894 - WASHINGTON- ARLINGTON- ALEXANDRIA, DC-VA-MD-WV	E	E/C	(D + E)	(D + E)/C	B	B/C
Race	4–5% Count	4–5%	3–5% Count	3–5%	Above 3% Count	Above 3%
White	22	1.6%	116	8.3%	119	8.5%
AfAm	6	2.1%	31	11.1%	31	11.1%
Ratio:		1.37%		1.34%		1.31%

FIGURE 4.33   WASHINGTON, DC, MSA RACE EXAMPLE (CONTINUED)

Figure 4.34 shows similar information for the Raleigh, North Carolina, metropolitan area.

Figures 4.33 and 4.34 show that the disparity ratio for above-threshold loans falling into the first tier (i.e., 1 percent above the 3 percent reporting threshold) is 1.60 percent versus 1.33 percent for Washington, D.C. The overall disparity ratio is 67 bp higher for Raleigh/Cary than for Washington, D.C., with the above-threshold loan pricing rate for African-American borrowers (16.2 percent) being twice that for white borrowers (8.2 percent).

If we define the upper income to be the control group for comparative purposes, then the 3 to 4 percent incidence disparities are: Mid 1.33, Mod 2.00, and Upper Inc 2.83 as shown in Figure 4.35.

PRICING INFORMATION FOR CONVENTIONAL HOME-PURCHASE LOANS, FIRST LIEN, 1- TO 4-FAMILY OWNER-OCCUPIED DWELLING (EXCLUDES MANUFACTURED HOMES), BY BORROWER OR CENSUS TRACT CHARACTERISTICS, 2004

MSA/MD = 39580 – RALEIGH – CARY, NC

BORROWER OR CENSUS TRACT CHARACTERISTICS	NO REPORTED PRICING DATA#	REPORTED PRICING DATA#	PERCENTAGE POINTS ABOVE TREASURY:ONLY INCL. LOANS WITH APR ABOVE THE THRESHOLD						MEAN	MEDIAN
			3 – 3.99 #	4 – 4.99 #	5 – 5.99 #	6 – 6.99 #	7 – 7.99 #	8 OR MORE		
BORROWER CHARACTERISTICS										
RACE										
AMERICAN INDIAN/ALASKA NATIVE	2	2	1	1					3.88	3.88
ASIAN	33	4	2	2					3.84	3.82
BLACK OR AFRICAN AMERICAN	98	19	13	6					3.71	3.58
NATIVE HAWAIIAN/OTHER PACIFIC ISLAND	8									
WHITE	738	66	56	9	1				3.50	3.35
2 OR MORE NON-WHITE RACES	15									
RACE NOT AVAILABLE	282	29	27	2					3.46	3.46
ETHNICITY										
HISPANIC OR LATINO	142	13	12	1					3.54	3.48
NOT HISPANIC OR LATINO	575	56	45	10	1				3.57	3.42
JOINT (HISPANIC OR LATINO/NOT HISPANIC)	13									
ETHNICITY NOT AVAILABLE	446	51	42	9					3.51	3.43
MINORITY STATUS										
WHITE NON-HISPANIC	738	66	56	9	1				3.50	3.35
ALL OTHERS, INCLUDING HISPANIC	438	54	43	11					3.59	3.49
INCOME										
LOW INCOME	24	7	7						3.35	3.34
MODERATE INCOME	87	8	7	1					3.49	3.40
MIDDLE INCOME	312	50	40	10					3.58	3.49
UPPER INCOME	753	55	45	9	1				3.55	3.43

FIGURE 4.34 Pricing Example: Raleigh/Cary MSA for Conventional, Owner Occupancy, Purchase, First Lien

39580 - RALEIGH/ CARY, NC	A	B	C	D	D/C
Race	Not Reported	Reported	Total Loans	3–4% Count	3–4%
White	738	66	804	56	7.0%
AfAm	98	19	117	13	11.1%
Ratio:					1.60%

FIGURE 4.35   RACE EXAMPLE FOR RALEIGH/CARY, NC

39580 - RALEIGH/ CARY, NC	E	E/C	(D + E)	(D + E)/C	B	B/C
Race	4–5% Count	4–5%	3–5% Count	3–5%	Above 3% Count	Above 3%
White	9	1.1%	65	8.1%	66	8.2%
AfAm	6	5.1%	19	16.2%	19	16.2%
Ratio:		4.58%		2.01%		1.98%

FIGURE 4.36   RACE EXAMPLE FOR RALEIGH/CARY, NC (CONTINUED)

39580 – RALEIGH/ CARY, NC	A	B	C	D	D/C
Income	Not Reported	Reported	Total Loans	3–4% Count	3–4%
Low inc	15	3	18	3	17%
Mod inc	64	10	74	9	12%
Mid inc	234	24	258	21	8%
Upper inc	575	49	624	39	6%

FIGURE 4.37   INCOME EXAMPLE: PRICING FOR CONVENTIONAL, OWNER OCCUPANCY, PURCHASE, FIRST LIEN

It is advisable to set thresholds on values of the indicators that will help you identify what to investigate further. More specifically, the disparity ratio for incidence of APR spread in various ranges specified in the FRB tables can be categorized by risk as low, medium, or high. These categorizations may be color-coded as green, yellow, or red, respectively. Within this discussion thresholds have been defined as: < 1.5 (green) for low risk, 1.5–2 (yellow) for medium risk, and > 2 (red) for high risk.

This definition of thresholds may vary by loan purpose (e.g., refinance, home purchase, home improvement), channel, or other factors. This helps answer questions such as: "What are some other examples for setting thresholds?" or "How might corporate policy be extended to accommodate

Protected Group	Disparity	Risk Category
Low	2.83	High
Moderate	2.00	Medium
Middle	1.33	Low

FIGURE 4.38   INCIDENCE DISPARITY BY INCOME RANGE

Group	Number of Loans (< 3.0)	Number of Loans ($>$ or $= 3.0$)	Number of Loans All (%)
Minority	20	15	35 (43%)
Control	40	25	65 (38%)
Total	60	40	100.00

FIGURE 4.39   ABOVE/BELOW-THRESHOLD LOAN COUNTS FOR MINORITY AND CONTROL GROUPS

Group	Mean Rate Spread (< 3.0)	Mean Rate Spread ($> = 3.0$)	Mean Spread All
Minority	1.50	3.70	2.44
Control	1.50	3.70	2.35
	Identical	Identical	Different

FIGURE 4.40   MEAN RATE SPREAD ANALYSIS BY MINORITY STATUS

specification of these sets of risk thresholds?" Figure 4.36 defines upper income as the control group, and shows the 3 to 4 percent incidence disparity for the remaining treatment groups. In this example, the result is that the lower the income, the higher the disparity and risk.

To ensure a complete analysis, all loans, above, at, or below thresholds should be included in the pricing analysis. A significant overall mean spread difference may exist when there is no significant mean spread difference for above-threshold loans. The following example (as illustrated in Figures 4.37 and 4.38) shows that the mean rate spread is the same for both high-priced loans and low-priced loans for minority and control groups. However, overall mean spread (all loans included) is higher for the minority group than that for the control group. This is because the percentage of the high-price loans for the minority group is higher than that of the control group. And if only high-price loans are included in analysis, no price disparity would be detected.

Directional patterns (i.e., constant, monotone increasing, monotone decreasing, or reversals) can be checked to determine if the direction can be established for all, or only certain, categories—and over time. We suggest that for income, one should order by low, moderate, middle, and high, while for race, one should see what patterns emerge and group accordingly (e.g., African-American, non-white Hispanic, Native-American, white Hispanic, and Asian-American). If testing for statistical significance, one may need to check whether the sample counts are sufficient. This process typically entails setting tolerances, determining materiality criteria (seek legal opinion), and prioritizing your investigation based on the resulting disparity levels.

Appendix 4B
PRICING AND LOAN TERMS ADJUSTMENTS

During the loan underwriting process there are may different accommodations that can be made as a result of negotiation with the borrower(s). These accommodations may take the forms as indicated in Figures 4.39 and 4.40. Figure 4.41 lists those fees that are included in the calculation of finance charges, and thus captured in the effective annual percentage rate reported for the loan. Other fees are not considered to be finance charges, but are associated with the loan transaction and they are identified in Figure 4.42. The reason this is important is that sometimes concessions are made relative to fees that may or may not be captured as part of the loan annual percentage rate, which makes monitoring more difficult. Instances also occur where the borrower is charged more than the actual cost to the lender for non-finance-related fees. In either circumstance, if non-finance-related fees are assessed on an inconsistent basis, there could be fair lending implications.

FACTORS	Rates: +/- to APR	Points: Fees or Discounts	Margin over Base Rate (e.g., Prime)	Comments on Factors
Promotional Offer				Should capture promotion code.
Other Offer				Should obtain authorization and document.
Origination		0 or -y%		Could be partial or total waiver.
Points-Buydown	-X%	0 or -y%		Could be partial or total waiver.
Discount Points		0 or -y%		Could be partial or total waiver.
Processing Fee		-$X		Could be partial or total waiver.
Admin Fee		-$X		Could be partial or total waiver.
Mortgage Ins Applic. Fee		-$X		Could be partial or total waiver.
Broker Yield Spread Premium		0 or -y%		Could be partial or total waiver.
Appraisal		-$X		Could be partial or total waiver.
Credit Report		-$X		Could be partial or total waiver.
Inspection		-$X		Could be partial or total waiver.
Post-Closing Admin Fee		-$X		Could be partial or total waiver.
Courier Fee		-$X		Could be partial or total waiver.
Incoming Wire Fee		-$X		Could be partial or total waiver.
Tax Lien		-$X		Could be partial or total waiver.
Flood Certificate		-$X		Could be partial or total waiver.
Title Search		-$X		Could be partial or total waiver.
State-Specific Fees		-$X		Could be partial or total waiver.

FIGURE 4.41 TYPES OF CONCESSIONS

FACTORS	Rates: +/– to APR	Points: Fees or Discounts	Margin over Base Rate (e.g., Prime)	Comments on Factors
Date locked				If a loan does not fund within the original lock period, and the rate lock expires, the loan must be repriced to avoid a loss by the lender.
# days locked				
Expiration date				
Interest Rate	x%			
Margin			x%	For 6-mo reset on ARM, or 2% if annual.
Ceiling			Y%	Interest rate ceiling, minus the original rate, caps the margin over the base rate.
Points (on rate sheet)		x%		Full or partial amount.
Origination fee		x%		Full or partial amount.
Discount points		x%		Full or partial amount.
Waive escrow (Y/N)		x%		Typically full amount.
Feature adjustment (+/−)		$X		Full or partial amount.
Overage		+1/8 to +?%		On the telemortgage side, AEs typically do not earn commissions on such loans.
Underage		−1/8 to −?%		Some are based upon established programs, such as: • Employee Program for Home Buyers/ Refinancers, • Relocation Program for Employees/Executives, • Private banking Program for Top-Tier Customers.

FIGURE 4.42 TYPES OF FEE WAIVERS[a]

[a]A comprehensive listing of fees at settlement appears in Ficek, Edmund F., Thomas P. Henderson, Ross H., Johnson, *Real Estate Principles and Practices*, Columbus, OH: Charles E. Merrill Publishing Company, 1976, pp. 279–283.

#	Type of Fee
1	Application fee (if not charged to all customers)
2	Assumption fee
3	Buydown cost
4	Closing fees (refinance only)
5	Commitment fee
6	FHA mortgage insurance product reserves
7	FHA mortgage insurance product
8	Flood hazard certification fee
9	Interest charged over the loan term
10	Prepaid interest
11	Private mortgage insurance reserve
12	Private mortgage insurance
13	Tax lien service fee
14	Termite/pest or inspection report (if lender required)
15	Underwriting fee
16	Wire transfer fee

FIGURE 4.43   FEES CONSIDERED TO BE FINANCE CHARGES

#	Type of Fee
1	Application fee (if charged to all customers)
2	Appraisal fee
3	Appraisal review fee
4	Closing fees (purchase only)
5	Credit and disability insurance premiums if:
	1. Insurance is not required as a condition of the loan, 2. Premium is disclosed at consummation, 3. After receiving disclosures, borrower signs affirmative request for insurance
6	Notary fee
7	Reconveyance fee
8	Recording fee
9	Seller paid closing costs
10	Subordination fee
11	Title insurance fee

FIGURE 4.44   FEES NOT CONSIDERED TO BE FINANCE CHARGES

Appendix 4C
OVERAGE/UNDERAGE DATA MODEL
(RESTRICTED TO INPUT FIELDS, BY CATEGORY)

At a minimum, certain data are required to monitor a lending institution's practices of charging overages or granting underages. Some of the data must be derived, such as an indicator that tells whether or not a loan officer, a branch, a region, or some other well-defined operating unit is exhibiting a statistically significant difference in amount, or incidence, associated with overages, or underages, for a protected class compared with some control group. Other data is more basic in nature and is used to derive the information that is needed to assess performance. We refer to the basic data as input fields and they make up a sufficient set of data elements from which a complete data model can be constructed. Figure 4.43 lists typical input fields by category for overage/underage data model:

Category	Field Name
Identifiers	• Mortgage loan number
Protected Class Information	• Primary race
	• Primary sex
	• Co-applicant race
	• Co-applicant sex
Transaction Information	• Loan amount
	• Closed date
	• Loan term in months
	• Employee loan flag
	• Overage/underage amount
	• Overage/underage expressed as points
	• Overage/underage sign
	• Reason code for overage/underage
	• Loan officer commission adjustment amount (debit if underage, credit if overage)
	• Loan officer commission adjustment reason (may differ from overage/underage reason, but usually not)
	• Loan officer sign (negative for underage, positive for overage)
Product Information	• Product code or loan plan/program code
	• Product/plan/program description corresponding to code
	• HMDA loan type
	• HMDA loan purpose
Loan Officer Information	• Loan officer number
	• Loan officer first name
	• Loan officer last name
	• Branch Information
	• Branch number
	• Branch name
Broker Information	• Broker code
	• Broker name
Channel Information	• Channel
	• Referral source code for call center originated mortgages that indicates special programs (e.g., employee mortgage program, job relocations)
	• Referral description associated with corresponding referral source code
Organization Information	• Sales region name
	• Sales region code
	• Legal entity

FIGURE 4.45 OVERAGE/UNDERAGE DATA MODEL

Appendix 4D
DETAILED OVERAGE/UNDERAGE REPORTING

Once input data are processed and the required fields derived, the results need to be reported. Reporting can and should be performed at different organizational levels within lines of business and in a proper business context within channel to facilitate remedial action, where needed. The business context varies by institution, but at a minimum must address adherence to overage/underage policy; the period of time over which history is maintained and the frequency of reporting; and appropriate segmentation to facilitate identification of suspect patterns and imbalances. Following are some examples of detailed overage/underage reports that are useful for monitoring performance relative to policy within each line of business and each channel.

- *Summary totals.* Current period (total number of loans reported, total number of overages, percentage of loans with overages, average overage for loans having an overage, total number of underages, percentage of loans with underages, average underage for loans having an underage); number of loans by HMDA loan type (conventional, VA, FHA, unknown). For each type, breakout (total number of loans reported, total number of overages, percentage of loans with overages, average overage for loans having an overage, total number of underages, percentage of loans with underages, average underage for loans having an underage); number of loans by HMDA loan purpose (purchase, refinance, home improvement, unknown) for each purpose, breakout (total number of loans reported, total number of overages, percent of loans with overages, average overage for loans having an overage, total number of underages, percent of loans with underages, average underage for loans having an underage).
- *Trend.* Four quarters (total number of loans reported, total number of overages, percentage of loans with overages, average overage for loans having an overage, total number of underages, percentage of loans with underages, average underage for loans having an underage).

Channel Specific

- Corporate level
  - Retail results by region
  - Wholesale results
- Within line of business
  - Call center
    - Reference frequency by type
    - Reference frequency by type by telephone branch
  - Retail branch
    - Frequency of processing delays for rate locks resulting in underages, by protected class

- o   Wholesale
  - ◆   Overage/underage frequency by state, by protected class
  - ◆   Overage/underage average amount by state, by protected class
- Loan officer level
  - o   Loan officers having "n" or more exceptions. Current period showing (name, office name, region, manager).
  - o   Loan officers having "n" or more exceptions. "n" or more consecutive reporting periods (name, office name, region, manager).
  - o   Loan officers with negative trend relative to identified exceptions. Current versus previous period showing (name, office name, region, manager).
  - o   Summary loan officer's exception report. — Overages (name, office name, region, manager, percentage difference in amount of overage for each protected class, percentage difference in incidence of overage for each protected class, total policy violations) [report total of number of exceptions by each category and percentage of possible categorized exceptions].
  - o   Summary loan officer's exception report. Underages (name, office name, region, manager, percentage difference in amount of underage for each protected class, percentage difference in incidence of underage for each protected class, total policy violations) [report total of number of exceptions by each category and percent of possible categorized exceptions].
  - o   Summary loan officer's report. — Total exceptions (name, office name, region, manager, amount-triggered overage exceptions, incidence-triggered overage exceptions, amount-triggered underage exceptions, incidence-triggered underage exceptions, total policy violations) [report total of number of exceptions by each category and percent of possible categorized exceptions].
  - o   Loan officer's trend report. Overage/underage exceptions (name, office name, region, manager, exceptions current period, exceptions prior period, exceptions two prior periods, increase over previous period) [report total of number of exceptions by each category and percent of possible categorized exceptions, number of loan officers flagged in each period].
  - o   Overages/underages exceeding cap report (region, branch, loan officer number, loan officer name, loan number, date closed, protected class, product code, loan amount, loan type, loan purpose, overage/underage amount, overage/underage indicator, loan officer reason code, loan officer commission amount.
  - o   Overage amount detail exception transaction report by loan officer, totaled by branch (loan officer number, loan officer name, loan number, date closed, product code, loan type, loan amount, overage percent, overage reason code, protected class, loan officer exception flag, branch office exception flag)
  - o   Underage amount detail exception transaction report by loan officer, totaled by branch (loan officer number, loan officer name, loan number, date closed, product code, loan type, loan amount, underage percent, underage reason code, protected class, loan officer exception flag, branch office exception flag)
  - o   Overage incidence detail exception transaction report by loan officer, totaled by branch (loan officer number, loan officer name, loan number, date closed, product code, loan type, loan amount, overage percent, overage reason code, protected class, loan officer exception flag, branch office exception flag).
  - o   Underage incidence detail exception transaction report by loan officer, totaled by branch (loan officer number, loan officer name, loan number, date closed, product code, loan type, loan amount, underage percent, underage reason code, protected class, loan officer exception flag, branch office exception flag).

- Branch level
  - Branch trend report. Overage/underage exceptions (branch number, branch name, region, manager, number of exceptions current period, number of exceptions prior period, number of exceptions two prior periods, increase over previous period) [report total of number of exceptions by each category and percent of possible categorized exceptions, number of branches flagged in each period].
  - Branch summary report. Branches with "n" or more overage/underage exceptions for current period (branch name, region, manager).
  - Branch negative trend report. Branches with "n" or more overage/underage exceptions for current period versus previous period (branch name, region, manager).
  - Summary branch exception report. Overages (branch number, branch name, region, manager, percentage difference in amount of overage for each protected class, percentage difference in incidence of overage for each protected class, total policy violations) [report total of number of exceptions by each category and percent of possible categorized exceptions].
  - Summary branch exception report. Underages (branch number, branch name, region, manager, percentage difference in amount of underage for each protected class, percentage difference in incidence of underage for each protected class, total policy violations) [report total of number of exceptions by each category and percent of possible categorized exceptions].
  - Summary branch report. Total exceptions (branch number, branch name, region, manager, amount-triggered overage exceptions, incidence-triggered overage exceptions, amount-triggered underage exceptions, incidence-triggered underage exceptions, total policy violations) [report total of number of exceptions by each category and percent of possible categorized exceptions].

Appendix 4E

SAMPLE SIZE DETERMINATION

Determining appropriate sample size is important to compliance testing. The sample size of a testing should be sufficient so to correctly identify any statistically significant difference across different classes or groups. The probability of correctly detecting the population difference is defined as the power of the statistical test. If the sample size is too small, it may not provide conclusive testing results. Thus, it may reduce the testing power and increase false negative error (Type II error probability $= \beta$). If the sample size is too large, it not only causes additional resource and costs, it may increase the probability of Type I error (false positive probability $= \alpha$) because an effect of a magnitude of little importance may appear statistically significant.

This section provides a few typical examples to illustrate how to determine required sample size for statistical testing.[66] In addition to statistical consideration, sample size requirements for compliance testing also need to meet OCC sampling guidance.[67]

Factors Determining the Sample Size

To determine the appropriate sample size for a statistical testing, we need to understand the factors that affect required sample size. Depending on the type of test, the following parameters are typically required to calculate the sample size:

- *Required power.* It is equal to $1 -$ value of β, Type II error, the risk of accepting a false null hypothesis when a particular value of the alternative hypothesis is true. Typically, the desired testing power is 0.9.
- *Required confidence level.* Value selected for α, the risk of rejecting a true hypothesis. In general, the desired confidence level is less than 0.05.
- *Value of the population standard deviation σ.* Everything else being equal, a higher population standard deviation can require a larger sample size. For multiple groups, variances can be equal or unequal.
- *Mean difference of effect size.* Everything else being equal, greater mean difference across testing groups requires a smaller sample size. Two-sample t-test of the standardized effect size can be calculated as d $= (\mu_1 - \mu_2)/\sigma$.

---

66. All of the examples were provided by using SAS POWER or GLMPOWR procedures. For computation details, see *SAS/STAT User's Guide*. For detailed descriptions on how to use SAS procedures for power and sample size determination for ANOVA and simple linear models, see Castlloe, J. M. "Sample Size Computation and Power Analysis with the SAS System," *Proceedings of the Twenty-Fifth Annual SAS Users Group International Conference*, Paper 265-26, SAS Institute Inc., 2000, and Castelloe, J. M., and R. G. O'Brien, "Power and Sample Size Determination for Linear Models," *Proceedings of the Twenty-sixth Annual SAS Users Group International Conference*, Paper 240-26, SAS Institute Inc., 2001. For theoretical considerations, see Cochran, William. *Sampling Techniques*, John Wiley & Sons, 1977, pp. 72–111.
67. Refer to *OCC Fair Lending Examination Procedures—Comptroller's Handbook for Compliance*, April 2006, pp. 47, 95–97.

- *Ratio of group sample sizes.* The ratio can vary depending on sample designs or available data.

Determining Minimum Required Sample Size

- *Determine sample size for two-sample t-test.* This is essentially the same as ANOVA with only two testing groups. Suppose we want to determine the total required sample size for one-sided sample t-test of two groups with different mean rate spread between protected group versus nonprotected group. Assume equal variance and equal sample size; the mean difference is 2.0. The required sample size will depend on required power and confidence level as shown in Figure 4.44.

  This figure shows that the minimum required sample size increases as the power increase and α decrease. For example, if we require power $= 0.9$ and $\alpha = 0.05$ then the minimum required total sample size will be 8.

- *Determining sample size for one-way ANOVA test.* The above example can be extended to the case of multiple groups for one categorical. Suppose we want to test whether mean differences across eight joint race groups are statistically significant. The testing scenario is shown in Figure 4.45. The statistical method is a one degree-of-freedom test of a contrast means for the nonprotected group versus each of the protected groups. The group means for seven protected groups $= 3.8, 3.9, 4.0, 4.1, 4.2, 4.3, 4.4$, respectively, and for the nonprotected group it is 3.5. Assume equal variance $= 0.3$. We require power $= 0.8 - 0.9$ and $\alpha = 0.01$ to 0.05, then the required sample sizes can be calculated as in Figure 4.46.

  Figure 4.46 shows that in this example, we will need at least 61 observations in order to perform the desired ANOVA test. For a paired comparison, the larger the mean difference, the smaller minimum sample size it may require.

- *Determining sample size for two-way ANOVA test.* The above example can be further extended to the case of two categorical variables. To test for mean difference in rate spread across protected groups versus protected group, often we need more than one classification

Computed N Total					
Index	Alpha	Std Dev	Nominal Power	Actual Power	N Total
1	0.04	1	0.85	0.903	8
2	0.04	1	0.9	0.903	8
3	0.04	1	0.95	0.964	10
4	0.04	1	0.85	0.903	8
5	0.04	1	0.9	0.903	8
6	0.04	1	0.95	0.964	10
7	0.05	1	0.85	0.928	8
8	0.05	1	0.9	0.928	8
9	0.05	1	0.95	0.974	10
10	0.05	1	0.85	0.928	8
11	0.05	1	0.9	0.928	8
12	0.05	1	0.95	0.974	10

FIGURE 4.46 SAMPLE SIZE TABLE FOR TWO-SAMPLE T-TEST

Fixed Scenario Elements	
Method	Exact
Alpha	0.05
Group Means	3.5 3.8 3.9 4.0 4.1 4.2 4.3 4.4
Standard Deviation	0.3
Nominal Power	0.9
Number of Sides	2
Null Contrast Value	0

FIGURE 4.47 TESTING SCENARIO FOR ONE-WAY ANOVA TEST

Computed N Per Group										
Index	Contrast								Actual Power	N per Group
1	1	−1	0	0	0	0	0	0	0.909	22
2	1	0	−1	0	0	0	0	0	0.92	13
3	1	0	0	−1	0	0	0	0	0.906	8
4	1	0	0	0	−1	0	0	0	0.922	6
5	1	0	0	0	0	−1	0	0	0.947	5
6	1	0	0	0	0	0	−1	0	0.951	4
7	1	0	0	0	0	0	0	−1	0.931	3

FIGURE 4.48 SAMPLE SIZE TABLE FOR ONE-WAY ANOVA TEST

Fixed Scenario Elements	
Dependent variable	Rate Spread
Alpha	0.05
Error standard deviation	0.9
Nominal power	0.9

FIGURE 4.49 TEST SCENARIO FOR TWO-WAY ANOVA

variable. For example, as shown in Figure 4.8, the rate spread is affected by the interaction of income level and race. So we need to subset applicants by race and income level. Using the example in Figure 4.8, if the test scenario is as shown in Figure 4.47, we can obtain the required sample size in Figure 4.48.

Figure 4.48 shows that to achieve desired power and confidence level for comparing mean difference across joint race and race indicator, we would need 19 applicants total or about 5 applicants in each group.

Computed Ceiling N Total							
Index	Type	Source	Test DF	Error DF	Fractional N Total	Actual Power	Ceiling N Total
1	Effect	Joint race	1	41	44.78498	0.901	45
2	Effect	Income indicator	1	23	26.60215	0.905	27
3	Effect	Joint race*income indicator	1	25	28.46511	0.906	29
4	Contrast	Non-Hispanic white low income vs. African-American low income	1	15	18.91464	0.902	19

FIGURE 4.50   SAMPLE SIZE TABLE FOR TWO-WAY ANOVA

Fixed Scenario Elements	
Method	Exact
Model	Random X
Number of predictors in full model	6
Number of test predictors	3
R-square of full model	0.6
R-square of reduced model	0.55

FIGURE 4.51   TESTING SCENARIO FOR MULTIPLE LINEAR REGRESSION ANALYSIS

Computed N Total				
Index	Alpha	Nominal Power	Actual Power	N Total
1	0.05	0.8	0.801	97
2	0.05	0.85	0.852	109
3	0.05	0.9	0.9	124
4	0.01	0.8	0.803	136
5	0.01	0.85	0.851	149
6	0.01	0.9	0.901	167

FIGURE 4.52   SAMPLE SIZE TABLE FOR MULTIPLE LINEAR REGRESSION ANALYSIS

- *Determining sample size for regression analysis.* Since regressions (such as least-square analysis) may involve multiple continuous variables, or categorical variables, sample size determination process can be more complicated. In addition to the required power and confidence level, and the factors we discussed above, we also need to consider required R^2 for the full model and reduced model, number and distribution of the variables used in the model, number of the variables to be tested, values of each categorical variables, and partial correlation between the tested variables and the response variable.[68]

A simple scenario for a multiple linear regression is shown in Figure 4.49, in which we require power = 0.9, and confidence level = 0.05. We can obtain the sample size table as shown in Figure 4.50, which indicates that we will need to have total number observations = 124 to perform the desired regression analysis.

For a logistic regression model, we also need to consider the effects of sample size on model goodness-of-fit statistics. A multiple logistic regression model requires larger sample size in order to detect testing effects due to possible correlations between indicators.[69] In practice, for fitting a main-effects model, a rough guess is that at least 5 to 10 observations per parameter is required.[70]

---

68. See Bartlett, James E. II, Joe W. Kotrlik, and Chadwick C. Higgins. "Organizational Research Determining Appropriate Sample Size in Survey Research," *Information Technology, Learning, and Performance Journal*, Vol. 19, No. 1, Spring 2001, pp. 5–6, for sample size consideration of categorical variables.
69. According to Agresti, 2002, p. 242, the sample size needs to be adjusted with $(1-r^2)$, here r is the correlation.
70. See Stokes, Maura E., Charles S. Davis, and Gary G. Koch. *Categorical Data Analysis Using the SAS System*. SAS Institute Inc., 1995, pp. 189–193, for sample size discussion on main-effects models.

5

REGRESSION ANALYSIS
FOR COMPLIANCE TESTING

Disparate impact is said to have occurred when there is evidence that a lender's policies and practices, although neutral on the surface, produced disproportionate and adverse effects on members of a protected class seeking a loan. In Chapters 3 and 4, we described how to identify specific protected-class groups of applicants that exhibit a disparate impact or higher risk of a potential fair lending violation. Those groups require further analysis to test if they are more likely to be treated differently than their nonprotected-class counterparts relative to underwriting and pricing decisions when all relevant factors having a bearing on the credit decision have been considered.

Disparate treatment is suspected when similarly situated borrowers have different lending outcomes, in particular, when a group of comparably qualified applicants are likely being declined or charged with higher interest rate than another group of applicants. Disparate treatment may occur among any applicants, independent of their credit qualifications. However, the risk of disparate treatment occurring is likely to be higher among middle-group applicants who are neither clearly qualified nor clearly unqualified for a loan. This may be attributed to the fact that there is more room for lender discretion, and also because lenders may provide assistance or encouragement in the preparation of an application, or propose solutions to weaknesses in the application, for some groups of applicants more than they do for others. This represents a significant challenge for disparate treatment testing. Finally, establishing disparate treatment does not require that it be demonstrated that the treatment was motivated by prejudice or a conscious intention to discriminate against an individual, or group of loan co-applicants, beyond the difference in treatment itself. To combat a claim of disparate treatment, it is necessary to demonstrate some credible, nondiscriminatory reason(s) to explain the difference in treatment that occurred.

Statistical modeling has played an increasingly important role in detecting possible disparate treatment in lending. Studies have shown that statistical testing and regression analysis can facilitate the detection of patterns in disparate treatment. However, there are also various criticisms and concerns regarding the use and limitations of statistical modeling in fair lending evaluation.[1]

Due to the fact that disparate testing requires a model that includes all factors that have predictive values for loan approval or pricing, regressions have been a natural modeling choice for this purpose.[2] In this chapter we present an alternative regression model formulation for disparate treatment testing called dynamic conditional process (DCP). We show how DCP can help overcome

---

1. See Calem, P. S., and S.D. Longhofer. "Anatomy of a Fair-Lending Exam: The Uses and Limitations of Statistics," FRB Working paper, 2000 for a discussion of main concerns and critics on the use and limitations of statistics for fair lending analysis.
2. Most commonly used are main-effects regression models. For example, logistic regression models are used for denial disparity while ordinary least square (OLS) models are used for loan pricing analysis.

some limitations inherent in traditional modeling, and how DCP dynamically categorizes lending decision–related factors and captures variation in policy thresholds among loan products, markets, or programs. We demonstrate how to create conditional and interaction structures in order to model the variant nature of decision factors in lending decision, while minimizing the complexity of model specification process and model maintenance. DCP can outperform competing modeling approaches by achieving a closer fit to business reality and using the data more efficiently. Finally, we discuss how DCP can be applied to monitoring and improving override processing to reduce associated compliance risk.

TRADITIONAL MAIN-EFFECTS REGRESSION MODEL APPROACH

Regression analysis is a statistical method that examines the relationship between a dependent (response) variable and one or more independent (predictors) variables, and it is widely used in fair lending analysis and compliance examinations.[3] Ordinary least-squares regression can be used for assessing disparate impact in loan pricing. Depending on how the problem is formulated, however, logistic regression can also be used to model and test for disparate treatment in loan pricing.[4] Logistic regression has been the statistical modeling technique of choice in testing for disparate treatment in loan underwriting, and that is our focus here. The dependent variable in the model is a field that takes on a value of 0 if the loan is approved and a value of 1 if the loan is denied. The predictor, or independent, variables are the most important factors considered during underwriting.[5] The concept of main effects was initially adopted from the analysis of variance (ANOVA) method and it represents a constant effect of the independent variable on the dependent variable.[6] The result of a logistic regression model is estimated probabilities of decline as a function of the independent variables. Therefore, for underwriting, logistic regression models are generally used to test whether the race of an applicant affects the probability that an applicant is declined.

The challenge is to obtain a model that has strong predictive power with predictor variables that are relevant to the underwriting decision. While it is typical to try to restrict the number of model variables to a dozen or fewer to avoid issues associated with collinearity, there are those who maintain that so long as the regression estimates are precise, then the degree of collinearity is irrelevant.[7]

It is important to segment by loan purpose, in addition to other variables that help to distinguish lender underwriting policy differences. Some use statistical sampling to gather observations for developing fair lending regression models. It is common for observations having missing values associated with one or more of the independent predictor variables to be dropped from consideration. This leads to situations where the sample structure is not representative of the general population and, in turn, can lead to biased results. Sometimes the logistic regression model development is based on a matched-pair sample of protected-class and nonprotected-class applicants. In order for a protected application to even have a chance to be included in the sample, it must

3. See *OCC Fair Lending Examination Procedures—Comptroller's Handbook for Compliance*, April 2006, p. 4.
4. A simple example would be to define the dependent variable to be the probability that a loan's spread over the comparable maturity Treasury yield curve is above a specific threshold amount, say 3 percent for a home purchase loan, or 5 percent for a home improvement loan.
5. See Figures 6.9 and 6.10 for a detailed list of credit application and credit bureau factors.
6. In contrast to the main effects, an "interaction effect" can indicate a separate effect of an independent variable on the dependent variable and is conditional on the value of other independent variable(s).
7. See Fox, John, *Applied Regression Analysis, Linear Models, and Related Topics*. Sage Publications, 1977, Chapter 13: Collinearity and Its Purported Remedies, § Introduction, p. 338. In some instances, models with dozens of variables are encountered, but that is the exception and model validation in these cases is usually at issue.

first closely resemble the profile of a nonprotected application in the applicant pool and possess complete information. The criteria for closeness are typically[8] applied to determine, for each protected-class applicant, the set of all nonprotected-class applicants who fall within the boundaries of the definition for a match. Ultimately, one nonprotected-class application is selected from each set and associated with its nonprotected-class counterpart to form a matched pair. After this is accomplished, a sample is drawn from the pool of protected-class applicants having a matched pair and that sample is used for the model development. Provided there is sufficient sample, a subsequent sample is drawn from the remaining protected-class matched pairs for the purpose of model validation.

If the P-value of the protected-class indicator variable indicates it is significant at the 95 percent confidence level, then the conclusion is that there is sufficient evidence of a problem to warrant construction of a matched-pair sample and conduct manual comparative file reviews. One important model diagnostic is to make sure the signs of the model coefficients for the independent factors make intuitive sense.[9] For example, if the dependent variable is the probability of decline, then the sign of high debt-to-income (DTI) and high loan-to-value (LTV) ratios should be positive, because the higher they become, the greater the probability of decline. Credit score, however, should have a negative coefficient sign, because the higher the credit score, the lower the probability of decline.

Before we describe DCP, we first discuss some challenges that have surfaced in the literature relative to fair lending disparate treatment testing and some limitations associated with main effects regression modeling methodology.

First, main-effects regression models may oversimplify the actual decisioning processes to the extent that they fail to reflect the actual loan-pricing and underwriting processes in practice in the field.[10] Consider the following example of how the main effects regression would assess disparate treatment in a simplified loan underwriting exercise. Suppose there are only two primary factors, say credit score and LTV, plus one secondary factor (e.g., monthly discretionary income) considered in decisioning a loan application. A primary factor is one that must be considered in all situations, whereas a secondary factor comes into play only when the applicant is weak in one or more of the primary factors. A main-effects model means that the effect of score does not depend on the LTV ratio. In reality, score and LTV are interdependent. In other words, high-scoring applicants are allowed to have higher LTVs than those who are low scoring. In this example, discretionary income would only be considered in circumstances where the applicant had a low credit score or high LTV.

Second, main-effects regressions may not allow sufficient flexibility in model specifications for variant effects of a decision variable. In main-effects regression, all factors are either included as main effects or excluded from the model. If included, its estimated impact on the outcome of loan decision is constant and does not depend on the values of other factors. For example, if a secondary factor such as discretionary income is included as a main effect, the estimated impact of discretionary on the loan application decision is a constant for all values of credit score and LTV. In reality, discretionary income should impact the outcome only when an applicant has a low credit scores or high LTVs. In this case, the independent variables in this example would be credit score, LTV, race, and possibly discretionary income. Therefore, if only main effects are considered and their estimated coefficients are invariant in all cases, the model predictability

8. See Avery, Robert B., Patricia E. Beeson, and Paul S. Calem. "Using HMDA Data as a Regulatory Screen for Fair Lending Compliance," *Journal of Financial Services Research*, Vol. 11, February/April 1997, p.13, for standard matching criteria: product, market, time, number of applicants, loan amount, income, for example, a rule of thumb for determining similarity of loan amounts or income is a range within 8 percent.

9. There are additional model diagnostics and validation methods that we will not elaborate on now that are covered in Chapter 8.

10. See Horne, David K. "Testing for Racial Discrimination," in Anthony M. Yezer (ed.), *Fair Lending Analysis: A Compendium of Essays on the Use of Statistics*. American Bankers Association, 1995, pp. 132–133.

will suffer, since the same estimated coefficients can be too hard on some applicants or too easy on other applicants. In testing for disparate treatment based on applicant race and ethnicity, it is necessary to test for individual race/ethnicity combinations (i.e., African-American compared with white non-Hispanic).[11] The regression model of Hunter and Walker found a statistically significant and positive effect of credit history on the index of creditworthiness for all sets of conditioning information.[12] In other words, having a good credit rating increased the probability of loan approval for both white and minority applicants and for males and females, which is intuitive. Interestingly, the effect was found to be stronger (the estimated coefficient was larger and the standard error smaller) for minority applicants than for white applicants. This leads to a conjecture that there is some racial effect present, since the magnitude of the common model parameter for credit history differs across racial groups.

Third, main-effects regression also presents difficulties in modeling interactions.[13] Interaction effects must be checked early in forming a model, because the model must contain all single independent variables that are found in significant interaction terms to be "hierarchically well structured." Consideration must be afforded to variables that interact with a protected class indicator variable, such as race. Hunter and Walker found an interaction between race and the ratio of total monthly obligations to total monthly income (OBRAT). Conditioning on "bad" levels of credit history and education, the effect of race was found to be small and statistically insignificant for a relatively low level of OBRAT.[14] They found that the coefficient became larger and statistically significantly different from zero when OBRAT increased. These results suggest that race was relatively unimportant to mortgage lenders for high-quality applicants (as indicated by OBRAT). As the OBRAT increased, the results suggested that white applicants were considered to be more creditworthy than their minority counterparts.

Finally, a practice of constructing matched pairs in advance of main effects regression model development can create problems. The rationale for this sampling approach is the fact it guarantees that in the event the protected class variable is found to be significant, then the ability to find matched pairs is certain. Essentially, application data are compiled and all minority applicants are matched to a similarly situated nonminority applicant. For example, each minority application would be matched with a nonminority application, which has a similar credit score (e.g., within ten points), and a similar LTV, say within 10 percent. To the extent that income is correlated with race, the matched pair scheme would have the potential to exclude high-income nonminority applicants and low-income minority applicants from the data used to develop the model. Also, matched applications that are missing any data are also excluded. As a result of restricting the data, the significance test results associated with main effects regression models can be unreliable.

---

11. Rachlis, M. B., "Nine Common Flaws Found in Statistical Models of the Loan Approval process," in Anthony M. Yezer (ed.), *Fair Lending Analysis: A Compendium of Essays on the Use of Statistics*. American Bankers Association, 1995, found that minorities are not homogeneous relative to fair lending. Including Hispanic, African-American, Native American, and Asian applicants together masks differences in lending behavior between those groups. Empirical evidence has indicated that, even after controlling for economic differences, rates associated with origination, withdrawal, rejection, and market penetration vary significantly among those groups.

12. See Hunter, William C., and Mary Beth Walker. "The Cultural Affinity Hypothesis and Mortgage Lending Decisions," *Journal of Real Estate Finance and Economics*, Vol. 13, No. 1, 1996, pp. 57–70.

13. An interaction implies that all involved main effects are present as well even if they may not be significant (because different parameterizations) in regression models. In other words, an interaction means that the effects of a variable differ across the levels of another variable. See Horne, David K. "Evaluating the Role of Race in Mortgage Lending," *FDIC Banking Review*, Vol. 7, No. 1, 1994, pp. 1–15; and Horne, David K. "Mortgage Lending, Race, and Model Specification," *Journal of Financial Services Research*, Vol. 11, 1997, pp. 43–68.

14. The model used two levels of the debt obligation ratio. See Hunter and Walker, 1996, pp. 57–70.

DYNAMIC CONDITIONAL PROCESS

In this chapter, we show how limitations associated with the more traditional regression testing approach can be overcome. The approach we describe more closely emulates the business realities in loan underwriting and pricing and it is more inclusive of observations having missing data items. Furthermore, it addresses other data problems, such as extreme values. In the real world of lending, there is more to consider than simply the factors that come into play in order to assess, or price, credit risk. This is because those factors often have combined effects relative to the dependent variable (e.g., the probability of borrower default). These combined effects can be captured by interaction terms in the regression model. For example, if you were to hold constant an applicant's DTI at 40 percent, then the level of the annual income would affect the risk weighting of DTI. All else being equal, a DTI ratio of 50 percent would indicate higher risk for someone earning $45,000 per year than it would for someone earning $200,000 per year. The extent to which factors are dependent varies.

The approach we are describing is called the dynamic conditional process (DCP). The "conditional" aspect refers to the fact that this method handles situations where there is a weakness in one or more primary factors by allowing other factors to come into play that otherwise would not be given any weight at all. The ability to condition the presence or absence of one or more additional factors, depending on the marginal risk associated with ranges of values exhibited by primary factors, is core to DCP. The resulting conditional framework among all primary factors and secondary factors essentially captures the true risk relationships and provides the most accurate modeling of the actual business processes involved. For example, suppose that an applicant had weaknesses in primary factors, such as a high DTI and a high LTV. To compensate, an underwriter may enforce secondary factor requirements including a demonstrated ability to service a higher debt burden, the existence and maintenance of considerable reserves and liquidity.

The "dynamic" aspect of DCP refers to its ability to compensate, within a single model, for variances in thresholds and business rules that dictate policy for different loan products and loan programs, and also different market and collateral-related distinctions. This aspect of the process is achieved through generalized primary factor definitions, coupled with very granular specification of those primary factor "generic" levels relative to each and every product, program, market, and collateral-specific policy thresholds and business rule. This translates to fewer models, and better overall coverage due to larger sample sizes. The ability to manage through sample size constraints in this way is critical in building multilayered segmentation models, and is the ability to include more observations that, on the surface, may appear to be incomplete, and hence unusable. In cases where there is a considerable amount of missing data for many observations, DCP can offer a variety of remedies, including tapping alternative data, conditionally applying different weightings for factors where data is present, or recognizing through the conditional structure that the observations having missing data are instances where the available data is actually sufficient and secondary, missing information is not required. In practice, one or more of the above situations often apply.

Capturing the Business Reality

Lending decisions involve a complicated interaction of factors that elude the more typical statistical regressions. In fact, the results of simple statistical approaches are often overturned when more advanced techniques are introduced to account for the complex nature of mortgage transactions. Stengel and Glennon[15] concluded that bank-specific policy guidelines need to be incorporated

---

15. Stengel, Mitchell, and Dennis Glennon, "Evaluating Statistical Models of Mortgage Lending Discrimination: A Bank-Specific Analysis," Economic & Policy Analysis Working Paper, 95–3, OCC, Washington, D.C., May 1995.

into statistical models. However, considerable differences in underwriting standards across banks exist, and the process of incorporating bank-specific underwriting guidelines can be difficult. In fact, those differences persist across lines of business within banks, channels within lines of business, and so on. In addition, experience has shown that sourcing policy guidelines alone may be insufficient to capture the true underwriting practices. Data quality and sampling issues further complicate matters. Rachlis[16] indicated that loan approval models must include all important financial and economic factors that reasonably affect a bank's lending decision. Economic theory and most lender mortgage applicant credit evaluation lending policies stress payment burden, creditworthiness, down payment, and collateral value as key characteristics. Many practitioners maintain that all important variables must be included in disparate treatment models and they assert that more sophisticated models are needed for fair lending analysis. Most empirical work to date has applied single-equation estimation techniques focusing on the underwriting process, independent of application process. The single equation model may provide a false indication of discrimination. With an efficient model consensus session (MCS) method, the regression models produced using DCP can more closely approximate the loan underwriting process than traditional regression models.

This result is achieved through several modeling techniques. First, DCP uses interaction terms to capture simultaneous effects of two or more decision factors. This reflects the fact that the partial relationship between one primary factor and the probability of decline depends on the value at which another primary factor is held constant. For example, the probability of applicants being approved can depend on the interaction between LTV and credit score. In other words, an applicant who has a high LTV would need a high credit score in order to get an approval. However, an applicant who has a low LTV can get approved even with a low credit score. This technique relies on a thorough understanding of business requirements and process. However, when subject-matter business knowledge is lacking for some variables, interaction detections through statistical methods may be used.[17] When more variables are involved, one can test simultaneously the joint importance of all interactions for one single predictor at a time.[18]

Second, DCP employs a conditional approach, which can control the presence or absence, of any factor, or combination of factors, depending on other givens. The process recognizes the fact that certain interactions exist, and some secondary factors only come into play depending on the values of certain "primary" factors. For example, an underwriter may not consider examining a secondary factor, such as discretionary income, before making a decision unless the applicant has a combination of high LTV and low credit score. This process will help better separate racial effects from nonracial effects.[19]

Third, DCP uses trimming to mute effects of extreme values or restrict values of factors to be within meaningful ranges, from an underwriting viewpoint. This is due to the fact that certain secondary factors have no further contribution to strengthening an application after some threshold value. An example of a secondary factor with a threshold is discretionary monthly income. It may turn out that any value beyond $10,000 in discretionary monthly income has no incremental contribution. In that case, a value of $20,000 or above for sample observations will be trimmed to $10,000.

16. Rachlis, 1995.
17. Some common variable selection methods are backward and stepwise. For details on selection strategies, see Agresti, Alan. *Categorical Data Analysis*. John Wiley & Sons, 2002, pp. 211–217.
18. See Harrell, F. E., K.L. Lee, and D. B. Mark. "Tutorial in Biostatistics, Multivariable Prognostic Models: Issues in Developing Models, Evaluating Assumptions and Adequacy, and Measuring Reducing Errors," *Statistics in Medicine*, Vol. 15, 1996, pp. 361–387.
19. While this was a concern for modeling mortgage redlining, it also applies to underwriting, pricing, and steering. See Rossi, Clifford V., and Fred. J. Phillips-Patrick. "Statistical Evidence of Mortgage Redlining? A Cautionary Tale," *Journal of Real Estate Research*, Vol. 11, 1996, pp. 13–24.

Utilizing Loan Information and Data

Typical compliance regression testing involves segmentation of loan data by program/product, channel, loan purpose, loan type, occupancy status, dwelling type, and market, in addition to other control variables. This often results in insufficient data for model development. Furthermore, when observations are excluded due to missing information, the problem is magnified. For example, racial status is oftentimes associated with many characteristics that have traditionally signaled higher credit risk, including lack of individual and family wealth and favorable long-term income prospects. Limited data sets and simple statistical approaches have proved to be inadequate to separate out the effects of these and other economic factors from race, ethnicity, sex, or marital status.[20] With DCP, it is possible to combine different segments with threshold variation in products, markets, or programs. This reduces the probability of having an insufficient number of observations for modeling and matched pair analysis,[21] and ensures that sufficient data is available in order to develop a more robust regression model. Specifically, this is achieved by handling missing values and mitigating the effects of omitted variables.

For applications having one or more missing data items, those missing data items may not even be required. This is because DCP may determine that the primary factors associated with those observations have sufficient strength to render the missing data unnecessary. In cases where an applicant was decisioned, but had missing information for a primary factor, those observations should be included in the model development sample for the following reasons. First, a more complete picture and comprehensive analysis is possible when all of the available information is used. Second, by incorporating the applications with missing data, it is then possible to determine how applicants having missing information are decisioned.

Omitted variables can have significant impact on model estimate and outlier identification.[22] In some cases, model variables may appear to be statistically significant, when in fact they are not. The cause may be correlation with predictive variables that are not present in the model. Net worth and depth and breadth of credit file are examples of borrower characteristics, which have a direct bearing on the lending decision and are also correlated with the protected class indicator variable. Statistical analysis of discrimination is exposed to the situation where some variable has been omitted that is correlated with race, which results in rejecting the hypothesis that race does not matter, when, in fact, it does matter.[23] Applications having a specific primary factor missing can be distinguished within the conditional structure in order to determine what, if any, impact

20. Yezer, Anthony M. "Bias in Tests for Redlining by Lenders," in Anthony M. Yezer (ed.), *Fair Lending Analysis: A Compendium of Essays on the Use of Statistics*. American Bankers Association, 1995, discussed that some initial studies using limited data sets and simple statistical models produced false positive results.
21. See Hosmer, D. W. and S. Lemeshow. *Applied Logistic Regression*. John Wiley & Sons, 2000, pp. 339–347, for sample size issues for logistic regression. See also Cochran, William G. *Sampling Techniques*, 3rd ed. John Wiley & Sons, 1977, pp. 75–78, for determining minimum sample size.
22. See Dietrich, Jason, "Under-Specified Models and Detection of Discrimination in Mortgage Lending, Office of the Comptroller of the Currency Economic and Policy Analysis," Working Paper, 2003, for a discussion of how using underspecified models can affect discrimination detection in mortgage lending.
23. See Browne, Lynne E., and Geoffrey M. B. Tootell. "Insights from the Boston Fed Study of Mortgage Discrimination," in Anthony M. Yezer (ed.), *Fair Lending Analysis: A Compendium of Essays on the Use of Statistics*. American Bankers Association, 1995. Also see Browne, Lynne E., and Geoffrey M. B. Tootell. "Race and Mortgage Lending—Dissecting the Controversy," *Regional Review*, Federal Reserve Bank of Boston, Vol. 5, No. 4, Fall 1995, p. 22, which discussed the default rates across race groups where three nonpublic variables, namely DTI, LTV, and credit history, were omitted from the analysis. Using a simulation approach, Ross, Stephen L. "Mortgage Lending Discrimination and Racial Differences in Loan Default: A Simulation Approach," *Journal of Housing Research*, Vol. 8, No. 2, 1997, pp. 277–297, indicated that a default model suffers from both omitted variable bias and selection bias when credit history variables were omitted from the model but those variables were used in underwriting process. Additionally, Rossi and Phillips-Patrick, p. 22, and Yezer, A.M. "The Role of FHA Data in the Lending Discrimination Discussion," *Cityscape: A Journal of Policy Development and Research*, Vol. 2, No. 1, February 1996, pp. 71–72, discussed concerns surrounding the "omitted-variables" problem.

the absence of information had on the underwriting outcome. In some cases, the effect of missing a primary factor can be compensated with one or more secondary factors (surrogates). Therefore, applicants with one or more missing primary factors can still be used in modeling, and the effects of omitted variable issues can be lessened.

Simplifying Model Development and Management

Traditional model development is time consuming since each model is required to capture different thresholds or policy guidelines for each different geography, product, or program. Maintaining or updating models is also resource-intensive. As Calem and Longhofer (2000) pointed out, much detailed information needs to be collected from the loan files and this results in a large number of variables, most of which are correlated with one another. This often results in the specification of a large number of different model scenarios based on combinations of protected class variables, geographical regions, product, or market to ensure the most meaningful business fit and also the best statistical fit. In practice, it is often very difficult and time consuming to manage this process. With DCP, since the values of primary factors, secondary factors, and their interactions are dynamically determined based on their thresholds, only one or few generic models are required to develop to capture variation in policy thresholds by products, programs, and so on. Thus, fewer models are required to develop and maintain. Updating models can be simply accomplished through a dynamic thresholds setting, and minimum changes in model specifications and model development. Furthermore, since model specifications are controlled by MCS, no additional variable selection and correlation analysis are required. This can speed up model development and assessment process.

DCP MODELING FRAMEWORK

The main DCP framework and components appear in Figure 5.1. Preliminary findings of compliance testing are important inputs for determining business and compliance focus, which identify analysis segments and important lending factors. The MCS captures business rules, conditions, and interactions for formulation of model specifications. During the model development

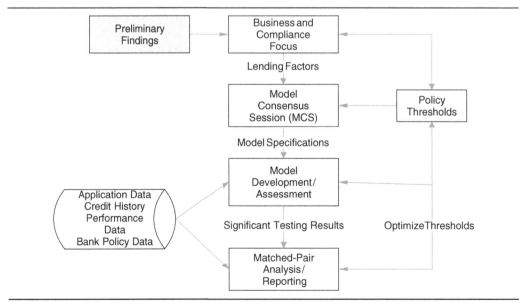

FIGURE 5.1   DCP FRAMEWORK

and assessment process, model specifications will be further tuned and evaluated to minimize false-negative/positive errors. Compliance testing is performed and, if significant, the results will be used to generate matched pairs for detailed review. Compliance testing result reporting is used to create new underwriting policy conditions or pricing rules, in addition to updating lending policy thresholds. The following sections detail each of the components in this framework.

Business and Compliance Focus

The DCP is driven by prior significant and material compliance testing results. Those results from a variety of sources including analyses described in Chapters 3 and 4, such as universal performance indicator (UPI) ranking at MSA level for a particular channel within a line of business, or above threshold differences in annual percentage rate (APR) spread from Home Mortgage Disclosure Act (HMDA) Federal Reserve Board tables.

Once the segments are determined, a thorough understanding of the loan decision process, or pricing relative to those segments is required. The loan decision process may vary by lender, market product, channel, and so on. In general, loan application and underwriting processes can be characterized as outlined in Figure 5.2. The main purpose of analyzing the loan decision process is to identify which factors are relevant to the loan decision and how those factors are used to make the loan decision. To specify a model using DCP, it is necessary to first specify the primary factors in the underwriting, or pricing process, and the interplay between those factors.

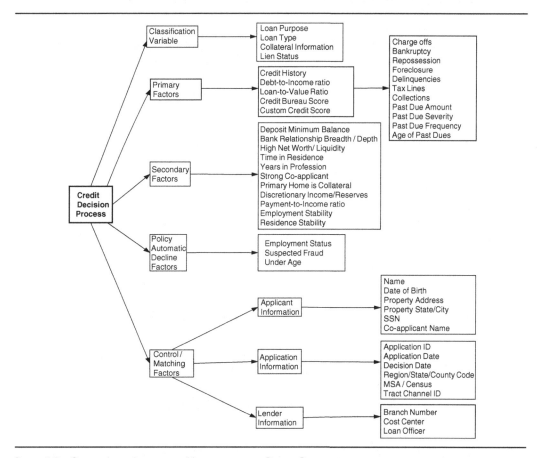

FIGURE 5.2 GENERAL LOAN APPLICATION, UNDERWRITING, OR PRICING PROCESS

One also needs to understand when, and how, any secondary factors can have a bearing on the final decision. The totality of mutually exclusive cases must be enumerated, based on all possible combinations of the primary factors, or subsets thereof. The outputs of the analysis often include the identified primary factors, secondary factors, control/segment variables, and the protected classes.

In a loan decision process, the *primary factors* are those important to loan decision and common to all lenders. For example, the primary factors for mortgage loan underwriting or pricing include:

- *Credit score.* The score is provided by the credit bureaus and obtained when the application is submitted to the application system. Cutoffs for passing this score can be established based on historic performance data and a bank's risk strategy. In the past, the credit bureau score used was some summary of the scores provided by three individual credit bureaus[24] (often, the core falling into the middle of the three reported scores would be used) since the credit bureaus can have different information in their respective files. Recently, the three credit bureaus have collaborated to create a new, consistent score that will be identical for all three credit bureaus.[25] In addition, many lenders create their own custom score that is specific to the institution and product line (e.g., there would be a different score for mortgage, auto loans, credit card, etc.). In those instances, both credit scores might be maintained as separate primary factors. Alternatively, in cases where loans are to be sold to the secondary market, the custom score may represent a proprietary score or recommendation from the loan purchaser's (e.g., Fannie Mae's or Freddie Mac's) underwriting system.

- *Customer credit history.* This is a summary of the history with the lending institution in question, encompassing all banking relationships (e.g., loans, deposits, and investments and services). It may be at the household, joint, or individual level. This may come into play as a primary factor to segregate banking customers according to profitability tiers. Lending institutions may experience problems with this type of policy standard if their customer base is skewed relative to protected classes.

- *LTV.* To calculate the LTV ratio, we need to calculate total liens to determine the numerator of the ratio. The denominator is calculated as the smaller of sales price or the appraisal value of the property. In the case of home improvement loans, the denominator must be consistently defined as value of the property "as is" or "after repairs are made." Secured loan products may differ in their maximum allowable LTV, that is, a zero down payment 3/1 adjustable rate mortgage (ARM) may have a maximum allowable LTV of 90 percent, whereas a conventional 30 year mortgage may have a maximum LTV of 80 percent, while a non-owner-occupied interest—only 5/1 ARM may have a maximum LTV of 70 percent.

- *DTI.* To calculate the DTI, the numerator is defined as the sum of monthly housing expense and monthly repayment of debt, while the denominator consists only of the monthly income. Often excluded from monthly repayment of debt are installment debts with only a few remaining payments and revolving debt where repayment will occur within a few months (assuming no new purchases). Like LTV, each product usually has an associated maximum allowable DTI.

Secondary factors are the variables that may or may not be used in loan decision, depending on the values of the primary variables. They are often used to assist decision making when a loan applicant exhibits some weakness in the primary factors. Examples of secondary factors include bank relationship, net worth, liquidity, whether the property financed is primary residence or not,

---

24. TransUnion, Equifax, and Experian.
25. Termed the *vantage score*.

strong co-applicant, years on job or in profession, low LTV (a specified number of points below policy maximum allowed), short-term loan (half of regular term or less), and so forth.[26]

Secondary factors can also be identified with the criteria for excusing bad credit. Lenders can take borrower explanations into account relative to pass due performance. For example, if the problem is due to a life event (major illness, accident, death of a family member, loss of job, etc.) or act of God (hurricane, etc.), then the problem may be excused. It should be noted that even when a loss was not booked, a failure to perform as agreed may have serious consequences. When losses are recorded, ultimate repayment of amounts owed is also taken into account.

After identifying primary and secondary factors and understanding how they are used in making loan decision, one needs to understand how the use of those primary or secondary factors is affected by control variables or classification variables. Typical control variables include loan type, loan purpose, property type, owner occupancy, and so on. Often, prior analytical testing results can be used as a guideline in selecting the control variables. For example, if an ANOVA testing indicates that denial rate or higher-priced loan incidences vary significantly by state across race groups, then state may be used as one of the control variables. Datasets created based on those variables can be identified with indicator variables and modeled with a generic model. In DCP, a control variable can be used with policy thresholds to dynamically categorize a continuous variable.

Pricing credit risk, and fair pricing analysis, also fits well within the DCP framework. Developing regression models for disparate treatment in loan pricing is analogous to that for loan underwriting. At the highest level it involves: (1) a daily or weekly market pricing component; (2) a rate sheet that specifies adjustments to the loan price, margin, or points, based on numerous factors, some taken in combination with one another; (3) add-on fees for additional products or services required by the lender or elected by the borrower; (4) point, price, or margin concessions, including fee waivers; (5) channel-related costs that are specific to the broker/agent, call center, retail branch, Internet-based unit, private banking division, and so on; and (6) a discretionary component that can vary by amount and may represent a cost adjustment in either direction (i.e., either an overage fee percentage or an underage credit percentage). The guidelines for pricing typically entail dozens of pages of detailed point, price, and margin adjustments that are specific to every product and program of mortgages offered by the lending institution. This information can be captured and, together with the daily generic market rate quote sheet from the institution's pricing desk and the items relating to items 3 to 5 above, it can be used to effectively simulate a large portion of the pricing process. The MCS focuses primarily on item 6, discretionary adjustments, but also explores item 3 to probe for fee-packing and general sales practices for borrower options, as well as exceptions granted to lender requirements; item 4 to identify reasons for exceptions to policy and their frequency and cause; and item 5 to ascertain as much information as possible that bears on distinctive pricing drivers and practices across channels.

In Chapter 4 typical mortgage models were examined that consisted of numerous single-factor adjustments. In contrast, DCP can provide a single adjustment based on all of the relevant information, considered jointly, instead of providing rate, points, or margin offsets. This improvement avoids the tendency for overstatement, or understatement, of credit risk associated with numerous factors, which are not independent of one another. This can become particularly evident when there are many factor adjustments based on borrower qualifications, plus elected product features, that result in a price spread that is "above threshold" for HMDA reporting purposes.[27] DCP provides a means to ensure that the risk is being priced appropriately, and lessens the likelihood that any segment of customers will be overpriced due to "double counting" certain risk factors that

---

26. For a more detailed list of primary and secondary factors, please refer to Figures 6.9 and 6.10.
27. A loan's rate spread must be reported if the spread exceeds the threshold set by the Federal Reserve Board in Regulation C. For first-lien loans, the threshold is three percentage points above the Treasury security of comparable maturity. For second-lien loans, the threshold is five percentage points.

are significantly correlated. The reader is referred back to the simple mortgage-pricing example in Figure 4.38, where individual adjustments are made, factor-by-factor. In contrast, DCP offers an all-together, all-at-once, alternative that avoids the overstatement of risk that results when single factors are layered on, one by one.

Model Consensus Session

Developing a model for disparate treatment detection is not a data mining project. The object of the exercise is not simply to develop a sufficiently predictive model for loan denials or above-threshold loans. Rather, the goal is to predict outcomes as accurately as possible by modeling the true loan underwriting and pricing processes, using the actual variables that come into play, and the associated qualification and pricing adjustment rules that are actually applied by loan officers and underwriters in the field. In the parlance of inferential statistics, our null hypothesis is: H_0: There are no protected class effects in underwriting (pricing). This hypothesis is typically tested at the 95 percent level of confidence. A Type I error (false positive) is said to occur if we reject H_0 when it is true. Accepting H_0 when it is false is called a Type II error (false negative).[28] Purely sourcing the "official" underwriting credit policy guidelines and pricing sheets can prove to be insufficient to ward off false negative errors. MCS is the vehicle used for debriefing experienced underwriters on the primary factors and secondary factors. MCS also documents what it will take to make the loan, or price the risk, when one or more weaknesses in the primary factors are present in a loan application. In this way, DCP utilizes the MCS method to control and manage model specifications, which include all effects of primary factors, their interactions, and all secondary factors. Model specifications determine how secondary factors interact with the primary factors. In this process, all possible loan decision scenarios are specified by the *handle*, which is a special categorical variable created based on the combinations of the primary variables. Then they are compared with the emulated case scenarios and the relevant and important lending scenarios are selected. Next, a set of indicators or flag variables are created based on those scenarios to control how the primary and secondary factors are used to make loan decisions. To specify which secondary factors come into play for each enumerated case, the primary factors need to be evaluated and ranked for their strength relative to the lending decision. For example, the underwriters may state that certain secondary factors cannot be used to overcome a recommended decline for score, but may be used to overcome a policy exception such as a high DTI. The overall process is described in Figure 5.3.

Accurate model specification is essential to achieving a successful result, and requires an in-depth interview of representative group(s) of underwriters.[29] Conducting a successful MCS requires preparation, and the allocation of sufficient time to navigate through all possible underwriting (or pricing) scenarios.[30] In addition to capturing all primary factors, their interactions, and all secondary factors, it is also important to identify automatic approval, or automatic decline, factors. In addition, the derivation of a simple three-valued (e.g., good, fair, or poor) variable such as credit history may require an hour to specify, depending on how underwriters evaluate a credit report. Credit history in practice has been derived from over 200 different variables, including bankruptcy, foreclosure, repossession, judgment, or charge-off; one time, two times, three or

28. Mood, Alexander M., Franklin A. Graybill, and Duane C. Boes. *Introduction to the Theory of Statistics*. McGraw-Hill, 1974, p. 405, defines error types.
29. Different lending subsidiaries tend to have distinct lending policies, and those lending policies may also differ by channel, loan purpose, owner occupancy, geographic market, etc.
30. For example, MCS may require two full days with six to eight underwriters to cover retail and call center channel sourced mortgage applications for owner-occupied residences spanning the following five loan purpose-related categories: home purchase, internal refinance, external refinance, home improvement with property valued after improvements are made, and home improvement with property valued before improvements are made. If there are different policies across regions, then this process may need to be repeated in full, or possibly designed to capture differences if the policies are fairly similar.

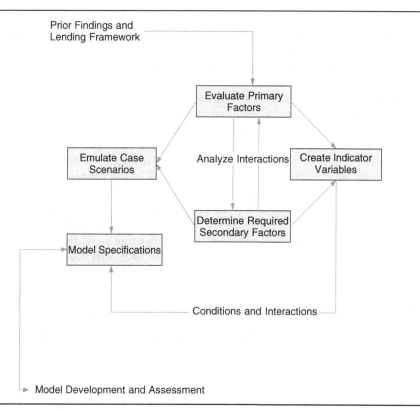

FIGURE 5.3 OVERALL MCS PROCESS

more times 30 days, 60 days, or 90 days past due; within the past year, within the past 13 to 24 months, beyond 2 years; for revolving, installment, and mortgage trade lines, and so on. The combinations quickly mount up, and summary ratings of credit history by trade lines must also be compiled prior to final assignment of a good, fair, or poor rating for an application. A good design of the MCS and thorough execution of it to capture every possible scenario is important. Poor MCS designs can result in incomplete, or erroneous, model specifications that will degrade the final regression model for DCP. Credit applications having a specific primary factor missing can be distinguished within the conditional structure in order to determine what, if any, impact the absence of information had on the underwriting outcome.

DCP must address missing data, flag exceptions, perform trimming, translate primary and secondary variables into discrete variables having few distinct values, and capture every possible business scenario through the handle structure. We proceed to describe these activities in no particular order.

Handling Missing Data

Loan application data often contain missing values, particularly for the secondary factors. In a typical regression analysis, missing data can be treated in several ways.[31] One can simply exclude observations with missing values from the analysis. Alternatively, one can apply various imputation

---

31. For a discussion of how to perform a complete statistical analysis with missing data, see Little, R. J. A., and D. B. Rubin. *Statistical Analysis with Missing Data*. John Wiley & Sons, 2002.

techniques to retain the data with missing values,[32] or treat missing values as a special value. Simply excluding the observations with missing values can result in loss of valuable information and insufficient data for analysis.[33] This can also result in false negative error as a simulation study shows in the section entitled "DCP Application: A Simulation" later in this chapter. However, imputing missing values with sets of values by regression or means may not be an efficient and reliable method. Often, this results in biased parameter estimates and errors. DCP allows observations with partial missing values to be included in the model as long as the nonmissing values, or the relations among them, are sufficient for making loan decisions. This is where MCS comes into play. Missing data scenarios are explicitly dealt with as additional cases within the business scenarios. In other words, for a scenario where any factor is considered to be "weak," the facilitator of the MCS asks the experts assembled what would happen if, instead of the factor being weak, it was unknown. The responses would provide the business rule for handling the missing data in question. Recognize that in the actual loan decision process, approvals, denials, or pricing adjustments can sometimes be made for applicants possessing very strong primary factors (i.e., credit bureau score, LTV, DTI, and credit history) without using the secondary factors. In some cases, conditional and interaction variables used in DCP may allow certain observations with missing values in primary factors to be included in modeling analysis and missing values of some primary factors may be compensated by some strong secondary factors. For those loan applications that fall into the "gray area" (e.g., not so strong, or so weak in primary factors), it is unnecessary to include all or most of primary and secondary factors to make the decision in the many cases. Thus, a significant number of observations having missing values can be used in modeling and analysis, whereas typically they would have been excluded.

Flagging Exceptions

In loan underwriting or pricing processes, exceptional values that are significantly above policy thresholds in some primary factors (such as exceptionally high/low LTV or DTI) may have additional or special effects on the loan decision. Those exceptions need to be flagged and reflected in model specifications with separate indicator variables. An example would be a loan-to-value ratio less than 50 percent on a mortgage loan, which would be an especially dominant factor in the underwriting decision. Another example would be a strong co-signer, or guarantor, on a small business loan that dramatically reduces risk in the transaction.

Performing Trimming

For secondary factors, values exceeding certain thresholds have no additional impact on loan decision (such as exceptionally high/low income, or net worth). In this case, those extreme values can be trimmed without affecting loan decision. This will help reduce the number of levels of the categorical variables that are derived from a secondary factor and also mute any undue impact of outliers on model parameter estimates. MCS provides business guidance on thresholds that can be applied to these situations. For example, suppose that some credit applicants have more than 24 months of reserves, where *reserves* refers to savings divided by the monthly loan payment amount (for mortgage loans this would include taxes and insurance in addition to principal and interest). The MCS may set key value thresholds to be 3 months and 6 months, and 12 months, where any higher amount does not matter. In this case, values in excess of the highest threshold, that is, a value of 12, would be set to the threshold value.

---

32. For detailed discussion of various imputation methods, see Little and Rubin, 2002, pp. 59–90. See also Chen, Gongyue, and Thomas Astebro. "How to Deal with Missing Categorical Data: Test of a Simple Bayesian Method," *Organizational Research Methods*, Vol. 6, No. 3, 2003, pp. 309–327.
33. In addition to missing data imputation, in some cases one can simply drop missing data from analysis cases if they are missing at random.

Categorizing Continuous Primary/Secondary Factors

An important step for DCP is to translate the primary factors and the secondary factors so as to make them take on just a few discrete summary values that covers the true range of their possible values. For a factor like credit history that has a large number of discrete values to describe every category of performance (e.g., late 30 days once during the past year, but never more than 30 days delinquent in the past 2 years and no public record items, etc.) the necessity of boiling down all of the possible behavioral combinations to arrive at a "good," "fair," or "poor" designation is obvious. In the case where the factor is a continuous variable, like credit score, the process is called "discretization," and the good range for a credit score may be determined to be greater than 680, whereas fair and poor designations may relate to ranges of 640 to 680, and less than 640, respectively. The MCS provides the rules for performing these variable transformations. In order to arrive at an underwriting or pricing decision the primary factors or secondary factor values for a loan application are compared with policy thresholds and also viewed in light of the underwriter's experience. Categorizing decision factors surfaces important interactions between the primary factors and secondary factors, which are often hidden in implicit joint policy thresholds. Categorization automatically, and dynamically, provides a means to explicitly assign a summary categorization of variables to reflect the variation in thresholds by different products, markets, or programs.[34] This process of creating model variables, and the analysis of those new behavioral, or summary, factors can surface a great deal of meaningful new information about the business process as a byproduct of model construction and subsequent compliance testing. When business requirements or policy thresholds are not available for some factors, and the MCS has difficulty reaching agreement on an answer, then statistical methods can be used determine the thresholds for categorization. For example, the thresholds at which Kolmogorov-Smirnov (KS) statistic is maximized may be used to categorize a continuous variable. Naturally, a result would be reviewed as part of MCS follow-up.

Using a Handle

A handle is a special categorical analysis variable that can be created based on the values of some key covariates such as DTI, LTV, or credit bureau score. It defines a set of design variables that represent the primary values of the covariates. The thresholds of these variables can be determined based on underwriting/pricing policy or statistical attributes of the variables. Each handle pattern represents a unique combination of these risk variables, or a group of loan applications that have similar attributes and represent similar risk. The handle variable provides a convenient way to combine, organize, and analyze a set of risk variables, and this concept can be used extensively in the modeling and reporting described herein. It is worth noting that there are two possible contexts associated with the usage of the term *handle*. First is a "primary" handle, which refers to the classification of a credit application based on the primary factors only. Second is the designation of the classification of the loan application after the result of the application of secondary factors is known. Detailed examples are provided in Chapter 6, but the point here is that the terms are used interchangeably throughout the book without any sacrifice in clarity because context makes any handle reference sufficiently clear. A matrix is the simplest means of displaying a handle, and Figure 5.4 shows an example, in which four analysis variables are used to create a handle variable and a risk category variable. The handle variable shown has 24 unique combinations and represents 6 different levels of default risk.

---

34. The Pearson chi-square statistic can be used to test the difference between expected probability (using policy thresholds) and calculated probability for optimal thresholds.

Handle Number	Risk Category	Bureau Score	Credit History	DTI	LTV
1	0	High	Good	Low	Low
2	1	High	Good	High	Low
3	1	High	Fair	Low	Low
4	2	High	Fair	High	Low
5	2	High	Poor	Low	Low
6	3	High	Poor	High	Low
7	1	Low	Good	Low	Low
8	3	Low	Good	High	Low
9	2	Low	Fair	Low	Low
10	3	Low	Fair	High	Low
11	3	Low	Poor	Low	Low
12	4	Low	Poor	High	Low
13	1	High	Good	Low	High
14	2	High	Good	High	High
15	2	High	Fair	Low	High
16	3	High	Fair	High	High
17	3	High	Poor	Low	High
18	4	High	Poor	High	High
19	3	Low	Good	Low	High
20	4	Low	Good	High	High
21	3	Low	Fair	Low	High
22	4	Low	Fair	High	High
23	4	Low	Poor	Low	High
24	5	Low	Poor	High	High

FIGURE 5.4   CAPTURING ALL SCENARIOS WITH THE HANDLE

To classify handle numbers/segments into different risk categories, you need to analyze the distribution of frequency of handle numbers. Since each handle number is a unique combination of decision factors, it also represents a homogenous data segment. Each data segment has a certain discriminatory power to separate, say, loan denials from approvals. Those unique segments can be further regrouped according to their hierarchies and decision scenarios. Unlike a typical KS test,[35] which is used to determine the threshold for maximum separation of a single decision variable, the KS approach referred to here is used in an iterative process to search for combination of multiple thresholds and decision factors based on the hierarchical and conditional structure of the data. The results are then used to create conditional and interaction terms that best simulate the real decision process, with minimum number of new variables.

The MCS must examine all scenarios enumerated by the handle number in order to determine what, if any, additional factors must be considered in order to approve the loan. For example, for

---

35. For detailed discussion of K-S test, refer to Siegel, S., and N. J. Castellan. *Nonparametric Statistics for the Behavioral Sciences*. McGraw-Hill, 1988, pp. 47–52.

the applicant segment corresponding to handle number 12, secondary factors, such as strong liquid assets and a LTV ratio below 60 percent, may be required to make up for weaknesses in the credit bureau score, credit history, and debt ratio primary factors. Explanations for delinquent payments, and other derogatory items on the credit history file, may also be factored into the decision.

Emulating Scenarios

The handle can capture all possible scenarios in which primary and secondary variables are used to make loan decision. In practice, not all scenarios specified by the handle are relevant or important to loan decisions. For example, scenarios represented by handle 12, 18, 20, and 22 to 24 or handles 1, 2, 3, 7, and 13 may be decisioned together. Therefore, those scenarios can be further aggregated and represented by a single scenario. This can be determined by matching handle scenarios with the actual business scenarios. To do this, one can use the handle variables to rank the strength of primary factors. For example, these following criteria can be used to rank decision variables:

- *Very weak application (risk categories 4 and 5).* The primary factors are too weak to allow for secondary factors to be considered. In this case since the secondary variables play no role in loan decision, those applications with missing values for secondary factors are still included in analysis (e.g., handles 12, 18, 20, 22, 23, and 24).
- *Very strong application (risk categories 0 and 1).* The primary factors are strong that no additional secondary factors are required. Similarly, since the secondary variables play no role in loan decision, those applications with missing values for secondary factors are still included in analysis (e.g., handles 1, 2, 3, 7, and 13).
- *Average application (risk categories 2 and 3).* One or more primary factors are not strong enough or have missing values, so that certain secondary factors are required to compensate for the primary factors in order to make the loan decision. In general, a large proportion of loan applications fall into this category. Therefore, a careful design of the conditional and interaction variables to rate the risk or capture distinctive business scenarios is critical for those applications with missing values to be used for modeling analysis (e.g., handle cells 4, 5, 6, 8, 9, 10, 11, 14, 15, 16, 17, 19, and 21).

Figure 5.5 further illustrates with four examples various underwriting scenarios where applicants with strong primary factors are approved without secondary factors, while those with weakness in primary factors require secondary factors for loan decision. In the MCS, those business scenarios are associated with the handles, which contain all possible scenarios based on the levels of each primary or secondary factor.

Scenario	Loan Purpose	Credit History Category	Bureau Score	DTI/LTV	Decision
1	Purchase	Good	High Score	LTV < 50%; DTI < 35%	**Approve**
2	Refinance	Good	High Score	LTV = 90%; DTI > 50%	**Need** high liquidity, good bank relations, high income
3	Home improvement	Fair	Solid Score	DTI < 40%	**Approve**
4	Purchase	Poor	Weak Score	DTI > 50%	**Need** high income, low payment shock, 6 months of reserves, good bank relations

FIGURE 5.5 EMULATE CASE SCENARIOS

In Chapter 6 we provide extensive examples for mortgage and small business lending and we enumerate all scenarios and describe factors that may be required to make the loan in each case.

Model Development

DCP dynamically manages model specifications with automated policy thresholds for specified control variables, and conditions of the primary factors and their interactions with the secondary factors. MCS is the process used to specify the interactions and conditions based on business rules and statistical methods as shown in Figure 5.6. The output of MCS is mainly a set of rules that govern which or how primary or secondary factors are included in modeling. Those rules specify, for instance, under what conditions a primary factor may have, or not have, an impact on a loan decision. These rules must also address the following questions:

- When are the primary factors alone sufficient to make a loan decision?
- In instances where the primary factors alone are not sufficient to make a loan decision, which secondary factors are required?
- Under what conditions a primary factor can have missing values?

The execution of these rules occurs via a set of categorical variables that capture the interactions and dynamics between the primary and secondary factors. The primary objective of model development for DCP is to formulate model specifications based on those conditional and interaction structures identified within MCS.

Typically, logistic regressions can be used to model underwriting decision process. For a main effects model, primary and secondary variables are included directly in the model via a variable selection process. Thus, data with missing values often are excluded. While in a DCP model, new variables conditional or interaction variables are derived based on the attributes and distribution of handle cells.[36] Those variables replace part of all of the primary or secondary variables and are used to predict the target variable (e.g., default or denial). As a result, the handle cells with

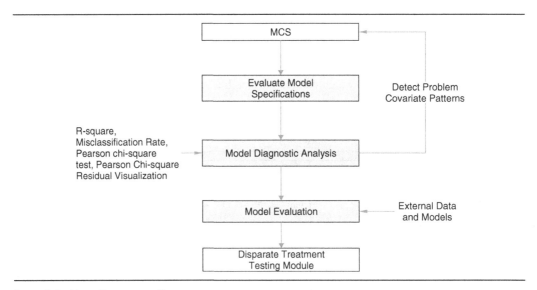

FIGURE 5.6   MODEL DEVELOPMENT OVERVIEW

36. Note that although those new interaction or conditional variables are used to replace the original variables, they are not typical "instrumental variables" since they are not derived based on the same assumptions (see, for example, Cheng, Chi-Lun, and J. W. V. Ness. *Statistical Regression with Measurement Error*. Oxford University Press,

similar values or similar attributes will be collapsed into a set of new groups or handle cells. The data with missing values in primary or secondary factors can still be used for developing models.

For DCP models, the underwriting decision process is modeled as a function of conditions and interactions derived from the *handle* within a specific context (e.g., region, channel, line of business, etc.). The effective sample size, covariate patterns, and model specifications are all associated with the *handle*. The numbers of covariate patterns and observations in each covariate patterns can be perturbed to enhance model performance, which is measured typically with the Pearson chi-square statistic, a summary measure of the Pearson residuals between the observed and fitted values.[37] In practice, this process can be conducted iteratively by means of scenario, or sensitivity analysis (e.g., by changing thresholds at which a primary or secondary variables are categorized, and the number of derived variables from handle cells). As a result, a set of covariate patterns can be produced that reduce model sensitivity to influential data.

Including these derived variables instead of primary and secondary variables can potentially mitigate or eliminate the effects of partial (quasi) or complete separation problem, which is a common data issue associated with logistic regressions having a binary response variable. This problem occurs when one or more independent variables can perfectly predict the outcomes of the response variable. Consider the case of the variable "credit history" is used to determine if an applicant will be approved for a loan. We will have a complete separation issue if all applicants with good credit history are approved while all applicants with a poor credit history will not be approved, without an overlap in data points.[38] When this happens, a model will have nonunique infinite maximum likelihood estimates, and this is reflected with large magnitude of the estimated parameter coefficients of standard errors.[39] For a main-effects model, a partial or complete separation problem often happens when sample size is insufficient, which results in no overlap in the distributions of the independent variables,[40] or when more primary and secondary factors are included in the model. While simply excluding some primary or secondary variables from the model may solve the complete separation issue, it may also cause the model to fail to capture the simultaneous effects among the variables. With logistic regressions developed with DCP, this issue is resolved by including derived conditional and interaction variables via analysis of primary and secondary factors within the MCS process. For example, a sole primary factor such as credit history, that could, by itself, completely predict the results of the final decision, should not be directly included in the model. Instead, one can use a derived variable that captures its relationship with other primary or secondary variables, such as LTV or co-applicant scores, and so on.

Another common modeling issue with main effects regression models is collinearities among the predictors included in the model. This happens when some variables included in the models are highly correlated. This is a common issue with linear regression models as well as logistic regressions, since there can be many interdependencies among lending decision variables

---

1999, pp. 94–132.) In this case, the covariate patterns formed from these new sets of variables will be different from those from the primary or secondary variables only.

37. For details about Pearson chi-square statistic, see Hosmer and Lemeshow, 2000, pp. 145–147.

38. A partial complete separation in this case would mean that a few applications with poor credit history are approved, and vice versa.

39. Complete and quasi-complete separation issues can be diagnosed and handled with SAS procedures such as the LOGISTIC procedure. See *SAS/STAT User's Guide*, 2003. A discussion on how SAS procedures handle quasi or complete separation in logistic regressions also can be found in Hosmer and Lemeshow (2000, pp. 138–141), and Webb, Mandy C., Jerey R. Wilson, and Jenney Chong. "An Analysis of Quasi-Complete Binary Data with Logistic Models: Applications to Alcohol Abuse Data," *Journal of Data Science*, Vol. 2, 2004, p. 274.

40. For a discussion on sample size determination for logistic regression, please see Agresti, 2002, pp. 242–243.

(e.g., primary and secondary factors). DCP includes in the model both conditional, and inter-action, variables that can reduce the effects of collinearities.[41] This topic will be further addressed in Chapter 8.

Model Assessment

In this section, we describe some basic model evaluation techniques aimed to ensure adequate model performance. The dynamic categorization of decision variables in the DCP model can minimize the effects of changes in the values of original variables, thus the effects of outliers, or missing values. From a model diagnostics perspective, this means we will see fewer prob-lem/extreme covariate patterns. This represents a significant benefit in practice, since it can save model development, validation, and maintenance time caused by changes in predictor variables over time. In practice, various model assessment and evaluation measures can be used for this purpose, depending on different modeling techniques used in the DCP. In the case where DCP models are developed using logistic regressions, we propose both summary measures and detailed diagnostics as described below.

Summary Measures of Model Assessment

A DCP model is first assessed with a set of summary measures, which can provide an initial overall assessment of how a particular model fit the data. For logistic regression modeling, summary measures can be based on goodness-of-fit statistics such as the Pearson chi-square residuals that describe the difference between observed and fitted values of the model. The results are used to calculate Pearson chi-square statistic, which is similar to the Hosmer-Lemeshow goodness of fit test.[42] The observations are sorted into increasing order or their estimated probability of having a particular outcome. The discrepancies between the observed and expected number of observations in these groups are summarized by the Pearson chi-square statistic. In general, large values of the statistic (and small P-values) indicate a lack of fit of the model. The goodness-of-fit statistics can be affected by sample size. Insufficient sample can result in elevated chi-square and a small P-value, and therefore poor model fit.[43] For main-effects models, it is important to use the appropriate number of groups and assign adequate observations in each of the groups. In the case of a DCP model, the number of groups and number of cases in each group are defined based on the handle cells.

Alternatively, the following three criteria are also used to evaluate the models:[44]

   1. *Model testing power.* This is measured by comparing false-positive/false-negative error rates against competing models in a simulated environment. The model that better captures any true effects of the factors the loan decision, or price, is considered to be superior to the others. Model estimates, including coefficients and their signs, are examined for validity.

---

41. This is a strategy similar to the use of prior information to improve data conditioning. For a detailed discussion and example of using prior information as remedies for collinearity, see Belsley, David A., Edwin Kuh, and Roy E. Welsch. *Regression Diagnostics: Identifying Influential Data and Sources of Collinearity.* John Wiley & Sons, 1980, pp. 203–212.

42. The Hosmer-Lemeshow tests normally involve dividing the data into a number of (usually 10) groups of roughly equal size based on the percentiles of the estimated probabilities. For details, see Hosmer and Lemeshow, 2000, pp. 147–156.

43. Person chi-square statistic is compared to a chi-square distribution with t degrees of freedom, where t is the number of groups minus n. By default, $n = 2$, and the total number of decile groups is 10. See Hosmer and Lemeshow, 2000, pp. 147–156. See also *Logistic Regression Examples Using the SAS System*, SAS Institute Inc., 1995, pp. 67–68; and Stokes, Maura E., Charles S. Davis, and Gary G. Koch. *Categorical Data Analysis Using the SAS System*, SAS Institute Inc., 1995, pp. 190–193.

44. See also Christensen, Ronald. *Log-Linear Methods and Logistic Regression*, Sprinter, 1997, pp. 127–136, for model fit assessment.

2. *Misclassification rate.* This is the most popular criterion used to judge model accuracy. Derived from the classification table, it is based on actual results.

3. *Adjusted R^2.* R^2 measures for logistic regressions having differing marginal distributions of their respective dependent variables cannot be compared directly with the R^2 from OLS regression. However, adjusted R^2 measures can provide insights. A number of logistic R^2 measures have been proposed,[45] for use when comparing the fit for competing models on the same data set.

These summary measures can be used together to assess model fit. Often, assessment based on one measure may be inconsistent with that based on another measure. For example, a model that fits the data well according to the Hosmer and Lemeshow test may exhibit poor classification. This is because the probability of misclassification is a function of the magnitude of the estimates and not the fit of the model.[46] In this case, one needs to determine which assessment measure(s) to choose. For DCP models, the Hosmer and Lemeshow tests based on Pearson chi-square statistics adjusted by the number of handle cells, coupled with underwriting scenarios, are most appropriate.

Detailed Diagnostics

Detailed diagnostics are used to examine if the summary measures described above are consistent throughout the entire covariate patterns, or how well the model fits individual covariate patterns. For logistic regressions, this process mainly relies on a set of visual plots for model covariate patterns. A series of plots can be created to aid visual inspection, including plots of Pearson and deviance residuals versus case number, leverage versus the estimated probability of default, distance versus the estimated probability of default, or changes in the diagnostic statistics and the estimated logistic probability.[47] Large changes in the Pearson chi-square statistic $\Delta X^2{}_j$, changes in deviance, $\Delta D^2{}_j$ or changes in estimated coefficient, $\Delta \beta^2{}_j$ represent poorly fit covariate patterns, or ones that have a significant influence on the values of estimated parameters.[48] Each of these diagnostic statistics addresses model fit from a particular aspect. Assessment of model fit can be performed with combination of numerical analysis and visualization.

In addition, sensitivity analysis is used to evaluate model stability by examining how model estimates are affected as the number of covariate patterns change. In this process, for example, the signs, or magnitudes, of the estimated coefficients for protected classes are examined in order to determine how they are influenced by changing model specifications, the number of covariate patterns, or deletion of the problem covariate patterns. Alternatively, this can be done using jackknife and bootstrap methods, which are two closely related data reuse and resampling methods. They are general nonparametric methods for estimating bias, variance, and a broad range of error measures.[49] The model that has more consistent and stable estimation is preferred. A simple illustration of the bootstrap method appears in Appendix 5A.

---

45. The LOGISTIC procedure in SAS computes a generalized coefficient of determination R square and an adjusted R square based on Cox and Snell's R square. The "Max-rescaled R-square," which divides the original R2 by its upper bound. See also SAS Institute Inc., 1995, p. 68.

46. See Hosmer and Lemeshow, 2000, pp. 156–157.

47. See SAS LOGISTIC procedure, and Hosmer–Lemehsow, 2000, op. cit., pp. 167–186. See also Cook, R. D. *Regression Graphics*. John Wiley & Sons, 1998, pp. 304–313, for various residual plots that can be used in regression model assessment.

48. In general, the Pearson residual values of greater than 2 are considered as possible lack of fit. See Hosmer and Lemeshow, 2000, pp. 167–186, for visual interpretation of logistic probability plots.

49. For an introduction to jackknife and bootstrap estimates of bias, see Efron, Bradley, and Robert J. Tibshirani, *An Introduction to the Bootstrap*. Chapman and Hall, 1993, pp. 124–150. For a more theoretical discussion on this topic, see Shau, J., and D. Tu. *The Jackknife and Bootstrap*, Springer, 1996, pp. 23–127. A simple illustration of the bootstrap method appears in Appendix 5A.

External Model Validation

Alternatively, a fitted model developed with the DCP can also be validated with external data (or holdout sample) and compared against the competing models such as the main effects regression model or decision tree models. The purpose of this step is to further evaluate the DCP model with different criteria. In this case, either the summary or detailed diagnostics methods, such as the Hosmer-Lemeshow statistic,[50] can be used to validate the models. In addition, typical data mining techniques can be used for this purpose.[51]

Interpretation of Model Findings

Interpretation of DCP model results depends largely on the modeling objectives. For disparate treatment testing, the primary goal is to examine whether or not protected class membership, represented by an indicator variable, has a significant impact on loan denial after controlling for all relevant borrower and loan characteristics. In case of logistic modeling, interpretation of model estimates typically involves the following aspects:

- *Examine the effects of protected-class membership on loan decisions.* The inferential goals of a disparate treatment testing are to examine model coefficient estimates of the protected variables and their significance level. This involves interpretation and presentation of model coefficients, standard error, Wald chi-square statistic, a related P-value, as well as odds ratios. For example, negative signs of the coefficients for the non-protected groups indicate a negative impact on the probability of decline, while positive signs for the protected groups indicate a positive impact on the probability of decline.
- *Test the significance of other estimated coefficients.* A DCP model may only include protected variables and their interactions with some covariates, and conditional and interaction variables for covariates. Thus, it is particularly important to test whether or not the estimated coefficients for those protected class-related variables are statistically significant, given the signs that are unfavorable to the protected groups. Typically, a positive coefficient that is significant at 5 percent significance level for a protected group may require further examination.[52]
- *Examine materiality of the estimated coefficients.* It is important to examine the materiality of the estimated coefficients and, interaction terms, and other dichotomous variables. Often, estimated odds ratios can be more convenient and intuitive for interpretation of the relative magnitude of the estimates. For example, an odds ratio of 1.5 for African-American group indicates that African-American applicants are 1.5 times more likely to be declined than a control group applicant (usually white non-Hispanic group).[53]

DCP APPLICATION: A SIMULATION

In this section, we illustrate the performance of a DCP model by comparing it with comparable main-effect models and testing to see which models can best capture true discriminatory patterns.[54] We constructed data in which discriminatory patterns are explicitly embedded. As a result, data

50. See Hosmer and Lemeshow, 2000, pp. 186–188.
51. For summary information, see SAS/Enterprise Miner 5.1, Fact Sheet, 2003, p.8, and for more technical details, see SAS Enterprise Miner Release 4.3 Predictive Modeling Documentation, SAS Institute Inc., 2002.
52. Various statistical tests, such as the Wald test, can be used for this purpose.
53. It was recently learned that the definition of the control group may be expanded by regulators to include gender (e.g., a white, non-Hispanic male group).
54. Simulation has been used in various mortgage lending discrimination studies. For example, Ross, 1997, used a simulation approach to examine the omitted variable bias and selection bias associated with the default model

with intended relationships among covariates and between the response variable and covariates can be examined for both the DCP model and main-effects models. It allowed testing for true effects of the protected class variable, and policy, variables, and evaluation of model performance relative to missing values and outliers.

More specifically, a simulation was conducted based on various scenarios in which the number of observations, percentage of missing values, and percentage of outliers were easily alternated, both independently and simultaneously, while keeping everything else the same. In other words, the relationships between covariates and the response variable, as well as the conditional and interaction structure among covariates, were held to be identical in different scenarios. This provided a means to determine how well a DCP model, versus a main-effects model, responds to those factors, noting key differences in the process.

One of the important simulation results was that the amount of missing data associated with covariates has a significant impact on model performance. This is particularly the case when the sample size is relatively small. DCP can mitigate missing data effects and improve model goodness-of-fit. The simulation shows that the main effects model and the DCP model can generate similar results, while having compatible goodness-of-fit, when there are no conditional, nor interaction, structures in the data, and the issue of missing values is not a concern. However, for the data containing complicated conditions and interactions, the DCP model outperforms the corresponding main effects models. The superior performance of the DCP model to other models is due to the fact that DCP retains almost all of the original data, and the fact that DCP model specifications are designed to capture interactions.

Data Processing

Generating Values for Selected Variables

To generate and prepare the variables and data for modeling, we assume each continous variable is normal random with mean μ and variance σ^2, that is $X \sim N(\mu, \sigma^2)$. All the observations in each of the cells are independent and have a normal distribution with certain percentage of outliers (usually 10 to 15 percent of the total number of observations). The distributions and statistical attributes (ranges, means, variance, etc.) of each covariate were generated so that they are as close to business reality as possible.[55]

Six distinctive decision scenarios or business rules similar to those shown in Figure 5.4 were simulated and used to formulate the interactions and conditions. The rest of process follows the description in Section Model Consensus Session (MCS). Figure 5.7 lists the variables as well as their summary statistics for selected primary and secondary variables.

Handling Missing Values

In a main-effects model, simply excluding the observations with missing values can result in the loss of valuable loan information. This almost always results in less reliable estimates, and poor model goodness-of-fit. Consider a dataset in Figure 5.8 with original 6,477 observations, where each of the 6 decision variables contained about 10 percent missing values. Main-effects regression models can only make use of 2,683 observations.

This means that only about 59 percent of the original data can be utilized. Alternatively, a DCP model with careful design of the interaction and conditional terms can make use of all of the

---

by Berkovec, James, A., Glenn B. Canner, Stuart A. Gabriel, and Timothy H. Hannan. "Race, Redlining, and Residential Mortgage Loan Performance," *Journal of Real Estate Finance and Economics*, No. 9, November1994, pp. 263–294.

55. To ensure the data reflect business reality, we incorporated the attributes of actual loan data that consisted of bank policy data, application data, and census data.

Variable Name	Mean	Minimum	Maximum	Standard Deviation
Credit bureau score	672.1374629	191	820	119.0450244
Loan-to-value ratio	0.634189933	0.0095	1	0.214770251
Debt-to-income ratio	0.280829427	0.0296	0.6489	0.09223612
Loan amount	240077.9441	24157	665459	122848.4788
Applicant income	114889.0298	18117	373850	67221.11251
Average check balance	10584.28491	1779	20077	2877.780979
Net worth	267029.6035	29756	501947	70811.68448
Co-applicant bureau score	666.6255658	100	820	137.3902768
Years in profession	7.367764082	1	13	2.032053538
Liquidity	258679.8825	35425	463885	71486.60019

FIGURE 5.7   VARIABLE STATISTICS

Model	DECLINE	Count
DCP Model	1–Yes	2,500
DCP Model	0–No	3,977
Main-Effects Model	1–Yes	888
Main-Effects Model	0–No	1,795

FIGURE 5.8   DATA PROFILE

Variable	Description	Codes/Values	Name
1	Missing LTV flag	Set to 1, else 0	MIS_LTV_IND
2	Missing DTI flag	Set to 1, else 0	MIS_DTI_IND
3	Missing income flag	Set to 1, else 0	MIS_INC_IND
4	Missing credit bureau score flag	Set to 1, else 0	MIS_CBS_IND
5	Missing custom score flag	Set to 1, else 0	MIS_CS_IND

FIGURE 5.9   FLAG MISSING VALUES

original observations. Simulation studies show that missing data, and the way in which observations with missing values are handled, can have a significant impact on model performance. In this simulation, missing values are flagged and used together as part of criteria to create interaction variables. Figure 5.9 shows the variables with missing values for primary factors. The first table entry defines a flag variable called "MIS_LTV_IND" that takes on a value of "1" in the event an observation has a missing LTV ratio, or it is set to the value "0" if a value for LTV is not missing in a particular observation. The other flag variables are set to values of "1" or "0" in a similar fashion.

Categorizing Primary and Secondary Variables

All continuous decision variables are categorized as 1 or 0, based on the thresholds which are dynamically determined by loan type, loan purpose, channel, products, or programs.[56] Those control variables are identified to create data segments or similarly situated loans. Figures 5.10 and 5.11 show categorized primary and secondary variables.

The variable credit history takes on one of only three possible values, but as we show later in Chapter 6, this variable is derived from over one hundred other variables. The process of boiling down information to useful proportion is an important aspect of keeping models simple, yet predictive. In short, there is a lot of information packed into the primary variable called "applicant credit history."

Variable	Description	Codes/Values	Name
1	Applicant credit history	Poor $= -2$, Fair $= 1$, Good $= 0$	CREDHIST
2	The level of DTI	High DTI $= 1$, Low DTI $= 0$	DTI_IND
3	The level of LTV	High LTV $= 1$, Low LTV $= 0$	LTV_IND
4	Credit bureau score	Low CBS $= 1$, High CBS $= 0$	CBS_IND

FIGURE 5.10   CATEGORIZE THE PRIMARY VARIABLES

Variable	Description	Codes/Values/Conditions	Name
1	High average checking account balance	If $\geq 10,000$, then 0; else $< 10,000 = 1$	AB_FLAG
2	High-net-worth indicator	net_worth $> = 250000$, then high_net_worth $= 1$; else high net worth $= 0$	HNW_IND
3	High liquidity	If current checking account balance $> 5,000$ or average checking account balance $> 2,500$ or checking account > 2 years old, then 0; else 1	BANK_DEPOSIT
4	Strong coapp. indicator	If credit bureau score > 680, then 1; else 0	COAPP_FLAG
5	High-liquidity indicator	If liquid assets $>$ loan amount, then 1; else 0	LIQUID_FLAG
6	Years in profession indicator	If years in profession > 4, then 1; else 0	YRS_PROF_IND
7	Primary residence indicator	No $= 1$, Yes $= 0$	PRIM_RES_IND
8	Under age indicator	Yes $= 1$, No $= 0$	UND_AGE_IND
9	Good bank relation indicator	If age of checking account > 2 yrs and average checking balance $> 5,000$, then 1; else 0	GOOD_BANK REL_IND
10	Low LTV indicator	If actual LTV $<$ (cutoff point $- 15$), then 1; else 0	LOW_LTV_IND

FIGURE 5.11   CATEGORIZE THE SECONDARY VARIABLES

---

56. For example, thresholds used to categorize DTI differ by loan product. For home purchase, a value of 34 percent can be classified as "High DTI" while for home improvement, a value of 42 percent may be considered as "High DTI."

Some continuous variables, such as high average checking account balance, are broken down into a few ranges. This process transforms the information into a new flag variable that, in this case, is called "AB_FLAG." That "boiled down" variable takes on only one of two values, depending on whether or not the value for high average check balance meets or exceeds a threshold value (in this example that value is $10,000).

Creating a Handle and Emulating Business Scenarios

A handle variable is created based on the combination of four primary variables as described above. The handles are then used to partition the data into six categories (0, 1, 2, 3, 4, and 5). Each category is matched to a scenario depending if or what primary factor(s) are required. Each scenario represents a group of loan applicants with a distinct level of default risk. Since this is a simulation and policy data is not available, we used the KS method to categorize those handle numbers, in addition to knowledge about loan risk factors.

Creating Dynamic Conditional and Interaction Terms

A set of indicator variables are created to capture the interactions and conditions for primary and secondary variables based on handle cell distribution. For example, based on the handle table, risk category, and the business scenarios, five additional indicator variables can be created as shown in Figure 5.12. Interpreting the estimated coefficients for those conditional and interaction terms is straightforward.

Simulation Results

For each of the models, we examined the estimated coefficients to analyze their effects on the probability of loan decline. Specifically, we examined whether the inclusion of the protected variable(s) improves model fit. We then analyzed the signs and magnitudes of the estimated coefficients for the protected variables and other related variables. Next we compared the odds ratio across all classes of the protected variables(s). Finally, we conducted sensitivity analysis to examine how the results respond to changes in covariate patterns. Since the true effects of one or more protected variables are designed in the data, those steps allowed us to evaluate performance with respect to false-negative errors.

DCP Model Goodness of Fit Assessment

We have conducted various simulations by alternating the number of observations. Those results show that, in general, DCP produces better model goodness-of-fit statistics, and it results in fewer

Variable	Loan Purpose	Credit History	Bureau Score	DTI	LTV	Risk Category	Handle Cells
1	Purchase	Good	High Score	DTI < 35%	Low LTV (< 50%);	0	1,2
2	Refinance	Good	High Score	High DTI	LTV > 90%;	1	14
3	Home Improvement	Fair	Fair Score	DTI < 40%	Others	2	21,22
4	Purchase	Poor	Low Score	High DTI (> 50%)	High LTV	4	24
5	Purchase	Good	Fair Score	Other	Other	3	15,16

FIGURE 5.12 CREATING CONDITIONAL OR INTERACTION VARIABLES EXAMPLE

false negative errors. As shown in Figures 5.13, the DCP model can achieve a 28 percent lower misclassification rate, a higher log-likelihood-based R^2, and a better Pearson chi-square statistic, compared with the main-effects model.

The main reason that the DCP model can achieve a better model goodness-of-fit is that we use a set number of interaction and conditional variables to capture the true relationships between response variable and covariate. The number of new model covariates is selected so that they minimize the deviance residual and also represent distinctive decision scenarios.

False-Negative Errors

When the data contain very little missing data, our simulation results show that both the DCP model and the main-effects model captured the true relations between the response variable and the covariates, although the model goodness-of-fit of the DCP model is much better than that of the main-effects model. When the amount of missing data is significant, the main-effects model failed to capture true effects and resulted in false negative error. Figure 5.14 shows that the impact of racial effect on denial rate for (African-American or black is significant (P-value = 0.0004). The corresponding main-effects model results, as shown in Figure 5.15, indicate that the racial effects are insignificant.

The main reason that the DCP model can achieve better performance is twofold. First, categorization reduces the effects of outliers on model performance in DCP. In contrast, data with outliers in a main-effects model may cause a greater number of false-positive errors. Second, the DCP model reduces the effects of missing values and retains valuable loan decision information, while the main-effects model approach excludes observations with missing values. Hence, the true impact of variables on loan decisions that are associated with the observations with missing values is lost.

DCP Model Diagnostics

The plots for changes in the diagnostic statistics versus the estimated logistic probability can help identify poorly fitted points or covariate patterns. The diagnostics ΔX^2 versus the estimated logistic probabilities for the main-effects model and the DCP model are shown in Figures 5.16 and 5.17, respectively.

The shapes of these plots are similar with the points falling in the top left or top right corners of the plot represent the covariate patterns that are poorly fit. Comparing the two plots, we see that there are more poorly fitted points usually are displayed in the top left and right corners of the plot for the main effects model than that for the DCP model.

Specifically, we see that the curves for DCP model contain fewer extreme points in the top left or top right corners of the plots and the very few values exceed 5. In contrast, there are a large number of covariate patterns that have a ΔX^2 value greater than 5 for the main effects model. This indicates that the DCP model can be more stable and less influenced by outliers in the data. As described in previous sections, it is not difficult to understand that this is due to the fact the DCP model is able to reduce the effects of outliers and missing values.

Model Number	Model Description	Misclassification Rate	Max-Rescaled R-Square	Chi-Square	DF	Pr > Chi-Square
1	DCP Model	0.21183	0.3565	7.8375	8	0.4495
2	Main-effect Model	0.29258	0.1385	19.169	8	0.014

FIGURE 5.13 SUMMARY OF MODEL FIT STATISTICS (HYPOTHETICAL)

Variable	Value of Class Variable	DF	Estimate	Standard Error	Wald Chi-Square	Pr > Chi-Square
Intercept		1	−5.4712	0.1518	1298.3012	< .0001
joint_race2	Two or more non-White races	1	−0.0164	0.1328	0.0152	0.9019
joint_race2	American Indian/Alaska Native	1	0.00259	0.0906	0.0008	0.9772
joint_race2	Asian	1	−0.1167	0.1063	1.2052	0.2723
joint_race2	Black or African-American	1	0.2777	0.0787	12.4583	0.0004
joint_race2	Hispanic white	1	−0.033	0.1315	0.0628	0.8021
joint_race2	Joint (white/non-white race)	1	−0.0966	0.1237	0.61	0.4348
joint_race2	Native Hawaiian/other Pacific Island	1	−0.0216	0.1093	0.0392	0.8431
joint_race2	Non-Hispanic White	1	−0.0329	0.0574	0.3281	0.5668
inter_term_1	0	1	1.3954	0.0515	734.3959	< .0001
inter_term_2	0	1	1.4644	0.0946	239.8518	< .0001
inter_term_3	0	1	1.3068	0.0457	816.3359	< .0001
inter_term_4	0	1	1.3009	0.0417	971.4386	< .0001
inter_term_5	0	1	1.3703	0.0545	632.1839	< .0001

FIGURE 5.14   ESTIMATED MODEL COEFFICIENTS FOR THE DCP MODEL

Matched-Pair Selection and Reporting

The purpose of constructing matched pairs is to examine in greater detail, on a case-by-case basis, results that are statistically significant in an attempt to determine root causes and conclude whether or not in a specific instance if disparate treatment has occurred.[57] No model is going to contain every scrap of information. The rationale for using statistical analysis is to efficiently and effectively isolate instances of persistent and unexplained differences in outcomes between protected and nonprotected classes of consumers. Hence, the starting point for identifying which observations of possibly disadvantaged protected class applicants to examine is the output from a statistical model, as opposed to, say, including every declined minority applicant for a mortgage loan. The output we are referring to comes in different forms, depending on the type of analysis being performed, as was previously shown in Figure 4.18.

Unlike the matched pairs for pricing analysis as discussed in Chapter 4, which created a matched-pair table solely based on predetermined criteria, the results from the DCP can be factored into the process of constructing matched pairs postregression. By using the estimated probability of denial, estimated probability of a high-cost loan, or estimated rate spread for each loan application, the matched paring process can sort the observations by who is most likely to be denied, to be given a high-cost loan, or to be charged the most as reflected in the rate spread. Matched-pair files may contain minority declines matched to both minority and nonminority approvals. The matched pairs are constructed by first matching minority declines to nonminority approvals using

57. In order for results to be conclusive, additional information in paper files that is not captured in the automated files may need to be sourced.

Variable	Value of Class Variable	DF	Estimate	Standard Error	Wald Chi-Square	Pr > Chi-Square
Intercept		1	4.2802	0.5867	53.2318	< .0001
applicant_income		1	1.54E-06	1.55E-06	0.9903	0.3197
bureau_score		1	−0.00289	0.000396	53.5214	< .0001
coapp_score		1	−0.00361	0.000335	115.9927	< .0001
chk_avg		1	−0.00009	0.000023	14.6473	0.0001
debt_income_ratio_af		1	0.9504	0.6031	2.4831	0.1151
joint_race2	Two Or more non-White races	1	0.2489	0.1953	1.6247	0.2024
joint_race2	American Indian/Alaska Native	1	0.00406	0.1281	0.001	0.9747
joint_race2	Asian	1	−0.2142	0.1557	1.8927	0.1689
joint_race2	Black or African-American	1	0.1497	0.1158	1.6705	0.1962
joint_race2	Hispanic white	1	−0.1093	0.214	0.2608	0.6096
joint_race2	Joint (white/non-white race)	1	−0.1118	0.1813	0.3801	0.5376
joint_race2	Native Hawaiian/other Pacific island	1	−0.1087	0.1464	0.5506	0.4581
joint_race2	Non-Hispanic White	1	−0.0311	0.0828	0.1409	0.7074
liquid		1	−7.41E-07	7.54E-07	0.9675	0.3253
loan_amount		1	1.93E-06	7.81E-07	6.105	0.0135
loan_to_value		1	0.382	0.2706	1.9934	0.158
net_worth		1	1.13E-07	8.64E-07	0.017	0.8963
years_bank_rel		1	−0.0265	0.0429	0.3813	0.5369
yrs_prof		1	−0.0874	0.0261	11.195	0.0008

FIGURE 5.15   ESTIMATED MODEL COEFFICIENTS FOR THE MAIN-EFFECTS MODEL

certain criteria for a specific time period, usually one quarter of the calendar year. There may be additional control variables that are applied in the initial selection, such as geographic market, or product in the case of mortgages, or perhaps collateral type in the case of home equity and automobile lending. Usually, six examples of less qualified[58] or similarly qualified nonminority approvals are identified and "matched" with each minority decline. In addition, analysts may also find five minority approvals that most closely "match" with each of the aforementioned minority declines. There is a pitfall that is important to call out here. Even if a "broader net is cast" to define matched pairs, there is a risk that more glaring examples of disparate treatment will be missed. For example, consider the case where the statistical criteria for sampling specify absolute differences of 15 points (instead of 5 points) on credit score as the allowable range for a match, and further suppose that a declined minority borrower matches identically with an approved nonminority borrower on all other matching criteria (e.g., DTI, LTV, loan amount, income), but the minority borrower has a credit score of 690 and the nonminority borrower has a credit score of 590. In

---

58. The term *optimal matched pairs* usually references those cases which are the most glaring (e.g., not just similarly, or even identically, situated borrowers, but instances where the approved nonminority applicant is maximally less qualified across all relevant factors in the credit decision [underwriting or pricing]).

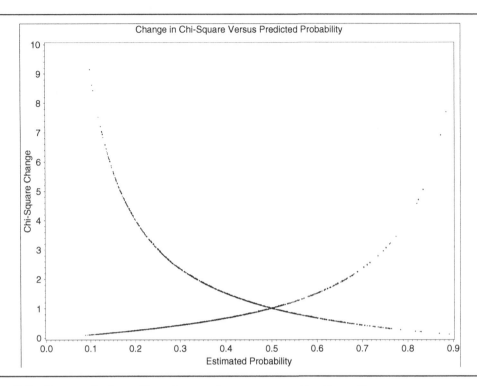

FIGURE 5.16   CHANGE IN CHI-SQUARE VERSUS PREDICTED PROBABILITY FOR THE MAIN-EFFECTS MODEL

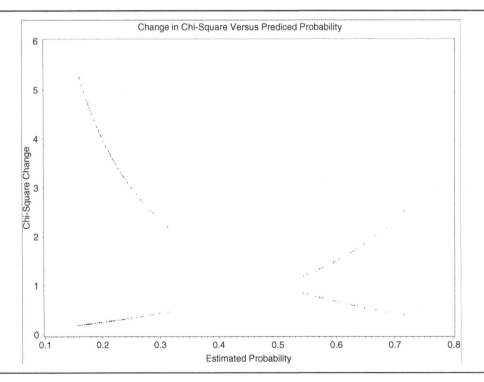

FIGURE 5.17   CHANGE IN CHI-SQUARE VERSUS PREDICTED PROBABILITY FOR THE DCP MODEL

that case, the glaring example will be missed as a matched pair for the observation in question, and may not get picked up in the sampling exercise at all.

An example of the logic used to construct matched pairs of minority declines to nonminority approvals is:

Matched-Pair Sampling Scheme 1

- The minority DCP-based probability of decline is less than the nonminority DCP-based probability of decline.
- The minority and nonminority bankruptcy, foreclosure, or repossession flags are equal. For example, if the minority and nonminority applicants have not had a bankruptcy, repossession, or foreclosure the condition would be satisfied.
- The minority and nonminority LTVs are within X points of each other. For example, if X equals 5, a minority applicant with a 95 percent LTV may be matched to refinance nonminority applicants with LTVs from 90 through 100 percent.
- The minority and nonminority credit bureau scores are within X points of each other. For example, if X equals 5, a minority applicant scoring a 690 may be matched to nonminority applicants scoring from 685 through 695.
- The minority and nonminority DTIs are within X points of each other. For example, if X equals 5, a minority applicant with a 35 percent DTI may be matched to nonminority applicants with DTIs from 30 through 40 percent.
- The minority and nonminority credit histories are the same. For example, the minority and nonminority applicants have been categorized as having a good credit history.

An alternative to the selection processes just described, an exhaustive approach is recommended. This is accomplished by a two-pass selection process. In the first pass, replace ranges of proximity with simple directional conditioning. For example, instead of requiring that the minority and nonminority credit bureau scores are within X points of one another, require that the nonminority score is less than or equal to the minority credit bureau score. In the second pass, a sampling is conducted on the observations isolated in the first pass, where selection is based on a priority of conditions that include rules for tie breaking based on an a prioritization of factors, or the DCP model's estimated probability of decline, and so forth. This process is described below:

Matched-Pair Sampling Scheme 2
  Pass 1

- The declined minority DCP-based probability of decline is less than the approved nonminority DCP-based probability of decline.
- The minority declined and nonminority approved applicants' bankruptcy, foreclosure, or repossession flags are equal or the minority declined applicant has one or more indicators that are more favorable than the approved nonminority counterpart.
- The minority credit bureau score is equal to or greater than the nonminority credit bureau score.
- The minority DTI is equal to or lower than the nonminority DTI.
- The minority LTV is equal to or lower than the nonminority LTV.
- The minority declined and nonminority approved applicants' credit histories are the same, or the minority declined applicant has a credit history that is better than the approved nonminority counterpart.

  Pass 2

For each minority declined applicant, select the five most extreme nonminority applicant matched-pairs where the nonminority applicant is the least creditworthy. The definition of *least creditworthy* is somewhat institution dependent, since there is no regulatory guidance that is this specific. An example would be to pick "the most important predictor first" as a means to rank the nonminority applicants by creditworthiness, say their credit bureau score. In an event of a tie, the next most important factor would be to pick nonminority applicants having the largest LTV ratio. LTV ties would be resolved by picking the nonminority with the largest DTI ratio, and so on.

The problem with picking a tie-breaking sequence is that there may be some "path dependency," that is, the order of variables considered in the tie breaking rules affects the outcome itself (e.g., which observations end up being selected). To ensure the methodology is sound, there should be an empirical basis for the rules and validation that they are, in fact, effective in determining the most extreme comparisons. Earlier in this chapter we introduced the notion of a handle that allows for simultaneous consideration of all factors making up the handle group and the handle groups themselves may be rank-ordered by credit risk. It is suggested that the choice for matched pairs therefore be driven by the empirical findings associated with applicant segments defined by the matched-pair factors. In this way, concern about possible path dependency is eliminated.

Sometimes the declines are matched with the approvals within the protected group to see if there are inconsistencies with other protected applicants, suggesting that any issue would involve other information not considered or simply a bad decision that was made without regard to the applicant's protected class membership. This is done using the following type of rules:

o   The declined protected class applicant's probability of decline is less than the protected class approved applicant's probability of decline.

o   The declined and approved protected class applicant's bureau scores differ by less than X points.

o   The declined and approved protected-class applicants' LTV percentages differ by less than X percentage points.

o   The declined and approved protected-class applicants' DTIs are within X percent of each other.

o   The declined and approved protected class applicants' bankruptcy, foreclosure, or repossession flags are equal.

o   The declined and approved protected class applicants' aggregate tradeline histories are the same.

Reporting

In addition to the matched pair listings themselves, a number of additional exception reports can be helpful. For example, it is helpful to tally how many matches were attempted and how many were successful for each matched-pair grouping, the number and percentage of declined applicants who were more likely to be approved based on the model, and the number and percentage of approved applicants who were more likely to be declined based on the model. An example of the first report appears in Figure 5.18.

Population of Interest	Minority Declines Where Match Attempted	Minority Declines Successfully Matched
Hispanic non-white	200	80
African-American	250	145
Asian-American	100	35

FIGURE 5.18 EXCEPTION REPORTS

MSA	White Non-Hispanic Applicants							African-American Applicants						
	Loan Number	Loan Amount	Bureau Score	Loan-to-Value	Income	Debt-to-Income Ratio	Probability of Decline	Loan Number	Loan Amount	Bureau Score	Loan-to-Value	Income	Debt-to-Income Ratio	Probability of Decline
10180 - ABILENE, TX	30	563731	679	0.2744	295320	0.1719	0.1889	5322	555963	686	0.2135	307169	0.1382	0.2411
10380 - AGUADILLA-ISABELA-SAN SEBASTIÁN, PR	74	534149	729	0.3269	282712	0.1482	0.1889	3136	560183	720	0.2418	279933	0.1136	0.2774
10380 - AGUADILLA-ISABELA-SAN SEBASTIÁN, PR	76	244331	820	0.6669	91980	0.3005	0.2176	3316	242181	820	0.7129	97560	0.3758	0.275
10420 - AKRON, OH	195	240174	751	0.5008	97022	0.1867	0.1687	5498	248168	760	0.564	97935	0.2697	0.2774
10420 - AKRON, OH	206	540341	820	0.2575	267906	0.1341	0.1889	7145	535991	816	0.207	271597	0.158	0.2774
10420 - AKRON, OH	115	248461	717	0.699	46651	0.2633	0.2196	2115	232871	727	0.7972	50388	0.3036	0.8381
10420 - AKRON, OH	187	173168	731	0.487	63321	0.2781	0.2176	4771	179904	740	0.4749	60988	0.2724	0.2774
10420 - AKRON, OH	154	208077	659	0.3976	71800	0.3062	0.7915	5624	222186	664	0.3699	77524	0.3383	0.2774
10420 - AKRON, OH	156	242617	507	0.6713	71029	0.2536	0.7915	3932	255301	508	0.5846	70007	0.3139	0.8381

FIGURE 5.19 Sample Matched-Pair Denial Report

The results of a matched pairing for denials is shown in Figure 5.19.

SUMMARY

In this chapter we introduced an alternative modeling methodology, dynamic conditional process (DCP), to model complex loan decisions. The essence of this modeling approach is to seek to emulate business reality to the greatest extent possible. One of the important techniques is to use a "handle" to segment the applicant population into heterogeneous groups with respect to primary and secondary factors for loan underwriting or pricing. A simplified handle, coupled with some distinctive business scenarios, can capably represent the complexity of risk rating process. This can reduce the number of marginal cases that otherwise would require subjective or manual analysis. In a simulated example, we also showed that DCP can improve the process of examining and explaining the outcomes of the mortgage lending process and testing for statistically significant disparate treatment of a protected class of mortgage applicants. This is accomplished by dynamically incorporating real business requirements and specific lending guidelines into the modeling process, aided by an efficient MCS that captures conditional structures of primary and secondary factors. The approach achieves a better model goodness-of-fit and lower error rate than other standard approaches. Furthermore, DCP can allow multiple products to be underwritten by a single, generic model that captures the key elements of borrower stability, payment track record, capacity, capital, and liquidity and also reflects collateral, terms and conditions, channel, geographic market, and other relevant considerations across the spectrum of proposed transactions. This is a departure from the traditional approach of developing specific scorecards for each product, combined with segmentation variables such as region, channel, and so on that require distinct development samples. As shown in Figure 2.10, in general, the deeper the analysis goes, the fewer number of observations are available and the greater number of variables is required for model development. DCP enables fewer models with more observations available for each model. This is important to avoid the situation where there are too many models and too little data for practical use.

In addition to disparate treatment testing, DCP can be used to predict the probability of default when "thin credit bureau files" and other data deficiencies are prevalent. Here, traditional credit scoring models can fall short due to their inherent inability to dynamically deal with the complex data structure and leverage on noncredit payment history. Essentially, users of credit scoring models may have limited capabilities to optimally risk rank all constituencies. In contrast, DCP mitigates the issues of missing values and omitted variables using dynamic and conditional structures that capture the way in which experienced credit underwriters reach their conclusions. In the next several chapters, we further extend these concepts and combine them with other methods to address credit risk management, override analysis, segmentation, and model validation.

Appendix 5A

ILLUSTRATION OF BOOTSTRAP ESTIMATION

Suppose you want to determine the standard error of an estimate without having a formula for the standard error. In the case of a sample average, there is a formula, but for other summary measures there is not. Consider the case where we want to estimate the typical minority annual income. Two ways to accomplish this are: (1) calculate the average income, *or* (2) calculate the median income. Which method will yield the best answer?

From experience, income distributions are skewed (i.e., most people have low-moderate incomes, and the distribution has a long right tail as depicted in Figure 5.20).

For skewed distributions, the median is a better estimate of a typical income, because the mean will be overly influenced by the fewer large incomes. This is an unfortunate circumstance, because there is a closed-form equation for the standard error of the mean, but not so for the median. In

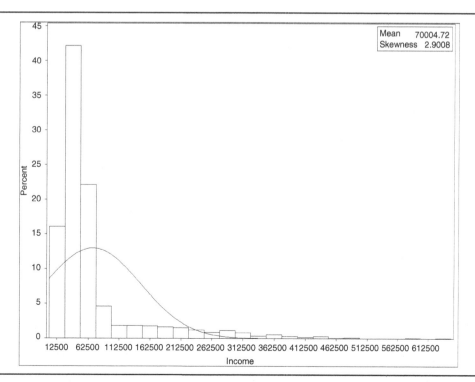

FIGURE 5.20 SKEWED INCOME DISTRIBUTION

this situation, we can turn to the bootstrap technique for an effective way to estimate the standard error of the median. The bootstrapping algorithm for this purpose is as follows:

Bootstrap Estimation of Standard Error of the Minority Median Income

Let n = number of observations

Step 1.	Randomly sample the set of n observations with replacement. The same observation can be sampled multiple times. This collection of data is called a bootstrap sample.
Step 2.	Calculate the median income of the bootstrap sample, called a bootstrap replicate.
Step 3.	Store the bootstrap replicate.
Step 4.	Repeat steps 1, 2, and 3 many times. The literature states that 200 repetitions is sufficient to estimate the standard error.
Step 5.	Calculate the standard deviation of the bootstrap replicates. This is the bootstrap estimate of the standard error of the minority median income.

For the DCP models, we can determine the number of observations for each sample based on handle cells, or covariate patterns. In addition, the jackknife method can be used to estimate coefficient bias by deleting one handle cell or covariate pattern each time from the data, and reestimating model coefficients from the rest of the covariate patterns.

6

ALTERNATIVE CREDIT RISK MODELS

In Chapter 5 we discussed how to conduct disparate treatment testing using a dynamic conditional process (DCP), which affords a closer fit to business reality and more fully utilizes credit information. In this chapter, we extend this concept to develop hybrid credit risk models that integrate aspects of both judgmental and credit scoring approaches, with particular implications for the underserved and underbanked segments of the consumer and small business markets. For credit scoring, two basic assumptions are (1) the future will be like the past, and (2) credit applicants having identical scores will perform the same way, despite significant differences in their circumstances, their goals and priorities, their lifestyle choices, and the sacrifices they are prepared to make to create some measure of wealth and a better life. The information value contained in alternative data[1] and community data[2] has made it increasingly apparent that significant ground can, and must, be gained in enhancing the state-of-the-art in consumer and small business lending. The end goal is to provide fair and equitable access to credit for all creditworthy consumers. Doing so will help them to meet their financing needs in order to achieve a better quality of life. The impact of successfully meeting this goal will be felt by consumers, lenders, regulators, and the economy at both community, and national, levels.

There is a great deal of financial reward awaiting those lenders who can improve how they transact with traditional consumer segments, while more effectively and accurately tapping, and fairly cultivating, the underbanked and emerging markets. A recent study by the Brookings Institution estimated that "lower income households in this country are now collectively worth more than $650 billion in buying power every year . . . greater than the budgets of Canada and Mexico combined. . . . ."[3] The study further reported that in 2005, 4.2 million lower-income households paid higher-than-average prices for their mortgages, and the same was true for 4.5 million lower-income households that took out auto loans. The report asserts that one of the most important sources of funding for antipoverty initiatives today is that portion of the $650 billion that can be redeployed by reducing the cost of basic necessities. We concur with this assertion, and take it a step further to illustrate how this may be accomplished relative to basic financial needs, by supplementing the prevailing credit underwriting and pricing paradigms with alternative credit risk data and models. At this time in the evolution of the credit markets, it is important that qualified borrowers in underserved markets obtain greater credit access in order to close the gap with their mainstream counterparts. We believe that the rewards associated with greater inclusiveness will most certainly surpass the financial benefits accompanying the business case.

---

1. For a list of alternative data, see Information Policy Institute, "Giving Underserved Consumers Better Access to Credit System—the Promise of Non-Traditional Data," July 2005, p. 11.
2. See www.socialcompact.org for more information.
3. See Fellowes, Matt. "Poverty, Opportunity; Putting the Market to Work for Lower Income Families," The Brookings Institution, Metropolitan Policy Program, 2006, p. 8.

This chapter starts with a description of the two common approaches for making credit decisions: judgment and credit scoring. It considers the strengths and weaknesses of each approach and then describes an alternative (hybrid) approach, considers its advantages, and provides examples in consumer and small business lending. The particular applicability of hybrid models in conjunction with alternative data is explored and examples are provided.

CREDIT UNDERWRITING AND PRICING

In general, the population of credit applicants falls into four groups: (1) willing and able, (2) unwilling and able, (3) unwilling and unable, and (4) willing and unable. Ideally, a lending institution should direct its credit officers to approve applicants who posses both the willingness and ability to repay a proposed obligation. However, determining which applicants fall into the first group presents a challenge. This entails the identification and analysis of risks that any given credit applicant is either unwilling or unable to repay the loan. Lending institutions possess credit policy manuals, underwriting systems, experienced loan officers, and secondary review staff to help them identify and quantify lending risks.

So the question is: "What criteria are (should be) considered to decision a loan application?" The answer to that question is: "It depends!" Loan approval and pricing criteria may vary substantially by product and lender. Historically, these criteria have reflected numerous relevant factors, which fall into one or more of the categories in Figure 6.1.

We will discuss loan underwriting and pricing factors in some detail in the section entitled Traditional Underwriting Criteria later in this chapter. Before doing so, we review the operational form of the decision process that they feed into and point to various shortcomings associated with commonly encountered models, and, indeed, the current state of the art.

Prior to the 1960s, human judgment, institutional guidelines, anecdotal evidence, competitor/market forces, and business objective and goals were primarily relied on. For the sake of simplicity, we will refer to these decision systems as *judgmental* systems.[4] In the 1960s and thereafter, *credit scoring* began its commercial evolution.[5] Where deployed, credit scoring replaced

Human Judgment	RMA Averages and Industry Data[a]
Lender's institutional guidelines and credit culture	Statistical analyses of historical/current credit applicant data
Regulatory guidance	Competitor/market forces
Anecdotal evidence and actual loss experience	Business objectives and goals
Collateral information (for secured loans)	Borrower relationship breadth/depth
Credit bureau files[b]	Channel

FIGURE 6.1   CATEGORIES OF LOAN UNDERWRITING AND PRICING CRITERIA

[a]RMA refers to Risk Management Association, formerly Robert Morris Associates.
[b]Often, lenders merge files from the three major credit bureaus, namely Equifax, Experian, and TransUnion.

---

4. Expert systems and subjective analysis were also widely used to assess the credit risk on corporate loans. See Altman, E. I., and A. Saunders. "Credit Risk Measurement Developments over the Last Twenty Years," *Journal of Banking and Finance*, Vol. 21, 1998, p. 1722.
5. In his introductory book on this subject, a friend and former colleague wrote that he joined Fair, Isaac and Company in 1960 just in time to witness the development of the first credit scoring model by that firm. See Lewis, Edward M. *An Introduction to Credit Scoring*, Athena Press, 1992.

human judgment and the influence of anecdotal evidence on individual lending transactions, with empirically developed and intuitively more objective criteria for decision making. Human judgment, however, does come into play in the scorecard development process, which is a mixture of art and science. Reflecting business objectives and goals in the scorecard development process will result in scorecards that are more realistic and pertinent to current operations. However, when business objectives change the scorecard may become obsolete. An easy example is a subprime finance company that specifies good/bad account definitions that are consistent with their ability to refinance loans to current customers, who are generally more delinquent in payments than the general population (prime plus subprime borrowers). In this instance, someone might still qualify as a "good" account if they were late 30 days four times over the past two years. Based on actual loss experience, if the finance company decides to tighten up their definition of what constitutes "good" behavior, the scorecard would have to be redeveloped.

Over subsequent decades, credit scoring has evolved from being primarily custom application scoring for a particular lender (with credit bureau information accessed only in cases where it could change the approve/decline decision), to scorecards with credit review overlays resulting in institutional overrides, to credit bureau–based scorecards, to dual score (custom and bureau-based) systems, to use of scoring in risk-based pricing, to incorporation into multistage decision processes comprised of various credit scores (custom, bureau, bankruptcy, behavior, etc.) plus sets of business decision rules to be applied at each stage. For simplicity, we refer to systems composed of credit scores and business rules as *hybrid* systems.

In the next section, we provide a brief review of these approaches and discuss the pros and cons of each. For simplicity, we consider the application of credit models for underwriting, but the same basic principles apply to loan pricing. As underwriting modeling approaches are being reviewed, the reader should seek to make the connection to the dynamic conditional process (DCP) for fair lending compliance testing described in Chapter 5. This will set the stage for the introduction of a new paradigm in the subsequent sections in this chapter.

OVERVIEW OF CREDIT RISK MODELS

Judgmental Systems

Traditional credit analysis uses human judgment to evaluate creditworthiness. Under a purely judgmental system, analysis of incoming credit applications is carried out by a credit officer in light of their own prior experience and their employer's institutional guidelines. In theory, the institution directs its credit officers to approve applicants having both the ability and willingness to repay a proposed obligation.

There are four basic steps in analyzing risks in the typical judgmental system:

Step 1. *Gather all pertinent information.* In some instances, this may require ensuring that the credit applicant(s) complete the application form properly and then having someone enter the pertinent information into a system. In an automated environment, this amounts to sourcing and extracting information from the loan origination system that pertains to the credit application information furnished by the credit applicant(s). It also entails obtaining information from credit bureaus and possibly furnishers of payment data for noncredit accounts and transactions, where applicable and available. Finally, for existing customers, it may also entail gathering information internally on other loans, deposit, or investment accounts, depending on the breadth and depth of the customer relationship.

Step 2. *Verification of information.* Activities here include contacting the applicant's employer, verifying bank accounts and balances, direct checking of existing liabilities, and combining and reconciling all three credit bureau report scores and trade line information.

Step 3. *Evaluation.* This entails weighing points of strength against any weaknesses perceived by the credit officer.

Step 4. *Accept/reject decision.* After a final review of all relevant factors, a final decision is rendered.

Focusing attention primarily on Step 3, we find many approaches toward analyzing the information gathered. In one common method, the loan officer considers five major factors. These five factors, because they all begin with the letter C, are known as the five "Cs" of credit, as explained in Figure 6.2. The first "C" of credit attempts to determine if the applicant is willing to meet a proposed obligation while the remaining "Cs" focus on their ability to repay the proposed loan as agreed.

Figure 6.3 displays the weaknesses of the judgmental approach. The main drawbacks associated with the judgmental system are inefficiency and subjectivity. In particular, subjectivity may have greater vulnerability to risk of personal prejudice. Additional weaknesses include lack of reliability and repeatability.[6] On balance, it is important to note that subjectivity is found in both the development process for credit scoring systems, and also in the scoring system override process.

Main Factor	Typical Components
1. Character	(a) Past payment record. (This includes such considerations as the frequency of past borrowings and the manner in which each obligation was paid.) (b) Mix and types of previous credit (c) Time in profession and type of employment (d) Length of employment and length of time at present address.
2. Capacity	(a) Income. The applicant must be capable of earning enough money, during the course of the loan, to be able to repay it. In addition to current earnings, the outlook for earnings to continue or increase in the future is examined. Mix of salary, commission, and bonus are considered. (b) Residence type / arrangement (c) Level of existing credit limits and degree of utilization (d) Debt to income ratio (e) Payment to income ratio
3. Capital	(a) Personal assets which constitute secondary sources of income. (b) Months of reserves (c) Liquid assets (d) Tangible net worth of borrower(s)
4. Collateral	(a) Savings accounts, stocks, bonds, automobiles, boats, etc. (b) Pledged portion of IRA / retirement assets (c) Life insurance (d) Loan to value ratio (e) Age and type of appraisal (f) Collateral attributes (age, location, etc.)
5. Conditions	(a) Loan conditions (term, interest rate, purpose, amount, etc.) (b) External conditions (the labor market, industry and economic conditions, etc.) (c) Borrower conditions, such as self-employment, start-up company, etc.

FIGURE 6.2 FIVE "Cs" OF CREDIT

6. Also see Hand, David. "Modeling Consumer Credit Risk," *IMA Journal of Management Mathematics*, Vol. 12, 2001, p. 141, for some shortcomings related to the judgment system.

Weakness	Explanation
1. Credit officer may have an imperfect recollection of past experience.	1. Cumulative collection and organization of applicant data in a form which is readily amendable to analysis is either ignored or accomplished in a very cumbersome way.
2. One very troublesome incident may distort the officer's view of a particular group.	2. There is a natural tendency to consolidate applicant profiles and then to generalize based on one or more isolated factors.
3. Inability to benefit from the institution's total accumulated lending experience in a timely fashion.	3. A judgmental system is composed of numerous subsystems where each credit officer corresponds to a separate subsystem, each having its own share of the total experience.
4. Fails to react well to changes in the composition and credit worthiness of the applicant population.	4. Over time, the emphasis placed on certain factors is not adjusted to reflect actual shifts in their importance. Furthermore, changes in the applicant population composition can significantly affect acceptance rates.
5. Inclusion of institutional guidelines that lack empirical verification.	5. Often, these guidelines have their foundation in traditional slogans which possesses some intuitive appeal.[a] Stereotyping of legal professions and other simple rules of thumb undoubtedly result in the loss of profitable accounts. Short of controlled research, the validity of institutional guidelines cannot be established.
6. Inability to quantify the risk associated with any given loan.	6. Percentage probabilities of default or repayment are not provided for individual applicant profiles or for groups of profiles.
7. Does not allow for a numerical statement of policy.	7. Although management may know the level of risk they are willing to operate at, they have no way to translate this information into an effective policy which can readily be enforced. Directives to credit officers such as "tighten up" or "loosen up" but do not convey policy in a precise quantitative fashion and are ambiguous.
8. Manual credit analysis is time consuming.	8. The process of gathering, verifying and evaluating information is lengthier than what is required with a credit scoring system. This results in higher operating costs and a lower volume of throughput than is possible with a scoring system.
9. Performance evaluation of the system is not available by applicants' initial profiles, rather it is typically the individual loan officer whose performance is monitored and reviewed.	9. In the absence of performance analysis, no feedback loop can exist, which hinders future development of better lending practices.
10. Incurs difficulty in assessing marginally acceptable cases.	10. Quantitative models can readily make "close calls" at the margin, because they translate relevant applicant information to an odds quote that either makes, or fails to make, the approval cutoff. If that cutoff value is, say, 200, then scoring systems can easily distinguish and approve applicants scoring 200 and are approved from those that score 199 and are declined.[b]

Figure 6.3 Weaknesses of A Judgmental System

[a]For example, the three "Bs": "Never lend to beauticians, bartenders, or barbers"; or the three "Ps": "Never lend to preachers, plumbers or prostitutes." Main, "A New Way to Score With Lenders," Money, Feb. 1977, p. 73; M. Irving, *The Bank Book* (1973) (suggesting other occupations as falling within the three "Ps").
[b]Any notion that judgmental systems are superior because they allow for "cherry picking" must be balanced by the fact that in the main stream of cases scoring systems will outperform them, and in special cases scoring systems do allow for various types of overrides, which we discuss later in this chapter.

Figure 6.4 displays the strengths of the judgmental system. The main advantages include interpretability and flexibility.

Credit-Scoring Systems

In this section, we present a brief overview of developments in credit-scoring systems and how they operate. For purpose of comparison, we also list associated strengths and weaknesses.

Overview of Typical Credit-Scoring Approaches

To date, credit-scoring models represent the most successful application of statistical modeling methods to assess consumer credit risk.[7] The main goal of credit scoring is to accurately predict which loans are likely to go bad. Credit-scoring systems seek to achieve this by maximizing the

Strength	Explanation
1. Each applicant is given specialized consideration in addition to being reviewed as to their general qualifications.	1. In this sense there really are no system overrides. However, if written policies are in place, then there may be exceptions to those policies.
(a) The approval decision is not based solely upon a predetermined set of factors as in the case of credit scoring. There is flexibility to give different weight to factors on a loan-by-loan basis. (b) Certain loans merit further study as may be determined by the loan officer during the course of his/her investigation.	(a) Applicants may be distinguished by their maturity relative to wealth accumulation, their safe and sound use of credit, etc. Mild delinquency, and other weaknesses, may have a good explanation, or may be considered inconsequential when viewed within a complete credit context. Additional items of information may be incorporated into the decision process. For example, the loan officer may wish to take the full customer relationships into account when evaluating a loan request, not just deposit relationship. (b) For factors such as bank references, where the applicant may indicate the existence of checking and savings accounts, the loan officer may wish to examine historical saving/spending patterns to assess the applicant's ability to pay. While debt ratios and cash flow analysis may indicate that sufficient funds are available, there may be other "hidden" sources of cash outflow.
2. Allows for specific reasons for decline as determined by the credit officer's analysis.	2. Isolation of deficiencies in the credit application is an integral part of judgmental credit analysis.
3. Loan approval criteria are logical and intuitive. Known causal relationships provide a basis for evaluation.	3. These criteria are based on sound lending principles, which make sense and can readily be explained.
4. Tailored to meet the needs of specific communities.	4. Local populations of credit applicants differ from regional samples. Demographics, economic conditions, standards and customs of living, local industry types, etc. All may vary to a greater or lesser extent.
5. Not solely dependent on the performance of customers granted credit in the past when determining the exact criterion and its relative weight in evaluating a specific loan. Can leverage on expert judgment that spans economic cycles and market conditions.	5. A credit scoring system's criterion and companion weights are determined using a sample of applicants which varies from being one to three (and sometimes five) years old at the time of system development. Avoids "noise in the data" that can influence quantitative methods.

FIGURE 6.4   STRENGTHS OF A JUDGMENTAL SYSTEM

7. There are numerous studies on this topic. See Mester, L. J., "What's the Point of Credit Scoring?" *Federal Reserve Bank of Philadelphia Business Review*, September/October 1997, pp. 3–16, for a quick review of credit scoring models on consumer and business lending.

divergence, or separation, between the score distributions of good and bad accounts. Within the general heading of credit scoring there are many different approaches utilized to arrive at a set of predictor variables and weights that allow the user to calculate the credit score for a credit application that relates mathematically to the odds that the credit will be repaid in a timely manner according to the terms of the loan agreement. "William R. Fair and Earl J. Isaac founded their company in 1956 ... to investigate the possibility of applying statistical methods to the field of consumer credit..."[8] Over time, they pioneered an information-theoretic approach using methods described by Solomon Kullback[9] to measure the information value of individual credit characteristics, and sets of credit characteristics, for predicting creditworthiness. By the mid-1970s, when one of the authors joined Fair, Isaac and Company, different scorecard development processes were being used to deal with situations where the scorecard was replacing a judgmental system, versus a credit-scoring system. This was necessitated by the fact that inferring the behavior of rejected credit applicants is a necessary part of building a statistically sound credit scoring system, and that task is made more difficult when there is less inconsistency in loan decisioning, such as when the system being replaced is credit scoring. Fair, Isaac and Company's variable weighting algorithm utilized nonlinear optimization techniques, and those methods have continued to evolve over time. The basic idea of optimization in credit underwriting is to adopt as an objective function a measure of the separation between creditworthy and noncreditworthy applicants[10] and then seek to maximize it over a sequence of iterations. There are many variations of optimization models for estimating creditworthiness. In one particular algorithm, each iteration corresponds to a change of one point in the value assigned to a particular response corresponding to a question on the credit application. When changes no longer result in an improvement, the process halts. Pitfalls include path dependency (the order in which variables are chosen or adjustments made to them can impact the final solution) and overfitting (model does not validate on a randomly chosen holdout sample).

Over time, approaches had to evolve to deal with the fact that system redevelopment, and post-credit scoring implementation posed increased difficulties due to a more consistent "no-experience" group of applicants. Kolesar and Showers developed a mathematical programming approach to credit screening.[11] Altman introduced a multiple discriminant analysis approach that includes the naïve Bayes model, which assigns a numerical weight to each category of a predictive variable and then computes a score for a new applicant by adding all weights over the variables.[12] As a credit management consultant in the 1970s, one of the authors encountered another approach that utilized univariate analysis to assess variable predictive content, correlation analysis to deal with multicollinearity and perform variable selection, and finally used regression to produce point values for the final scoring model. Yet another basic approach was to use a linear regression model to predict the probability of default based on a set of financial and demographic variables that have statistical explanatory power. There are some inherent weaknesses to these basic scoring

---

8. See Lewis, 1992, p. xii.

9. See Kullback, Solomon. *Information Theory and Statistics*, Dover, 1959, pp. 83–85, for a discussion of a Bayesian classification approach for assigning samples to one of several populations (in the credit case, creditworthy and non-creditworthy applicants), pp. 109–140 for a discussion of discrete estimation approach for multinomial samples, and pp. 189–207 for a discussion of the continuous analog for sampling from multivariate normal populations.

10. $D = [\mu_G - \mu_B]^2/(1/2)[\sigma_G^2 + \sigma_B^2]$, where σ_G, σ_B are the variances of the good and bad score distributions, respectively, and μ_G, μ_B are the means of the good and bad score distributions, respectively.

11. Kolesar, Peter, and Janet L. Showers. *A Robust Credit Screening Model Using Categorical Data*, *Management Science*, Vol. 31, No. 2, February 1985, pp. 123–133.

12. See Altman, E. I. "Financial Ratios, Discriminant Analysis and the Prediction of Corporate Bankruptcy." *Journal of Finance*, September 1968, pp. 589–609. Also see Hand, 2001, pp. 144–146, for a description of the naïve Bayes model for credit scoring.

approaches including data limitations and assumptions of properties of the sampled data and resulting score distributions including linearity, normality, symmetry, equal variance, and so on.[13]

In addition to those basic predictive tools, many other sophisticated mathematical and statistical models and tools have been developed to address credit risk from different perspectives over the past several years. Thomas, Edelman, and Crook described some new ways to build credit-scoring models including nontraditional statistical methods for credit scoring.[14] Those methods include ensemble models, indirect credit scoring, linear programming, integer programming, and neural networks, as well as nearest-neighbor and genetic algorithms. They also described how to use Markov chain probability models to infer consumer segment default behavior. Hand provided a comprehensive review of different qualitative prediction tools or approaches that are being used in modeling consumer credit risk. He discussed both traditional scorecard methods and some of the more recent developments, such as neural network and decision trees,[15] and typical performance measures for these prediction tools. It has been noted that neural networks are an advanced form of regression for modeling nuances and interactions, and may provide greater separation between the classes. However, this technique has been criticized for its complexity and inefficiency in computation, and difficulties in interpretation of the estimated coefficients. Decision trees offer some advantages in handling missing values and interpretation in credit scoring context and taking into consideration interactions between the variables. Astebro and colleagues explained three new modeling approaches: models segmenting the dynamics and level of the default losses, models exploiting conditional independence, and models similar to the reduced form and survival analysis approaches.[16] Additionally, survival analysis has been introduced into credit behavior scoring and loss estimation.[17] As markets continue to develop, we will continue to see more methods applied in new and innovative ways to this area. In Appendix 6A we explain how credit-scoring models are developed by way of a simple example of scorecard with two characteristics. Our aim is to enable the nontechnical reader, who is unfamiliar with the mechanics of credit scoring, to grasp the essentials.[18]

Operational Description

The two fundamental components to a scoring system are scorecard and cutoff score. The scorecard defines all of the various subclassifications within each category appearing on the scorecard, and points are assigned to each response on the credit application as it is classified. For credit bureau characteristics, the information is obtained from a credit report. After this process of classifying responses and recording point scores is completed, the individual scores for each characteristic are totaled and compared with a cutoff score. This cutoff score determines whether the application is accepted, rejected, or referred on to a review. Based on the results of the review, the application is approved or rejected. Figure 6.5 shows a scorecard that was typical in the days where scoring

---

13. See Allen, Linda. "Credit Risk Modeling of Middle Markets," working paper, Zicklin School of Business, Baruch College, CUNY, p. 7.
14. See Thomas, L. C., D. B. Edelman, and J. N. Crook. "Credit Scoring and Its Applications," SIAM Monographs on Mathematical Modeling and Computation, 2002, pp. 187–208.
15. Hand, 2001, pp. 139–155.
16. See Astebro, T., P. A. Beling, D. Hand, R. Oliver, and L. C. Thomas. Banff Credit Risk Conference Paper, October 11–16, 2003.
17. See Stepanova, M., and L. C. Thomas. "PHAB Scores, Proportional Hazards Analysis Behavioral Scores," *Journal of the Operational Research Society*, Vol. 52, pp. 1007–1016; Thomas, Edelman, and Crook, 2002, pp. 203–208; and Calem, Paul S., and Michael LaCoar-Little. "Risk-Based Capital Requirements for Mortgage Loans," *Journal of Banking and Finance*, 2004, pp. 647–672. See also Allison, Paul D., *Survival Analyzing using the SAS System: A Practical Guide*. SAS Institute Inc., 1995, for proportional hazard estimation using SAS procedures.
18. An in-depth discussion of how credit-scoring models are developed is outside the scope of this book. However, a recent treatment of the subject can guide interested readers through the process. See Siddiqi, Naeem. *Credit Risk Scorecards: Developing and Implementing Intelligent Credit Scoring*. John Wiley & Sons, 2006.

OWN/RENT	Owns Buying 21	Rents 15	Parents/All Other 15	Mobile Home 18		
TIME AT PRESENT ADDRESS	Under 1 year 10	1–2 years 17	2.01–4.5 yrs 15	4.51–8.5 years 14	8.51 Up 21	
YEARS ON JOB	Under 6 months 10	6 months–1.5 years 18	1.51–2.5 years 16	2.51–4 years 19	4.01 Up 25	
DEPT STORE/OIL CO/MAJOR CC	None 0	Any One 7	Any Two 9	All Three 18		
FINANCE CO. REFERENCES	None 1	One 5	Two or More 0			
CHECK/SAV ACCT	None 0	Checking Only 2	Savings Only 7	Both 12		
AGE OF AUTO	None 0	0–2 years 20	3 years 25	4 years 15	5 years or more 2	
DEBT-TO-INCOME RATIO	No Debts 50	1–5% 25	6–15% 15	16–25% 5	26% Up 25	
TYPE OF BORROWER	Former 15	Present 10	New 8			
WORST REFERENCE RATINGS (CREDIT BUREAU)	No File 0	Any Major Derogatory –120 One Excellent/Satisfactory 1	Any Minor Derogatory –10 2–4 Ex/Sat 10	5–Up Ex/Sat 15		

FIGURE 6.5   SCORECARD

relied primarily on application information and a credit bureau report was only ordered if it had the potential to make a difference in the credit decision. The concept of how a scorecard works is identical to that used today. The only difference is that the characteristics have changed to reflect greater emphasis of credit bureau information.

The acceptance cutoff score is determined in one of three ways with the aid of the statistical table in Figure 6.6. One strategy for setting the acceptance cutoff is to choose the credit score that corresponds to the mix of good and bad loans that will yield a net present value of zero (the breakeven point). Referring to Figure 6.6, we note that if the economic value of 30 good loans is offset by one bad loan, then an acceptance cutoff score of 201 would be assigned, which corresponds to good/bad odds of 30.5 to one.

Often, leverage and mix of business considerations force volume constraints, which may dictate the score at which the acceptance cutoff should be set. Again, referring to Figure 6.6, we see that, under the column labeled TOTAL POPULATION PCNT, an acceptance rate of 61 percent corresponds to a score of 220. Finally, under a growth strategy, management may undertake to maximize their approval rate while taking the same number of bad loans as the firm had been accepting under its previous system. Suppose that prior experience showed that 295 bad loans resulted from a 65 percent acceptance rate. Then Figure 6.6 forecasts that under our growth strategy, the acceptance cutoff score would be set at 197, resulting in an 80 percent acceptance rate.

Score Range	GOOD RISKS		BAD RISKS		TOTAL POPULATION		GOOD/ BAD
	NBR	PCNT	NBR	PCNT	NBR	PCNT	ODDS
276–280	243	2.6	1	0.1	244	2.4	372.5
...	...	...	...	...	...	...	...
223–225	5817	62.9	122	16.2	5939	59.4	47.5
220–222	5984	64.7	133	17.6	6117	61.2	45.0
217–219	6292	68.1	154	20.4	6446	64.5	40.9
214–216	6462	69.9	166	22.0	6629	66.3	38.9
211–213	6570	71.1	175	23.2	6745	67.4	37.6
208–210	6758	73.1	190	25.2	6948	69.5	35.6
206–207	6768	73.2	191	25.3	6959	69.6	35.4
204–205	6803	73.6	194	25.7	6997	70.0	35.1
203–203	6952	75.2	208	27.6	7160	71.6	33.4
202–202	7114	76.9	225	29.8	7339	73.4	31.7
201–201	7231	78.2	237	31.4	7468	74.7	30.5
200–200	7527	81.4	270	35.8	7797	78.0	27.9
199–199	7607	82.3	279	37.0	7886	78.9	27.3
198–198	7618	82.4	281	37.2	7889	79.0	27.2
197–197	7712	83.4	293	38.8	8005	80.0	26.4
196–196	7813	84.5	306	40.6	8119	81.2	25.5
194–195	8013	86.7	336	44.5	8349	83.5	23.9
192–193	8038	86.9	340	45.0	8337	83.8	23.7
190–191	8102	87.6	351	46.5	8453	84.5	23.1
187–189	8156	88.2	361	47.9	8517	85.2	22.6
184–186	8186	88.5	367	48.7	8553	85.5	22.3
...	...	...	...	...	...	...	...
150–155	9246	100.0	754	100.0	10000	100.0	12.3

FIGURE 6.6　DESCENDING CUMULATIVE SCORE DISTRIBUTIONS BY PERFORMANCE GROUP SPECIFYING SCORE ODDS RELATIONSHIP

Strengths and Weaknesses of Credit-Scoring System

Beginning in the 1980s, generic credit scores were developed based on credit bureau data. This expanded credit scoring coverage, with industry options added later for auto lending, credit card, mortgage, and small business lending. Some credit grantors adopted a dual-score strategy, wherein they used their own internal application factors for their custom score and covered the credit bureau history with the single credit bureau score. Approval for a loan, in these instances, required meeting a separate cutoff for each of the two scores. The strengths of credit scoring are outlined in Figure 6.7.

Before proceeding to discuss the weaknesses of credit-scoring systems, it is appropriate to consider the ways in which their effectiveness can diminish. Credit scorecards are designed to predict the "norm" based on historical performance and environmental factors that were prevailing at the time. As such, any deviations from the norm may diminish their effectiveness. Symptoms range

Strength	Explanation
1. Credit applications are evaluated uniformly and in a consistent manner.	1. The scorecard embodies a universal standard which reflects the credit grantor's past lending experience. The approval decision is taken out of the hands of the credit officer.
2. Reduction in application processing time.	2. The evaluation process has been reduced to a clerical function.
3. Reduction in delinquent accounts (increase in the number of satisfactory accounts).	3. In the long run, an empirically derived, statistically sound scoring system will out perform any judgmental system in identifying bad risks. This greater precision in risk assessment stems from the fact that a scoring system can associate a percentage probability of repayment with every loan application.
4. Management control over credit extension is greatly enhanced.	4. This results from having: (a) Standard approval criteria (b) A means of fine-tuning credit volume (c) A clean-cut means of expressing policy in quantitative terms
5. Better management reports.	5. Types of reports include: (a) End of month operational summaries: 　(i) branch activity 　(ii) regional activity 　(iii) organizational activity 　(iv) exception reports (b) Early warning report monitoring acceptee, reject, and applicant score distributions (c) Maturity tracking report (d) Delinquency reports giving year to date and inception to date figures
6. Better system performance measurement.	6. Scoring system users can check the accuracy of loss forecasts, determine if the composition of the applicant population has changed from that of the development sample, and monitor adherence to the acceptance cutoff score policy by field personnel.

FIGURE 6.7 STRENGTHS OF EARLY CREDIT-SCORING MODELS

from unpredicted increases or decreases in the volume of loans approved to rises in delinquency and charge-off rates. Variation in scoring system forecasts can be attributed to two root causes, namely: (1) the percentage of applicants having a specific score, or range of scores, changes (evidenced by a change in acceptance rate); and (2) the bad loan risk associated with a specific score, or range of scores, changes. This may or may not be evidenced by recent delinquency experience.

Recall that all applicants have a specific "profile" with respect to the characteristics on a system scorecard. Now, in either case above, these shifts may be associated with all profiles assigned to a specific score that is affected, or they may be associated with only some of the profiles assigned to that score. Bearing in mind the difference between applicant score and applicant profile, we proceed to examine the weaknesses of credit scoring in Figure 6.8.[19]

We recognize that some of the weaknesses attributed to credit scoring may be addressed by improving current practices relative to both its development and use. Instead, we focus on the strengths of credit scoring and judgmental methods to mold a new approach.

---

19. For a high-level overview of credit scoring system and its limitations, see also Mester, 1997.

Weakness	Explanation
1. Adjustment of a scoring system to accommodate changes in the composition of the applicant population is limited to making a change in the acceptance cutoff score.	1. The exact nature of these changes cannot be determined at the applicant profile level, except in a limited view through individual scorecard variables that may be examined taken one at a time.[b] Dual and three-way effects, or even higher multiway shifts, cannot be isolated.
2. Credit scoring systems may be invalidated by internal as well as environmental changes affecting the loan applicant population.	2. A basic premise of credit scoring is that future events will resemble events occurring anywhere from one to five years prior to system installation.
3. Adjustment of a scoring system to accommodate changes in the degree of risk associated with a given score range consists of either of the following actions: (a) Change the acceptance cutoff score. (b) Replace the scoring system.	3. Changes cannot be isolated at the applicant profile level. Changing the cutoff score is only appropriate in certain special circumstances.
4. Assessment of the impact of a change in acceptance policy.	4. Individual applicant profiles affected by such a change cannot be explicitly identified. For example, if the cut-off score is changed from 205 to 200, all that can be said is that profiles for applicants scoring in the range 201 to 205 are no longer acceptable, without really identifying what credit characteristics distinguish them. Thousands of different profiles are associated with an identical credit score. A credit score, by itself, does not identify anything specific about the applicant relative to any of the credit factors that make it up.
5. The policy embodied in a scorecard is statistically, not logically, based. Credit scoring systems model the performance of borrowers without analyzing the reasons for their performance. The existence of causal linkages is neither assumed nor investigated.	5. In manual scoring days, irrational-looking point criteria on a scorecard put the credit granting institution in an unfavorable light with both the public, who were judged by the criteria, as well as their own operations staff, who oftentimes tried to second-guess the system. Even in an automated-scoring environment, the lack of intuitive sensibility of a scorecard can cause management, and regulators, concern. A philosophy of accepting a model based on predictive strength alone can pose unanticipated risks, including failure to distinguish transitional performance patterns or to anticipate long-lasting effects attributable to "late-breaking" developments. So-called "predictive variables" may not have any real "causal linkage" to the creditworthiness of borrowers, and, in fact, may adversely impact protected classes of applicants. Transitional performance patterns can be caused by an illness, injury, divorce, or temporary unemployment.

FIGURE 6.8 WEAKNESSES OF CREDIT-SCORING SYSTEM[a]

[a]See also Mester (1997) for a high level overview of credit scoring system and its limitations.
[b]This is commonly referred to as a characteristic analysis.
[c]El Boghdady, Dena, "Lenders Put Great Store in Credit Score—A Bit of Advice for Mortgage Seekers," *Washington Post*, appeared in *Raleigh News & Observer*, Sunday, January 28, 2007. In the Credit Myths Section, "Myth 4: If you have a good FICO score, one late payment won't hurt. Fact: A first-time delinquency can drag down your score by at least 100 points." The credit scores used by credit bureaus are scaled so that 20 points approximately doubles the odds, so 100 points equates to $2^5 = 32$ times the risk of default simply due to one late payment!

Weakness	Explanation
6. Only the performance of customers granted credit in the past is available for analysis. The premise is that consistency is synonymous with objectivity. Unfortunately, what can evolve is a system that is "consistently unfair!"	6. As a result, samples are naturally biased to a greater or lesser extent depending upon past loan approval criteria. Reject inference can correct for a portion of this bias, but by no means all of it. The residual bias is perpetuated by credit scoring in a very consistent manner. The impact of that bias may be disproportionately felt by millions of credit applicants that fall outside of the mainstream.
7. The incidence of even mild delinquency can have a significantly disproportionate impact on model estimates of default odds. As a result, the scoring model overstates the risk associated with one late payment.[c]	7. In credit scoring system development, a common practice is to exclude observations associated with borrowers that have exhibited *indeterminate behavior* (i.e., behavior that is insufficient to be classified as "good" but not severe enough to be labeled as "bad"). This can lead to the elimination of a significant proportion of the observations. Furthermore, if "good" observations have little or no delinquency, then the incidence of even mild delinquency could greatly increase the estimated probability of becoming "bad."
8. Credit applicants having identical scores will perform the same way, despite the fact that they may fall into different consumer segments that are not considered explicitly in the scoring system.	8. Credit applicants scored by the identical scorecard may differ significantly in their circumstances, their goals and priorities, their lifestyle choices and the sacrifices they are prepared to make to create some measure of wealth and a better life.
9. Automatic universal default trigger.	9. The lending practice of changing the terms of a loan from the normal to default rates by a lender when borrowers have missed payments with another lender, despite good payment records. This could worsen the situation and damage the customer relationship. In contrast, judgmental system can consider specifics involved and avoid charging the customer if they are having other problems.
10. Identical weight is given to factors in every applicant segment, resulting in consistency that has the effect of overstating the risk for some segments, while understating it for others.	10. Applicants are not distinguished at system development time by their maturity relative to wealth accumulation, their safe and sound use of credit, etc. If an applicant has used credit for 30 years and has repaid obligations as agreed and has had steadily increasing net worth, then the likelihood of default associated with a 30 day late payment, or an above threshold number of credit inquiries, is different than that for a recent college graduate or someone with a blemished credit history. By pooling all applicants together, the resulting scorecard will likely underpenalize the more risky applicants and overpenalize the good credit applicants. This can result in significant fluctuations in credit scores among creditworthy applicants that can unnecessarily put a higher cost on their transactions due to their lower credit score.

FIGURE 6.8   (*continued*)

Traditional Underwriting Criteria

Earlier in this chapter, we noted that loan approval and pricing criteria may vary substantially by product. There are many reasons for this. The distinction between consumer lending and small business lending is fairly straightforward, since business and individuals possess many differing attributes. Unsecured credit differs from secured lending, where an important consideration is the amount of equity the borrower has at stake in the transaction, which is usually captured by a loan-to-value ratio (LTV). This is fairly straightforward for a home purchase mortgage (e.g., LTV) and may be defined as the requested mortgage amount divided by the lesser of the sales price and the property's appraised value. Typical guidelines for this ratio vary by product, and additional processing is performed in situations where the LTV exceeds 80 percent, where mortgage insurance may be required.

LTV is a good example of a primary factor that interacts with other aspects of the transaction. For example, if other primary factors are marginal, or if the loan amount falls into a high tier, then a low value for the LTV will strengthen the borrower's chances of approval. In the case of home equity lending there is the added twist of whether the value used in the calculation is based on the property appraisal preimprovement, or after improvements are made. This has implications for fair lending disparate treatment testing, because this distinction can be significant, depending on the nature of the improvements and associated anticipated change in property value. Separate models may be developed to control for the possible effect of how LTV is calculated on tests for disparate treatment in underwriting.

Figures 6.9 and 6.10 provide a sampling of commonly encountered underwriting factors for seven categories of loans that represent lines of business. In practice, there is considerable more granularity than portrayed and there are variances in criteria within a particular line of business (e.g., home purchase versus refinancing within the mortgage category). A large bank may have hundreds of credit-scoring models that cover consumer and small business lending. Common segmentation schemes drive off of geographic splits (regional or state), channel,[20] programs and product tiers (classic, gold, platinum credit cards; a multitude of different mortgage products and programs with differing underwriting standards and criteria thresholds), property and collateral types and attributes (e.g., conventional single family dwellings versus mobile homes, new versus used autos, motorcycles, boats), and so on. For simplicity, we consider aggregate models; in practice, credit underwriting is more specific to the credit offering and marketplace.

These are by no means exhaustive lists! An immediate question that arises is "How does one determine which factors are primary and which ones are secondary in importance?" The answer is that an in-depth understanding of the business problem is achieved through rigorous analysis and discussions among expert practitioners. In the case of credit scoring, all candidate variables are evaluated at development time, with no prior notion of which ones will have greater weight in the final scorecard. Hence, scoring represents more of a pure data-driven approach and certainly has the appeal of apparent objectivity. In the case of hybrid models, the model consensus session (MCS) would be the primary mechanism for assigning variables to primary and secondary categories. This is covered in the next section.

A core argument against judgment was that a scoring model could consider many more recent cases of good and bad credits than any individual loan officer. Loan officers were challenged to decision ten loans of known performance, but unknown to the loan officers making the approve/decline decision. Then a credit scorecard, developed on a historical pool of good, bad, and rejected loans, was used to score the same loans, and a cutoff score was used that reflected the current acceptance rate, or maximum acceptable odds of default. Anecdotally, nine times out of ten, the scorecard beat the loan officer on identifying bad credits.

Back to the notion that credit scoring affords greater objectivity. While this may be true if one limits one's criteria to those found in the scorecard, the argument loses clarity when one questions the scope of information considered for the scoring model, or when data that the model is expecting is unavailable. Also, a significant amount of discretion is used during scorecard development. It is those discretionary aspects, not the mathematical underpinnings or scoring algorithms, that would likely benefit the most from a thorough vetting among all constituencies. They include sampling

---

20. For example, for credit card there are branch applications, direct mail pre-approvals, and call center originated, affinity/reward-based, business card; for mortgage there are branch, private banking, call center, internet, broker, and correspondent-based applications; for auto lending there are branch, call center, internet, and dealer-sourced applications.

Factors	Portfolios						
	Direct Auto	Indirect Auto	Credit Card	Home Equity	Mortgage	Other Secured IL	Small Business
Credit history	P	P	P	P	P	P	P
Credit bureau score	P	P	P	P	P	S	S
Debt-to-income ratio	P	P	P	P	P	P	S
Payment-to-income	S	P	S	n/a	n/a	n/a	n/a
Loan-to-value	P	S	n/a	P	P	P	n/a
Payment shock	n/a	n/a	n/a	n/a	S	n/a	n/a
Credit limit/Mo. Inc.	n/a	n/a	S	n/a	n/a	n/a	n/a
Net worth	n/a	n/a	n/a	n/a	S	n/a	S
Liquidity	S	S	S	S	S	P	P
Months of reserves	n/a	n/a	n/a	n/a	S	n/a	n/a
Employment stability	S	S	S	S	S	S	S
Housing ratio	n/a	n/a	n/a	S	S	n/a	n/a
(Trade in + cash)/price	P	P	n/a	n/a	n/a	n/a	n/a
Co-app bureau score	S	S	S	n/a	n/a	S	n/a
Loan term	P	S	n/a	S	S	S	S
Custom credit score	P	P	P	P, n/a	P	P	P
Years in profession	S	S	S	S	S	S	S
Residence stability	S	S	S	n/a	n/a	S	n/a
Deposit relationship	S	S	S	S	S	S	S
Prior loan experience	S	S	S	S	S	S	S
Age of vehicle	S	P	n/a	n/a	n/a	n/a	n/a
Loan amount	S	S	S	S	S	S	S
Owner-occupancy	n/a	n/a	n/a	S	S	n/a	n/a
Add-ons-to-unpaid bal.	n/a	S	n/a	n/a	n/a	n/a	n/a
Income tier	n/a	n/a	S	n/a	n/a	S	n/a
Financial performance tier/trend	n/a	n/a	n/a	n/a	n/a	n/a	P
Quick ratio	n/a	n/a	n/a	n/a	n/a	n/a	S
Current ratio	n/a	n/a	n/a	n/a	n/a	n/a	S
Working capital	n/a	n/a	n/a	n/a	n/a	n/a	S
Debt/net worth ratio	n/a	n/a	n/a	n/a	n/a	n/a	S
Return on assets	n/a	n/a	n/a	n/a	n/a	n/a	S
A/R inv AP turn	n/a	n/a	n/a	n/a	n/a	n/a	S
Receivables aging	n/a	n/a	n/a	n/a	n/a	n/a	S
Management quality	n/a	n/a	n/a	n/a	n/a	n/a	P

FIGURE 6.9 TRADITIONAL DECISION VARIABLES AND THEIR IMPORTANCE

Importance: P, primary; S, secondary; n/a, not applicable.

Factors	Direct Auto	Indirect Auto	Credit Card	Home Equity	Mortgage	Other Secured IL	Small Business
	Portfolios						
Industry	n/a	n/a	n/a	n/a	n/a	n/a	P
Life ins./credit life ins.	S	S	S	S	S	S	S
Geographic concentration	n/a	n/a	n/a	n/a	n/a	n/a	P
Market diversity	n/a	n/a	n/a	n/a	n/a	n/a	P
Type of ownership	n/a	n/a	n/a	n/a	n/a	n/a	S
Disability ins.	S	S	S	S	S	S	S
Prof. ins./bonding	n/a	n/a	n/a	n/a	n/a	n/a	S
LTV below threshold	S	S	n/a	S	S	S	n/a
Strong co-applicant	S	S	S	S	S	S	S
Savings pattern	n/a	n/a	n/a	S	S	S	n/a
Cash flow analysis	n/a	n/a	n/a	n/a	S	n/a	S
Relationship	S	S	S	S	S	S	P
Diversification of customer base	n/a	n/a	n/a	n/a	n/a	n/a	S
Education	n/a	n/a	S	S	n/a	n/a	S
Own/rent	S	S	S	n/a	n/a	S	S

FIGURE 6.9   (continued)

window and criteria, population performance definitions,[21] scope of data and choice of variables, order in which variables are allowed to come into the scorecard,[22] palatability considerations for variables,[23] and handling of missing data.[24] Any variation in those and other discretionary aspects may result in significantly different scorecards, meaning, not only different point assignments by attributes, but also different factors. For example, using the same data, you may have eight factors on both scorecards A and B, but only four of them are common. For credit applicants falling close

---

21. For example, exclusion, inactive, indeterminate, bad, and good performance groups.
22. This can determine what is/is not included in the model. While correlation makes this more of a nonissue from the standpoint of distinguishing goods and bads, it may have a disproportionately unfavorable impact on a protected class. Put another way, there exists a family of scorecards that achieve virtually the same predictive ability for default and identical ranking of risk among credit applications, but that differ in their impact on various population segments. The effects test in Regulation B is a special case, where one must demonstrate the existence of an alternative credit approval system that has less of a disparate impact on a protected class and also predicts creditworthiness with equal or greater success than the scoring system in use by the lending institution. See Hsia, David. "Credit Scoring and the Equal Credit Opportunity Act," *Hastings Law Journal*, Vol. 30, No. 2, September 1978, p. 418, and a consideration of the practical hurdles to making a successful application of the effects test are discussed on pages 421–422.
23. (1) Dealing with nonintuitive patterns, such as reversals on years on job, years at address, years in profession, etc.; new trends in information value or weight of evidence that are not in step with the status quo or intuition and (2) dealing with variables that will be more costly or a hassle to deal with, such as income, because it is inflation bound, etc.; housing ratio payment shock in cases where there are three to four mortgage co-applicants.
24. (1) Failure to include observations with missing data can bias the development sample; (2) assigning no-information "neutral" points for variables with missing values implies the approval decision will be based on a more restricted set of variables, rather than substituting a proxy or considering secondary factors; (3) conditional structure among variables is not exploited and interactions among them are not explicitly considered.

Factors	Portfolios						
	Direct Auto	Indirect Auto	Credit Card	Home Equity	Mortgage	Other Secured IL	Small Business
# Tradelines	S	S	S	S	S	S	S
# New recent tradelines	S	S	S	S	S	S	S
# Satisfactory ratings	S	S	S	S	S	S	S
% Satisfactory trades	S	S	S	S	S	S	S
# 30-day late revolving	S	S	P	S	S	S	S
# 30-day late installment	P	P	P	S	S	S	S
# 30-day late mortgage	P	P	P	P	P	P	P
Total # 30-day late	S	S	S	S	S	S	S
# 60-day late revolving	S	S	P	S	S	S	S
# 60-day late installment	P	P	P	S	S	S	S
# 60-day late mortgage	P	P	P	P	P	P	P
Total # 60-day late	S	S	P	S	S	S	S
# 90-day late revolving	S	S	P	S	S	S	S
# 90-day late installment	P	P	P	P	P	P	P
# 90-day late mortgage	P	P	P	P	P	P	P
Total # 90-day late	P	P	P	P	P	P	P
# Open trades by type	S	S	P	S	S	S	S
# Liens or judgments	P	P	P	P	P	P	P
# Foreclosures or repos	P	P	P	P	P	P	P
Bankruptcy last 5 years	P	P	P	P	P	P	P
# Derog items	P	P	P	P	P	P	P
# Current past dues	P	P	P	P	P	P	P
Ratio sat/tot trades	P	P	S	S	S	S	S
# Inquiries < 6 mos	S	S	P	S	S	S	S
# Inquiries < 12 mos	S	S	P	S	S	S	S
Ratio of bal/cred lmt	S	S	P	S	S	P	S
Age of oldest trade	S	S	S	S	S	S	S
# Collections > $X	S	S	S	S	S	S	S
# Derog > $X	S	S	S	S	S	S	S
Condition on last 12 mos	S	S	S	S	S	S	S
Condition on last 24 mos	S	S	S	S	S	S	S
Ratio of type/tot trades	S	S	S	S	S	S	S
Prev ratios by type trd	S	S	S	S	S	S	S

FIGURE 6.10   COMMON CREDIT BUREAU DECISION VARIABLES AND THEIR IMPORTANCE

Importance: P, primary; S, secondary; n/a, not applicable.

Factors	Portfolios						
	Direct Auto	Indirect Auto	Credit Card	Home Equity	Mortgage	Other Secured IL	Small Business
Depth of credit file	P	P	P	P	P	P	P
Ratio of install/tot trds	P	P	S	S	S	P	S
Ratio of rev/tot trds	S	S	P	S	S	S	S
Revolving tot utilization	S	S	P	S	S	S	S
Total major derogs	P	P	P	P	P	P	P
Ratio nondelinq/tot trd	P	P	P	P	P	P	P
Mos since last past due	P	P	P	P	P	P	P

FIGURE 6.10   (continued)

to the cutoff odds (assume the same odds for both scorecards), we observe that some applicants are approved using one scorecard but denied on the other.

Hybrid Systems

Hybrid systems integrate statistically based criteria with business rules, in light of the organization's objectives and goals. Operationally, they may take many forms. What is presented here is one particular type of system whose structure lends itself naturally to tap the strengths of the two previously discussed approaches, while minimizing the weaknesses associated with credit scoring that were detailed earlier. We use the terminology risk evaluation and policy formulation system (REPFS) for this particular hybrid model form.

The flexibility afforded by a hybrid system is especially important when new products, new markets, and new channels, or any combination of them, are present. In that regard, two especially important aspects of hybrid models are:

1. Initial model criteria and weights may be estimated or judgmentally determined. Judgmental determination may be justifiable when data simply does not exist, or there is no modeling experience to quantify the relationship between known sociological, demographic, geo-economic, investment, or legislative factors and actual loan performance. For example, post Katrina, the underwriting criteria for small business loans in New Orleans and other affected communities might benefit from this approach.

2. Hybrid models are adaptive (i.e., relationships among model factors, and their linkage to performance, can be monitored, quantified, and updated continuously over their life). This helps them to maintain their predictive power and stay in step with changes in consumer segments. Specifically, initial risk estimates based on the development sample are augmented with actual performance information and the performance window can be fixed or rolling. For example, if the development sample is an accumulation of five years of experience, the model estimates could drop the oldest month in the five-year window as each new month is added. Another scheme would involve saving and using all historical data, with or without weighting.

Before describing the form of the hybrid system and their applications in detail, we briefly outline how they are developed.

HYBRID SYSTEM CONSTRUCTION

Hybrid systems have roots in quantitative analysis and their construction has close parallels to credit scoring development.[25] In this section, we describe the hybrid system development process. We note that some similar concerns and processes are involved that are present in scorecard development. A schematic of the hybrid system development process appears in Figure 6.11.

Our focus here is on the modeling methodology, and that is where the process described begins (Phase 1). The first step in system construction is to conduct meetings with all of the appropriate stakeholders and participants in the lending process. The purpose of these sessions is to identify automated and paper data and business rule sources, primary and secondary factors in the lending decision, and to gain a complete understanding of credit policies for the loan product in question. If the current system in place is scorecard driven, the scorecard factors and their predictive performance should also be gleaned from these meetings.

It is important to determine whether a family of systems, or segmentation, is required. This can occur based on policy, legal, product, program, organizational, channel, customer, geographic, or

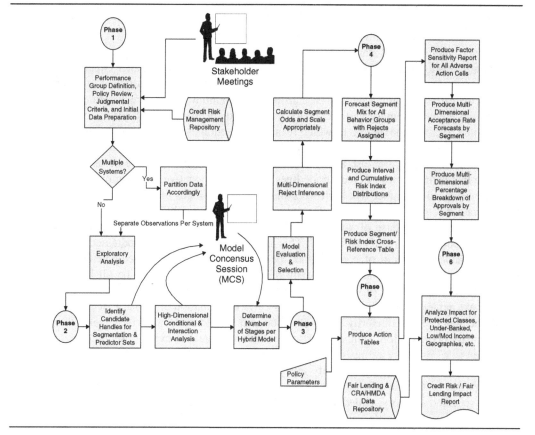

FIGURE 6.11 HYBRID SYSTEM DEVELOPMENT PROCESS

---

25. See Siddiqi, 2006, pp. 11–17, for a description of the persona involved and a complete treatment of the scorecard development process, which emphasizes that the exercise is a collaboration between a number of different personas.

market factors. For example, in mortgage lending, different systems may be required for refinance, home purchase, and home improvement loans. Channel and region can also be important factors. Programs tailored for specific segments, such as first-time home buyers, may also merit a separate system.

Once the scope of loans for a specific hybrid system are determined, the data are analyzed and initial *candidate handles* are formulated, using insight gained from the initial meetings with stakeholders (Phase 2). Choice of predictor variables can be considered from perspectives that encompass conditional relationships between risk factors, envision policy variables that are customized to leverage on alternative data and dynamically reweighted when indicated, and recognize that two underwriting systems that are equivalent relative to credit risk prediction can vary in fair lending and community reinvestment performance. During an MCS, the primary factors are determined, and an exhaustive enumeration of combinations is considered in a model facilitation session with line and policy staff. This process drives out how many stages will be required.

At that point, model evaluation and selection is performed (Phase 3). This is an important part of the system construction process. It is where the model is fitted to the basic handle structure. We have found that this can be best accomplished via a structural modeling of credit data.[26] Credit data are complicated by the number and interrelationships of the many factors that come into play in credit-related activities such as underwriting, pricing, and marketing. The structural model is a mathematical representation that provides parameters that allow for interpretation and deep understanding of the particular activity and its associated data. Structural models in this context are developed under the assumption that the group of subject matter experts can identify the primary and secondary factors, and their conditional relationships, sufficient to specify a base model. There are two main drawbacks to substituting data mining, and pure quantitative techniques for MCS to identify primary and secondary factors and specify a model. First is the reliance on the sampled data and the degree to which it may not accurately represent observations from new and emerging populations, such as predominantly noncredit transactors seeking loans. Second is the concern that simply because a factor has predictive strength, it should be used. An example might be that certain types of credit trade lines may have a negative connotation because they are typically accessed by higher risk borrowers and their sales offices may be typically found in low- to moderate-income neighborhoods. If a particular borrower established credit with one of those trade lines because of ease of access, then they could be penalized by the model even if they paid their obligation perfectly as agreed. This second concern could be addressed by designating certain variable to be "out of bounds," but the reality is that model development typically only excludes factors that have been specifically designated by regulators to be off-limits (e.g., ZIP code of residence, because of a direct correlation to a prohibited factor, such as applicant race).

The base model identified earlier enumerates every combination of primary factors, and whether or not the applicant satisfactorily meets all associated secondary factor requirements that apply to their primary classification. Hence, the structural model classifies every observation into one and only one of "n" mutually exclusive and exhaustive risk-homogenous handle cells.

Once we have the ability to classify every observation, we then want to know the likelihood of occurrence of the classification (i.e., the odds that a randomly chosen observation will fall into the specified category, called a *handle cell*). We also want to know the degree of credit risk to associate with the handle cell. For these purposes, and for the case of credit approval, it is important to reconstruct the credit applicant population coming "through the door" of the lender, and we will outline shortly, in general terms, how that is done. Essentially, observations of good, bad, and rejected credit applicants are classified into their respective handle cell and structural

---

26. Bishop, Yvonne M., Stephen E. Fienberg, and Paul W. Holland. *Discrete Multivariate Analysis: Theory and Practice*. MIT Press, 1975, pp. 42–48, on models for four or more dimensions, and pp. 57–122 on maximum likelihood estimation and model fitting.

models are developed for each one. The MCS in Phase 2 specifies the dimensions that make up the handle and also the sufficient conditions in order to render an outcome in handle cells requiring evaluation of secondary factors.[27] What remains in order to specify the structural model is to derive the expected handle cell counts m_θ (where θ represents the handle subscripts) for the good, bad, and rejected credit applicants. This is done using maximum likelihood estimation techniques. In some instances, direct (closed form) estimates for the expected cell counts are possible, but in other cases iterative methods must be used. A more in-depth discussion here would require the development of statistical concepts used in the process, such as the notion of a sufficient statistic,[28] minimal sufficiency,[29] model comprehensiveness, hierarchical models, nonelementary cells, configurations, and minimally sufficient configurations.[30] We will not burden the reader with those more theoretical details. Instead, we proceed to consider some simple examples to illustrate the nature of structural models, and then we complete our coverage of the remaining steps in Phase 3 of the hybrid model development process.

In the simplest case, suppose the credit-granting system had only one predictor, namely, high debt ratio, with possible values of "yes" and "no" depending on whether the credit applicant had a debt ratio less than or equal to 36 percent, respectively. In this case there are two cells in the handle, as shown in Figure 6.12.

Bringing the known outcomes into this framework, we have the 2-by-2 table of frequencies in Figure 6.13,

Where:

p_{11} = the frequency of credit applicants having a high debt ratio in the bad group
p_{12} = the frequency of credit applicants not having a high debt ratio in the bad group

High debt ratio	1. Yes	2. No

FIGURE 6.12 HANDLE CORRESPONDING TO A ONE-FACTOR STRUCTURAL MODEL

High debt ratio	1. Yes	2. No	Totals
Outcome			
1. Bad	p_{11}	p_{12}	p_{1+}
2. Good	p_{21}	p_{22}	p_{2+}
Totals	p_{+1}	p_{+2}	1.00

FIGURE 6.13 SIMPLE FOURFOLD TABLE OF HANDLE FREQUENCIES FOR GOOD AND BAD GROUPS

27. Secondary factors may be represented by a single indicator variable relating to any number of business rules that are sufficient to qualify a borrower for a loan, provided that one or more rules are satisfied. This may include rules that relax thresholds on primary factors. For example, if the DTI threshold is 40% for the primary factor, a secondary factor rule may allow up to a 50% value for DTI, provided that certain conditions are met. In other words, primary factors may reappear as one or more secondary factors at varying thresholds. The same principle applies to override analysis as shown in Figure 6.45.
28. Mood, Alenander M., Franklin A. Graybill, and Duane C. Boes. *Introduction to the Theory of Statistics*, McGraw-Hill Series in Probability and Statistics, 1974, pp. 299–307.
29. Mood, Graybill, and Boes, pp. 311–312.
30. See Mood, Graybill, and Boes, pp. 64–84, for a discussion of how to derive sufficient statistics, theorems dealing with the existence of direct estimates (complete with proofs), maximum likelihood estimation, and iterative proportional fitting of log-linear models.

p_{21} = the frequency of credit applicants having a high debt ratio in the good group
p_{22} = the frequency of credit applicants not having a high debt ratio in the good group
p_{+1} = the frequency of credit applicants having a high debt ratio
p_{12} = the frequency of credit applicants not having a high debt ratio
p_{1+} = the frequency of bad credit applicants
p_{2+} = the frequency of good credit applicants

It turns out that the structure of the relationships in Figure 6.13 is completely specified by p_{1+} and p_{+1} and the cross product ratio $\alpha = (p_{11} * p_{22})/(p_{12} * p_{21})$.[31] Also known as the "odds ratio," the interpretation of α in our credit example is as follows: The odds that you have a debt ratio greater than 36 percent, given that you have a bad credit risk, is p_{11}/p_{12}. The odds that you have a debt ratio greater than 36 percent, given that you have a good credit risk, is p_{21}/p_{22}. Then α is the ratio of these odds (i.e., $\alpha = (p_{11}/p_{12})/(p_{21}/p_{22}) = (p_{11} * p_{22})/(p_{12} * p_{21})$). Let us look at a specific example shown in Figures 6.14 and 6.15.

Suppose in this example that the odds in the general population of being a good versus bad credit risk are 9 to 1 and suppose for this example that we do not have to contend with rejects. Then we multiply the first row in Figure 6.15 by (0.1) and we multiply the second row by (0.9) with the result shown in Figure 6.16.

An odds ratio of 1.0 would imply that high debt ratio and outcome are independent. In this example, the odds ratio (α) is calculated to be $(.0944)(.540)/(.360)(.0056) = 0.050976/0.002016 = 25.286$. This means that the rate of having a high debt ratio is approximately 21 times higher among bad credit risks compared with good credit risks.

We can extend this simple model to one that is linear in the logarithmic scale. This log-linear model is analogous to the analysis of variance (ANOVA) models, and it can be used to express a

High debt ratio	1. Yes	2. No	Totals
Outcome			
1. Bad	1,400	100	1,500
2. Good	600	900	1,500
Totals	2,000	1,000	3,000

FIGURE 6.14   CREDIT EXAMPLE OF SIMPLE FOURFOLD TABLE OF SAMPLE COUNTS STRATIFIED ON GOOD/BAD

High debt ratio	1. Yes	2. No	Totals
Outcome			
1. Bad	0.944	0.056	1.00
2. Good	0.400	0.600	1.00
Totals	1.344	0.656	2.00

FIGURE 6.15   CREDIT EXAMPLE OF SIMPLE FOURFOLD TABLE OF RAW FREQUENCIES STRATIFIED ON GOOD/BAD

---

31. Bishop, Fienberg, and Holland, p. 13. In addition to the cross-product ratio, there are four other functions of probabilities in the table that, like the cross product ratio, are sufficient for complete specification of the table. The reason for choosing the cross product ratio is due to properties that it alone possesses, as discussed on pp.14–15.

High debt ratio	1. Yes	2. No	Totals
Outcome			
1. Bad	0.0944	0.0056	0.100
2. Good	0.360	0.540	0.900
Totals	0.4544	0.5456	1.00

FIGURE 6.16 CREDIT EXAMPLE OF ESTIMATED FREQUENCIES ASSUMING 9-TO-1 ODDS OF GOOD/BAD

High debt ratio	1. Good performance	2. Bad performance
1. No	300	100
2. Yes	150	50

FIGURE 6.17 CREDIT EXAMPLE OF ESTIMATED FREQUENCIES ASSUMING 9-TO-1 ODDS OF GOOD/BAD

structural model for our simple table of frequencies as follows:[32]

$$\log p_{ij} = u + u_{1(i)} + u_{2(j)} + u_{12(ij)}, \quad \text{for i = 1, 2 and j = 1, 2,} \qquad (6.1)$$

where: $u = $ the grand mean of the logarithm of the frequencies $\sum_{ij} [(\log p_{ij})/4]$

$$u_{1(i)} = \tfrac{1}{2}[\log p_{i1} + \log p_{i2}] - \tfrac{1}{4}[\sum_{ij} [(\log p_{ij})] \text{ for i = 1, 2}$$

$$u_{2(j)} = \tfrac{1}{2}[\log p_{1j} + \log p_{2j}] - \tfrac{1}{4}[\sum_{ij} [(\log p_{ij})] \text{ for j = 1, 2}$$

and $u_{12(ij)}$ is an interaction term that is absent when variables 1 and 2 are independent

$$u_{12(ij)} = \log p_{ij} - \tfrac{1}{2}[\log p_{i1} + \log p_{i2}] - \tfrac{1}{2}[\log p_{1j} + \log p_{2j}] + \tfrac{1}{4}[\sum_{ij} [(\log p_{ij})]$$

Note that: $u_{12(11)} = -u_{12(12)} = -u_{12(21)} = u_{12(22)}$

The ANOVA analogy would be that u is the "grand mean," $u_{1(i)}$ and $u_{2(j)}$ are "main effects" and $u_{12(ij)}$ is the "interaction term." In these examples we have operated with a table of probabilities that sum to one. With a little algebra, it can be shown that the structural model for the corresponding expected counts $\{m_{ij}\}$ that sum to "N" is identical to the structure of the probabilities except for a constant term equal to log N. In other words, we have that if $\sum_{ij} m_{ij} = N$ then $m_{ij} = Np_{ij}$. And so we have that:

$$\text{Log } m_{ij} = \log[Np_{ij}] = \log N + \log p_{ij} = (u + \log N) + (u_{1(i)} + u_{2(i)} + u_{12(ij)}) \qquad (6.2)$$

and hence the odds ratio α can be defined as the cross product of expected counts instead of probabilities.[33] We provide a simple example (see Figure 6.17), again to drive home the concepts.

Here:

$u = $ the grand mean of the logarithm of the frequencies $= \sum_{ij} [(\log p_{ij})/4] = 600/4 = 150$

$$u_{1(1)} = \tfrac{1}{2}[300 + 100] - 150 = +50; \quad u_{1(2)} = \tfrac{1}{2}[150 + 50] - 150 = -50$$

---

32. Ibid., p. 17.
33. Ibid., p. 19. The interested reader is encouraged to read further in the text through pp. 42–45 for an explanation of how the simple dichotomous variable model can be generalized to four or more dimensions.

$$u_{2(1)} = \tfrac{1}{2}[300 + 150] - 150 = +75; \quad u_{2(2)} = \tfrac{1}{2}[100 + 50] - 150 = -75$$

$$u_{12(11)} = [300 - 50 - 75 - 150] = +25; \quad u_{12(12)} = [100 - 50 + 75 - 150] = -25$$

$$u_{12(21)} = [150 + 50 - 75 - 150] = -25; \quad u_{12(22)} = [50 + 50 + 75 - 150] = +25$$

Given u, $u_{1(1)}$, $u_{2(1)}$, and $u_{12(11)}$ the remaining five parameters can be determined. The simple 2-by-2 table of counts is characterized by four independent parameters. This model is termed a *saturated model* since the number of parameters equals the number of cells in the table. Saturated models can represent the table of counts exactly. There is a connection between log-linear representations and the logistic regression model described in Chapter 5.[34]

Log-linear models allow you to test individual interactions among combinations of credit factors for significance, conditional on the presence of other known effects, via a partitioned likelihood ratio test statistic.[35] Beyond the summary of goodness of fit, individual cell residuals can be examined in the hybrid models. This is important to identify poorly fit cells, even when the overall model fit is good, and to identify patterns in the signs of the action table cell deviations that might indicate the presence of a superior model. Residuals and model parameters can be standardized for this purpose.

Log-linear models are fit to observed credit data for good, bad, and reject populations individually in order to construct structural models for those groups.[36] These models specify the final estimated counts as functions of a set of parameters that correspond to the various individual predictor dimensions (called main effects) as well as the multiway interactions among the predictor dimensions. Consider a one-stage system having six dimensions as described earlier in this chapter. Let the indices 1, 2, 3, 4, 5, and 6 correspond to these dimensions, and let θ (theta) represent the index set, which is comprised of just these indices. Let (θ) denote the power set of θ (this is the set of all possible combinations of the indices taken one at a time, two at a time, three at a time, ..., up to six at a time). Let $M_1\theta$, $M_2\theta$, and $M_3\theta$ denote, respectively, the final estimated cell counts for the (i, j, k, l, m, n) cell for the good, bad, and unknown behavior groups, respectively. Then the structural models previously referred to are of the form:

$$M_{1(\theta)} = \exp\left[\mu_1 + \sum_{i \in I} u_{1i}(\theta)\right], I \subseteq P(\theta); \tag{6.3}$$

wherein "I" is a subset of the power set of "θ"

$$M_{2(\theta)} = \exp\left[\mu_2 + \sum_{j \in J} u_{2j}(\theta)\right], J \subseteq P(\theta) \tag{6.4}$$

$$M_{3(\theta)} = \exp\left[\mu_3 + \sum_{k \in K} u_{3k}(\theta)\right], K \subseteq P(\theta) \tag{6.5}$$

Where μ_1, μ_2, μ_3 are the grand mean effects.

34. Logistic regressions are just special cases of log-linear models. See Christensen, Ronald. *Log-Linear Methods and Logistic Regression*, Springer, 1997, p. 1.
35. Bishop, Fienberg, and Holland, pp. 125–130, and a discussion of the advantages of comparing successive log-linear models on p. 148.
36. Imrey, Peter B., Gary G. Koch, and Maura E. Stokes. "Categorical Data Analysis: Some Reflections on the Log-Linear Model and Logistic Regression. Part I: Historical and Methodological Overview," *International Statistical Review*, Vol. 49, 1981, pp. 271–276.

An example of the outcome of that process for the example used in this chapter is as follows:

Bad Population Model:

$$\log(m_{ijklmn}^B) = u + u_{236}(jkn) + u_{256}(jmn) + u_{123}(ijk) + u_4(l) \tag{6.6}$$

Good Population Model:

$$\log(m_{ijklmn}^G) = u + \sum_{ijkl}(\ldots) \text{ (all first, second, and third-order } u\text{-terms)} \tag{6.7}$$

Reject Population Model:

$$\log(m_{ijklmn}^R) = u + u_{13}(ik) + u_{16}(in) + u_{23}(jk) + u_{24}(jl)$$

$$+ u_{26}(jn) + u_{35}(km) \tag{6.8}$$

These models are hierarchical in the u-terms; that is, if an interaction term is present, then by implication all lower-order interaction terms involving the same subscripts must be present. For example, the hierarchical parametric equation for the reject population above translates to the fully specified form of:

$$\log(m_{3(\theta)}) = \mu_3 + u_1^{(3)}(\theta) + u_2^{(3)}(\theta) + u_3^{(3)}(\theta) + u_4^{(3)}(\theta) + u_5^{(3)}(\theta) + u_6^{(3)}(\theta)$$

$$+ u_{13}^{(3)}(\theta) + u_{16}^{(3)}(\theta) + u_{23}^{(3)}(\theta) + u_{24}^{(3)}(\theta) + u_{26}^{(3)}(\theta) + u_{35}^{(3)}(\theta) \tag{6.9}$$

where the superscripts are used to indicate the behavior group in order to avoid confusion with the subscripted dimension indices. The above model for the reject population was fit to the 754 observations in the reject sample used to develop the sample system that illustrates the method in this chapter. Figure 6.18 shows the sample observation counts, fitted estimates, and standardized residuals for the first four handle cells in the hybrid model. Similar tables for the good and bad population samples, based on the structural models appropriate for those groups, are also generated during the development process.

The estimated risk in a particular segment is a function of these fitted models. Furthermore, we hypothesize that these models may vary by protected class (i.e., the distribution of good, bad, and rejected credit applicants in the handle scheme is different for different groups). By law, this fact cannot be used even if the intent is to better understand the empirically estimated risk associated with a protected class within each segment in such a way as to give more favorable consideration relative to those differences.[37]

Bank Ref	Credit File Depth	Housing	Low # Credit Inquiries	Utility Ref Rent Payment	None 1 + Late 2 yrs	None On Time	One-up 1 + Late 2 yrs	One-up On Time
None	Low	Rent/Other	No	Data	23.0	10.0	2.0	1.0
				Fit	20.2709	9.2697	2.1231	0.9709
				Residual	0.6062	0.2399	−0.0845	0.0293

FIGURE 6.18 CREDIT EXAMPLE OF THE HANDLE DISTRIBUTION ESTIMATE DERIVED FOR THE REJECT POPULATION

37. See Barefoot, Jo Ann S., "Shooting the Rapids of Credit Scoring and Fair Lending," *ABA Banking Journal*, September 1997.

These methods may, however, be applied to other classifications of consumers, such as "thin file" credit applicants. Hence, models for good, bad, and rejected thin-file credit applicants may be derived separately from more mainstream credit applicants in order to derive risk estimates that better reflect their true performance than if they were lumped in with the mainstream pool of credit applicants. As a result, even when considering identical credit factors, the weight of utility, rent, and other alternative data may be greater in the model for underbanked consumers than for more traditional borrowers. The primary advantage that hybrid models offer over a separate credit-scoring model developed specifically for this segment is the ability to incorporate judgment-based predictors and associated judgment-based risk estimates in the underwriting and pricing model. Because of the explicit nature of the hybrid model, these assumptions can be directly monitored and tested for validity on a continual basis. This enables lenders to avoid barriers to lending caused by missing or incomplete data. In this way, it combines the strengths of both scoring and judgmental approaches. In the following section, we describe the form of the hybrid models.

The next steps in Phase 3 consist of the following:

1. Convert the fitted cell count estimates to percentages separately for the performance groups.
2. Calculate the log-odds ratio based on good/bad percentages for every cell to produce a table of unscaled cell risk estimates.[38]
3. Input the acceptance rate (e.g., 55 percent) and bad rate for the known population (e.g., 4.2 percent).
4. Calculate the expected number of sampled goods and bads in the unknown population.[39]
5. Calculate the population odds, which was found to be 12.3 to 1.
6. Output the table of inferred cell estimates.

Figure 6.19 displays the output for the first four handle cells. Counts for all hybrid model segments are scaled to produce model results based on 10,000 applicants. This results in known goods of 5,269, inferred goods of 3,977, and total goods of 9,246. In addition, there are 231 known bads, 523 inferred bads, and 754 total bads.

This concludes Phase 3. An important component of this phase was reject inference. Possible approaches for utilizing the information on rejected credit applicants include: (1) reweighting the observations of the accepted population (with known performance); (2) extrapolating the likelihood

Bank Ref	Credit File Depth	Housing	Low # Credit Inquiries	Utility Ref Rent Payment	None 1 + Late 2 yrs	None On Time	One-up 1 + Late 2 yrs	One-up On Time
None	Low	Rent/Other	No	UNKNOWN	20.2709	9.2697	2.1231	0.9709
				EXPT. BDS	9.3802	3.3723	0.4849	0.1514
				EXPT GDS	10.8907	5.8974	1.0383	0.8195

FIGURE 6.19 CREDIT EXAMPLE OF THE HANDLE DISTRIBUTION ESTIMATE DERIVED FOR THE REJECT AND EXPECTED GOOD AND BAD POPULATIONS

38. For our sample system, the range of values, and average, for the unscaled indices were: minimum of −2.978, maximum of +2.848, and an average index of +0.024.
39. In this example, the bad rate for the unknowns was determined to be 11.62 percent and the number of unknown bads was 88, while the total number of unknowns was 754.

Bank Ref	Credit File Depth	Housing	Low # Credit Inquiries	Utility Ref Rent Payment	None 1 + Late 2 yrs	None On Time	One-up 1 + Late 2 yrs	One-up On Time
None	Low	Rent/Other	No	Goods	71	43	17	16
				Bads	61	24	5	3
				% Applicants	1.32	0.67	0.21	0.19
				Index	203	211	224	234

FIGURE 6.20 CREDIT EXAMPLE OF THE HANDLE DISTRIBUTION OF GOODS AND BADS, FACTORED UP TO 10,000 APPLICANTS WITH REJECTS ASSIGNED, PERCENTAGE OF TOTAL APPLICANTS, AND SCALED RISK INDICES

of bad performance for rejected applicants based on the performance of the accepted applicants;[40] (3) using MCS-based judgmental factors; and (4) utilizing the structural model's multilayered segmentation (MLS) to associate rejects with their good and bad applicant counterparts and proceed to apply secondary factors, including alternative data, to estimate the good/bad odds ratio for the rejects, on a cell-by-cell basis. The mechanism for reject inference with the hybrid approach in this example was to leverage the structural model as indicated in the fourth approach.

Phase 4 marks the successful reconstruction of the "through-the-door" applicant population, at which time forecasts of the percentage distribution of applicants falling into each segment are generated. Specifically, scaled risk indices are calculated by cell and table is produced giving good and bad risk distributions by cell (scaled to 10,000 applicants), applicant percentages by cell and risk index by cell, as shown in Figure 6.20.

Multidimensional views are then created to provide a top-down analysis of each dimension viewed individually, and then in combination with every other dimension taken two at a time, three at a time, and so on. For example, an individual dimension forecast of the applicant population mix relative to the number of credit bureau inquiries for our example is:

Applicant Forecast Low Number of Credit Inquiries	Percent
No	54.38
Yes	45.42

There are 5 more one-dimensional and 15 additional two-dimensional forecasts. An illustration of a three-dimensional forecast for the housing, credit inquiry, and utility reference dimensions of our sample hybrid system is:

Applicant Forecast Low Credit Inquiries By Utility Reference By Housing				
Housing	Utility Ref.	Low Inq:	No	Yes
Rent/other	1 + Late		17.64	12.36
Rent/other	On-Time		12.82	12.42
Own/buy	1 + Late		12.76	9.62
Own/buy	On-Time		11.35	11.02

40. There are various studies on this topic (e.g., see Hand, D. J., and W. E. Henley, "Can Reject Reference Ever Work?" *IMA Journal of Management Mathematics*, 1993, Vol. 5, No. 1, pp. 45–55; doi:10.1093/imaman/5.1.45).

There are 19 additional three-dimensional forecasts, plus 15 four-dimensional, and additional 6 five-dimensional marginal forecasts in all. Essentially every possible marginal table is calculated and reported so that segment aggregates can be analyzed.

Next, risk index distribution tables are created that associate segments with risk of default, as shown in Figure 6.21. The column labeled "Odds" provides the risk of default (e.g., for risk index 203, the first row entry for the risk index, there are 71 goods for every 61 bads for an odds ratio of 1.2-to-1 goods for every bad).

By sorting the risk index in Figure 6.21 into descending order from top to bottom so that the higher the risk function value, the lower the risk of default, we obtain the table in Figure 6.22. Figure 6.22 is central to the formulation of policies whereby the applicants representing the lowest risk (starting with risk index 320) are taken for a given acceptance rate policy. Each of the 84 lines in this figure corresponds to a distinct action table. The point at which management determines to be the credit approval threshold corresponds to a row in that figure, which is usually selected based on a target acceptance rate or bad rate. The final step in Phase 4 is to produce a cross reference table that we explain in detail in a later section on assessing the change in policy cutoff.

For example, consider a cutoff at risk function value 258, with associated 54.7 percent approval rate, odds of 56.5 to 1, and approval actions associated with 107 distinct entries in the decisioning table. If the cutoff were moved to 245, a 74.7 percent approval rate would result, with associated odds of 30.6 to 1, and 46 additional distinct table entries would now have action "approve" specified.

Phase 5 involves production of the action table (see Figures 6.23 and 6.24). Recall the concept of a handle, which was introduced in Chapter 5. For this simple one-stage example, Figures 6.23 and 6.24 depict a two-dimensional representation of a six-dimensional handle, where the strata in each dimension run alternately, and mutually exclusively, across the rows and columns of a decisioning table whose unique entries correspond to a particular homogenous grouping of credit applicants. Every credit applicant in this example can be assigned to one, and only one, entry in the table by a set of business rules and by their successful classification within each handle dimension. Also, each such entry has a unique integer identifier, a probability of default, and an applicant population percentage associated with it. Each instance of a table embodies a credit approval strategy that corresponds to how much risk the lending institution is willing to take. It can accommodate such strategies as taking the same number of bad loans, while increasing the approval rate; maintaining the current acceptance rate, but take fewer bads; or taking the same number of bad loans, while increasing approvals within certain designated applicant segments.

This simple example may be extended to incorporate any type of criteria and any number of stages. For example, those applicants who have a thin credit file and do not own a home, but have paid rent on time for 24 months and have a solid utility reference and payment history, may be automatically approved for a particular type of loan, in which case the action table would indicate "Policy Approval." With reference to multistage systems, the indicated action may be "proceed to stage two," "call landlord or utility for verification," "perform cash flow analysis," "route to senior loan officer," and so forth. We may further generalize to multiple systems based on any type criteria (e.g., applicant characteristics, geographical region, product line, and any combination of criteria, for example, "borrower type within product line by branch"). The need for multiple systems can either be established by exploratory data analysis at system development time or dictated by the user, or both.[41]

In addition, for each decision strategy, the system provides a sensitivity report for all adverse action cells that gives the maximum improvement in risk attained by a change in a single factor for every handle entry corresponding to a "decline" decision. In each case, the four most significant

---

41. This is consistent with all Basel II Use Test requirements. See Basel II paragraph 417 relating to pertinent judgmental and data aspects.

Index Number	Good		Bad		Total		Odds	Cells
	Number	Percent	Number	Percent	Number	Percent		
203	70	0.7	61	86.5	131	1.3	1.2	1
209	50	0.5	31	44.8	81	0.8	1.6	1
211	115	1.2	66	94.5	181	1.8	1.7	2
215	29	0.3	13	19.1	42	0.4	2.1	1
218	91	0.9	37	52.5	128	1.3	2.5	2
220	61	0.6	22	31.1	83	0.8	2.8	1
222	66	0.7	22	31.9	88	0.9	2.9	1
224	45	0.5	14	19.5	59	0.6	3.3	2
226	103	1	28	39.8	131	1.3	3.7	2
228	35	0.4	9	12.7	44	0.4	4	1
230	61	0.6	14	19.6	75	0.7	4.4	2
231	181	1.8	39	55.4	220	2.2	4.7	1
232	154	1.5	30	43.2	184	1.8	5.1	2
233	31	0.3	6	8.7	38	0.4	5.1	1
234	57	0.6	11	15.1	67	0.7	5.4	2
235	63	0.6	11	15.6	74	0.7	5.8	2
237	25	0.3	4	5.5	29	0.3	6.5	1
238	202	2	30	42.4	231	2.3	6.8	3
240	100	1	14	19.3	113	1.1	7.4	1
241	95	1	12	17.5	108	1.1	7.7	3
242	13	0.1	2	2.2	14	0.1	8.2	1
243	80	0.8	9	13.3	90	0.9	8.6	1
244	295	3	33	46.9	328	3.3	9	5
245	116	1.2	12	17.2	128	1.3	9.6	2
246	163	1.6	17	23.6	179	1.8	9.8	2
247	151	1.5	14	20.2	165	1.6	10.7	2
248	36	0.4	3	4.6	40	0.4	11.3	2
249	11	0.1	1	1.3	12	0.1	11.4	1
250	186	1.9	15	21.8	201	2	12.1	5
251	112	1.1	9	12.4	121	1.2	12.8	4
252	172	1.7	13	17.9	184	1.8	13.7	4
254	308	3.1	21	29.7	329	3.3	14.8	7
255	173	1.7	11	15.6	184	1.8	15.8	7
256	205	2.1	12	17.7	217	2.2	16.4	4
257	253	2.5	15	20.7	268	2.7	17.4	6
258	17	0.2	1	1.3	17	0.2	18.4	1

FIGURE 6.21 INTERVAL STATISTICS FOR HYBRID SYSTEM

Index Number	Good Number	Good Percent	Bad Number	Bad Percent	Total Number	Total Percent	Odds	Cells
259	62	0.6	3	4.7	65	0.6	18.8	2
260	270	2.7	13	19.2	283	2.8	20	7
261	20	0.2	1	1.3	21	0.2	20.7	1
262	193	1.9	9	12.4	202	2	22.2	9
263	160	1.6	7	9.8	166	1.7	23.2	4
264	55	0.6	2	3.2	57	0.6	24.6	2
265	40	0.4	2	2.2	42	0.4	26.2	2
266	156	1.6	6	8.2	161	1.6	27.2	3
267	26	0.3	1	1.3	27	0.3	28.4	1
268	143	1.4	5	6.8	148	1.5	30	3
269	105	1.1	3	4.7	108	1.1	31.8	4
270	194	2	6	8.3	200	2	33.3	7
271	18	0.2	1	0.7	19	0.2	35.3	1
272	68	0.7	2	2.7	70	0.7	36.4	3
273	16	0.2	0	0.6	16	0.2	38.1	1
274	111	1.1	3	3.9	113	1.1	40.3	3
275	55	0.5	1	1.8	56	0.6	42.3	2
277	28	0.3	1	0.9	28	0.3	46.2	1
278	132	1.3	3	3.9	135	1.4	48.7	2
279	49	0.5	1	1.4	50	0.5	51.7	2
281	103	1	2	2.6	104	1	57.1	3
282	63	0.6	1	1.5	64	0.6	61.7	1
283	114	1.1	2	2.6	116	1.2	62.6	2
285	43	0.4	1	0.9	44	0.4	69.7	1
286	101	1	1	1.9	102	1	74.9	2
287	72	0.7	1	1.3	73	0.7	76.5	1
288	161	1.6	2	2.8	163	1.6	81.7	2
289	58	0.6	1	0.9	58	0.6	87.6	1
290	146	1.5	2	2.3	147	1.5	89.9	2
291	62	0.6	1	0.9	63	0.6	94	1
292	204	2.1	2	2.9	206	2.1	99.8	2
293	226	2.3	2	3.1	228	2.3	103.8	4
294	109	1.1	1	1.4	110	1.1	109.8	2
295	36	0.4	0	0.5	37	0.4	114.4	1
296	195	2	2	2.3	197	2	122.2	2
297	194	1.9	2	2.2	195	2	127.5	2
298	76	0.8	1	0.8	76	0.8	134.6	1

FIGURE 6.21 (*continued*)

Index Number	Good		Bad		Total		Odds	Cells
	Number	Percent	Number	Percent	Number	Percent		
300	230	2.3	2	2.2	231	2.3	147.3	2
301	87	0.9	1	0.8	87	0.9	158	1
302	133	1.3	1	1.2	134	1.3	163.5	2
304	221	2.2	1	1.7	222	2.2	180.1	2
305	72	0.7	0	0.5	72	0.7	187.9	1
306	221	2.2	1	1.6	222	2.2	198	2
309	76	0.8	0	0.5	76	0.8	232.7	1
311	187	1.9	1	1	188	1.9	254.4	2
315	150	1.5	0	0.7	150	1.5	309.1	1
317	99	1	0	0.4	100	1	344.1	1
320	150	1.5	0	0.5	151	1.5	393.5	1

FIGURE 6.21   (continued)

factors are ranked in order of importance, and the resulting net gain in reduction of risk is indicated for each factor. Also included are the actions that would result in each instance. A table for the current example is displayed in Figure 6.25.

Multidimensional acceptance rates by handle segment and a forecast of the resulting acceptee population mix relative to handle segments are also produced so that strategy implications can be examined in advance and in detail.

This example hybrid system allows management to identify and select the best strategy to meet their current business objectives and goals. At any point in time, all alternative policies under evaluation are completely specified to allow for detailed trade-off analyses. It accommodates internal changes, such as new corporate business and compliance objectives or marketing emphasis. It also accommodates environmental changes, such as shifts in the composition of the applicant loan population. Furthermore, such systems can address questions about the effect of recent changes in risk relationship structures (such as the degree of risk associated with a specific handle segment or set of handle segments). Finally, hybrid systems such as these can forecast the impact of a planned change (possibly a relationship-based promotion to broaden, deepen, or retain valued customers).

The foregoing simple example may be easily extended to incorporate any type of criteria and any number of stages for both underwriting and pricing. For example, those applicants that fall into a particular handle segment could be approved as a matter of policy, or they may be routed on to a second table having secondary criteria for approval. Possible actions might include consideration of secondary borrower credit risk factors; changes to pricing, terms, conditions, and other product features; performing a suitability analysis to assess if other product/program might be better for the customer and the lender; inclusion of alternative data;[42] consideration of geographical location at varying levels of granularity; either promoting or limiting transactions at a portfolio, branch, or loan officer level to control concentrations, accommodations, or incremental fees; or consideration of total relationship information. The list goes on, and the secondary factors may be combined

---

42. This refers to remittance information, or non-credit payment information. See Turner, Michael, S. Alyssa Lee, Ann Schnare, Robin Varghese, and Patrick D. Walker. "Give Credit Where Credit Is Due—Increasing Access to Affordable Mainstream Credit Using Alternative Data," Political and Economic Research Council and The Brookings Institution Urban Markets Initiative, 2006, pp. 16–21.

Cumulative Statistics (Descending)								
Risk	Good		Bad		Total			No.
Index	No.	Pct	No.	Pct	No.	Pct	Odds	Cells
320	148	2	0	0	148	2	393.5	1
317	245	3	0	0	245	3	372.5	2
315	397	4	1	0	398	4	345.3	3
311	580	6	2	0	581	6	310.4	5
309	652	7	2	0	654	7	299.3	6
306	874	9	2	0	876	9	264.9	8
305	944	10	2	0	946	9	257.0	9
304	1163	13	4	1	1166	12	237.9	11
302	1288	14	5	1	1293	13	227.7	13
301	1372	15	5	1	1377	14	221.8	14
300	1601	17	7	1	1608	16	206.8	16
298	1673	18	8	1	1681	17	202.1	17
297	1867	20	9	1	1876	19	190.4	19
296	2059	22	11	1	2070	21	181.0	21
295	2094	23	11	1	2104	21	179.3	22
294	2197	24	11	2	2209	22	174.0	24
293	2414	26	14	2	2427	24	164.1	28
292	2617	28	16	2	2633	26	156.3	30
291	2681	29	17	2	2697	27	153.6	31
290	2826	31	18	2	2844	28	148.4	33
289	2881	31	19	3	2900	29	146.4	34
288	3045	33	21	3	3066	31	140.5	36
287	3119	34	22	3	3141	31	137.7	37
286	3215	35	23	3	3238	32	134.4	39
285	3258	35	24	3	3282	33	132.7	40
283	3371	36	26	3	3397	34	127.8	42
282	3431	37	26	4	3457	35	125.5	43
281	3527	38	28	4	3555	36	121.5	46
279	3574	39	29	4	3603	36	119.4	48
278	3704	40	32	4	3736	37	113.6	50
277	3730	40	32	4	3762	38	112.5	51
275	3779	41	34	5	3813	38	110.1	53
274	3888	42	37	5	3925	39	105.2	56
273	3901	42	37	5	3938	39	105.6	57
272	3965	43	38	5	4003	40	103.1	60
271	3983	43	39	5	4022	40	101.6	61

FIGURE 6.22   DESCENDING CUMULATIVE RISK INDEX DISTRIBUTION FOR HYBRID SYSTEM

Cumulative Statistics (Descending)							
Risk	Good		Bad		Total			No.
Index	No.	Pct	No.	Pct	No.	Pct	Odds	Cells
270	4172	45	45	6	4217	42	92.2	68
269	4272	46	48	6	4320	43	88.5	72
268	4412	48	53	7	4465	45	83.6	75
267	4439	48	54	7	4493	45	82.9	76
266	4589	50	59	8	4648	46	78.0	79
265	4625	50	60	8	4685	47	76.7	81
264	4680	51	63	8	4743	47	74.8	83
263	4837	52	69	9	4906	49	69.7	87
262	5017	54	78	10	5095	51	64.6	96
261	5036	54	78	10	5114	51	64.2	97
260	5299	57	91	12	5390	54	58.1	104
259	5358	58	94	13	5452	55	56.8	106
258	5372	58	95	13	5467	55	56.5	107
257	5623	61	109	15	5732	57	51.4	113
256	5819	63	121	16	5940	59	47.9	117
255	5987	65	132	18	6119	61	45.4	124
254	6295	68	153	20	6448	64	41.1	131
252	6465	70	165	22	6630	66	39.2	135
251	6573	71	173	23	6746	67	37.9	139
250	6760	73	189	25	6949	70	35.7	144
249	6770	73	190	25	6960	70	35.6	145
248	6805	74	193	26	6998	70	35.3	147
247	6954	75	207	28	7161	72	33.5	149
246	7116	77	224	30	7340	73	31.8	151
245	7233	78	236	31	7469	75	30.6	153
244	7529	81	269	36	7798	78	28.0	158
243	7609	82	278	37	7887	79	27.3	159
242	7620	82	280	37	7900	79	27.2	160
241	7714	83	292	39	8006	80	26.4	163
240	7814	85	305	41	8119	81	25.6	164
238	8014	87	335	44	8349	84	23.9	167
237	8039	87	339	45	8378	84	23.7	168
235	8103	88	350	46	8453	85	23.2	170
234	8157	88	360	48	8517	85	22.7	172

FIGURE 6.22   (continued)

Cumulative Statistics (Descending)								
Risk	Good		Bad		Total			No.
Index	No.	Pct	No.	Pct	No.	Pct	Odds	Cells
233	8187	89	366	49	8553	86	22.4	173
232	8341	90	396	53	8737	87	21.1	175
231	8521	92	434	58	8955	90	19.6	176
230	8578	93	447	59	9025	90	19.2	178
228	8613	93	456	61	9069	91	18.9	179
226	8719	94	485	64	9204	92	18.0	181
224	8763	95	498	66	9261	93	17.6	183
222	8831	96	522	69	9353	94	16.9	184
220	8892	96	544	72	9436	94	16.4	185
218	8983	97	581	77	9564	96	15.5	187
215	9011	97	594	79	9605	96	15.2	188
211	9125	99	661	88	9786	98	13.8	190
209	9175	99	693	92	9868	99	13.2	191
203	9246	100	754	100	10000	100	12.3	192

FIGURE 6.22   (continued)

with one another, such as thresholds on transactions that are calculated cumulatively for a given monitoring horizon by borrower type, within product line, by branch, on a daily, or possibly real-time, basis.

HYBRID SYSTEM MAINTENANCE

Every system is based on historical data that is analyzed and synthesized in order to produce an initial set of alternative policies. Maintenance efforts provide the means whereby a risk evaluation and policy formulation system can adapt over time in a nonstationary environment.

There are two ways in which a system's effectiveness can diminish. Either the distribution of applicants corresponding to specific profiles changes, or the risk associated with specific profiles changes (i.e., the assumption of "the future will be like the past" is no longer valid). In both cases, application of the proper system maintenance techniques will uncover these shifts so that fluctuations in the system's performance can be anticipated, understood, and corrected.

Applicant Profile Analysis

Significant shifts in the structure of the applicant population with respect to any individual profile or group of profiles can be dealt with effectively by means of this analysis. All that is required is a tally of the number of applicants corresponding to each individual cell in the action table. The profiles are identified easily by their action table reference numbers. This technique is far more powerful than the corresponding early warning measures employed by scoring system users to explain shifts in score distributions as they relate to various strata in the applicant population. This should be done on a monthly basis. Each profile analysis, with the exception of the first, examines the results for the given period separately as well as cumulatively when combined with all previous tallies. A variance analysis is performed using this data coupled with system development-time

Bank Ref	Credit File Depth	Housing	Low # Credit Inqs	Utility Ref Rent Payment	None 1 + Late 2 yrs	None On Time	One-up 1 + Late 2 yrs	One-up On Time
None	Low	Rent/other	No	Cell no. Action	1. Decline	2. Decline	3. Decline	4. Decline
None	Low	Rent/other	Yes	Cell no. Action	5. Decline	6. Decline	7. Decline	8. Decline
None	Low	Own/buy	No	Cell no. Action	9. Decline	10. Decline	11. Decline	12. Decline
None	Low	Own/buy	Yes	Cell no. Action	13. Decline	14. Decline	15. Decline	16. Decline
None	Moderate	Rent/other	No	Cell no. Action	17. Decline	18. Decline	19. Decline	20. Decline
None	Moderate	Rent/other	Yes	Cell no. Action	21. Decline	22. Decline	23. Approve	24. Approve
None	Moderate	Own/buy	No	Cell no. Action	25. Decline	26. Decline	27. Decline	28. Decline
None	Moderate	Own/buy	Yes	Cell no. Action	29. Decline	30. Decline	31. Approve	32. Approve
None	High	Rent/other	No	Cell no. Action	33. Decline	34. Decline	35. Decline	36. Decline
None	High	Rent/other	Yes	Cell no. Action	37. Approve	38. Approve	39. Approve	40. Approve
None	High	Own/buy	No	Cell no. Action	41. Decline	42. Decline	43. Decline	44. Approve
None	High	Own/buy	Yes	Cell no. Action	45. Approve	46. Approve	47. Approve	46. Approve
Save	Low	Rent/other	No	Cell no. Action	49. Decline	50. Decline	51. Decline	52. Decline
Save	Low	Rent/other	Yes	Cell no. Action	53. Decline	54. Decline	55. Decline	56. Approve
Save	Low	Own/buy	No	Cell no. Action	57. Decline	58. Decline	59. Decline	60. Approve
Save	Low	Own/buy	Yes	Cell no. Action	61. Approve	62. Approve	63. Approve	64. Approve
Save	Moderate	Rent/other	No	Cell no. Action	65. Decline	66. Decline	67. Decline	68. Decline
Save	Moderate	Rent/ other	Yes	Cell no. Action	69. Decline	70. Decline	71. Approve	72. Approve
Save	Moderate	Own/buy	No	Cell no. Action	73. Decline	74. Decline	75. Approve	76. Approve
Save	Moderate	Own/buy	Yes	Cell no. Action	77. Approve	78. Approve	79. Approve	60. Approve
Save	High	Rent/other	No	Cell no. Action	61. Decline	62. Decline	63. Decline	64. Decline
Save	High	Rent/other	Yes	Cell no. Action	85. Decline	86. Decline	87. Approve	88. Approve
Save	High	Own/buy	No	Cell no. Action	89. Decline	90. Decline	91. Approve	92. Approve
Save	High	Own/buy	Yes	Cell no. Action	93. Approve	94. Approve	95. Approve	96. Approve

FIGURE 6.23   ACTION TABLE 1: ONE-STAGE SYSTEM STRATEGY MAINTAIN CURRENT ACCEPTANCE RATE

forecasts. If significant enough changes are detected among the applicant population at any time, then a new action table with accompanying statistical tables would need to be produced.

System Updating

Hybrid systems are easier to update than scoring systems. Updates can also be made more frequently since smaller sample sizes are required (i.e., individual cells in the action table may be updated).

System updating focuses on a reexamination of the degree of risk that the system associates with various applicant profiles specified in the action table. A performance audit is carried out for all accounts opened since the date of system installation. Results from the audit are analyzed to determine whether the overall distribution of newly acquired creditworthy and noncreditworthy

Bank Ref	Credit File Depth	Housing	Low # Credit Inqs	Utility Ref Rent Payment	None 1+Late	None On Time	One-up 1 + Late 2 yrs	One-up On Time
Check	Low	Rent/other[1]	No	Cell no. Action	97. Decline	98. Decline	99. Decline	100. Decline
Check	Low	Rent/other	Yes	Cell no. Action	101. Approve	102. Approve	103. Approve	104. Approve
Check	Low	Own/buy	No	Cell no. Action	105. Decline	106. Decline	107. Decline	108. Approve
Check	Low	Own/buy	Yes	Cell no.	109. Approve	110. Approve	111. Approve	112. Approve
Check	Moderate	Rent/other	No	Cell no. Action	113. Decline	114. Decline	115. Decline	116. Approve
Check	Moderate	Rent/other	Yes	Cell no. Action	117. Approve	116. Approve	119. Approve	120. Approve
Check	Moderate	Own/buy	No	Cell no. Action	121. Decline	122. Approve	123. Approve	124. Approve
Check	Moderate	Own/buy	Yes	Cell no. Action	123. Approve	126. Approve	127. Approve	126. Approve
Check	High	Rent/other	No	Cell no. Action	129. Decline	130. Decline	131. Decline	132. Approve
Check	High	Rent/other	Yes	Cell no.	133. Approve	134. Approve	135. Approve	136. Approve
Check	High	Own/buy	No	Cell no. Action	137. Approve	138. Approve	139. Approve	140. Approve
Check	High	Own/buy	Yes	Cell no. Action	141. Approve	142. Approve	143. Approve	144. Approve
Both	Low	Rent/other	No	Cell no. Action	145. Decline	146. Decline	147. Decline	146. Approve
Both	Low	Rent/other	Yes	Cell no. Action	149. Approve	150. Approve	151. Approve	152. Approve
Both	Low	Own/buy	No	Cell no. Action	153. Decline	154. Approve	155. Approve	156. Approve
Both	Low	Own/buy	Yes	Cell no.	157. Approve	156. Approve	159. Approve	160. Approve
Both	Moderate	Rent/other	No	Cell no. Action	161. Decline	162. Decline	163. Decline	164. Approve
Both	Moderate	Rent/other	Yes	Cell no. Action	165. Approve	166. Approve	167. Approve	166. Approve
Both	Moderate	Own/buy	No	Cell no. Action	169. Decline	170. Approve	171. Approve	172. Approve
Both	Moderate	Own/buy	Yes	Cell no. Action	173. Approve	174. Approve	175. Approve	176. Approve
Both	High	Rent/other	No	Cell no. Action	177. Decline	178. Decline	179. Approve	160. Approve
Both	High	Rent/other	Yes	Cell no. Action	161. Approve	162. Approve	163. Approve	164. Approve
Both	High	Own/buy	No	Cell no. Action	165. Approve	166. Approve	167. Approve	166. Approve
Both	High	Own/buy	Yes	Cell no. Action	189. Approve	190. Approve	191. Approve	192. Approve

FIGURE 6.24   ACTION TABLE 1 (CONTINUED)

customers is significantly different from that of the previously sampled creditworthy and non-creditworthy customers. Finally, appropriate adjustments are made so as to assure accurate risk estimates for those profiles that are affected.

Hybrid System Policy Formulation

Management has a great deal of flexibility in formulating policy that is consistent with the entire organization's goals and objectives. Policy can be based on the following types of criteria (which may vary in a multisystem environment):

- Acceptance rate
- Number of bad loans taken
- Individual applicant profile (handle cell) emphasis
- Product emphasis

Action Table Ref. No.	Factor 1 Net Gain Result	Factor 2 Net Gain Result	Factor 3 Net Gain Result	Factor 4 Net Gain Result
1	Cred inq 47. Decline	Bank ref 30. Decline	Util ref 21. Decline	CF depth 18. Decline
2	Cred inq 40. Decline	Bank ref 34. Decline	Util ref 23. Decline	CF depth 16. Decline
3	Cred inq 28. Decline	Bank ref 19. Decline	Mo, inc. 19. Decline	Rent pay 9. Decline
4	Bank ref 26. Approve	Cred inq 21. Decline	CF depth 18. Decline	Housing 4. Decline
5	Bank ref 38. Approve	CF depth 13. Approve	Util ref 3. Decline	Housing 2. Decline
6	Bank ref 45. Approve	CF depth 12. Approve	Util ref 4. Decline	Rent pay 0. Decline
7	Bank ref 30. Approve	CF depth 15. Approve	Rent pay 3 Decline	Housing 1. Decline
8	Bank ref 37. Approve	CF depth 14. Approve	Rent pay 0. Decline	Util ref 0. Decline
9	Cred inq 42. Decline	Bank ref 38. Decline	Mo, inc. 23. Decline	Util ref 21. Decline
10	Bank ref 45. Approve	Cred inq 35. Decline	Oil co, 22. Decline	CF depth 22. Decline
11	Bank ref 30. Approve	Cf depth 25. Decline	Cred inq 24. Decline	Rent pay 7 Decline
12	Bank ref 36. Approve	Cf depth 24. Approve	Cred inq 17. Decline	Rent pay 0. Decline
13	Bank ref 49. Approve	Cf depth 19. Approve	Util ref 3. Decline	Rent pay 0. Decline
14	Bank ref 55. Approve	Cf depth 18. Approve	Util ref 4. Decline	Rent pay 1 . Decline
15	Bank ref 40. Approve	Cf depth 21. Approve	Rent pay 1. Decline	Util ref 0. Decline

FIGURE 6.25   ADVERSE ACTION SENSITIVITY REPORT

- Geographic region
- Customer relationship
- Any other well-defined criteria

Referring back to our simple example, Figure 6.21 displays the total percentage of applicants falling within each of eighty-four different risk levels and the action table in Figure 6.23 corresponds to a risk index cutoff of 258 with resulting acceptance rate of approximately 55 percent. In this hypothetical case, the credit grantor's previous delinquency experience with a 55 percent acceptance rate was a 4.2 percent bad rate. Since the table in Figure 6.22 is based on 10,000 applicants, we note that the previous number of bad loans made was 231 and this most closely corresponds to a cutoff risk index of 245.

At a risk level of 245, the credit grantor would experience a 75 percent acceptance rate while taking the same number of bad loans as before. The action table corresponding to this latter acceptance policy is easily generated, along with its companion decline factor analysis, multi-dimensional acceptance rates, and acceptee population mix corresponding to the new approval strategy.

A hybrid system allows for immediate identification of individual profiles affected by a change in approval policy. A table specifying all profiles corresponding to each and every risk level is provided for this purpose, and is displayed in Figure 6.26.[43]

Figure 6.26 allows you to examine the risk function/handle entry relationship explicitly. For example, a change in policy from risk level 258 to 245 discussed in the previous section would

---

43. This is the segment/risk index cross reference table referenced in Figure 6.11 in the box just preceding Phase 5. This provides more transparency for underwriting process.

209	1	9					
211	2	2	17				
215	1	10					
218	2	18	25				
220	1	33					
222	1	49					
224	2	3	26				
226	2	65	81				
228	1	34					
230	2	11	50				
231	1	145					
232	2	41	97				
233	1	82					
234	2	4	66				
235	2	19	57				
237	1	42					
238	3	12	99	161			
240	1	113					
241	3	51	58	73			
242	1	27					
243	1	98					
244	5	20	35	129	147	177	
245	2	89	105				
246	2	74	146				
247	2	83	153				
248	2	67	115				
249	1	28					
250	5	5	52	90	100	114	
251	4	6	13	14	107		
252	4	7	36	131	162		
254	7	15	21	59	106	121	130	163
255	7	8	16	22	43	53	84	85
256	4	30	55	86	169		
257	6	29	54	68	69	70	178
258	1	87					
259	2	56	179				
260	7	23	71	88	116	148	154	155
261	1	108					

FIGURE 6.26 SEGMENT IMPACT OF A POLICY CHANGE IN CUTOFF

262	9	24	31	32	44	60	72	122	123	132
263	4	37	38	75	137					
264	2	61	62							
265	2	63	78							
266	3	64	91	185						
267	1	77								
268	3	39	94	170						
269	4	40	46	76	164					
270	7	45	79	80	93	103	138	139		
271	1	124								
272	3	92	96	171						
273	1	95								
274	3	48	156	180						
275	2	47	104							
277	1	119								
278	2	111	186							
279	2	135	140							
281	3	112	120	187						
282	1	151								
283	2	101	136							
285	1	172								
286	2	102	127							
287	1	117								
288	2	128	149							
289	1	167								
290	2	118	133							
291	1	109								
292	2	152	165							
293	4	110	134	143	183					
294	2	159	188							
295	1	144								
296	2	125	150							
297	2	126	181							
298	1	168								
300	2	157	166							
301	1	184								
302	2	160	175							

FIGURE 6.26 (*continued*)

304	2	141	182
305	1	142	
306	2	158	173
309	1	176	
311	2	174	191
315	1	189	
317	1	192	
320	1	190	

FIGURE 6.26 (continued)

result in the inclusion of 46 additional segments. In contrast, raising of the cutoff from 261 to 262 results in the elimination of one segment from the portfolio, identified by action table reference number 108. Referring to the action table in Figure 6.20, we see that profile 108 corresponds to an applicant with a checking account, in the low credit file depth group, who owns a home, has a high number of credit inquiries, but has both a utility reference and good rent payment history. This is an example where a Stage 2 series of factors based on alternative data could possibly qualify an entire segment where credit history is thin and a high number of credit inquiries has an adverse impact.

HYBRID UNDERWRITING MODELS WITH TRADITIONAL CREDIT INFORMATION

At this point, we will make the foregoing discussion more concrete by considering several detailed examples of what a realistic hybrid model would look like relative to the lines of businesses identified. We start with unsecured lending and illustrate a hybrid home purchase mortgage approval model. In these examples, we focus on the credit factors that can be used in a hybrid model and not on the technical details in Phases 3 through 6 of the development process. Essentially, we illustrate handles for these types of loan products and we share several additional hybrid model formulations using traditional credit factors in Appendix 6C.

Home Purchase Mortgage Example

The following example is for home purchase mortgages originated through a lender's retail channel (i.e., branch, call center, internet, etc.). Models for refinancings or home improvement loans would have differing sets of criteria, as would wholesale channel mortgages. This specific example affords an opportunity to expose how complicated the calculation of categories for criteria represented by consumer behavioral variables can be. Consider the credit history factor. It takes on values of good, fair, or poor, which seem simple enough on the surface. However, it is important to weigh both the type of trade line and the time since delinquency. Figures 6.27 and 6.28 represent a derivation of the credit history classification.

As one might expect, credit history is a primary underwriting factor in mortgage lending. This has implications for credit applicants who do not possess either sufficient breadth, or depth, to calculate a value for this credit history factor. We will address approaches for overcoming that problem in the next section on nontraditional credit underwriting. Figure 6.29 provides primary factors for this example, and Figure 6.30 shows the corresponding handle structure for primary factors.

Delinquency Time Frame	Mortgage Trades				Installment Trades				Revolving Trades			
Frequency:	0	1	2	3+	0	1	2	3+	0	1	2	3+
Less than 12 months												
30 days past due	G	F	F	P	G	G	F	F	G	G	F	F
60 days past due	G	P	P	P	G	F	P	P	G	F	P	P
90 days past due	G	P	P	P	G	P	P	P	G	P	P	P
12–24 months												
30 days past due	G	G	F	P	G	G	G	F	G	G	G	F
60 days past due	G	P	P	P	G	F	F	P	G	F	F	P
90 days past due	G	P	P	P	G	P	P	P	G	P	P	P
Over 24 months old												
30 days past due	G	G	G	F	G	G	G	G	G	G	G	G
60 days past due	G	F	P	P	G	G	G	G	G	G	G	G
90 days past due	G	P	P	P	G	F	F	P	G	F	F	F

FIGURE 6.27 CREDIT HISTORY DIMENSION: RATINGS FOR THREE TRADE LINES WITHIN THREE TIME PERIODS

Examples of secondary factors are shown in Figure 6.31. We now proceed to explain how the primary factors and secondary factors are combined to make loan-underwriting decisions.

Figure 6.32 specifies the two-stage action table for this example. There are 36 primary handle cells based on the handle dimensions. The reason that there are 72 entries in the table is that the last 36 entries correspond to Stage 2 decline decisions based on secondary factors not being satisfied. When primary handle cells (i.e., those cells with numbers less than or equal to 36) indicate "Stage 2" instead of "Accept" or "Decline" as an action, then those handle numbers are reserved for those applicants that satisfy the Stage 2 rules for loan approval.

Consider the examples in Figure 6.33, which were simply extracted from Figure 6.30. For each handle cell, we now examine how the secondary factors in Figure 6.31 would be applied to the primary factor combinations (handle cells). It is necessary that every handle cell relationship to secondary factors be defined, even if the definition specifies approve or decline with no secondary factors required, or a general rule such as any two secondary factors with good (G) ratings.

Referring to Figure 6.33, we now will examine the secondary factor qualifications associated with the six handle cell examples shown. Beginning with handle cell 3, we see that in order for a credit applicant to be approved, no secondary factors are required. However, for handle cell 12 to be approved, a history of successfully handling higher debt (e.g., meeting obligations timely at similar total debt ratio) must be G-rated with months of reserves at least F-rated, or, alternatively, history of handling higher debt must be F-rated with months of reserves at least G-rated. In the third example, in order for handle cell 27 to be approved, one G-rated secondary factor is required. In the fourth example, for handle cell 28 to be approved, similar housing expense (e.g., ratio of new mortgage payment to prior rent or mortgage payment) would need to be G-rated with months of reserves at least F-rated, or, alternatively, similar housing expense would have to be F-rated with months of reserves at least G-rated. In the fifth example, for handle cell 33 to be approved, months of reserves must be G-rated, discretionary income must be at least F-rated, and relationship must be at least F-rated. Also, there are additional factors that can have their associated thresholds calibrated for loan approval, such as the extent to which LTV is below threshold, or the explanation of derogatory credit ratings, or any alternative credit or noncredit trade lines that have been satisfactorily paid for two or more years, or a savings account with

Case	Credit History Rating	Mortgage	Installment	Revolving
1	G	G	G	G
2	F	G	G	F
3	P	G	G	P
4	F	G	F	G
5	F	G	F	F
6	P	G	F	P
7	P	G	P	G
8	P	G	P	F
9	P	G	P	P
10	F	F	G	G
11	F	F	G	F
12	P	F	G	P
13	F	F	F	G
14	F	F	F	F
15	P	F	F	P
16	P	F	P	G
17	P	F	P	F
18	P	F	P	P
19	P	P	G	G
20	P	P	G	F
21	P	P	G	P
22	P	P	F	G
23	P	P	F	F
24	P	P	F	P
25	P	P	P	G
26	P	P	P	F
27	P	P	P	P

FIGURE 6.28   CREDIT HISTORY DIMENSION: TIME PERIODS ELIMINATED AND COLLAPSING ALL THREE TRADE LINE CATEGORIES TO THREE VALUES

significant regular payments. Finally, for handle cell 35 to be approved, LTV must be less than 70 percent and liquid assets must be G-rated. If approved, the action cell reference number is 71, otherwise it will remain at 35.

From an operational standpoint, this hybrid model could be easily deployed in a decision engine that is encased in a comprehensive model management environment.[44] In this way, the adaptive nature of hybrid models can be exploited to the fullest extent possible. Next, we consider an

---

44. See Chu, Robert, David Dulling, and Wayne Thompson, "Best Practices for Managing Predictive Models in a Production Environment," SAS Institute Inc., 2007.

Primary Factors	Categories, Definitions, and Value Assignments		
Credit bureau score[a]	G- 700 +	F- 621–699	P- < 620
Credit payment history for all trade lines in credit bureau report(s)	G- See Figure 25 for detailed definition based on past due occurrence for < 1r, 1–2 years, > 2 year sep. for rev., IL, mtg.	F- See Figure 25 for detailed definition based on past due occurrence for < 1r, 1–2 yrs, > 2 yr sep. for rev., IL, mtg.	P- See Figure 25 for detailed definition based on past due occurrence for < 1r, 1–2 years, > 2 year sep. for rev., IL, mtg.
DTI	L- < 44%	H- 44% +	
LTV ratio[b]	L- 80% or less	H- 81% +	

FIGURE 6.29   HOME PURCHASE MORTGAGE LOAN PRIMARY FACTORS

[a]Usually based on the credit score associated with the applicant having the highest income, in the case of joint applicants. Usually, scores from all three credit bureaus are ordered and the high and low scores are thrown out (e.g., TransUnion = 742, Equifax = 720, and Experian = 684, then bureau credit score = 720).
[b]Loan-to-value ratio calculated as loan amount divided by the Blue Book value of the collateral.

example that demonstrates the applicability of hybrid models to business, in addition to all forms of consumer, lending.

Small Business Unsecured Term Loan Example

Credit scoring has been successfully used in small business lending by some large banks.[45] There are many forms of small business lending. We picked a simple case (e.g., no collateral to consider) for the purpose of ease of illustration, but the same general approach holds in more complicated transactions. Models for small business real estate loans and other forms of secured loans would have differing sets of criteria, as would loans in higher loan amount tiers, community development qualified loans under the Community Reinvestment Act, and so on.

The following example is for an unsecured small business term loan. These loans have maturities in excess of one year and are made to increase working capital, purchase fixed assets, or possibly retire capital. In contrast to the consumer loans discussed previously, there are additional types of risks posed by these loans that relate to the ability of the business to service the debt, namely:

- *Industry.* Relates to the industry in which the business is classified[46] or sector risk as a whole, often denoted by Standard Industrial Classification (SIC) codes.
- *Geographic.* Relates to the economic well-being of the area where the business is located, competitive forces, government or private sector programs aimed at funding revitalization efforts and community development, demographic/immigration trends, multicultural and social fabric of the residents and businesses, and so on.
- *Market.* Relates to the economic well-being of the customer/prospective customer base (in many instances, this coincides with geographic risk), the diversity of the market, the complexity and granularity of customer segmentation, the business' prevailing market share in

45. See Akhavein, Jalal, W. Scott Frame, and Lawrence J. White, "The Diffusion of Financial Innovations: An Examination of the Adoption of Small Business Credit Scoring by Large Banking Organizations." White Paper, The Wharton Financial Institutions Center, 2001, pp. 1–30.
46. For example, agriculture, forestry and fishing; construction; manufacturing; transportation, communication and utilities; wholesale trade; retail trade; finance and insurance; real estate; services.

Handle	Risk Category	Credit Bureau Score	Credit Payment History	Debt-to-Income Ratio	Loan-to-Value Ratio
1	0	G	G	L	L
2	1	G	G	H	L
3	1	G	F	L	L
4	2	G	F	H	L
5	2	G	P	L	I
6	3	G	P	H	L
7	1	F	G	L	L
8	2	F	G	H	L
9	1	F	F	L	L
10	2	F	F	H	L
11	2	F	P	L	L
12	3	F	P	H	L
13	2	P	G	L	L
14	3	P	G	H	L
15	2	P	F	L	L
16	3	P	F	H	L
17	3	P	P	L	L
18	4	P	P	H	L
19	1	G	G	L	H
20	2	G	G	H	H
21	2	G	F	L	H
22	3	G	F	H	H
23	3	G	P	L	H
24	4	G	P	H	H
25	2	F	G	L	H
26	3	F	G	H	H
27	2	F	F	L	H
28	3	F	F	H	H
29	3	F	P	L	H
30	4	F	P	H	H
31	3	P	G	L	H
32	4	P	G	H	H
33	3	P	F	L	H
34	4	P	F	H	H
35	4	P	P	L	H
36	5	P	P	H	H

FIGURE 6.30   HANDLE TABLE

Months of reserves	G- 6 months +	F- 3–5 months	P- 2 months or less
Similar housing expense	G- 120% or less of previous payment	F- > 120–135% of previous payment	P- > 135% of previous payment
Time in profession	G- 5 years +	F- 3–4 years	P- < 3 years
Strong liquid assets	G- > 10% loan amt.	F- 5–9% loan amt.	P- 4% or less loan amt
History of handling higher debt	G- 3 + years	F- 1–2 years	P- < 1 year
Discretionary Income[a]	G- > $2 M/month	F- $1 M to 2 M/month	P- < $1 M/month
Relationship	G- 2+ loan, deposit, investment accounts	F- 1 loan, deposit, or investment account	P- None

FIGURE 6.31 SECONDARY FACTORS (WEIGHT IN FINAL DECISION OF 5–15 PERCENT EACH)

[a]Defined as total monthly income less total monthly debt. A minimum, say $1 M, is usually required to qualify.

key segments, the opportunity to gain additional share in profitable segments via repartitioning of the market for competitive advantage, concentration risk (i.e., what percent of the business comes from a single or top three customers as well as suppliers).

- *Management.* Relates to management competency and experience in running a successful business.
- *Financial.* Financial performance and structure of the firm, sourced from balance sheet and income statements (e.g., gross annual revenue, net worth, and liquid assets). The elements are combined via standard financial ratios that address profitability, liquidity, and leverage.
- *Relationship and credit track record.* Length of relationship, time in business, balances maintained in business savings, checking, and other deposit accounts.[47]

This specific example affords an opportunity to expose the complexity of the calculation of categories for criteria represented by business financial variables. Furthermore, the complexity is deepened when the industry dimension above is included. This is accomplished by specifying the definition of good, fair, and poor values for the various financial ratios in such a manner as to reflect known averages for the industry, or the lender's own historical performance for comparable loans in the respective industry.[48]

Consider the ratio analysis factor, which addresses financial risk. It takes on values of good, fair, or poor, which seem straightforward enough. However, it is important to weigh both balance sheet and income factors over time, relative to the type of business, or industry. The following is a representative derivation of a ratio analysis factor that combines liquidity (L), indebtedness (I), and profitability (P) in order to form a combined ratio factor (C).

---

47. In most small business loans, the personal credit history of the principle is also considered.

48. A commonly encountered source of financial and operating ratios for over 700 industries is the RMA Statement Studies (originally branded the Annual Statement Studies) available from the Risk Management Association, formerly Robert Morris Associates. This information is based on over 190,000 statements of financial institution borrowers and prospects directly from member banks that get their data straight from their customers. Other suppliers of this type of information include Dun & Bradstreet Business Economics Division, Moody's Investor Service, and Standard & Poor's Corporation. In addition, some retail and wholesale trade associations regularly compile and publish ratio statistics. This is much less so with manufacturing associations, but a quarterly report is available from the Federal Trade Commission that contains ratio analysis for manufacturing and mining companies. There are many other federal government sources for industry financial data including the Small Business Administration, U.S. Department of Commerce, Internal Revenue Service, and the Department of the Treasury.

Credit Score	Credit History	DTI	Stage 1		Stage 2	
			Low LTV	High LTV	Low LTV	High LTV
Good	Good	Low	1. Accept	19. Accept	37. n/a	55. n/a
Good	Good	High	2. Accept	20. Stage 2	38. n/a	56. Denial
Good	Fair	Low	3. Accept	21. Stage 2	39. n/a	57. Denial
Good	Fair	High	4. Stage 2	22. Stage 2	40. Denial	58. Denial
Good	Poor	Low	5. Accept	23. Stage 2	41. n/a	59. Denial
Good	Poor	High	6. Stage 2	24. Denial	42. Denial	60. n/a
Fair	Good	Low	7. Accept	25. Accept	43. n/a	61. n/a
Fair	Good	High	8. Accept	26. Stage 2	44. n/a	62. Denial
Fair	Fair	Low	9. Accept	27. Stage 2	45. n/a	63. Denial
Fair	Fair	High	10. Stage 2	28. Stage 2	46. Denial	64. Denial
Fair	Poor	Low	11. Accept	29. Stage 2	47. n/a	65. Denial
Fair	Poor	High	12. Stage 2	30. Denial	48. Denial	66. n/a
Poor	Good	Low	13. Accept	31. Stage 2	49. n/a	67. Denial
Poor	Good	High	14. Accept	32. Stage 2	50. n/a	68. Denial
Poor	Fair	Low	15. Stage 2	33. Stage 2	51. Denial	69. Denial
Poor	Fair	High	16. Stage 2	34. Denial	52. Denial	70. n/a
Poor	Poor	Low	17. Stage 2	35. Decline	53. Accept	71. n/a
Poor	Poor	High	18. Stage 2	36. Decline	54. Accept	72. n/a

FIGURE 6.32   TWO-STAGE ACTION TABLE FOR MORTGAGE LOAN EXAMPLE

Handle	Risk Category	Credit Payment History	Credit Bureau Score	Debt-to-Inc Ratio	Loan-to-Value Ratio
3	1	G	F	L	L
12	3	F	P	H	L
27	2	F	F	L	H
28	3	F	F	H	H
33	3	P	F	L	H
35	4	P	P	L	H

FIGURE 6.33   SELECTED HANDLE CELLS FOR SECONDARY FACTOR QUALIFICATION DISCUSSION

Liquidity

- *Current ratio.* This is an indication of a company's ability to meet short-term debt obligations, and is defined as the total current assets/total current liabilities. The higher the ratio, the more liquid the company is:
  - Good: 1.7 or greater
  - Fair: 1.25–1.69
  - Poor: Less than 1.25
- *Quick ratio.* This is a measure of a company's liquidity and ability to meet its obligations. Quick ratio is viewed as a sign of company's financial strength or weakness, and is defined as (Cash + Marketable securities + Reserves + Net accounts receivable)/Total current liabilities). A higher number means stronger, and a lower number means weaker:
  - Good: 0.75 or greater
  - Fair: 0.45–0.74
  - Poor: Less than 0.45

  Liquidity is a function of current ratio and quick ratio as shown in Figure 6.34.
- *Indebtedness.* This is represented by debt ratio, and defined as [Tangible net worth/(Total liabilities − Subordinated debt)], which tells you how much the company relies on debt to finance assets:
  - Good: 0.6 or greater
  - Fair: 0.35–0.59
  - Poor: Less than 0.35
- *Profitability.* This is defined as: [(Net income + (Interest expense − Income taxes saved in interest expense))/Average total assets]:
  - Good: 0.09 or greater
  - Fair: 0.055–0.089
  - Poor: Less than 0.055

Trending is important in ratio analysis, and the value of the combined ratio must be determined for each of the past three years of history (column labeled "C" in each of three columns in Figure 6.35, where the columns are grouped by year for each of the three individual ratios and their respective combined ratio).

Case	Current Ratio	Quick Ratio	Liquidity Ratio
1	G	G	G
2	G	F	G
3	G	P	F
4	F	G	G
5	F	F	F
6	F	P	P
7	P	G	F
8	P	F	P
9	P	P	P

FIGURE 6.34 LIQUIDITY DIMENSION

Case	12- Month Time Frame				12–24 Month Time Frame				24–36 Month Time Frame			
	Liqui-dity	Indebted-ness	Profit-ability	Combi-ned	Liqui-dity	Indebted-ness	Profit-ability	Combi-ned	Liqui-dity	Indebted-ness	Profit-ability	Combi-ned
1	G	G	G	G	G	G	G	G	G	G	G	G
2	G	G	F	G	G	G	F	G	G	G	F	G
3	G	G	P	F	G	G	P	F	G	G	P	G
4	G	F	G	G	G	F	G	G	G	F	G	G
5	G	F	F	F	G	F	F	F	G	F	F	F
6	G	F	P	P	G	F	P	P	G	F	P	P
7	G	P	G	F	G	P	G	G	G	P	G	G
8	G	P	F	F	G	P	F	F	G	P	F	F
9	G	P	P	P	G	P	P	P	G	P	P	P
10	F	G	G	G	F	G	G	G	F	G	G	G
11	F	G	F	F	F	G	F	F	F	G	F	F
12	F	G	P	F	F	G	P	F	F	G	P	F
13	F	F	G	F	F	F	G	F	F	F	G	F
14	F	F	F	F	F	F	F	F	F	F	F	F
15	F	F	P	P	F	F	P	P	F	F	P	P
16	F	P	G	F	F	P	G	F	F	P	G	F
17	F	P	F	P	F	P	F	P	F	P	F	P
18	F	P	P	P	F	P	P	P	F	P	P	P
19	P	G	G	F	P	G	G	G	P	G	G	G
20	P	G	F	F	P	G	F	F	P	G	F	F
21	P	G	P	P	P	G	P	P	P	G	P	P
22	P	F	G	F	P	F	G	F	P	F	G	G
23	P	F	F	F	P	F	F	F	P	F	F	F
24	P	F	P	P	P	F	P	P	P	F	P	P
25	P	P	G	P	P	P	G	F	P	P	G	G
26	P	P	F	P	P	P	F	P	P	P	F	P
27	P	P	P	P	P	P	P	P	P	P	P	P

FIGURE 6.35   FINANCIAL DIMENSION COMBINING LIQUIDITY, INDEBTEDNESS, AND PROFITABILITY WITHIN EACH OF THREE TIME PERIODS

Finally, the combined ratio values are determined by collapsing performance over time, based on the business rules embodied in Figure 6.36. The most weight is given to the most recent information, but in some instances even the oldest year can make a difference in the final result.

In addition to the industry and financial factors, there are management and market/geographic factors.

Management past experience, background, and depth are a focus. Issues tend to surround key manager competency, succession planning, management ability and effectiveness. Another aspect is the degree of commitment on the owner's part(s) and how much sacrifice they are

Case	Current Year	12–24 Mos.	24–36 Mos.	Collapsed
1	G	G	G	G
2	G	G	F	G
3	G	G	P	G
4	G	F	G	G
5	G	F	F	G
6	G	F	P	F
7	G	P	G	G
8	G	P	F	F
9	G	P	P	F
10	F	G	G	G
11	F	G	F	F
12	F	G	P	F
13	F	F	G	F
14	F	F	F	F
15	F	F	P	F
16	F	P	G	F
17	F	P	F	F
18	F	P	P	P
19	P	G	G	F
20	P	G	F	P
21	P	G	P	P
22	P	F	G	P
23	P	F	F	P
24	P	F	P	P
25	P	P	G	P
26	P	P	F	P
27	P	P	P	P

FIGURE 6.36   FINAL COLLAPSING OF FINANCIAL DIMENSION ACROSS TIME TO THREE VALUES

prepared to make in order to ensure the success of the enterprise. For example, limits on executive compensation, distribution of profits, borrowing base, and so on may be captured as part of the loan agreement. For this area, management classification has been simplified to strong or weak.

The topic of market and geographic risk assessment is a particularly interesting one and it also represents perhaps the greatest opportunity for outreach to entrepreneurs who operate in, or consider expanding into, economically depressed areas, or cater to low to moderate income customers. Initial perceived deficiencies in management or financial strength may be surmountable if the businesses economic franchise is especially strong. Using a computer-based, multiperiod stochastic financial simulation model, different business scenarios can be constructed using a combination of company-specific, management/owner-related, industry, and environmental factors (macroeconomic, demographic, sociological/cultural related, market based, geographic, competitive, etc.).

Cash flows can be constructed under each scenario, which is either probability weighted, or comprised of variables that take on values according to known probability laws (e.g., normal, triangular, multinomial, exponential, Poisson), or combinations thereof (e.g., lognormal, lognormal-gamma). The model can calculate the odds that the small business applying for a loan will default on the obligation at some point during the term of the loan agreement.

In-depth discussion of environmental factors is beyond the scope of this book, but the implications for prudent financing in the wake of natural disasters, such as Hurricane Katrina, are substantial.[49]

Finally, relationship and credit track record are also of primary importance. The age, breadth, and depth of the relationship and the extent to which loans have been paid on time and as agreed can weigh heavily, especially if there is a weakness in one or more of the other factors. The consumer credit history and credit bureau scores associated with principal owners and operators of the small business also frequently come into play.

Figure 6.37 summarizes the end results of the categorization process for all of the derived primary factors for small business lending.

At this point, the handle for the small business unsecured term loan is completely specified. Figure 6.38 shows the handle dimensions for the hybrid model based on the factors determined by MCS.

Figures 6.9 and 6.10 list dozens of candidate secondary factors for small business lending using traditional credit bureau and non–credit bureau sources. The reader is encouraged to review those figures for specific examples. Factors listed as primary can also serve as secondary factors, depending on the information values of related factors, the degree of correlation with primary

Primary Factors		Categories and Definitions	
Credit history (internal/external for both business trade lines and owner personal consumer accounts)	G-Positive with sufficient breadth and depth of reporting and experience	F/P-Weak: Negative information or insufficient record to permit assessment	
Financial strength/industry	G- Gross, operating, pretax margins above RMA median; leverage and liquidity ratios above RMA median	F- Gross, operating, pretax margins in third RMA quartile; leverage and liquidity ratios margins in third RMA quartile	P- Gross, operating, pretax margins in fourth quartile RMA avgs.; leverage and liquidity ratios margins in fourth quartile RMA avgs
Geographic/market Influences	P- Positive	N- Neutral to Negative	
Management	S- Strong	W- Weak	

FIGURE 6.37   PRIMARY FACTORS FOR SMALL BUSINESS LENDING

49. The Brookings Institution's "Urban Markets Initiative (UMI) aims to improve the quality of the information available on urban communities to unleash the full power of those markets while connecting them to the economic mainstream ." See Sabety, Pari. "Fulfilling the Promise: Seven Steps to Successful Community-Based Information Strategies," discussion paper prepared for the 2006 Council on Foundations Annual Conference, The Brookings Institution, May 2006, p. iii.

Handle Number	Risk Category	Credit History	Market Effects	Management Quality	Financial Strength
1	0	Good	Strong	Positive	Good
2	1	Good	Strong	Positive	Fair
3	2	Good	Strong	Positive	Poor
4	1	Good	Strong	Neutral/Negative	Good
5	2	Good	Strong	Neutral/Negative	Fair
6	3	Good	Strong	Neutral/Negative	Poor
7	1	Good	Weak	Positive	Good
8	2	Good	Weak	Positive	Fair
9	3	Good	Weak	Positive	Poor
10	2	Good	Weak	Neutral/Negative	Good
11	3	Good	Weak	Neutral/Negative	Fair
12	4	Good	Weak	Neutral/Negative	Poor
13	1	Fair/Poor	Strong	Positive	Good
14	2	Fair/Poor	Strong	Positive	Fair
15	3	Fair/Poor	Strong	Positive	Poor
16	2	Fair/Poor	Strong	Neutral/Negative	Good
17	3	Fair/Poor	Strong	Neutral/Negative	Fair
18	4	Fair/Poor	Strong	Neutral/Negative	Poor
19	2	Fair/Poor	Weak	Positive	Good
20	3	Fair/Poor	Weak	Positive	Fair
21	4	Fair/Poor	Weak	Positive	Poor
22	3	Fair/Poor	Weak	Neutral/Negative	Good
23	4	Fair/Poor	Weak	Neutral/Negative	Fair
24	5	Fair/Poor	Weak	Neutral/Negative	Poor

FIGURE 6.38   HANDLE TABLE FOR SMALL BUSINESS LOAN EXAMPLE (PRIMARY FACTORS)

factors, and the segmentation scheme used. A small business-specific credit score designed specifically for use for certain products, industries, geographies, and so forth could incorporate many factors and serve in a secondary capacity. Hybrid systems and credit scoring are effectively used in unison.

The next step in the process is to specify, for every handle cell whether secondary factors are required to render a decision to approve the loan. If secondary factors are not required, then the approve or decline decision appears in the handle cell. If secondary factors are required, then the business rules for qualifying the loans falling into the handle cell are specified fully and the handle cell action is designated as "Stage 2."[50] This is illustrated in Figure 6.39.

---

50. The stage 2 action table has handle cell numbers beginning with the number equal to the number of cells in the handle plus one. In the current example, the stage 2 action table would begin with action cell number 25. Suppose in the example that handle cells with risk category 0 were approved and those with risk category 4 were declined, and that handle cells with risk categories 1, 2, and 3 are referred on to stage 2. Then there are 20 stage 2 action table cells, numbered 25 through 44. Loans approved in stage 2 maintain the stage 2 action cell number. Those

Other Factors			Financial Strength – Stage 1			Financial Strength – Stage 2		
Credit History	Mkt/Ind.	Mgmt. Exper.	Good	Fair	Poor	Good	Fair	Poor
Good	Strong	Positive	1. Appv.	2. Stg 2	3. Stg 2	n/a	25. Apv	26. Apv
Good	Strong	Neutral/Neg.	4. Stg 2	5. Stg 2	6. Stg 2	27. Apv	28. Apv	29. Apv
Good	Weak	Positive	7. Stg 2	8. Stg 2	9. Stg 2	30. Apv	31. Apv	32. Apv
Good	Weak	Neutral/Neg.	10. Stg 2	11. Stg 2	12. Decl	33. Apv	34. Apv	n/a
Fair/Poor	Strong	Positive	13. Stg 2	14. Stg 2	15. Stg 2	35. Apv	36. Apv	37. Apv
Fair/Poor	Strong	Neutral/Neg.	16. Stg 2	17. Stg 2	18. Stg 2	38. Apv	39. Apv	40. Apv
Fair/Poor	Weak	Positive	19. Stg 2	20. Stg 2	21. Stg 2	41. Apv	42. Apv	43. Apv
Fair/Poor	Weak	Neutral/Neg.	22. Stg 2	23. Decl	24. Decl	44. Apv	n/a	n/a

FIGURE 6.39 TWO-STAGE ACTION TABLE FOR SMALL BUSINESS LOAN EXAMPLE

The conditional business rules associated with the stage 2 action table shown in Figure 6.39 are not provided, but those rules are dictated by MCS. Following the process outlined in Figure 6.11, the remaining portion of the small business loan example for underwriting consists of statistical model building to estimate the handle cell frequency and risk estimates.

HYBRID UNDERWRITING MODELS WITH NONTRADITIONAL CREDIT INFORMATION

In Chapter 1 we noted that consumer, and to some extent small business, access to credit depends largely on point scoring models that were developed based on samples that may not well represent out-of-the-mainstream consumers who are now attempting to qualify for a loan. We raised the question: "How can lenders qualify certain segments of the consumer population that have not historically been users of traditional credit, and hence do not have associated credit payment performance histories in credit bureau databases?" The answer to this question may reside in recent research conducted by PERC and the Brookings Institution,[51] which concluded that mainstream lenders can use alternative or nontraditional data to evaluate the risk profile of a potential borrower. It appears we now have strong empirical evidence that noncredit payment data can help predict credit risk.

Alternative data has always existed but has not been readily accessible. So consumers have had to put themselves into debt and then make timely payments in order to demonstrate that they are creditworthy! Alternative data can help qualify consumers who pay their cash obligations as agreed, and its use represents the next logical step in the evolution of consumer credit models. Alternative data can help to speed the process of *mainstreaming* financially responsible cash-paying consumers whose dreams of a better life, including homeownership, continue to elude them. We believe the

that are declined revert back to their primary handle cell number. For example, suppose that a loan falling onto handle number 22 is approved in stage 2. Then we can derive the associated action table reference number by adding the primary handle action table number (22) to the number of entries in the stage 2 table (20) and add the number of non–stage 2 handle cells that possess a higher handle cell number (2) = 44. For a loan falling onto handle number 2 approved in stage 2, the associated action table reference is calculated to be the primary handle action table number (2) plus the number of entries in the stage 2 table (20), plus the number of non–stage 2 handle cells that possess a higher handle cell number (3) = 25.

51. See Turner, et al., 2006.

propagation of new alternative credit models throughout the financial system will afford better and fairer chances for all borrowers and greater revenue for lenders, and deliver broader economic prosperity in communities across the nation.

Including more comprehensive data should improve credit-scoring models. We expect that more lenders will start to use alternative data in conjunction with traditional data to develop credit-scoring models. We assert that it will be important for modeling methodology to evolve in order to enable best use and incorporation of the nontraditional data.[52]

In this section, we assert that hybrid models can help speed that evolution. Hybrid credit models combine subject matter expertise with the best science. They can effectively tap alternative sources of data associated with all facets of the loan-underwriting and pricing process so that greater access to credit can be afforded to deserving consumers without generating unacceptable incremental risk.[53]

Factors	Portfolios						
	Direct Direct	Indirect Dealer	Credit Card	Home Equity	Mtg	Other Sec IL	Small Business
Utility payment history	P	P	P	P	P	P	P
Bill-pay score	S	S	S	S	S	S	S
Phone payment history	P	P	P	P	P	P	P
Noncredit payment-to-income ratio[a]	S	S	S	S	S	S	S
Insurance payment history[b]	S	S	S	S	S	S	S
Ratio of noncredit accounts with no current or historical delinquency to total noncash accounts	S	S	S	S	S	S	S
Time since most recent late noncredit payment	S	S	S	S	S	S	S
Total late payments for open noncredit accounts	S	S	S	S	S	S	S
Number of noncredit accounts requiring monthly payment	S	S	S	S	S	S	S
Rent/lease payment history	P	P	P	P	P	P	P
Checking account w/min $500 balance maintained	S	S	S	S	S	S	S
Checking overdrafts/NSFs	S	S	S	S	S	S	S

FIGURE 6.40   NONTRADITIONAL DECISION VARIABLES AND THEIR IMPORTANCE

[a]Sum of monthly noncredit payment obligations (including, but not limited to, rent, electricity, water/sewer, garbage collection, phone, security, renter's insurance, auto insurance, etc.) divided by gross monthly income.
[b]Include all forms of insurance (e.g. term life, auto, disability, health, casualty, etc.).

---

52. It is also important to develop a model validation framework to validate model developed with nontraditional data. This will be discussed in Chapter 8.
53. Turner, Michael A., Ann B. Schnare, Robin Varghese, and Patrick Walker. "Helping Consumers Access Affordable Mainstream Credit: Measuring the Impact of Including Utility and Telecom Data in Consumer Credit Reports," IPI Research Publication, 2006.

The alternative data often come from energy and water utility payments, phone bills, rental payments, remittance payments, and stored value cards, and certain types of retail payment. The data can fit the same analysis framework based on either traditional credit scoring or hybrid models. Figure 6.40 shows an example of nontraditional underwriting criteria. The criteria or variables can be substituted for their traditional counterparts in the previous two examples or the portfolio-specific examples in Appendix 6C of this chapter. The substitution is accomplished by replacing traditional primary or secondary variables with nontraditional ones. The columns in Figure 6.40 indicate the primary and secondary status by portfolio. In this way, readers can design their own alternative models. We are not advocating a "blind substitution" of credit factors in these alternative models. For example, if there were a question of borrower capacity, then that issue would not be addressable by an alternative data variable that demonstrates a regular $50 payment. Payment on time, like a credit delinquency history variable, shows borrower willingness to pay, but not necessarily borrower ability to pay. The reader is referred to our earlier discussion on the five Cs of credit that underpin the judgemental approach. Alternative data substitutions should be performed within like categories. Hence, in lieu of a DTI, an alternative data equivalent might be an aggregate alternative monthly obligation to income ratio that combines the proposed loan payment with the numerator of the noncredit payment to income ratio described in the fourth row of Figure 6.41. In fact, the ratio just described and the payment-to-income ratio (without the

Utility payment history	G- 0 times late past 12 months	F- 1–2 late past 24 months	P- 3 + times late past 24 months
Bill payment score	G- > 720	F- 660–720	P- < 660
Phone payment history	G- 2 years +	F-1–2 years	P- < 1 year
Noncredit payment-to-income ratio[a]	G- < 40%	F- 41–59%	P- 60% +
Insurance payment history[b]	G- 0 times late past 12 months	F- 1–2 late past 24 months	P- 3 + times late past 24 months
Ratio of noncredit accounts with no current or historical delinquency to total noncash accounts	G- 80% +	F- 50–79%	P- < 50%
Months since most recent late noncredit payment	G- 12 months +	F- 7–12 months	P- < 6 months
Total late payments for open noncredit accounts	G- 0 or 1 late payment last 24 months	F- 2–4 late payments last 24 months	P- 5 + late payments last 24 months
Number of noncredit accounts requiring monthly payment	G- 4 + accounts	F- 2–3 accounts	P- None or 1 account
Rent/lease payment history	G- 0 times late past 12 months	F- 1–2 late past 24 months	P- 3 + times late past 24 months
Checking account w/min balance maintained	G- Min bal > $1 M	F- Min bal $500-1 M	P- Min bal < $500
Checking overdrafts/NSFs	G- None	F- 1–2 last 6 months	P- 3 + last 6 months

FIGURE 6.41   GROUPINGS AND RATINGS FOR NONTRADITIONAL FACTORS

[a]Sum of monthly noncredit payment obligations (including, but not limited to, rent, electricity, water/sewer, garbage collection, phone, security, renter's insurance, auto insurance, etc.) divided by gross monthly income.
[b]Include all forms of insurance (e.g., term life, auto, disability, health, casualty, etc.).

loan payment amount included) could be an indicator of payment shock that could be used as a secondary factor, provided it proves to have sufficient statistical relevance.

Nontraditional primary or secondary factors are classified into homogenous groups based on policy, which can be either empirically or judgmentally based. Figure 6.41 provides hypothetical examples for a dozen typical variables.

HYBRID MODELS AND OVERRIDE ANALYSIS

As we have shown in the previous sections, the hybrid model contains both quantitative and qualitative elements to reduce model risk and compliance risk. In this section, we discuss the relationship between hybrid models and loan overriding, which is a subjective loan underwriting practice associated with credit scoring. We first describe how loan overrides occur and explain the different types of override. We then, provide examples, and discuss their impact on credit risk management and fair lending compliance. We then describe how the hybrid model can be applied to lower the overall incidence of overrides. By monitoring them in detail and fine tuning secondary factor criteria, negative impacts from both a credit and compliance perspective may be lessened. Furthermore, by incorporating override criteria into the hybrid model, policy overrides can be minimized or eliminated. We note the majority of individual circumstantial overrides can be minimized by capturing specific examples over time and creating business rules to trap legitimate cases as secondary factors.

Override Types and Examples

Override analysis is used in conjunction with credit scored loans. While it is intended to provide a means to help implement loan underwriting policy consistently and fairly, it can also open the door to potential discrimination since this involves mainly subjective analysis and judgment. Therefore, it is necessary to examine and monitor override process and results, and identify and correct any potential discriminatory practices. Bank examiners evaluate the reasonableness of the bank's override practices from three aspects: bank policy, required information, and intuition. In operation, credit-scoring underwriting decisions overrides fall into three main categories: informational, policy, and individual subjective.[54] Management should be able to identify the type and volume of overrides by category and measure the quality of their performances.[55]

Informational overrides occur when additional information that was not captured in the scorecard and is material and known about the applicant causes the scoring system decision to be overturned, or product terms and conditions for which the scorecard was developed are at variance with what the customer wants. A commonly cited example of an underwriting informational override is when it becomes known that the applicant has just been sentenced to a prison term. An example relative to credit-scoring pricing decisions might be that a borrower asks for a different term or condition than the product being priced off a pricing sheet (e.g., a 72-month term instead of a 60-month term) which may increase/decrease risk of default. In this case, the loan officer may override the price sheet and require a higher rate than the score would indicate for the standard product offering.

Policy overrides occur when the lender sets up business rules that are to be applied as an automatic review rules. A common low-side override factor is customer relationship. Policy overrides are preferable to individual subjective overrides as discussed next. This is because individual subjective overrides may not be applied consistently and this exposes the lender to potential disparate

---

54. See Lewis, 1992, II.3.4 Overrides, pp. 89–93.
55. See OCC Bulletin, 97–24, *Examination Guidance on Credit Scoring Models*, May 20, 1997, p. 6.

treatment allegation. In contrast, policy overrides are applied uniformly and, in the worst case, expose the lender to disparate impact.

Individual subjective overrides occur when a loan officer decides to override a scorecard decision for reasons other than policy. This occurs in risk-based pricing when the score and other criteria are not sufficiently granular to fit a particular situation. Suppose that a pricing adjustment is 100 basis points for a purchase mortgage loan is based on the credit score being in a certain range, the LTV being below a certain threshold, and the debt to income ratio being greater than 40 percent. In a situation where the applicant scores in the particular range and meets the LTV requirement, but has a DTI of 42 percent, they will be penalized the full 100 basis points by policy. In this circumstance, the loan officer may decide to make an override and only assess an additional 25 basis points, because the applicant is certainly not as risky as someone who has a DTI greater than 70, 60, or even 50 percent. This can happen in many ways where it appears to the loan officer that the risk-based score recommendation over/underpenalizes the borrower in question.

Overrides occur both for applicants scoring at, or above, the cutoff that are declined (termed *high-side overrides* [HSOs]) and those scoring below cut-off that are approved (termed *low-side overrides* [LSOs]). As one might expect, the highest percentage of overrides occur within a 15-point range on either side of the cutoff score, with fewer overrides occurring the further the score is from the cutoff point.

Some detailed examples of policy overrides appear in Figures 6.42 and 6.43. Pricing overrides are too numerous to cite, so the following examples of low-side and high-side overrides pertain to loan underwriting, but many have direct application to pricing adjustments that are commonly found on rate sheets for various consumer loan products.

There will be many situations where applicants fall into multiple override reason categories (i.e., multiple policy override factors may apply). In these instances, usually only a single override code is captured. It is important, therefore, that the lender imposes a hierarchy of severity ranking of override reasons so that the most severe reason is always selected for every override reason. Otherwise, arbitrary selection of the override reason where multiple factors apply will occur, and the result will be to introduce bias into override monitoring by reason code. Limitation to a single

---

- *Account Transfer.* When a new product replaces a pre-existing one. These are operational in nature, and should not be counted in system monitoring for credit and compliance exceptions!
- *Application Voided.* Used to handle operational errors, such as when an application is scored using an incorrect scorecard, or duplicated, etc. These are operational in nature, and should not be counted in system monitoring for credit and compliance exceptions!
- *Bank Relationship.* Refers to applicants who qualify for special consideration due to the profitability of their personal banking relationship. Key metrics may be specified, e.g., profitability tier membership, or relationship/product specific thresholds (e.g., maintenance of minimum average monthly deposit balances over a set period of time, utilization rates, aggregate loan amounts, etc.).
- *Employee.* Applicant is an employee of the lending institution.
- *Executive Referral.* Applicant has a recommendation from a bank executive that has been granted approval authority.
- *Guaranteed Account.* Refers to when a person, or business, guarantees the credit.
- *High Bureau Score.* Applicant possesses a credit bureau score that exceeds a policy threshold.
- *Strong Co-applicant.* If substituting the co-applicant credit bureau score would qualify the credit application and the co-applicant score also exceeds a policy threshold value.
- *Very High Net Worth/Very High Liquidity.* Occurs when the applicant possesses a very significant financial condition with verifiable assets or a large amount of assets that can easily be converted to cash.

FIGURE 6.42 EXAMPLES OF UNDERWRITING LOW-SIDE OVERRIDE REASONS

- *Application Voided.* Used to handle operational errors, such as when an application is scored using an incorrect scorecard, or duplicated, etc. *These are operational in nature, and should not be counted in system monitoring for credit and compliance exceptions!*
- *Bankruptcy, Judgment, Tax Lien, Foreclosure, Repossession.* Public record for one of the foregoing found in the applicant's credit bureau file that is less than a policy threshold in age, usually 4–7 years.
- *Counter-Offer Made.* Used to cover cases where the applicant is approved for another product and declined for the product requested.
- *Debt to Income Ratio.* Refers to DTI ratios exceeding a policy threshold.
- *High Exposure.* Refers to situations where the applicant has high aggregate loan balances and high utilization of credit lines spanning all lending institutions. A high income or credit score could factor into the override criteria.
- *Inadequate Income.* Applicant income falls below the policy minimum amount
- *Income Not Verified.* Questionable, or temporary, income that cannot be verified.
- *Major Derogatory.* Refers to when a trade line is 60 days past due or more within the past policy-specified time frame
- *Non-Permanent Resident.* The applicant is not a permanent resident of the United States.
- *Poor Credit History With the Lender.* The applicant's payment history is unsatisfactory per policy guidelines.
- *Suspected Fraud.* Possible fraudulent application is identified. *These are operational in nature, and should not be counted in system monitoring for credit and compliance exceptions!*
- *Thin File/No Credit Bureau File.* Little or no credit history exists.
- *Unacceptable Bureau Score.* Although the applicant's credit score passes the cutoff, the Credit Bureau Score falls below policy guidelines

FIGURE 6.43   EXAMPLES OF UNDERWRITING HIGH-SIDE OVERRIDE REASONS

reason for capturing the override result has implications for the choice of testing procedure. A possible way around the limitation would be if the lender expanded the list of override codes to include a way to capture all combinations of override policy factors that apply in a given situation, but this would put a larger burden on the operational staff. Alternatively, additional fields could be sourced that relate to all policy factors so that the override reason could be derived independently. In this case, a logistic regression model could be developed, where the dependent variable represents the probability of being an override. The method is analogous to that described in the previous chapter.

The impact of HSOs and LSOs on portfolio profitability and quality is an important topic. Another concern is the risk they pose for regulatory noncompliance relative to fair lending.[56] Fair lending laws are vigorously enforced, and violations pose serious financial consequences and reputation risk. Regulatory agencies have put forth guidance on the use of credit scoring.[57] Management should be able to identify the type and volume of overrides by category and measure the quality of their performances.[58]

Override Analysis Areas

The purpose of override analysis is twofold. First, it ensures a bank's credit underwriting exceptions are within acceptable levels and do not pose credit quality problems. Second, it seeks to determine

56. Applicable Federal laws for equal credit access and mortgage lending include Federal Housing Act (1968), Equal Credit Opportunity Act (1974), Home Mortgage Disclosure Act (1975), the Community Reinvestment Act (1977), and the Civil Rights Act of 1866 (Section 1981).
57. Enforcement of these laws, relative to credit scoring, has been addressed by regulatory exam guidelines of the FFIEC and the OCC—see OCC Bulletin 97–24, 1997.
58. OCC Bulletin, 97–24, 1997, pp. 6–7.

whether or not a bank's credit-scoring override practices have been uniformly applied across pre-defined protected/unprotected groups and to ensure that any disparate impact relative to the incidence of overrides can be explained when all related credit factors are taken into account.[59] In particular, override analysis addresses the following credit-scoring issues:

- Ensuring the frequency if occurrence of overrides does not exceed the corporate policy threshold. Override rates are monitored by scoring model on a periodic basis to ensure that they fall within policy thresholds (e.g., 5 percent for low-side overrides and 10 percent for high-side overrides).[60] In instances where override rates are excessive, the frequency of overrides by override reason is examined to determine the factors that are contributing to the policy threshold exception. Trends from period to period are also examined by scorecard. Every effort should be made to eliminate an "Other" category for override reason, as this can often become a "catch-all" bucket for individual subjective overrides that may, in hindsight, appear to be arbitrary or unjustified. In the event that the override reason is specific, such as bank deposit relationship, then detaining qualifications such as account open for at least 12 months with an average balance of $2,000, a secondary factor can be developed and incorporated into the underwriting model after sufficient time has passed to determine the quality/profitability of the overrides in question.

- Determining if the actual performance of non-score-qualified loans that were approved support the override decision. Collectively, they should have a default rate equal to, or lower than that associated with the score cutoff for loan approval. Low-side overrides should be tracked to capture delinquency and default experience, both on an incidence and dollar basis. This information is usually captured in delinquency by score tracking reports, and also portfolio vintage cohort analysis that examines roll rates and charge-offs on a loan and dollar basis. On the cohort analysis, overrides of a specific vintage can be isolated and examined for their contribution to any deterioration in performance of back-testing scorecards using low-side overrides. Having a minimum of two years of history can serve to validate the override processing rules for incorporation into a hybrid model or justify the continuation of the type of overrides included in the analysis.

- Assessing performance of above-cutoff score bounds for possible adverse impact of rejecting score-qualified applicants. High-side override score distributions should be tracked to determine if the score bands they fall into achieve the scoring model performance targets. If performance falls short, then the indication would be that declining those score-qualified applicants may not have been warranted, and that, if approved, they could have helped to achieve the predicted performance. If performance is better than anticipated, then the override process may be credited in part for the result.

- Identifying disparate impact on a protected class of applicants. Scoring model-specific override disparities associated with protected classes of credit applicants should be examined. The purpose is to see whether there is a statistically significant difference in override rates between each protected class and its corresponding control group. This analysis may be further broken down by geographical level in the event different score cutoff are used for different regions. The same would be true for channel breakouts or other scorecard segmentation schemes. For example, if there is a statistically significant differences in high-side override rates for the Asian, African-American, and Hispanic groups with respect to the

---

59. In Chapter 8 we will discuss how override analysis can be used for model validation.
60. The low-side override rate is defined as the number of applicants failing the credit score cutoff that are approved divided by the number of applicants failing the credit score cutoff. The high-side override rate is the number of applicants scoring above credit score cutoff that are declined divided by the number of applicants scoring above the credit score cutoff.

white non-Hispanic group at a regional, state, or MSA level, then disparate treatment testing may be indicated, as described in Chapter 5.

Override Analysis Process for Fair Lending

Overrides of credit score Home Mortgage Disclosure Act (HMDA) loans are analyzed for possible fair lending violations. Management monitors these overrides to spy any imbalances between protected and nonprotected classes to ensure score-qualified, protected-class customers are not disproportionably denied credit. Conversely, management also needs to ensure that score unqualified, protected class customers are proportionally approved for credit, compared with their nonprotected class counterparts. Policy rules are maintained to reflect any significant results of statistical analysis and changes in the business environment. Override monitoring can be performed at various levels of details with respect to individual policy rules. The overall analysis process is depicted in Figure 6.44.

Data Collection and Summary Reporting

Depending on the volume of overrides, the analysis may be performed quarterly, semiannually, or annually. In terms of selection criteria, observations are typically removed for various reasons, including: (1) restriction to single family dwellings; (2) restriction to certain collateral code types; (3) drop observations having invalid protected class codes; (4) final action results of withdrawn, incomplete; (5) application was purchased; (6) applications having missing credit scores; and (7) restriction to only certain states if performing a regional analysis. It is important to restrict the analysis to individual scorecards. All relevant data pertaining to override policy must be obtained. Merely sourcing override reason codes is not sufficient for the analysis.

For management reporting and macro trending, a summary of HMDA-reportable real estate–secured, credit-scored loan overrides, for both high and low sides, should be performed. This

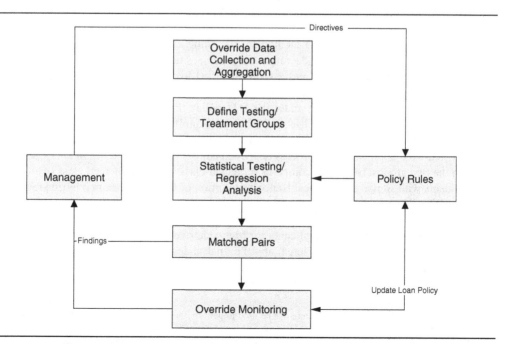

FIGURE 6.44 OVERRIDE ANALYSIS PROCESS

would be done at the enterprise level in total, and for each legal entity, and perhaps region, within the legal entity for each borrower protected-class group.

Defining Risk Factors, Test and Control Groups

As was the case for overage/underage analysis, the first step in setting up a monitoring capability is to define which groups of borrowers are in one or more protected classes and which ones are in one or more control groups. See Figures 3.2 and 3.3 in Chapter 3 for details.

Statistical Testing and Regressions

Some simple statistical tests can be used to examine the difference in observed versus expected proportions between the control and treatment group for low-side and high-side overrides.[61] The process used to perform the required testing considers one policy factor at a time in a particular iteration, starting with the factor that explains the largest amount of variation between the test and control group. A three-way cross-tabulation of policy override factor group, override indicator, and protected-class membership is specified. Missing values should be interpreted as nonmissing and should be included in the calculation of percentages and other statistics. This process produces summary statistics including total applications, number of protected-class and nonprotected-class score-qualified applications, number of protected-class and nonprotected-class overrides, and percentage of protected-class and nonprotected-class overrides.[62] The process culminates when no significant differences exist, when no further factors are available to consider, or when the sample is exhausted.

A visual example would be similar to a tree having branches defined by partitioning based on value ranges of the override policy variables. The number of branches associated with each policy override factor is data dependent. This is analogous to the binning problem faced by credit-scoring developers when they transform a continuous variable, like debt ratio, into a discrete variable comprised of several ranges of values that debt ratio can assume. In practical application, the number of bins is limited to four and the sample counts are spread as uniformly as possible across the bins. The depth of the branching process is usually constrained to consider at most five levels, or policy factors.

The process described provides a method for obtaining an unbiased comparison of protected-class and nonprotected-class override rates. Consider a situation where no disparate treatment occurs in the underwriting process and a score qualified loan applicant requesting a DTI higher than the DTI cutoff for a product is more likely to be declined as a high-side override compared with those applicants scoring under the DTI policy threshold value. If a higher frequency of protected-class loan applicants has a DTI above cutoff, relative to the nonprotected-class group, then protected-class applicants will have a greater high-side override frequency than nonprotected-class applicants. The process described adjusts for the difference in DTI distributions between the two groups, because it compares protected-class and nonprotected-class override rates for applicants with similar DTI values. Hence, the portion of the difference in override rates that is linked to DTI differences is effectively eliminated from the comparison. A tabular representation of an override partitioning tree is shown in Figure 6.45, which reflects the result of the branching process for a protected group of applicants for high-side override analyses.

Once the process has been completed, and the final nodes determined, frequency analysis can create three-way cross-tabulation of final node, override indicator, and protected-class membership.

---

61. For example, the SAS FREQ procedure can be used to perform the required testing. See *SAS/STAT User' Guide*, SAS Institute Inc., 2003.
62. For example, Fisher's exact test P-values where small samples are present, while the Pearson chi-square test statistic is used for sufficiently large samples.

Final Node	Partition 1	Partition 2	Partition 3	Partition 4	Partition 5	Partition 6
1	LTV Delta < 3.0	DTI Delta > = 20.0	LTV Delta < 1.0			
2	LTV Delta < 3.0	DTI Delta > = 20.0	LTV Delta > = 1.0			
3	LTV Delta > = 3.0	DTI Delta > = 10.0	Score Delta < 40			
4	LTV Delta > = 3.0	DTI Delta > = 10.0	Score Delta > = 40			
5	LTV Delta < 3.0	DTI Delta < 20.0	DTI Delta > = 5	Score Delta < 10		
6	LTV Delta < 3.0	DTI Delta < 20.0	DTI Delta > = 5	Score Delta > = 10		
7	LTV Delta < 3.0	DTI Delta < 20.0	DTI Delta < 5	Score Delta < 40	DTI Delta < 1	
8	LTV Delta < 3.0	DTI Delta < 20.0	DTI Delta < 5	Score Delta < 40	DTI Delta > = 1	
9	LTV Delta < 3.0	DTI Delta < 20.0	DTI Delta < 5	Score Delta > = 40	LTV Delta > = 2	
10	LTV Delta < 3.0	DTI Delta < 20.0	DTI Delta < 5	Score Delta > = 40	LTV Delta < 2	Score Delta < 60
11	LTV Delta < 3.0	DTI Delta < 20.0	DTI Delta < 5	Score Delta > = 40	LTV Delta < 2	Score Delta > = 60

FIGURE 6.45   OVERRIDE PROCESS NODE DEFINITIONS FOR HIGH-SIDE OVERRIDE ANALYSIS

Note: Delta represents the absolute value of the difference between the indicated values for protected and nonprotected class score-qualified declines.

Results that are significant at the 95 percent confidence level indicate the need for a matched-pair file review. The examples provided have pertained mainly to underwriting, but the same holds true for pricing overrides. A high-side pricing override occurs when the borrower is assessed a higher rate or fee that would otherwise be expected according to the scoring system result. A low-side override in pricing is when the borrower is afforded a price break relative to the scoring system recommended price. Another aspect would be the relative variability of the prices charged to different groups, viewed perhaps as a secondary analysis.

Purely on race/ethnicity basis, we can test for significance of the two types of override rates as shown in Figures 6.46 and 6.47. But, typically, there are several factors to be considered for both high-side and low-side override analyses, and more than one factor may apply for a specific credit applicant. For example, a high-side override may exhibit a high DTI greater than certain threshold value and also a lower credit score that is below a policy threshold. In instances where a protected class has a higher proportion of applicants that satisfy a particular high-side override rule, compared with a nonprotected group, the result will be the appearance of discrimination. Regression analysis can be used to test for significance of protected class variables (e.g., race, ethnicity), policy variables, and all relevant interactions of the variables relating to the override decision. The regression process and the more powerful variant, DCP, were discussed in detail in Chapter 5.

Credit Scored Loan Applications			
Group	Score Qualified Applicants	High-side Override Rate (%)	Fisher's Exact Test (p-value)
Native American	15	27.8	0.070
Asian	265	16.5	*0.050*
African-American	376	24.9	*< 0.001*
Hispanic	1,819	18.2	*< 0.001*
Nonminority	6,045	12.7	N/A

FIGURE 6.46   HIGH-SIDE OVERRIDE RATES BY ETHNICITY

Credit Scored Loan Applications			
Group	Applicants below Score Cutoff	Low-side Override Rate (%)	Fisher's Exact Test (p-value)
Native American	1	0.0	0.943
Asian	33	0.0	0.151
African-American	296	1.7	*0.002*
Hispanic	629	1.3	*< 0.001*
Nonminority	754	5.7	N/A

FIGURE 6.47   LOW-SIDE OVERRIDE RATES BY ETHNICITY

An example of low-side override factor analysis is shown in Figure 6.48, which reports actual override counts and frequency by minority status and override factor. For example, we see that 23 percent of the overrides due to good credit score are for white non-Hispanic applicants, while 27 percent of the overrides due to good strong co-signer are captured by protected class. This may indicate that override factors may have different impact on different applicant groups.

When there are multiple and interrelated override factors, regression analysis can be used to answer the following questions:

- Which factors have significant impact on override decision? The identified override factors will be validated against the override code in underwriting policy.[63]
- Are those factors related to protected factors such as race or ethnicity?
- Are overrides exercised consistently with policy?
- Whether or not one group of applicants (treatment group) is more likely to receive overrides that another group (control group) after controlling for geographic and risk attributes?

Overrides can be assigned to an MLS segment and then their predicted impact on performance can be assessed from a credit perspective. Secondary factors may be used to assign to a handle cell and infer default probabilities that validate with the base model (hybrid, scoring, etc.). For compliance risk assessment, the distribution of overrides in the MLS can be compared for protected and nonprotected groups.

---

63. See Figures 6.42 and 6.43 for a list of typical policy override codes.

Table of Override Code by Minority Status				
		ms_race_ethnic		
Override Code	Statistic	White Non-Hispanic	All Others, Including Hispanic	Total
	Frequency	221	818	1039
	Percent	8.72	32.28	41
	Row Pct	21.27	78.73	
00: Unknown	Col Pct	26.92	47.75	
	Frequency	4	0	4
	Percent	0.16	0	0.16
	Row Pct	100	0	
10: Cash Secured	Col Pct	0.49	0	
	Frequency	120	463	583
12: Co-applicant	Percent	4.74	18.27	23
Bureau Score 100 +	Row Pct	20.58	79.42	
pts. above Cutoff	Col Pct	14.62	27.03	
	Frequency	2	0	2
	Percent	0.08	0	0.08
14: Strong Bank	Row Pct	100	0	
Relation	Col Pct	0.24	0	
	Frequency	182	127	309
	Percent	7.18	5.01	12.2
15: High Net	Row Pct	58.9	41.1	
Worth	Col Pct	22.17	7.41	
	Frequency	106	39	145
	Percent	4.18	1.54	5.72
	Row Pct	73.1	26.9	
16: High Liquidity	Col Pct	12.91	2.28	
	Frequency	186	266	452
18: Custom Credit	Percent	7.34	10.5	17.8
Score 50 + pts.	Row Pct	41.15	58.85	
Above Threshold	Col Pct	22.66	15.53	
		821	1713	2534
Total		32.4	67.6	100

FIGURE 6.48   LOW-SIDE OVERRIDE FACTOR ANALYSIS

Matched Pairs

Where indicated, various approaches can be used to construct samples of matched pairs corresponding to each statistically significant end nodes for the control and treatment group in question. The purpose of this exercise for high-side overrides is to select the "n" most extreme cases where nonprotected-class applicants were accepted but had the worst credit quality matched against protected-class overrides. There is an implied hierarchy for defining "worst credit quality" that is determined by policy. An example would be to consider first absolute point differences in credit scores, then various policy variables in order of importance, such as percentage difference in LTVs, percentage difference in DTI, and so forth.

The process can involve a number of models, considering the number of protected classes involved, the number of regions, the number of scorecards, and the need to analyze low-side and high-side overrides separately. Consideration of channel would also potentially increase the number of models required. Figure 6.49 shows matched pairs of high-side overrides side by side with primary credit criteria values for each paring and the associated override reason.

Override Monitoring

Override monitoring process can be used to identify and mitigate the risk associated with disparate treatment in underwriting or pricing of loans to consumers who are members of protected classes. Periodic reports track policy violations. A process for determining the appropriate actions to be undertaken to address violations is described in Appendix 6D. The reports generated from this process are typically produced for presentation and review by management. Those reports include:

- *Summary totals*. Current quarter for total line of business, by region or by state (total applications, number of protected-class and nonprotected-class score-qualified applications, number of protected-class and nonprotected-class overrides, percentage of protected-class and nonprotected-class overrides, significance of the difference based on Pearson or Fisher's exact chi-square test).
- *Results by policy override factor*. Current quarter by factor bins, for example, for score difference the bins would be point ranges above and below cutoff, while for customer relationship the bins could correspond to number, type, and length of relationships, for credit history the bins could represent number of satisfactory, slow or derogatory ratings for trade lines (total applications, number of protected-class and nonprotected-class score-qualified applications, number of protected-class and nonprotected-class overrides, percentage of protected-class and nonprotected-class overrides, significance of the difference based on Pearson or Fisher's exact chi-square test).
- *Results across all policy override factors*. Current quarter by factors, examples of which appear in Figures 6.46 and 6.47 (total applications, number of protected-class and nonprotected-class score-qualified applications, number of protected-class and nonprotected-class overrides, percentage of protected-class and nonprotected-class overrides, significance of the difference based on Pearson or Fisher's exact chi-square test).
- *Exceptions and matched-pair reports*. Example in Figure 6.49.
- *Trend*. Four quarters noting where there have been significant findings, and where file reviews have supported findings by line of business, by scorecard, by region, by protected class, for high-side and low-side overrides, respectively.
- Frequency of override analysis can vary, but a minimum frequency would be twice per year based upon the most recent six months of data. In cases where national scorecards have been developed, override samples are typically drawn separately for large states (e.g. CA, NY, TX), and on a regional basis for lower volume states (e.g. VA/ DC/MD). Obviously, the sampling plan would vary by lending institution based on their geographic emphasis.

Matched Pair Number	Non-Protected Group	FICO/Non-Protected Group	LTV/Non-Protected Group	DTI/Non-Protected Group	Protected Group	FICO/Protected Group	LTV/Protected Group	DTI/Non-Protected Group	Override Reason
1	White Non-Hispanic	681	0.879	0.3269	All others, Including Hispanic	742	0.2737	0.1581	High exposure
2	White Non-Hispanic	699	0.7263	0.3572	All others, Including Hispanic	820	0.2469	0.207	Nonpermanent resident
3	White Non-Hispanic	600	0.8318	0.2994	All others, Including Hispanic	785	0.2798	0.136	High exposure
4	White Non-Hispanic	581	0.7298	0.1764	All others, Including Hispanic	820	0.2966	0.0919	Nonpermanent Resident
5	White Non-Hispanic	649	0.6865	0.3156	All others, Including Hispanic	683	0.2991	0.1822	Bankruptcy, Judge, tax lien, fore, repo, MMD
6	White Non-Hispanic	547	0.9361	0.3818	All others, Including Hispanic	764	0.8027	0.2932	High exposure
7	White Non-Hispanic	674	0.8219	0.3146	All others, Including Hispanic	687	0.2656	0.1425	Poor credit history with lender
8	White Non-Hispanic	552	0.9085	0.3805	All others, Including Hispanic	621	0.7834	0.2084	Nonpermanent resident

FIGURE 6.49 MATCHED PAIRS AND EXCEPTIONS REPORT FOR HIGH-SIDE OVERRIDES

Hybrid Model and Override Analysis

The relationship between hybrid model and override analysis as well as how they impact each other can be described with Figure 6.50. The basic idea is initially to incorporate all secondary review, and any override policy, considerations directly into the hybrid model structure. Instead of having overrides associated with policy rules, we now have handle cells in the hybrid model. Compared with Figure 6.44, this process is significantly simplified, and in many cases, overrides can be eliminated. Simply by identifying particular treatment groups in a hybrid model, we can immediately perform statistical testing for significance of any disparities relative to the control group.

   Statistical testing and regression analysis results will be periodically applied to the hybrid model. As a result, the need for override analysis can be significantly reduced, as compared with a credit-scoring environment.

SUMMARY

Developing credit risk management models is both science and an art, and it requires solid statistical techniques and sound business judgment. In this chapter we have reviewed current credit risk–scoring systems and their strengths and weaknesses. We then presented a hybrid credit risk–management system, which takes advantage of both statistical scoring models and judgmental and business criteria. We have also illustrated how to use this system to enhance loan underwriting criteria with both traditional and nontraditional credit information.[64] Using this hybrid modeling

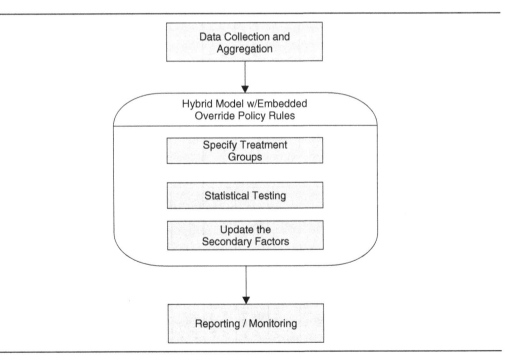

FIGURE 6.50   HYBRID MODEL SIMPLIFIES OVERRIDE ANALYSIS

---

64. The same concept can also be applied to loan pricing.

approach, the fair lending disparate treatment process described in Chapter 5 becomes more transparent. The hybrid model, together with DCP, creates an integrated approach that effectively and efficiently meets the dual objectives of credit risk management and fair lending compliance. There is an un-banked lending conundrum, in other words, use judgment with associated pitfalls (inconsistency/experiential bias) or use credit scoring with associated shortcomings (one-size fits all/historical data dependency). A hybrid modeling approach addresses the un-banked lending conundrum and better qualifies non-mainstream borrowers. Hybrid models leverage a "handle" segmentation specified by experts in a model consensus session (MCS), and effectively identify sets of like-borrowers from a credit risk perspective. Hybrid models become more predictive over time, as loan performance accumulates within the handle and full action table framework. In addition, we have described override analysis for scored HMDA loans, and how the hybrid model can greatly simplify, or possibly eliminate, the need for overrides.

Appendix 6A

LOAN UNDERWRITING WITH CREDIT SCORING

We provide a progression of examples to illustrate how a credit-scoring system is developed under various simplified assumptions. The purpose of credit scoring is to increase the number of correct decisions in granting credit. A key underlying assumption is that past behavior is a determinant of future behavior. Past experience is organized into a form that is amenable to analysis. Analysis focuses on the significant factors that predict future behavior. The result is a numerical score, or odds quote, that allows an applicant to be identified as a good or poor risk.

Basic Terms

The term *odds* is used to describe a measure of the relative percent of goods to bads in a group (e.g., Odds = Percentage of goods in group 1/percentage of bads in group 1). The population odds are the odds that an arbitrary member of the applicant population will be good (i.e., it is a measure of the relative number of goods to bads in the entire population). The information odds are the odds developed from various applicant information sources. The overall odds are the product of the information odds and the population odds. The weight of evidence (WOE) is defined to be the logarithm of the information odds.

Scoring System 1: Assume the population odds are 16 to 1. Assume the profit from a typical good account is $100 and the loss from a bad account is $2,000, on average. This implies that the breakeven odds are 20 to 1. In other words, it takes 20 good accounts to pay for the loss from a single bad account. In the absence of any other information, we would reject anyone who applies for credit!

Scoring System 2: Assume we know one applicant risk factor, say credit depth is either none, thin, moderate, or thick as shown in Figure 6.51.

We can calculate the overall odds for an applicant with (1) no file: $16/1 \times 1/4 = 4/1$ and (2) thick file: $16/1 \times 4/1 = 64/1$. Since breakeven is at 20/1, we would accept the thick-file applicant and reject the thin-file applicant.

Credit File Depth	Good	Bad	Information Odds
No file	10%	40%	1/4
Thin file	20%	40%	1/2
Moderate	30%	10%	3/1
Thick	40%	10%	4/1

FIGURE 6.51 CREDIT FILE DEPTH GOOD/BAD ODDS

Housing Status	Good	Bad	Information Odds
Own	60%	30%	2/1
Rent	30%	60%	1/2
Other	10%	10%	1/1

FIGURE 6.52   HOUSING STATUS GOOD/BAD ODDS

X	$Log_2 X$	X	$Log_2 X$	X	$Log_2 X$
1/4	−2	3	1.58	20	4.32
1/2	−1	4	2	32	5
1	0	8	3	64	6
2	1	16	4	128	7

FIGURE 6.53   TABLE OF BASE 2 LOGARITHMS

Credit File Depth	Good	Bad	Information Odds	WOE
No file	10%	40%	1/4	−2
Thin file	20%	40%	1/2	−1
Moderate	30%	10%	3/1	1.58
Thick	40%	10%	4/1	2

FIGURE 6.54   CREDIT FILE DEPTH GOOD/BAD WEIGHT OF EVIDENCE

Scoring System 3: Assume we now know two applicant risk factors, say credit depth and housing status, which is either own, rent, or other, as shown in Figure 6.52.

We can calculate the overall odds for an applicant with (1) *no-file* applicant who rents: 16/1 × 1/4 × 1/2 = 2/1 and (2) *thick-file* applicant who owns: 16/1 × 4/1 × 2/1 = 128/1. Since breakeven is at 20/1, we would accept the thick-file applicant and reject the thin-file applicant. For simplicity, we have assumed that credit depth and housing status are independent, when in fact, that is not the case. The odds quote range for scoring system 3 has expanded from the range 4/1 to 64/1 to the range 2/1 to 128/1. These calculations can be simplified so that we do not have to multiply all of these probabilities, which is cumbersome and time consuming. Logarithms allow us to transform these multiplications to additions. Recall that the logarithm of a number is the power to which another number (called the *base*) is raised to find the number. For example, a table of logarithms in base 2 appears in Figure 6.53.

Recall that the logarithm of a product is the sum of the logarithms (i.e., log (ab) = log(a) + log(b)). For example, if a = 4 and b = 8, then log (4 × 8) = log(4) + log(8); simplifying we obtain log (32) = 2 + 3; and finally the expressions on both sides of the equality reduce to 5 = 5, which is correct. Now we can add a column to Figures 6.51 and 6.52, as shown in Figures 6.54 and 6.55.

The population weight of evidence is $log_2 16 = 4$ and the breakeven weight of evidence is $log_2 20 = 4.32$. Now, for a *no-file* applicant that rents we can calculate the log (odds) as: log[(population

Housing Status	Good	Bad	Information Odds	WOE
Own	60%	30%	2/1	1
Rent	30%	60%	1/2	−1
Other	10%	10%	1/1	0

FIGURE 6.55   HOUSING STATUS GOOD/BAD WEIGHT OF EVIDENCE

X	$(Log_2 X) + 3$	X	$(Log_2 X) + 3$	X	$(Log_2 X) + 3$
1/4	1	3	4.58	20	7.32
1/2	2	4	5	32	8
1	3	8	6	64	9
2	4	16	7	128	10
X	$[(Log_2 X) + 3]x20$	X	$[(Log_2 X) + 3]x20$	X	$[(Log_2 X) + 3]x20$
1/4	20	3	92	20	146
1/2	40	4	100	32	160
1	60	8	120	64	180
2	80	16	140	128	200

FIGURE 6.56   SCALING WITH A LINEAR TRANSFORMATION OF LOGARITHMS

Credit File Depth	Good	Bad	Odds	WOE	+2	x20
No file	10%	40%	1/4	−2	0	0
Thin file	20%	40%	1/2	−1	1	20
Moderate	30%	10%	3/1	1.58	3.58	72
Thick	40%	10%	4/1	2	4	80

FIGURE 6.57   CREDIT FILE DEPTH SCORING POINTS

odds) × (thin file odds) × (renter odds)] which equals $4 + (−2) + (−1) = 1 < 4.32$ so we reject the *no-file* renter. For a *thick-file* applicant who owns, we can calculate the log (odds) as: $4 + 2 + 1 = 7 > 4.32$, so we accept the *thick-file* owner.

We can further ease the calculations by getting rid of negative numbers and decimals. Examining the table of logarithms in Figure 6.53, we see that this can be accomplished by adding 3 and multiplying by 20, as shown in Figure 6.56.

For the population odds, all that is needed is to multiply by 20; the odds = 16/1; the log odds $= log_2 16 = 4$; $4 × 20 = 80$ points. Similarly, the breakeven odds = 20/1; log odds $= log_2 20 = 4.32$; $(4.32 + 2 + 1) × 20 = 146$ (approximately). Now, looking at each of the predictor variables, we see that for credit file depth we must add 2 and multiply by 20, whereas for housing status we must add 1 and multiply by 20. The results are shown in Figures (6.57 and 6.58).

For the no-file renter, we calculate the credit score as $80 + 0 + 0 = 80 < 146$ (reject).

For the thick-file owner, we calculate the credit score as $80 + 80 + 40 = 200 > 146$ (accept).

Housing Status	Good	Bad	Odds	WOE	+1	x20
Own	60%	30%	2/1	1	2	40
Rent	30%	60%	1/2	−1	0	0
Other	10%	10%	1/1	0	1	20

FIGURE 6.58   HOUSING STATUS SCORING POINTS

Credit File Depth	No File	Thin File	Moderate	Thick
Housing Status				
Own	Decline 120	Approve 160	Approve 192	Approve 200
Rent	Decline 80	Decline 100	Approve 152	Approve 160
Other	Decline 100	Decline 120	Approve 172	Approve 180

FIGURE 6.59   SCORING SYSTEM DECISION MATRIX WITH CUTOFF = 146

If we examine every possible combination, we see that the scoring system is equivalent to the following collection of discrete decision rules shown in Figure 6.59.

Again, this is a simplified example that has ignored correlation of variables, the fact that there are many more factors to consider, and the rejected population of credit applicants must also be taken into account in the scoring model. The focus of this book is on the introduction of alternative methods, and space limitations preclude our pursuit of those more in-depth scoring system development topics in this edition.

Appendix 6B
LOG-LINEAR AND LOGISTIC REGRESSION MODELS

We describe the connection between the log-linear model and the logistic regression models described in Chapter 5 in the simplest case, which generalizes to "n" dimensions.[65] Referring to the example in Figure 6.17, we fix the row totals (i.e., $m_{1+} = 400$ applicants not having a high debt ratio and $m_{2+} = 200$ applicants having a high debt ratio). By doing so, we can then examine the relative proportions of good and bad credit applicants within the rows. We define the logit L_i = ln $[p_{1(i)}/(1 - p_{1(i)}] = \ln[m_{i1}/m_{i2}]$. With some algebraic manipulation of the expression for the saturated log-linear model (equation 6.2), we have that $L_i = u_{2(1)} - u_{2(2)} + u_{12(i1)} - u_{12(i2)}$ and by substituting $(w/2)$ for $u_{2(1)}$ and $(w_{1(i)}/2)$ for $u_{12(i1)}$, we obtain a linear model in the logits, namely: $L_i = w + w_{1(i)}$, where $w_{1(1)} + w_{1(2)} = 0$.

This facilitates a comparison with the one-way ANOVA, where the presence of a high debt ratio is viewed as an independent predictor variable and the column in the table corresponding to good and bad credit performance represents the dependent variable. In this way, the term $w_{1(i)}$ is interpreted to measure the effect of a high debt ration on good/bad performance. The result extends easily to where "n" predictor variables are present and stratified samples of good, bad, and rejected credit applicants are taken.

---

65. Bishop, Fienberg, and Holland, 1975, pp. 22–23, specifically equations (2.2–49) and (2.2–51).

Appendix 6C

ADDITIONAL EXAMPLES OF HYBRID MODELS WITH TRADITIONAL CREDIT INFORMATION

Direct Auto Example

Figure 6.60 identifies primary factors for this direct auto example, and their associated categories, definitions, and value assignments.

Figure 6.61 depicts the handle cells for this direct auto example, and their associated risk category and distinct covariate pattern relative to primary variable values. The handle specifies all possible combinations of values for the primary factors.

Figure 6.62 identifies secondary factors for this direct auto example, and their associated categories, definitions, and value assignments.

Primary Factors	Categories, Definitions, and Value Assignments		
Credit payment history	G- < 2 trades 30DPD last 24 months; 0 trades 60DPD last 24 months	F- 2+ trades 30DPD last 24 months; 1+ trades 60DPD last 24 months	P- Public record[a] – last 2 years, bankruptcy – last 5 years
Credit bureau score	G- 680+	F- 620–680	P- < 620
DTI	L- < 42%	M- 42–48%	H- > 48%

FIGURE **6.60**   Direct Auto Loan Primary Factors

[a]Judgments, tax liens, repossessions, foreclosures, all qualify as public records.

Handle #	Risk Category	Credit Payment History	Credit Bureau Score	Debt-to-Income Ratio
1	0	G	G	L
2	1	G	G	M
3	2	G	G	H
4	1	G	F	L
5	2	G	F	M
6	3	G	F	H
7	2	G	P	L
8	3	G	P	M
9	4	G	P	H
10	1	F	G	L
11	2	F	G	M
12	3	F	G	H
13	2	F	F	L
14	2	F	F	M
15	3	F	F	H
16	2	F	P	L
17	3	F	P	M
18	4	F	P	H
19	2	P	G	L
20	2	P	G	M
21	4	P	G	H
22	2	P	F	L
23	3	P	F	M
24	4	P	F	H
25	4	P	P	L
26	4	P	P	M
27	5	P	P	H

FIGURE 6.61   DIRECT AUTO LOAN HANDLE TABLE: PRIMARY FACTORS

Term of loan	G- < 49 months	F- 49–60 months	P- > 60 months
LTV ratio[a]	G- < 75%	F- 75–100%	P- 100%+
Down payment pct[b]	H- 20%+	L- < 20%	
Employment stability	G- 2 years+	F- 1–2 years	P- < 1 year
Vehicle new/used	L- New	H- Used	
PTI ratio	G- < 10%	F- 10–14%	P- 15%+
Strong co-applicant	G- Bureau score 680+	F- Bureau Score > 640	
Deposit relationship	G- 2 years; Avg bal $2 M	F- 1 year; No NSFs	

FIGURE 6.62   DIRECT AUTO LOAN: SECONDARY FACTORS (WEIGHT IN FINAL DECISION OF 5–15 PERCENT EACH)

[a]Loan-to-value ratio calculated as loan amOwnt divided by the Black Book value of the collateral.
[b](Trade-In + Cash Down) / Price

Indirect Auto Example

These loans (retail installment sales contracts) originate through a lender's network of automobile dealers. Consumers typically arrange financing for a new or used vehicle that they wish to purchase and sign the loan agreement at the dealer's showroom. The dealer offers these loans to the lending institution for purchase and servicing.

Figure 6.63 identifies primary factors for this indirect auto example, and their associated categories, definitions, and value assignments.

Figure 6.64 depicts the handle cells for this indirect auto example, and their associated risk category and distinct covariate pattern relative to primary variable values. The handle specifies all possible combinations of values for the primary factors.

Figure 6.65 identifies secondary factors for this indirect auto example, and their associated categories, definitions, and value assignments.

Bank Card Example

Figure 6.66 identifies primary factors for this bank card example, and their associated categories, definitions, and value assignments.

Figure 6.67 depicts the handle cells for this bank card example, and their associated risk category and distinct covariate pattern relative to primary variable values. The handle specifies all possible combinations of values for the primary factors.

Primary Factors	Categories, Definitions, and Value Assignments		
Credit payment history	G- < 2 trades 30DPD last 24 months; 0 trades 60DPD last 24 months	F- 2+ trades 30DPD last 24 months; 1+ trades 60DPD last 24 months	P- Public record[a] – last 2 years, bankruptcy – last 5 years
Credit bureau score	G- 680+	F- 620–680	P- < 620
DTI	L- < 42%	M- 42–48%	H- > 48%

FIGURE 6.63   INDIRECT AUTO LOAN: PRIMARY FACTORS

[a]Judgments, tax liens, repossessions, foreclosures, all qualify as public records.

Handle #	Risk Category	Credit Payment History	Credit Bureau Score	Debt-to-Income Ratio
1	0	G	G	L
2	1	G	G	M
3	2	G	G	H
4	1	G	F	L
5	2	G	F	M
6	3	G	F	H
7	2	G	P	L
8	3	G	P	M
9	4	G	P	H
10	1	F	G	L
11	2	F	G	M
12	3	F	G	H
13	2	F	F	L
14	2	F	F	M
15	3	F	F	H
16	2	F	P	L
17	3	F	P	M
18	4	F	P	H
19	2	P	G	L
20	2	P	G	M
21	4	P	G	H
22	2	P	F	L
23	3	P	F	M
24	4	P	F	H
25	4	P	P	L
26	4	P	P	M
27	5	P	P	H

FIGURE 6.64   INDIRECT AUTO LOAN: PRIMARY FACTOR HANDLE TABLE

Credit file depth	G- 2+ years; 2 + sat.	F- 1–2 years or < 2 sat.	P- < 1 year; or 0 sat.
Dealer advance[a]	G- < 100%	F- 100–115%	P- 115%+
Down payment pct[b]	H- 20%+	L- < 20%	
Employment stability	G- 2 years+	F- 1–2 years	P- < 1year
Vehicle age	G- < 2 years	F- 2–4 years	P- 4+ years
PTI ratio	G- < 10%	F- 10–16%	P- 17%+

FIGURE 6.65   INDIRECT AUTO LOAN: SECONDARY FACTORS (WEIGHT IN FINAL DECISION OF 5–15 PERCENT EACH)

[a]Calculated as the ratio of finance amount to collateral value, where the finance amount may include such add-ons as multiyear warranty, undercoating, special equipment upgrades, life and disability insurance, etc.
[b](Trade-In + Cash Down) / Price

Primary Factors	Categories, Definitions, and Value Assignments		
Credit payment history	G- < 2 trades 30DPD last 12 months; 0 trades 60DPD last 24 months	F- < 4 trades 30DPD last 12 months; 0 trades 60DPD last 12 months	P- 4 + trades 30DPD last 12 months; 1 + trades 60DPD last 24 months
Credit bureau score	G- 720+	F- 640–719	P- < 639
DTI	L- < 36%	M- 36–50%	H- > 50%

FIGURE 6.66 BANK CARD: PRIMARY FACTORS

Handle #	Risk Category	Credit Payment History	Credit Bureau Score	Debt-to-Income Ratio
1	0	G	G	L
2	1	G	G	M
3	2	G	G	H
4	1	G	F	L
5	2	G	F	M
6	3	G	F	H
7	2	G	P	L
8	3	G	P	M
9	4	G	P	H
10	1	F	G	L
11	2	F	G	M
12	3	F	G	H
13	2	F	F	L
14	2	F	F	M
15	3	F	F	H
16	2	F	P	L
17	3	F	P	M
18	4	F	P	H
19	2	P	G	L
20	2	P	G	M
21	4	P	G	H
22	2	P	F	L
23	3	P	F	M
24	4	P	F	H
25	4	P	P	L
26	4	P	P	M
27	5	P	P	H

FIGURE 6.67 BANK CARD PRIMARY FACTOR HANDLE TABLE

Credit file depth	G- 2+ years; 3 + sat.	F- 1–2 years or < 2 sat.	P- < 1 year; or 0 sat.
Credit limit/mo. income	L- < 130%	H- > 130%	
Years on job	G- 2+ years	F-1+ years	P- < 1 year
PTI ratio[a]	L- < 5.5%	H- 5.5%+	
Residence stability	G- Own/Buying	F- Renting/Living w/relatives	
Strong co-applicant	G- Bureau score 700+	F- Bureau score > 660	
Deposit relationship	G- 2 years; avg bal $3 M	F- 1 year; avg bal $2 M	

FIGURE 6.68 BANK CARD: SECONDARY FACTORS (WEIGHT IN FINAL DECISION OF 5–15 PERCENT EACH)

[a]Payment-to-income ratio estimated at 4% times credit limit divided by gross monthly income.

Figure 6.68 identifies secondary factors for this bank card example, and their associated categories, definitions, and value assignments.

Home Equity Loan Example

Figure 6.69 identifies primary factors for this home equity loan example, and their associated categories, definitions, and value assignments.

Figure 6.70 depicts the handle cells for this home equity loan example, and their associated risk category and distinct covariate pattern relative to primary variable values. The handle specifies all possible combinations of values for the primary factors.

Figure 6.71 identifies secondary factors for this home equity loan example, and their associated categories, definitions, and value assignments.

Other Secured Installment Loan Example

Figure 6.72 identifies primary factors for this other installment loan example, and their associated categories, definitions, and value assignments.

Primary Factors	Categories, Definitions, and Value Assignments		
Credit payment history	G- < 2 trades 30DPD last 24 months; 0 trades 60DPD last 24 months	F- 2 + trades 30DPD last 24 months; 1+ trades 60DPD last 24 months	P- Public record[a] – last 2 years, bankruptcy – last 5 years
Credit bureau score	G- 660+	F- 621–660	P- < 620
DTI	L- < 44%	H- 44%+	
LTV ratio [b]	L- 80% or less	H- 81%+	

FIGURE 6.69 HOME EQUITY LOAN: PRIMARY FACTORS

[a]Judgments, tax liens, repossessions, foreclosures, all qualify as public records.
[b]Loan-to-value ratio calculated as loan amount divided by the Blue Book value of the collateral.

Handle #	Risk Category	Credit Payment History	Credit Bureau Score	Debt-to-Income Ratio	Loan-to-Income Ratio
1	0	G	G	L	L
2	1	G	G	H	L
3	1	G	F	L	L
4	2	G	F	H	L
5	2	G	P	L	L
6	3	G	P	H	L
7	1	F	G	L	L
8	2	F	G	H	L
9	1	F	F	L	L
10	2	F	F	H	L
11	2	F	P	L	L
12	3	F	P	H	L
13	2	P	G	L	L
14	3	P	G	H	L
15	2	P	F	L	L
16	3	P	F	H	L
17	3	P	P	L	L
18	4	P	P	H	L
19	1	G	G	L	H
20	2	G	G	H	H
21	2	G	F	L	H
22	3	G	F	H	H
23	3	G	P	L	H
24	4	G	P	H	H
25	2	F	G	L	H
26	3	F	G	H	H
27	2	F	F	L	H
28	3	F	F	H	H
29	3	F	P	L	H
30	4	F	P	H	H
31	3	P	G	L	H
32	4	P	G	H	H
33	3	P	F	L	H
34	4	P	F	H	H
35	4	P	P	L	H
36	5	P	P	H	H

FIGURE 6.70   HOME EQUITY LOAN: PRIMARY FACTOR HANDLE TABLE

Credit file depth	G- 2+ years; 2+ sat.	F- 1–2 years or < 2 sat.	P- < 1year; or 0 sat.
Down payment pct[a]	H- 20%+	L- < 20%	
Employment stability	G- 2 years + or 3 years + in same profession	F- 1–2 years + or 2 years + in same profession	P- < 1 year or < 2 years in same profession
PTI ratio	G- < 10%	F- 10–14%	P- 15%+
Strong co-applicant	G- Bureau score 700+	F- Bureau score > 660	
Relationship	G- DDA 2 years; avg bal $2.5 M	F- Similar loan paid off; first mtg held	

FIGURE 6.71   HOME EQUITY LOAN: SECONDARY FACTORS (WEIGHT IN FINAL DECISION OF 5–15 PERCENT EACH)
[a](Trade-In + Cash Down) / Price

Primary Factors	Categories, Definitions, and Value Assignments		
Credit payment history	G- < 2 trades 30DPD last 24 months; 0 trades 60DPD last 24 months	F- 2+ trades 30DPD last 24 months; 1+ trades 60DPD last 24 months	P- Public record[a] – last 2 year, bankruptcy – last 5 year
Credit bureau score	G- 670+	F- 640–670	P- < 640
DTI	L- < 50%	H- 50%+	
LTV ratio [b]	L- 90% or less	M- 91–95%+	H- 96%+

FIGURE 6.72   SECURED INSTALLMENT LOAN: PRIMARY FACTORS
[a]Judgments, tax liens, repossessions, foreclosures, all qualify as public records.
[b]Loan-to-value ratio calculated as loan amount divided by the Blue Book value of the collateral.

Figure 6.73 depicts the handle cells for this other secured installment loan example, and their associated risk category and distinct covariate pattern relative to primary variable values. The handle specifies all possible combinations of values for the primary factors.

Figure 6.74 identifies secondary factors for this other secured installment loan example, and their associated categories, definitions, and value assignments.

Handle #	Risk Category	Credit Payment History	Credit Bureau Score	Debt-to-Inc Ratio	Loan-to-Value Ratio
1	0	G	G	L	L
2	0	G	G	L	M
3	1	G	G	L	H
4	1	G	G	H	L
5	1	G	G	H	M
6	2	G	G	H	H
7	1	G	F	L	L
8	1	G	F	L	M
9	1	G	F	L	H
10	1	G	F	H	L
11	2	G	F	H	M
12	2	G	F	H	H
13	1	G	P	L	L
14	1	G	P	L	M
15	2	G	P	L	H
16	2	G	P	H	L
17	2	G	P	H	M
18	3	G	P	H	H
19	1	F	G	L	L
20	1	F	G	L	M
21	1	F	G	L	H
22	1	F	G	H	L
23	1	F	G	H	M
24	2	F	G	H	H
25	1	F	F	L	L
26	1	F	F	L	M
27	2	F	F	L	H
28	2	F	F	H	L
29	2	F	F	H	M
30	3	F	F	H	H
31	1	F	P	L	L
32	2	F	P	L	M
33	2	F	P	L	H

FIGURE 6.73   SECURED INSTALLMENT LOAN HANDLE TABLE

Handle #	Risk Category	Credit Payment History	Credit Bureau Score	Debt-to-Inc Ratio	Loan-to-Value Ratio
34	2	F	P	H	L
35	3	F	P	H	M
36	3	F	P	H	H
37	1	P	G	L	L
38	1	P	G	L	M
39	2	P	G	L	H
40	2	P	G	H	L
41	2	P	G	H	M
42	2	P	G	H	H
43	1	P	F	L	L
44	1	P	F	L	M
45	2	P	F	L	H
46	2	P	F	H	L
47	2	P	F	H	M
48	3	P	F	H	H
49	2	P	P	L	L
50	2	P	P	L	M
51	3	P	P	L	H
52	3	P	P	H	L
53	3	P	P	H	M
54	4	P	P	H	H

Figure **6.73**   (*continued*)

Credit file depth	G- 2 + years; 2 + sat.	F- 1–2 years or < 2 sat.	P- < 1 year; or 0 sat.
Employment stability	G- 2 years+	F-1–2 years	P- < 1 year
Years at residence	G- > 2years	F- 1–2 years	P- < 1 year
Co-applicant	G- Bureau score 680+	F- Bureau score > 660	
Relationship	G- DDA 2 years;avg bal $2.5 M	F- Other loan, deposit, investment account	

Figure **6.74**   Secured Installment Loan: Secondary Factors (Weight in Final Decision of 5–15 Percent Each)

Appendix 6D
GENERAL OVERRIDE MONITORING PROCESS

It is important that lending institutions put a process in place that will ensure overrides are legitimate and kept within acceptable ranges, as determined by the lender's written policies and by regulators who are responsible for ensuring that the lender's credit granting processes are fair, safe, and sound. Concerning the impact of overrides on credit portfolio performance, we recommend that low-side overrides be tracked and their performance measured over time. We also recommend that the potential impact of high-side overrides on observed bad rates, by score, be assessed periodically. It is of fundamental importance to measure the incidence of both low and high-side overrides relative to each individual scorecard, or underwriting system, and we provide an example in the section entitled Model Validation and Override Analysis in Chapter 8 that also illustrates the connection with fair lending performance. We outline in this appendix section the essential components that should be put in place and documented by lenders to enable them to monitor their performance relative to the fair lending aspects of their override policy.

Step 1. Line management reviews Web-accessible reports to identify high-level statistically significant differences (disparate impact) by protected class by type of override, by scorecard, by region, and possibly by channel. Graphical representations of potential disparate treatment relative to overrides, such as color-highlighted end-nodes of tree-like structures, can accompany statistical reporting of findings.

Step 2. A statistically significant result from the override analysis is not conclusive concerning the fairness of the lender's override practices relative to protected classes of applicants. As discussed previously, individual subjective overrides may be the root cause. It is also possible that additional credit factors affecting loan application decisions were omitted from the analysis. Wherever significant findings persist, matched-pair samples should be drawn to facilitate a manual file review.

Step 3. Because the degree of similarity between the sets that are being matched is not known *a priori*, the process for selecting matched pairs typically involves two steps. First, protected-class applicants are matched to nonprotected-class applicants using collateral code, credit score, bureau score, LTV, and DTI. A second step reduces the number matched pairs so that the number of files requiring manual review is manageable.

Step A: Select matched pairs.

1. For low-side analysis, all nonprotected-class low-side overrides are matched with protected class applicants below the credit score cutoff who did not receive an override. Similarly, for high-side analysis, all protected-class high-side overrides are matched with nonprotected-class applicants above the credit score cutoff who did not receive an override.

2. For both analyses, the nonprotected-class collateral code must equal the protected-class collateral code.

3. For both analyses, the protected-class custom score difference must be greater than or equal to that for the nonprotected class. Custom score difference is defined as the difference between the custom score and the custom score cutoff, which can result in a positive or negative number.

4. For both analyses, the remaining policy variables, each in turn, must demonstrate that the protected-class applicant being matched has a value that is equal to or more favorable than that for the nonprotected-class applicant being matched.

Step B: Select a subset of the matched pairs from Step A.

For the low-side analysis, select the "n" most extreme protected class applicants matched to each low-side override nonprotected-class applicant. Here, *extreme* refers to the "n" highest qualified protected class applicants. As noted earlier, the notion of "highest qualified" requires definition. For example, protected-class applicants possessing the largest credit score differential could be considered to have the highest credit qualifications. Therefore, when a tie occurs, other criteria could be used as a tie breaker, such as the credit bureau score. Credit bureau score ties could then be resolved by selecting the protected class applicant having the smallest difference in loan to value ratio. Further ties in LTVs could be resolved by choosing the protected-class applicants having the smallest difference in DTI.

For the high-side analysis, select the "n" most extreme protected class applicants matched to each high-side override protected class applicant. Here, extreme refers to the "n" least qualified nonprotected-class applicants. *Least qualified* requires definition. For example, nonprotected-class applicants having the most negative credit score differential could be considered to be least qualified. Custom score difference ties could be resolved by selecting the nonprotected-class applicant having the smallest credit bureau score. Credit bureau score ties could be resolved by selecting the nonprotected-class applicant with the largest DTI difference. Next, DTI difference ties might be broken by picking the nonprotected-class applicant with the largest loan to value ratio difference.

Matched pairs would be selected only for end-nodes in the override analysis where a statistically significant difference exists between protected-class and nonprotected-class groups. A report indicating the number of applications eligible to be matched and the actual number of applications matched for each end-node may also be produced.

Step 4. Manual file reviews should be conducted to account for the reasons behind the statistically significant results in every case.

Step 5. The organization implements corrective actions based on the information and insight obtained from the monitoring process. Wherever possible, consideration should be given to "institutionalizing" legitimate kinds of individual subjective overrides, to reduce their number and ensure a more consistent experience across all credit applicants.

7

MULTILAYERED SEGMENTATION

This chapter describes an integrated segmentation approach and its implications for risk management and compliance. In Chapter 2 we described briefly how segmentation fits within the context of the systematic approach. The importance of reliable and sufficient data was emphasized with examples drawn from fair lending compliance. In subsequent chapters, we illustrated numerous times the fundamental role segmentation plays in compliance testing and credit risk modeling. In Chapter 6 we further discussed alternative credit risk models and how they can be applied to consumer and small business lending, particularly in the emerging markets. The alternative hybrid credit risk models leverage upon the methodologies described in Chapter 3 (universal performance indicator [UPI]) and Chapter 5 (dynamic conditional process [DCP]). The interplay between segmentation, credit decisioning, and compliance is made particularly transparent through the use of these methods. In this chapter, we describe the segmentation approach and offer several illustrations of segmentation schemes that are in keeping with the central theme of previous chapters in the book. We show the role that segmentation plays in dynamic relationship pricing, community development lending, and in predicting loan portfolio performance. In the chapter summary, we tie together these examples with some overarching observations.

While credit risk management, fair lending compliance, and emerging market opportunity assessment are usually addressed by distinct corporate areas, they are inextricably intertwined. It is our hope that the concepts and suggestions presented will lead to more integrated and coordinated efforts among them and facilitate the development and execution of improved risk/return strategies, particularly in relation to underserved markets.

SEGMENTATION SCHEMES SUPPORTING INTEGRATED VIEWS

The basic idea of segmentation is to separate a population of interest into distinct homogenous groups according to similarities that have been judged, or demonstrated, to be of significance in achieving one or more objectives. For example, if the goal is to maximize credit card account profitability, then the criteria might include such factors as account age, utilization, and payment behavior. A goal of loan approval might include several of the underwriting factors reviewed in Chapter 6, with choice of specific factors partially dependent on the type of loan. A loan marketing goal would also need to consider the type of loan and might include factors describing life cycle and customer wants and needs, in addition to community-level factors such as housing stock availability and affordability. If the population of interest is the underserved consumers in a particular market, then factors which will help distinguish them from the universe of consumers is the breadth and depth of their credit bureau report, credit score, age, income level, whether they own or rent their residence, citizenship status, and so on.

Segmentation is used to support business purposes that are both tactical and strategic in nature. Generally speaking, "strategic" segmentation occurs in situations where a company segments its entire franchise (across all products and lines of business, including separate "holding companies" and/or corporations.[1] A corporate level "strategic" segmentation would look at customers holistically (considering their entire relationship). From a customer's perspective, this makes sense! A customer that has a bank checking account, and also a credit card from the same bank, considers himself as that bank's customer (even though these products may be offered by two separate legal entities).

In contrast, "tactical" segmentation schemes are often conducted at a product level, where the goal is to find, and efficiently sell, prospects a product that they will use profitably. Historically, much of the segmentation work that organizations have done has been at this level. Tactical segmentation can lead to bad decisions from an enterprise level. For example at the product/line of business level, a tactical decision might be to sell more equity bank lines in order to boost the profitability of the loan portfolio. While this may be effective (e.g., more equity bank lines may be sold and the profitability of the loan portfolio enhanced, the downside of this tactic is that perhaps 20 percent of the new equity bank lines sales actually eliminate the bank's higher margin credit card balances).

A key distinction we want to make here is that strategic segmentation can effectively be the "rudder" to guide the investment of organizational resources toward customers that have the capacity and propensity to be profitable over the long term, whereas tactical (product/LOB level) segmentation can provide the means to incrementally foster those relationships. Segmentation is a very powerful instrument. It can be used to help shape and manage the "customers' experience" across multiple products/LOBs and contact channels. Segmented populations can be tapped in order to create "metrics" and key performance indicators (e.g., changes in profitability over time in high-opportunity segments). Segmentation schemas can be used to move from a "product-centric" to a "customer-centric" organization by creating "portfolios" of customers and then assigning portfolios to segment managers at the corporate level and account executives at a customer-facing level. Naturally, this necessitates the redesign of corporate measurement and incentive programs so that they are based on customer segment performance.

An integrated multilayered segmentation plays an important role in forecasting loan performance and estimating the timing and amount of losses and payouts associated with their loans. Later in this chapter, we will discuss a modeling method for estimating near-term credit losses. Portfolio loss forecasting is of particular importance, because the ability to accurately forecast the ultimate disposition of current outstanding loan balances is an essential component of lending and also for sale to investors or another lending institution. For hybrid models relying on judgmental factors, the ability to quickly spot loan portfolio quality problems is critical in order to adjust handle-based risk estimates. Development of a secondary market for emerging market and alternative data-based loans will allow issuers to diversify risk, enhance liquidity, and increase their loan volume by expanding their lending to these underserved markets. As a result, a far greater number of deserving consumers and entrepreneurs will be able to meet their financing needs.

In the Changing Markets section of Chapter 1, we highlighted the significant opportunity to bring more consumers into the mainstream of financial products and services. Enhancement of credit policy and the information infrastructure that supports loan underwriting and pricing can help bring greater access, and fairer pricing, to individuals and households that fall outside of the more traditional credit-based financing model. What is needed is a way to more rapidly assimilate the massive number of consumers who are currently either excluded from qualification by the current system, or end up paying significantly more for their financing needs, due to deficiencies in the way the market currently operates.

---

1. For example, a bank holding company has separate lines of businesses within the "retail bank" and also has separate companies (e.g., a credit card company, a mortgage company, an insurance company, etc.).

The solution entails three significant areas. The first is the ability to locate underserved communities possessing quantifiable potential for profitable investment and financing, and consumers and small businesses residing in those underserved markets, based on a wide range of economic, financial, and consumer data at varying levels of geographic granularity. Second is the identification and tapping of alternative data sources that can provide significant information value relative to qualifying unbanked and underbanked consumers and businesses for financial products and services. The third area deals with the ability to develop models that can accommodate missing information and alternative data via innovative mechanisms that deliver prudent and better ways to qualify, risk rate, and fully evaluate consumers and small businesses for mainstream products and services. The third area also includes the challenge of predicting outcomes for new populations that are qualified in alternative ways, where there is little historical performance to go on. The applications described later in this chapter shed some additional light on these areas.

Supporting the three areas is an integrated approach of segmentation schemes, which is designed for different purposes, can be leveraged to create dynamic, integrated, multidimensional views of customers and communities both globally and locally. In other words, the segmentation schemes are designed within the entire enterprise and by business line, within territory and outside of territory, and across channels and products relative to profit, growth, product utilization, relationship breadth and depth, attrition, market share and penetration, delinquency, loss, expense, resource demands, and volatility. Albert Einstein asserted that "Imagination is more important than knowledge." Coming up with an effective segmentation scheme is a very demanding exercise that combines knowledge and imagination. Knowledge is acquired by access to relevant and reliable information, coupled with experience working in the field. Imagination is necessitated by the fact that the world is constantly changing and that change requires new paradigms at critical junctures.

PROPOSED SEGMENTATION APPROACH

This section introduces an integrated segmentation approach that utilizes the methodologies discussed in previous chapters. This provides a more complete picture of compliance and credit risk at various levels of granularity, for example, as illustrated later in this chapter, consumer level versus community level.

Segmentation Process

Any segmentation scheme begins with one or more stated objectives and some identifying factors that will distinguish the population of interest, while partitioning the universe within which the population resides. A segmentation specification consists of a population definition and a collection of dimensions that partition the population into an exhaustive set of mutually exclusive segments. It is important to note that segmentation should have an associated set of measures that provide the ability to assess segment performance relative to any of a number of objectives. Now, consider the *handle* concept that was introduced in Chapter 5. A handle is associated with a population,[2] and partitions the population into every possible combination of the dimensions that comprise it. In Chapter 6 we built on the concept of the handle to introduce hybrid credit models, and provided numerous examples. Every one of those examples consisted of a handle, followed by collections of secondary factors that facilitated the evaluation of loan default risk and subsequent recommended course of action. In those segmentation examples, the associated set of measures would include the

---

2. Populations can be as broadly, or as narrowly, defined as desired (e.g., a population could consist of all consumers with steady employment, or consumers with household incomes above $100,000, or subprime borrowers who have recently been denied credit, or loan applicants that do not have a checking account or home phone).

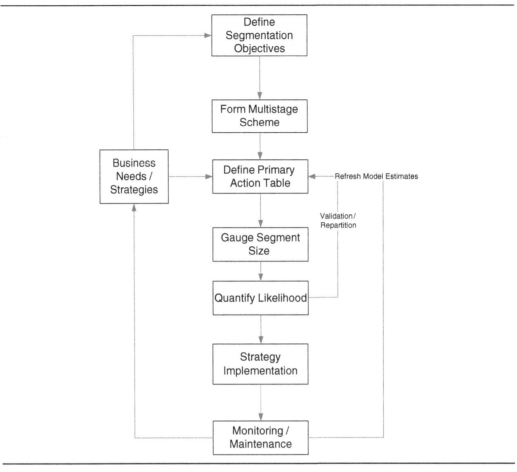

FIGURE 7.1   SEGMENTATION DEVELOPMENT

incidence of good and bad loans in the segment, the number of approved and declined applications in the segment, and the odds of default associated with the segment.

Figure 7.1 describes the general process for developing and maintaining valid segmentation schemes. This is an iterative process that is updated and validated across business scenarios in order to create a minimum set of homogenous segments. These segments can be measured relative to a broad spectrum of business objectives, and the effectiveness of specific strategies that support those objectives can be isolated at the individual segment level. The resulting outcomes are used to evaluate strategies and to identify those segments that are top performers or most influenced by specific strategies.

Define Segmentation Objectives

The first step of segmentation is to define the objective(s), and identify primary factors associated with the population that either distinguish subpopulations of interest or relate to the attainment of the objectives themselves.

Suppose the objective is to determine customer potential for a proposed bundle of products/services that a bank wishes to promote and customize, across market segments. The immediate question that must be addressed is: "What primary factors are relevant to distinguishing the like-groups of customers that would have a potential interest in the offering and what would be the best approach for each group?" The answer to this question is usually a by-product of both expert judgment and analysis of current and historical data. In addition, customer surveys may be conducted to further explore the importance of one or more primary factors.

Multistage Segmentation Scheme

Once identified, the primary factors are used to form a multi-stage segmentation scheme. If there are a half dozen or so factors, then a one stage scheme is possible. The following examples represent the end product of combining domain knowledge, corporate policy considerations, legal/compliance constraints, and data mining to derive factors that not only are relevant to the objective, but also will provide sufficient numbers of observations based upon the distribution of customers. This step is nontrivial and requires sufficient effort in practice. A segmentation scheme is also not something that you want to constantly redefine because it can represent a foundational view of customers and markets, it is often imbedded in many programs, and changing it makes comparisons difficult, especially relative to trend analysis.

Example of Stage 1 Scheme (32 combinations)

- Relationship Threshold[3]: Below, At/Above
- Available Credit Utilization Threshold: Below, At/Above
- Payment Behavior: Min. Payer, Accelerated Payer
- Product Breadth Threshold: Below, At/Above
- Capital Reserves[4]: Less than 5, 5 or more

A larger number of factors can result in two or more stages that relate to the basic segmentation scheme.

Example of Stage 2 Scheme (32 additional combinations)

- Contractual Obligations Threshold[5]: Below, At/Above
- Own/Buying Residence: Yes, No
- Bureau Credit Score: 660 or Below, 661+
- Yrs. In Profession: Under 5, 5+
- Full/Part-Time Student: Y/N

Example of Stage 3 Scheme (eight additional combinations)

- Customer Location Relative to Franchise Physical Footprint: In, Out
- Community Potential: Below Parity, At/Above Parity
- Sector of Employment[6]: Vulnerable/Volatile, Secure

---

3. Would span loans, deposits, investments, and insurance and be based on detailed criteria, such as duration, size of exposures/deposit balances/aggregate holdings/policy amounts, customer profitability, and so forth.
4. Defined by the ratio: $(1.5 \times$ Net worth$)$ / Combined household annual income.
5. This is typically measured by a debt ratio, but the intent here is broader and also seeks to capture noncredit obligations, such as rent and utility payments, as well as insurance premiums, scheduled retirement savings payments, planned medical expenses, planned child care expenses, educational expenses, and so forth.
6. Retirement would be considered secure, whereas self-employment might be an overriding concern even if the sector is considered secure, unless a sufficient track record had been established. The business rules would assign sectors to either of the two groups and a self-employment flag would be checked, along with a flag to indicate whether or not sufficient time and adequate performance standards had been met by the customer. If so, the value would be assigned based on the sector assignment. If not, the value would default to vulnerable/volatile for the

Define Primary Action Table

The next step is to define a primary action table, as described in Chapter 6 (see Figure 6.23), and possibly one or more subsequent action tables that account for every segment. The action table assigns a corresponding action, or model, to every segment. In the foregoing two-stage example, it certainly would be the case that the number of actual segments would be less than every possible combination of the factors.[7] Collapsing of segments could be based upon customer behavior relative to a pilot or initial testing that would precede a strategy rollout.

Consider the implications of using a ten-point scale, rather than high/medium/low, or simply high/not high, to specify a dimension variable. If there are six segmentation variables, use of the ten groups for each dimension would lead to $10 \times 10 \times 10 \times 10 \times 10 \times 10 = 1$ million segments! Attempting to manage this many distinct segments would pose serious difficulties and would not be practical. On the other extreme, a two-way distinction for each factor would lead to $2 \times 2 \times 2 \times 2 \times 2 \times 2 = 64$ distinct segments. This is certainly manageable. The curse of dimensionality forces modelers to abandon segmentation schemes that are too detailed. Still, there are many practical economies that can be found, such as instances where the same model applies to 75 percent of the segments, and only 10 to 25 percent of the segments exhibit nuances that require fine-tuning or special attention. The additional effort to construct these models pays off in significantly superior predictive performance than a *one-size-fits-all* approach.

Gauge the Relative Size of Each Segment

The fourth step is to gauge the relative size of each segment (e.g., if there are five dimensions comprised of dichotomous variables, and if each segment were equally likely to be assigned to a member of the population, then the relative size of any segment would be approximately 3 percent of the total population). The model used to estimate the frequency associated with a particular segment takes into account not only the individual dimensions, but also their first-order, second-order, ..., n^{th}-order interactions. For the more technical reader, we note that the model for estimating i^{th} population segment counts for a one-stage segmentation scheme composed of six-dimensions is of the general form:

$$M_{i(\theta)} = \exp \left[\mu_i + \sum_{j \epsilon I} \mu_{ij}(\theta) \right], I \subseteq P\{1, 2, 3, 4, 5, 6\} \qquad (7.1)$$

where $M_{i(\theta)}$ refers to the estimated count in a segment, μ is the grand mean for the ith population, the subscript i denotes a particular population, the subscript j denotes a particular combination of dimensions, the index set I is the collection of all combinations of the dimensions that are present in the model, θ (theta) represents the segment, and P denotes the power set.[8]

The type of model described is hierarchical and log-linear, and it can represent problems that possess very complex data structures. This log-linear model was covered in detail in Chapter 6 (refer to Equations 6.3–6.5), and its application to customer, marketing, and promotions is analogous to that for credit underwriting and also credit collection/recovery activities. Its properties, uses, and methods for applying it (e.g., determining how many variables and terms are necessary and which, if any, can be safely removed) are fully described in the literature.[9] In addition to

---

customer in question, even though the sector itself may be secure. The self-employment root cause of the value assignment could always be captured via detailed reporting.

7. In the 2-stage example, there are $2 \times 2 \times 2 \times 2 \times 2 \times 2 \times 2 \times 2 \times 2 \times 2 = 1,024$ possible factor combinations.
8. The power set of a collection of objects is the set that would result from forming every combination of the original collection of objects. For example, the power set of the set of objects {1,2,3} is the set {1,2,3,12,13,23,123}. Power set is defined in Halmos, Paul, *Naïve Set Theory*, 1960, Section 5, pp. 19–20.

business criteria, statistical significance tests of individual interactions among factors can be used to collapse dimensions for the purpose of estimating segment distribution and outcome probabilities.

Quantify the Likelihood of Success

The fifth step is to quantify the likelihood of success (captured by a response index) for every segment. In the case where a strategy drives directly off of the response index (i.e., when segment selection is predicated on choosing a response index cutoff), there are a number of statistical tables that are immediately applicable and they are perfectly analogous to the risk index described in Chapter 6, except that in this example, the outcome is acquisition of a product/service bundle, greater capture of wallet share, or increased profitability, instead of default on a credit obligation. These tables include:

- A response index cumulative (descending/interval/ascending) distribution function that provides the marginal odds of success over the entire range of values. See Figure 6.22.
- A reference table that maps all segments to a corresponding response index. See Figure 6.26.
- A reference table providing model sensitivity to the four most important segmentation dimensions for every segment where a "no treatment" action is recommended and also the resulting recommended treatment, given that the most desirable group was indicated relative to each of the four dimensions, considered one at a time. See Figure 6.25.
- Multidimensional forecasts of response rates and segment product/service bundle mix, including variance from what is expected by segment, segment concentrations, and so on. See the section entitled Hybrid System Construction in Chapter 6 for two examples that appear immediately after Figure 6.20.

An obvious question is: "How do you know the response index values in advance for treatment and nontreatment cells?" The answer is that the model is adaptive and the initial estimates of response index values are historically based on whatever treatments those cells were recipients of in the past. For example, the response index might be customer attrition likelihood, probability of activation, the likelihood a customer will acquire an additional product or service in a set period of time, or the likelihood that the customer will move to the next profitability tier. In all cases the initial response index values would be calculated on actual historically observed rates for each cell in the segmentation. Results from initial field tests and pilot programs may provide this data. Certain relevant consumer data may be purchased from a third party provider. In circumstances where data are unavailable, judgmental-based estimates can be substituted.

In the general case, multiple response index functions may be defined, in which case there are multiple sets of the above tables. Moreover, the tables can be integrated, based on a combined response function that measures the likelihood of every possible combination of responses. Alternatively, tables can be constructed serially. Serial tables are required when time must elapse to observe behavior in order to classify subjects, or select segments, for the next strategy. An example would be direct response marketing of a credit card where the first strategy may focus on getting the consumer to respond to the offer and activate their card, while the second strategy might be to encourage them to make purchases with their card so as to achieve a target account profitability tier by attaining and maintaining a target utilization.

The main goal is to develop segmentation strategies that allow for more effective programs aimed at one or more customer marketing goals and also a companion methodology that affords

---

9. See Bishop, Fienberg, and Holland, *Discrete Multivariate Analysis: Theory and Practice/* MIT Press, 1975, pp. 9–11, and Goodman, *Analyzing Qualitative/Categorical Data: Log-Linear Models and Latent Structure Analysis*, Abt Books, 1978, pp. 159–161.

accurate forecasting of results. One of the key business challenges is to devise treatments that will encourage customers to migrate toward a more sustaining and profitable relationship. In the case where segment definitions include behavioral factors, then the inducements may be aimed at migrating customers away from less desirable segments to more desirable ones.

Strategy Implementation

The vehicle described for defining and for implementing strategy is the Risk Evaluation and Policy Formulation System (REPFS) described in the section on hybrid models in Chapter 6. The action table component of the REPFS would correspond to a particular strategy that is to be applied. The segmentation is specified by the handle, or collection of all action table cells. The indicated action within each cell in the action table indicates the treatment to be applied. This system can be fashioned to simultaneously sort segments in increasing order of desirability, by any number of different criteria. An example of a profit-driven criterion might be formulation of policy on nuisance fee waivers on the most profitable cells, in conjunction with attrition measures. Figure 7.2 provides additional examples of strategies in a half dozen different application areas.

Some of these examples may require further refinement. For example, the last example on reissue tightening may benefit from a product breakout to isolate a segment of reward-linked product consumers that may want to secure additional rewards for higher usage. Reward card users may be exempted from the balance reduction initiative (first example). It is recommended that pilot tests be conducted on a representative sample of accounts prior to a full-scale rollout of a given strategy. Segment performance in these contexts spans attrition, loss, utilization, acquisition, and profit.

Application	Strategy	Dimension 1 Relationship Threshold	Dimension 2 Available Credit Utilization Threshold	Dimension 3 Payment Behavior	Dimension 4 Product Breadth Threshold	Dimension 5 Capital Reserves
1. Line Increase	Gradual Increments: $2M/yr	At/Above	At/Above	Accelerated Payer	At/Above	All
2. Authorization Pad Reduction	New Limit of 50% Current Pad	Below	At/Above	Minimum Payer	Below	All
3. Fee Wavier	Automatic on first two instances of late fees	At/Above	At/Above	Accelerated Payer	All	All
4. Balance Reduction via Elected Change in Terms	Increase to 5% Min Payment & Drop rate 300bp	All	At/Above	Minimum Payer	All	Less Than 5
5. Cash Restrictions	Set Maximum to 25% of Line Amount	All	All	Minimum Payer	All	All
6. Reissue Tightening	Raise Annual Fee	Below	Below	Accelerated Payer	Below	All

FIGURE 7.2 SEGMENT TARGETING STRATEGIES

In practice, you are not limited to a single strategy per action table. However, careful design of your experiments is required to enable you to identify and measure the impact of individual strategies on outcomes, as well as the combined effect of multiple strategies. This can be accomplished in a number of ways, the most simple of which is to randomly assign subjects who are qualified for multiple treatments to a series of test cells where some, or possibly every, permutation of treatments are assigned and results tracked. In the case of the six strategies listed in Figure 7.2, if a particular cell qualified for all six strategies, then in theory you would need to break the treatment cells into a group of 64 cells to cover every possible combination of treatments, including the case of no treatment at all.[10] Usually, strategies are more narrowly targeted, and this becomes less of an issue. In other cases, it is less important to break out individual effects. Another alternative would be to conduct tests serially, instead of in parallel, which would result in a separate action table for each strategy.

Monitoring/Maintenance

Strategy maintenance relative to segmentation can be achieved via continuous refreshing of estimates of segment performance and mix in order to maintain and improve predictive power. It also provides feedback and input to enhance business strategies. Typically, segment mix is updated monthly, and segment performance is updated quarterly. Data availability is the primary constraint. Concerning segment performance monitoring, as response likelihoods are refreshed with new performance data, the log-linear model can periodically be assessed to determine if the interaction structure has changed. If scoring models are incorporated in an REPFS, such as embedding various score ranges in a segment dimension, the scoring models themselves will still require validation and periodic redevelopment. Redevelopment frequency can be significantly reduced, however, if the scoring system does a good job of rank-ordering, despite loss of some power in the performance score distribution separation metric (e.g., divergence, Kolmogorov-Smirnov test). A reexamination of model predictive strength, in light of actual results (post-model development response data), is an exercise that can afford deep insight into how a particular strategy can affect different segments. Chapter 8 explains what is involved in this process.

The process of rolling out segmentation is inherently iterative. A full cycle involves the use of the best science for knowledge discovery, which, in turn, helps to build greater domain expertise. More specifically, knowledge gained is used to improve forecasts that can be compared and tested by taking actions taken under a champion/challenger segmentation-testing framework. Customer segment performance measurement and portfolio impact are quantified, along with any residual effects. These steps are followed by more analysis/reporting/refinement, resulting in improved models, taking a new set of actions, measuring the impact of those new actions, and the entire cycle repeats itself. In this evolutionary process each successive iteration incorporates what has been learned in the preceding, and all prior, iterations.

APPLICATIONS

In this section we present several examples to illustrate how the proposed segmentation schemes can be used to develop business strategies.

---

10. Expressed mathematically, the required number of cells is the number of ways you can choose, anywhere from none (zero) up to all six possible treatments, without regard to the order in which the treatments are applied, for example,

$$\sum_{i=0}^{6} \binom{6}{i} = 1 + 6 + 15 + 20 + 15 + 6 + 1 = 64 \; combinations.$$

Dynamic Customer Relationship Management

We outline a simplified example to illustrate application of a segmentation framework. Dynamic customer relationship management (DCRM) is an area that presents many business challenges, but holds the promise of significant rewards if mastered.

Rewards	Challenges
Protect valued relationships	Appropriately reward customer loyalty
Profitably grow the business	Refrain from penalizing profitable accounts
Win business away from competitors	Manage short- versus long-term trade-offs

We want to mention at the onset that one facet of the problem is the potential for unintentionally adversely impacting a protected class of customers, per fair lending laws. We advocate the use of fair lending statistical analysis methods described in Chapters 3 through 6 as a means to either avoid, or quickly identify and correct, potential issues. We also advocate the use of alternative data and hybrid modeling methodologies described in Chapter 6 to help identify qualified borrowers in emerging markets that can bring greater diversity and significant long-term profitability to the franchise. We address credit promotion and account management later in this chapter. Using our segmentation model framework described earlier, we proceed to define the necessary components.

Population   Existing customer base for a full-service financial institution.

Key objectives   Either promote, maintain, or control customer segments within the current portfolio of the firm's products and services (banking, brokerage, insurance).

Dimensions	Segment-Defining Variables/Key Measures
1. Borrower credit risk profile	Payment performance Indebtedness/exposure
2. Borrower wealth profile	Monthly household spend tier Deposit/investment tier Income tier/noncredit payment tier
3. Borrower insurance profile	Income replacement coverage percentage Asset/wealth protection coverage percentage[11] Competitor share of insurance portfolio
4. Borrower noncredit payment profile	Payment performance Noncredit Payment-to-Income ratio
5. Household demographics	Homeownership/value/loan term value (LTV) Number occupants/minors/dependents
6. Customer needs	Consumer life cycle positioning Goals/timing/perceptions/attitudes

Next, we examine customer goals and the attributes of products that can help them attain their goals. In Figure 7.3, we have grouped products under three main headings, namely those that help customers meet their wealth accumulation, financing, and insurance needs. In each column, the product offerings are ordered so that the products having lower purchase and usage propensity, and greater liquidity and stability, are at the top, while those having higher purchase and usage propensity, and lower liquidity and stability, are at the bottom.

Associated segment measures   These include, but are not limited to lifetime value, longevity, potential annual revenue, propensity to acquire additional products and services, attrition risk, credit risk competitor share of financing portfolio, competitor share of wealth management portfolio, and current year profitability. These may require the sourcing and combining of literally hundreds of data elements. Examples appear in Appendix 7B.

---

11. For example, coverage for automobile, homeowners, renters, health, travel, and life.

Wealth Enhancement	Financing Needs	Financial Protection
Payment/Deposit Mechanisms • DDA-checks/debit card • Reward credit card transactors • Bill-pay w/triggers	**Revolving Credit** • Credit card • DDA overdraft	**Event Risk** • Credit life • Unemployment • Health
Liquid Investments • Savings, CDs, T-bills • MMDAs, MMMFs • Options	**Term Loans, Installment, and Lines** • Auto (direct/indirect) • HELOC • Exec credit line	**Major Assets** • Auto • Homeowners • Property casualty umbrella
Higher-Return Investments • IRAs, annuities • T-bonds and notes, bond funds, corp. bonds • Equity funds, stocks • Trust svs	**Mortgages** • Residential (first lien) • Primary • Secondary (owner occup/rental) • second–Nth lien	**Income & Estate** • Disability • AD&D • Life (whole/term) • Safe deposit/custody

FIGURE 7.3   PRODUCT MATRIX USAGE/LIQUIDITY VERSUS CUSTOMER NEEDS

Focus on Dynamic Relationship Pricing

For this example, let's assume that pricing product and service offerings is a primary focus. Dynamic relationship pricing (DRP) entails pricing products in ways that take into account the total customer relationship value to the enterprise as a whole, rather than viewing the customer value to each line of business in isolation. The horizon over which the relationship is viewed can vary, and may be restricted to a one-year window, or the maturity of the product having the shortest time to maturity, or the estimated lifetime horizon for customers having identical profiles. Relationship pricing may take many forms, such as:

- Rate or margin concessions.
- Fee waivers (e.g., fees associated with certain product features, late fees, etc.).
- Special discounts.
- Special "bundling" of products and services.
- Rewards, such as cash back, points redeemable for merchandise or services.
- More personalized or priority service (requires activity-based costing to translate to dollar terms).
- Other accommodations that impact product, service, or transaction pricing based on the breadth and/or depth of customer relationship.

From the financial services company's perspective, the objective of DRP is to increase the company's share of wallet by providing an economic incentive to the customer. In essence, reward the customer for giving you more business. The basic concept is to provide increasing "value" to the customer as the customer concentrates more of his/her assets with your company. For companies that are financial services "supermarkets," this is a powerful concept because it enables them to compete more effectively with the mono-line[12] "category killers" that can offer better features and pricing at a product level.

---

12. For example, an independent credit card company, an independent mortgage company, a captive finance company for an automobile manufacturer, and so on.

One of the more interesting aspects of DRP is "customer empowerment." It enables the customer to control the "value equation" by decisions that they make. For example, you can ponder what will happen to your auto loan rate if you obtain your mortgage from your auto loan company. You, the customer, can weigh "trade-offs" and come to a well-reasoned conclusion that, overall, is most advantageous to you.

Relationship pricing may occur serially, as products are acquired by the consumer, or jointly when two or more products are acquired simultaneously.

DRP Implications

For cross-selling, a relationship manager should be able to offer any products available through any of the individual sales channels, LOBs, and so on and would be able to price products in an advantageous fashion so as to induce customers to bring more of their business to the institution (e.g., credit card balance transfers, mortgage refinancing, time deposits, etc.). Depending on the breadth of product offerings, there would undoubtedly be innovative combined product value propositions that would exploit possible product synergies, for example:

- Pledge CD, or 401(k) assets, for X percent of mortgage down payment to avoid mortgage insurance with a less than 20 percent down payment while still earning interest on the pledged asset.
- Credit card estimated lifetime triples from three to eight years with addition of mortgage, so a pricing concession may be made when a mortgage is booked.

DRP Challenges

Handling missing data is a big challenge. Too often, segmentation schemes associate values of "unknown" as indicating "undesirable." In other instances, models are developed purely on the customer records that are "complete" and in many instances very significant portions of the customer base has been excluded from the analysis. Small wonder that many attempts to build models that deliver results have failed to meet expectations. The use of hybrid models and dynamic conditional process can significantly help to address the problem.

Capturing the enterprise customer relationship presents another challenge. Organizations need an information infrastructure that facilitates the movement of information from operational systems to a customer intelligence platform. It is important that organizations conduct a formal assessment of their capabilities in this area, which will enable them to "chart a systematic path to sustainable growth and innovation thanks to optimized, strategic use of enterprise-wide business intelligence."[13] The process for accomplishing this task is well documented in the reference cited in the previous footnote and the reader is encouraged to take advantage of the detailed questionnaires that covers both the infrastructure dimension[14] and knowledge process dimension.[15]

There are multiple dimensions to pricing, in addition to customer segments, that relate to a number of factors which include the following: the product terms and conditions, the transaction type/purpose/costs, the organizational subentity's business model (especially required rates of return), channel cost structure, geographic area, competitive offers, attributes of any collateral,

---

13. Davis, Jim, Gloria J. Miller, and Allan Russell. *Information Revolution: Using the Information Evolution Model to Grow Your Business*, John Wiley & Sons, 2006, Chapter 10, Information Evolution Assessment Process, pp. 115–132.

14. This encompasses the hardware, software, networking/internet-based tools, and technologies that create, manage, store, distribute and utilize information.

15. This includes concepts covered in Chapters 1 and 2, such as governance, corporate policies, standards, and best practices that determine how information is created, validated and used; how it is tied to performance indicators and incentive systems; and how it supports the strategic use of information.

and the prevailing interest rate environment. DRP models must reflect these associated costs and risks when making adjustments to pricing. The complexity of the pricing adjustment mechanism for accomplishing this depends on how information is aggregated and at what level of detail product costs are captured and allocated.

Monitoring is another critical challenge associated with DRP. Business impacts must be measured and disparities from plan calibrated and aggregated across dimensions so that exposures can be identified, in addition to areas where results are exceptionally good. Timely analysis must be fine-tuned to reflect the dynamic business environment. The only constant is change with respect to consumer behavior, market conditions, competitive forces, and so forth and their impact on risk profiles and revenue generation. Analysis must be timely and policies and strategies must be kept in sync with the business reality.

DRP Application Process

Figure 7.4 depicts an application process that supports an enterprise risk and relationship-based pricing program. The UPI takes as inputs the group and disparity index definitions as described in Chapter 3. In statistical experiments, typically, the treatment group consists of customers who received some treatment, and the control group consists of customers who did not receive the treatment. However, in the sense we use the terms here, we are considering identical groups and measuring performance relative to either different points in time, or to identically defined industry segments, and so on. For example, group definitions for the treatment group might consist of actual results based on number of sales or number of customers, relative to the current period

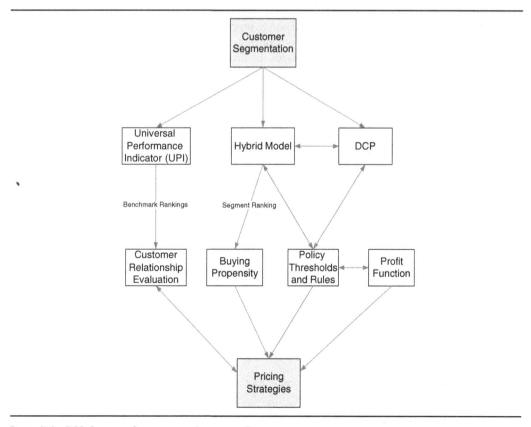

Figure 7.4   DRP Customer Segmentation Application Process

spanning organizational entity, channel, geography, customer segments, or risk pools. Whereas group definitions for the control group might consist of the identical definitions except that instead of actuals, the groups would be defined relative to budget, current year forecasts, industry peers, historical norms, or strategic plans.

Similarly to those disparity indices described in Chapter 3, DRP disparity indices can also be defined as either results based or decision based. Examples of results-based indices include low loan margin, high loan default, high prepayment, zero revolving balance, large number of transactions, additional products purchased, total exposure significantly increased, global customer loan to value across all loan exposures greater than 90 percent, and so on. Examples of decision-based indices include borrower profile of risk, wealth, insurance, and noncredit payment, borrower negotiation strength, terms and conditions, geographic, economic and market influences, customer relationship breadth/depth, and competitive forces.

For the decision-based indicator, the disparity indices are defined to reflect whether the treatment rewarded the customer or penalized the customer. This type of strategy visualization makes it possible to quickly spot what is working better than expected, versus "as expected," and which pricing strategies are not working as expected.

UPI can be derived relative to any segmentation scheme across multiple layers of aggregation, or within multiple layers of specification, in order to assess customer relationship status at the enterprise level. Some generic benchmark reports include ranking reports,[16] quadrant analysis,[17] spatial maps,[18] UPI decomposition,[19] and UPI trend analysis.[20] Relative to the quadrant analysis, the interpretation for results versus decision-based indicators making up UPI for relationship-based pricing might be as shown in Figure 7.5.

Dynamic conditional process (DCP) can be used to capture the pricing business rules and can be used periodically to revalidate them based upon actual results, changes in policy, and prevailing market conditions and customer behaviors. Buying propensity specifies how inclined the customer is to purchase based on price, including both rates and fees. This can be predicted using DCP and hybrid models. The profit function captures the distribution of revenue and cost as a function of product price for each product within a line of business. The resulting pricing strategies can be deployed and maintained within the hybrid model context using the risk evaluation and policy formulation systems described in Chapter 6.

Neighborhood and Underbanked Lending/Investment Assessment

The same segmentation techniques used to distinguish subpopulations of consumers may be applied at higher levels of aggregation, such as at a neighborhood level, for measuring and evaluating

Decision-Based Indicator	Results-Based Indicator	
	Better	Worse
Favored the customer	Strategy validates	Strategy fails—investigate!
Neutral or unfavorable	Unexplained improvement	Predictable outcome

FIGURE 7.5 CUSTOMER PRICING STRATEGY QUADRANT ANALYSIS

16. e.g. most profitable, responsive, highest attrition, or least profitable areas.
17. Refer to Figure 3.15.
18. Refer to Figures 3.22–3.23.
19. Refer to Figures 3.19 and 3.22.
20. Refer to Figure 3.25.

community development opportunities. The basic idea is to develop and utilize market intelligence to determine how much economic power a community possesses and to formulate strategies to better tap that power to foster greater economic prosperity and sustainable growth. This can be accomplished by (1) making a strong business case to suppliers and financial institutions for the delivery of goods and services to inner city and underserved community residents that are accessible and priced at par when compared with more affluent neighborhoods; (2) developing, tapping, and making accessible to all stakeholders sources of information on markets at all levels (federal, state, and local); and (3) creating improved methodologies, tools, and models to spur market innovation.[21] One of the pioneers in this area is the Social Compact, with their highly praised and field-proven *DrillDown* technique that creates business-oriented profiles of neighborhood markets.[22] The methodology taps transactional data and refines and brings current a diverse set of information from commercial, government and proprietary sources.

Neighborhood Segmentation Specification

Using our segmentation model framework described earlier, we proceed to define the necessary components for neighborhood lending and investment segmentation.

Population Neighborhoods where occupants are compelled to operate at subpar economic levels despite the existence of significant untapped potential for profitable growth through appropriate investment and financing.

Key objectives and associated measures Develop and utilize market intelligence to determine how much economic power a community possesses and to formulate strategies to better tap that power to foster greater economic prosperity and sustainable growth.

Dimensions	Segment-Defining Variables/Key Measures
1. Market size/growth	Number of households; population Aggregate neighborhood income Neighborhood turnover/growth trend
2. Housing profile	Home values/housing availability Occupancy/HMDA credit trends Housing construction Foreclosures
3. Commercial profile	Stores and retail space/location Revenue/employment Business turnover/failures
4. Public-sector profile	Institutions/space No. parks/recreational facilities/libraries Number of schools/enrollment Mass transit access and capacity
5. Stability/risk profile	Crime Aggregate informal economy[23]
6. Consumer behavior profile	Consumer credit Products/services usage Credit bureau data/spending patterns Bankruptcies

21. The Metropolitan Program at the Brookings Institution has produced numerous studies over the years that address the problems and issues surrounding urban development and economically challenged consumer groups and communities. Refer to the bibliography for specific references.

22. See remarks by Chairman Ben S. Bernanke, "By the Numbers: Data and Measurement in Community Economic Development," at the Greenlining Institute's Thirteenth Annual Economic Development Summit, Los Angeles, California, (via satellite), April 20, 2006, p. 16.

There are numerous related applications that center on locating underserved pockets of opportunity for consumer and small business lending. Having current data and very granular information on communities is perhaps the most important factor in developing models that are realistic and achieve broad acceptance by stakeholders. That said, even at a higher level of aggregation, such as metropolitan statistical area (MSA), studies have shown that there is opportunity to find qualified mortgage loan applicants in home ownership deficient low-/moderate-income metropolitan areas across the country.[24] The next example in this same vein focuses on the consumer level.

Underbanked Consumer Segmentation Specification

A survey of close to a million households conducted in 2005 in low-/moderate-income neighborhoods of Los Angeles, Washington, D.C., and Chicago underscored the notion that underbanked consumers are not a homogeneous group of consumers relative to attitudes, preferences, and experiences and their use of financial services represents more of a continuum than an dichotomy (e.g., use of mainstream vehicles for some services and products, while not for others, but not an "all or nothing" usage pattern). The study in question found ten distinct market segments for the underbanked. The following segmentation example is based on this, and similar studies over the past decade.[25]

Population   Residents and businesses operating within a particular neighborhood.

Key objectives   Develop and utilize customer intelligence to determine how to meet the needs of the underbanked households.

Dimensions	Segment-Defining Variables/Key Measures
1. Demographics	Age
	Ethnicity/race
	Educational level, incl. vocational school
	Income level
	Household size
	U.S. born/immigrant status
	Own/rent status
	Own car
2. Current financial services usage	Existence of checking account
	Existence of savings account
	Method of bill payment
	Insurance coverage
	Breadth of product usage
	Formerly banked but no longer bank
	Have friends and/or family that bank
	ATM usage
3. Credit usage/source	Credit card balances/utilization
	Student loans
	Payday loans
	Pawn shop loans
	Existence of credit bureau file/thin file
	Have secured credit card

23. See Alderslade, Jamie, John Talmage, and Yusef Freeman. "Measuring the Informal Economy—One Neighborhood at a Time." Brookings Institution Metropolitan Policy Program discussion paper, September 2006, for further details on measuring the informal economy.

24. Abrahams, Clark R., Frank R. Burnett, and Jin-Whan Jung. "Using Data Mining Technology to Identify and Prioritize Emerging Opportunities for Mortgage Lending to Homeownership-Deficient Communities," *SESUG 2000 Proceedings*, October 2000 in Charlotte, pp. 307–316.

25. See Seidman, Ellen, Moez Hababou, and Jennifer Kramer. *Getting to Know Underbanked Consumers: A Financial Services Analysis*. The Center for Financial Services Innovation, September 2005.

Dimensions	Segment-Defining Variables/Key Measures
4. Work status/savings habits	Savings rate
	Saving activity during past 12 months
	Number of adults working in HH
	Recipient of benefits
	Retirement indicator
	Self-employment indicator
	Disabled indicator
	Send money to homeland
5. Remittance payment profile	History of utility/telecom bill payment
	Rent payment history
	Other payment history
	Use of stored value cards
	Use of debit card/dual debit card
	Use of nonbank money transfer vehicles

An appropriately designed segmentation scheme can help banks expand into underbanked markets and, from all accounts in the literature, the volume of potential profitable customer transactions is enormous.

Credit Portfolio Analysis

The adoption of a new model for assessing credit on a consumer, or individual loan transaction level, has implications for credit portfolio management. This is true whether the model is simply a newly validated existing credit scoring model, which has been adapted to treat alternative trade lines as equivalent to traditional credit accounts, or in the case where a completely new model, perhaps in the hybrid classification, has been deployed. The chief goal of credit portfolio management is to measure and monitor the behavior of the credit portfolio in question relative to actual and projected losses and prepayment. Precursors of default, such as delinquency, credit bureau score deterioration, credit grade degradation, violations of loan agreement terms, above threshold frequency of exceptions to underwriting/pricing policies, account reaging, skip-payment usage, and reductions in behavior scores may all be monitored at the account level and summarized at and aggregate level. It is common also to examine and forecast collective account behavior relative to a behavioral segment, vintage cohort, dual score band, business line, channel, region, product, rate tier, loan amount or limit tier, and so on.

An important aspect of designing credit models that can accommodate emerging markets, or consumers and small businesses operating outside of the mainstream credit market, is the ability to forecast loan performance and estimate the timing and amount of losses and payouts associated with their loans. In this section we discuss a modeling method for estimating near-term credit losses. This approach can be used to track performance month-to-month and estimate losses in the short run. In practice, several methods would be used to forecast losses, such as vintage cohort analysis, ordinary least squares (OLS) regression with macro-economic and portfolio variables, account-level loss projection using credit/behavior/bankruptcy scores that are summed over all accounts, Markov chain reduced form models combining macro economic and market variables,[26] and so on. Some portfolio risk managers take a weighted average of the results from multiple approaches in order to arrive at a final dollar-loss estimate.

---

26. This method uses a discrete state space, continuous time, time-homogeneous Markov chain in credit ratings. See, for example, Jarrow, Robert A., Martin Lando, and Stuart M. Turnbull, "A Markov Model for the Term Structure of Credit Risk Spreads," *Review of Financial Studies*, Oxford University Press for Society for Financial Studies, Vol. 10, No. 2, 1997, pp. 481–523.

Up until now, the development of a secondary market in small business lending has been slow. Hybrid models can be used to effectively underwrite small business loans that have proven more challenging to decision using traditional methods. A recent Small Business Administration (SBA) research found that "despite the ability to obtain a quantified risk estimate through a credit score, other factors, such a lack of homogeneity in the loan pool, may slow the development of secondary markets."[27] Segmentation, or the handle grouping, can provide the ability to put loans into homogenous segments relative to default risk that can be subsequently tracked in order to help validate expected, and similar, delinquency behavior and projected losses.

Behavioral Simulation Method

Monitoring the performance of a portfolio relative to loan grades and past due status is the focus of this section. The topic is important for two main reasons. First is the need to understand the root causes of any adverse spikes, or trend in performance deterioration and the second is to ensure that a proper loan loss reserve level is maintained. To those ends, we describe a methodology that requires two months of history[28] on accounts to calculate their rate of movement among the various states of performance, where each performance state has an associated default risk. The need to keep up with these transition rates, or *roll rates*, as they are often termed, has been underscored by regulators. For example, OCC Bulletin 99–15 requires that "Analysis of portfolio quality should capture ... roll rates [Note 3: Roll rates refer to the movement of accounts from one payment status to another, e.g. the percentage of 60-days-past-due accounts that "roll" to 90 days past due, or, conversely, from 60 days past due to current. Calculations should capture both forward (worsening) and backward (improving) performance]. ..."[29]

A method that captures these month-to-month portfolio *forward, backward, and stay-put* rates has proven to be effective in predicting short-term losses.[30] It is "one step beyond" the typical roll-rate model that is commonly used at many banks. The model is a behavioral simulation method (BSM).[31] There are more powerful variants of this modeling technique than what is presented in

---

27. Cowan, Charles D. and Adrian M. Cowen. *A Survey Based Assessment of Financial Institution Use of Credit Scoring for Small Business Lending*, November 2006, 62 pages, SBA Office of Advocacy, Under Contract Number SBAH-04-Q-0021.

28. While two months of history is required to compute the model transition rates, the method presumes that the portfolio is of sufficient age to infer "steady-state" behavior. This usually implies that the portfolio has aged two to five years, depending on the loan product because they vary in the average time to bad debt for new accounts. For loan loss reserve estimation, GAAP rules and current viewpoints from FASB, AICPA, SEC, and bank regulators should be taken into account during model development. For application to unbanked populations, statistics from comparable portfolios that are more seasoned may be applicable, when available. Another option would be for a consortium of lenders to pool a representative sample of their respective emerging market portfolio data in a "blind" database to enable joint portfolio performance estimation and loss forecasting.

29. OCC Bulletin 99–15, April 5, 1999, Subprime Lending Risks and Rewards.

30. The authors' firsthand experience with this method has spanned four distinct segmentation schemes, which include: 1) Multi-region (3), Multi-Product (6) segmentation for a $1 billion Consumer Finance Portfolio. There were 18 distinct models for installment portfolios using contractual (C) and regency (R) based account-aging methods. Specific products were direct auto ($70 MM-R), indirect auto ($210 MM-C), mobile home ($190 MM-C), home equity/improvement ($250 MM-R), other direct installment ($150 MM-R) sales finance ($60 MM-C), respectively. Accuracy averaged 2.5 percent error on 12 month-forecast horizon 2) Account Age (3), Utilization (3), Payment Behavior (3), Product (2) segmentation (54 segments) for an $8B revolving credit portfolio. Accuracy ranged from 1 percent to 5 percent error, depending on behavioral segment, on 12-month forecast horizon. 3) Numerous additional Markov models developed to evaluate bid proposals. Accuracy not available, but forecasts were in proximity with average of several competing approaches. 4) Two models corresponding to program segments for an $80 MM nationwide credit card portfolio. Accuracy ranged from 1 percent to 3 percent error, depending on behavioral segment, on 12-month forecast horizon.

31. The model is technically referred to as a first order discrete-time Markov Chain. See Cyert, R. M., H. J. Davidson, and G. L. Thompson. "Estimation of Allowance for Doubtful Accounts by Markov Chains," *Management Science*, Vol. 8, 1962, pp. 287–303.

this book. What we seek to illustrate is the *simplest version* (no attempt is made to control for vintage effects, cyclical influences, forced versus voluntary attrition, account management policy changes, cash flow discounting, receivables growth, time-dependent properties of model parameters, etc.). Even the *simple version* has been found to be a very reliable and useful modeling technique, which allows for a deeper understanding and assessment of the true risk dynamics of a credit portfolio than the roll-rate approach.

The purpose of this exercise is to apply the method using realistic data, coupled with domain expert judgments, and compare the results with projections based on a typical current roll-rate model. In contrast to the simple roll rate model, the simulation model explicitly details how portfolio past due levels evolve, and allows the analyst to quantify the impact, and effectiveness, of collection strategies on segments of accounts in the various stages of delinquency.

First, we describe model inputs and outputs, using a credit card example, followed by a small business example. In addition, model sensitivity to key inputs is examined in some detail, while Appendix 7A provides the mathematical and statistical underpinnings of the method for the more technically inclined reader.[32]

Credit Card Portfolio Analysis

In this example, we examine a consumer credit card portfolio that has $100 million dollars in balances that are current, and $9,630,000 in delinquent balances, as shown in Figure 7.6. The model input requirements are specified below, followed by a description of model output and sensitivity to changes in selected input data values.

Required Input

In a nutshell, this method requires classification of outstandings by past due cycle as shown in Figure 7.6. In this example, outstandings at the beginning of November 2007 total $109,630,000, with $100 million current, $5 million 30 days past due, $1,700,000 60 days past due, and so forth.

The model next requires probabilities, which describe the likelihood that a dollar in a given delinquency cycle will transition, or move, to any other delinquency cycle. For example, the

State	Definition	Total Dollars	Percentages
1	Current	100,000,000	91.22
2	30 Days	5,000,000	4.56
3	60 Days	1,700,000	1.55
4	90 Days	1,200,000	1.09
5	120 Days	650,000	0.59
6	150 Days	550,000	0.50
7	180 Days	480,000	0.44
8	210 Days	25,000	0.05
	Total portfolio	$109,630,000	100.00

FIGURE 7.6   DISTRIBUTION OF DOLLARS BY DELINQUENCY STATE

32. The initial work on BSM was based on the lecture notes from the following college courses: Computational Algebra, Undergraduate Mathematics Department at UC Berkeley—Professor Beresford Parlett, and Stochastic Processes I & II, Graduate Statistics Department at Stanford University—Professor Rupert Miller.

	1	2	3	4	5	6	7	8
1	0.9500	0.0404	0.0000	0.0000	0.0000	0.0000	0.0000	0.0000
2	0.4000	0.2800	0.3218	0.0000	0.0000	0.0000	0.0000	0.0000
3	0.0097	0.0977	0.0900	0.7001	0.0000	0.0000	0.0000	0.0000
4	0.2176	0.0000	0.0000	0.0000	0.7801	0.0000	0.0000	0.0000
5	0.2974	0.0000	0.0000	0.0000	0.0000	0.7000	0.0000	0.0000
6	0.1774	0.0000	0.0000	0.0000	0.0000	0.0000	0.8201	0.0000
7	0.2021	0.0000	0.0000	0.0000	0.0000	0.0000	0.0000	0.0975
8	0.0696	0.0000	0.0000	0.0000	0.0000	0.0000	0.0000	0.2301

FIGURE 7.7   MONTHLY ACCOUNT TRANSITION RATES

probability of an account: remaining current is 95.00 percent; cycling from current to 30 days past due (DPD) is 4.04 percent; remaining 30 DPD is 28.00 percent; curing from 30DPD to current is 40.00 percent; cycling from 150 DPD to 180 DPD is 82.01 percent and so forth (see Figure 7.7). Accuracy is improved when the rates are estimated based upon *account*, rather than dollar, transitions. This example is based on the modeler's experience, but in practice would be calculated on 12 historical averages.

Finally, the model requires the likelihood that an account is absorbed (closed with zero balance) through attrition, bankruptcy, or contractual charge-off in a month's time. For example, the probability of contractual charge-off at 180 DPD is 70.00 percent, while the probability of bankruptcy at 90 DPD is 28 basis points (bp) (see Figure 7.8). The simulation model assumes that all paydowns occur after an account is brought current, which explains the one percent rate in the attrition column corresponding to the *current* state. The bankruptcy rate is assumed to be a bit higher in the early and late stages of delinquency. In fact, these assumptions can be replaced with actual observed rates, if it is cost effective to develop a management information system (MIS) to deliver what is required. Finally, the contractual delinquency charge-off rate assumes that there is no charge-off activity unless accounts age to 180 + DPD. Some regulators have suggested that accounts on fixed payment, or special hardship, programs that fall behind should be charged off at 90 DPD.

In this scenario, the portfolio is in a runoff mode, with no new outstandings.

State	Definition	Attrition	Delinquency C/O	Bankruptcy
1	Current	0.0100	0.0000	0.0057
2	30 Days	0.0000	0.0000	0.0056
3	60 Days	0.0000	0.0000	0.0028
4	90 Days	0.0000	0.0000	0.0028
5	120 Days	0.0000	0.0000	0.0028
6	150 Days	0.0000	0.0000	0.0028
7	180 Days	0.0000	0.7000	0.0050
8	210 Days	0.0000	0.7000	0.0050

FIGURE 7.8   MONTHLY ACCOUNT ABSORPTION RATES

State	Definition	Attrition	Delinquency C/O	Bankruptcy
1	Current	0.598	0.307	0.174
2	30 Days	0.490	0.380	0.151
3	60 Days	0.354	0.467	0.114
4	90 Days	0.383	0.550	0.121
5	120 Days	0.324	0.620	0.102
6	150 Days	0.209	0.754	0.068
7	180 Days	0.126	0.854	0.042
8	210 Days	0.054	0.937	0.022

FIGURE 7.9 ULTIMATE ABSORPTION PROBABILITIES

Model Output

By solving a series of simultaneous equations, the likelihood of a dollar being paid out, charged off due to aging past 180 days past due, or charged off due to bankruptcy, given the initial state at the beginning of the forecast period, is shown in Figure 7.9. Hence, the probability of a 60 days past due account being charged off due to severe delinquency is 46.7 percent, whereas the probability of default would be 58.1 percent (the sum of the probabilities of delinquency charge-off and bankruptcy in the 60 days past due state).

The *bankruptcy/nonbankruptcy split* (both dollar and percentage) is shown in Figure 7.10, along with cumulative total losses (i.e., both contractual and bankruptcy) of $83.75 MM for the 12-month period ending October 2008. Bankruptcies make up 38 percent of total losses. Cumulative losses for the first 12 months of the forecasting horizon are $8,375 on a $109,630,000 portfolio.

Month	Percent DELNQNT	Share BNKRPT	Dollars DELNQNT	($000) BNKRPT	Cumulative Total Loss ($000)
November 2007	56.58	43.42	371	285	656
December 2007	55.93	44.07	357	281	1,293
January 2008	52.10	47.90	301	277	1,872
February 2008	60.00	40.00	411	274	2,556
March 2008	60.74	39.26	418	270	3,244
April 2008	61.94	38.06	433	266	3,944
May 2008	64.62	35.38	479	263	4,686
June 2008	65.64	34.36	494	259	5,439
July 2008	66.01	33.99	495	255	6,188
August 2008	66.12	33.88	489	251	6,928
September 2008	66.14	33.86	482	247	7,657
October 2008	66.14	33.86	475	243	8,375

FIGURE 7.10 MONTHLY CURRENT CHARGE-OFF SHARES: DELINQUENCIES VERSUS BANKRUPTCIES

One-Year Loss Impact			
Key Roll Rate	**Δ Amount (bp)**	**$Δ**	**%Δ**
• Current-to 30DPD	+100	↑$ 452 M	5.4
• Current-to 30DPD	+200	↑$ 863 M	10.1
• 30-to-60DPD	+200	↑$ 109 M	1.3
• Bankruptcy	Double Rate	↑$2,144 M	25.6
• 30DPD-to-Current	+2,000	↓$2,630 M	31.4
• 60DPD-to-Current	+1,000	↓$2,625 M	31.1

FIGURE 7.11   MODEL SENSITIVITY TO KEY INPUTS

Several key inputs were tested to determine the impact on losses, and the results are displayed in Figure 7.11. The sensitivity of results to hypothesized inputs demonstrates the importance of accuracy in sourcing required data and estimating model input values.[33]

Small Business Portfolio Analysis

In this example, we examine a small business loan portfolio. As shown in Figure 7.12, the states are risk ratings, rather than past due categories. This is a hypothetical $1.1 billion portfolio of revolving lines of credit, of which $41.1 million is rated below acceptable quality.

The roll rates associated with this portfolio appear in Figure 7.13. For example, of the $300 million in loans risk rated as a "4," 3 percent of the dollars will move to the special-mention classification in the next period, whereas 2 percent of the dollars in the special mention category will move back into the risk rating 4 category.

Risk Rating	Definition	Total Dollars	Percentages
1	High quality	3,000	0.36
2	Good quality	150,000	18.20
3	Average quality	600,000	72.81
4	Acceptable quality	300,000	3.64
5	Special mention	10,000	1.21
6	Substandard	30,000	3.64
7	Doubtful	1,000	0.12
8	Loss	100	0.01
	Total Portfolio	$1,094,100	100.00

FIGURE 7.12   DISTRIBUTION OF DOLLARS BY RISK RATING

33. These data can be inferred via statistical sampling or by using actual historical data that is created by joining consecutive month-end master files containing the required account-level data and performing the necessary variable derivations.

	1	2	3	4	5	6	7	8
1	0.9500	0.0200	0.0000	0.0000	0.0000	0.0000	0.0000	0.0000
2	0.0000	0.9300	0.0200	0.0000	0.0000	0.0000	0.0000	0.0000
3	0.0000	0.0000	0.9000	0.0500	0.0000	0.0000	0.0000	0.0000
4	0.0000	0.0000	0.0100	0.9300	0.0300	0.0100	0.0000	0.0000
5	0.0000	0.0000	0.0000	0.0200	0.8400	0.0580	0.0000	0.0000
6	0.0000	0.0000	0.0000	0.0100	0.0850	0.8800	0.0210	0.0000
7	0.0000	0.0000	0.0000	0.0000	0.0050	0.1000	0.7800	0.0400
8	0.0000	0.0000	0.0000	0.0000	0.0000	0.0000	0.0050	0.0050

FIGURE 7.13   MONTHLY ACCOUNT TRANSITION RATES BY RISK RATING

In any given month, the dollar-based payout and charge-off rates, based on credit grade, are shown in Figure 7.14. For example, 8 percent of the account balances in the special mention category are paid off, while 99 percent of the balances in the loss category are charged off.

A typical loan loss reserve constraint used in commercial portfolios, in the absence of empirical evidence, is at a minimum to maintain reserve levels that will cover 5 percent of the balances in the special mention category, plus 15 percent of the balances in the substandard category, plus 50 percent of the balances for loans in the doubtful category. The model forecast for loss rates corresponding to those rating categories in Figure ?? is *lower* than the 5-15-50 Rule. It is helpful to track, over a minimum of five years, the probability that loans in a particular grade will end in a loss, and the average time to loss for loans resulting in a loss. Per Basel II, a minimum of five years of history is required to estimate probabilities of default (PDs), and seven years for estimates of losses given default (LGDs).

The forecast of the *steady-state* bad rate for the portfolio is 125 bp (computed as 13,656/[1,086,772 + 13,656]).

Controlling for Account Heterogeneity via Segmentation

For the purpose of illustration, suppose we have conducted some statistical analysis and found that in order to control for cardholder heterogeneity we need to segment the credit card

State	Definition	Payout	Loss
1	High quality	0.0300	0.0000
2	Good quality	0.0500	0.0000
3	Average quality	0.0500	0.0000
4	Acceptable quality	0.0200	0.0000
5	Special mention	0.0800	0.0020
6	Substandard	0.0000	0.0040
7	Doubtful	0.0000	0.0500
8	Loss	0.0000	0.9900

FIGURE 7.14   MONTHLY ACCOUNT ABSORPTION RATES

State	Definition	Charge-Off
1	High quality	0.000
2	Good quality	0.001
3	Average quality	0.005
4	Acceptable quality	0.014
5	Special mention	0.045
6	Substandard	0.171
7	Doubtful	0.476
8	Loss	0.997
Estimated bad debt rate		1.25%
Paid		$1,080,444
Loss		$13.656

FIGURE 7.15 ULTIMATE ABSORPTION PROBABILITIES

portfolio based on account age, utilization, payment behavior, and card type, which we define as follows:

- *Payment behavior:* Minimum payers/revolvers/transactors
- *Vintage:* < 1 year/1–3 years/3 + years
- *Utilization:* < 25 percent/25–79 percent/ 80 + percent
- *Product:* Standard/premium

Relative to the payment behavior dimension, we impose the following definitions. Minimum payers are defined as accounts that have had a balance and finance charge at least once during the last three months and where the last payment on the account was not more than 1.25 times the minimum payment due. Revolvers are defined as accounts that have had a balance and finance charge at least once during the last three months and where the last payment on the account was equal or more than 1.25 times the minimum payment due. Transactors are defined as accounts having had a balance, but no finance charges, during the last three months. Dormant accounts are defined as accounts that have had no balance during the past three months.

The vintage dimension is simply based on the age of the account, with the stipulation that the account must be an open account. The utilization dimension is defined for each account as the current cycle balance divided by the current credit limit. Accounts are grouped into one of three possible categories, namely utilization levels that are less than 25 percent, at least 25 percent and less than 80 percent, or 80 percent or more. Finally, the product dimension serves to distinguish between two types of credit cards, having different terms and conditions.

The shorthand for segment identification is the four-digit index based on these dimensions. The indexing scheme is shown Figure 7.15.

There are 54 distinct elementary segmentation cells in this example. The segmentation cells are identified as ordered quadruplets; for example, Case 1 [1111] corresponds to minimum payers that have an account less than one year old, are less than 25 percent utilized, and have the standard product. Case 4 [3334] corresponds to transactors whose accounts are over three years old, who are 80 percent or more utilized, and who have either the stand or premium product. Case 5 [4444] corresponds to all segments.

Next, suppose you wanted to visualize credit risk as a function of segments and you colored the segments according to ranges of default rates (e.g., green for less than 4 percent credit losses,

Case	Indices				Dimensions			
					1	2	3	4
					Behavior	Vintage	%Utilized	Card Type
1	1	1	1	1	Min Payer	< 1 year	< 25	Standard
2	2	2	2	2	Freq Revolver	1 < 3 years	25 < 80	Premium
3	3	3	3	1	Transactor	3+ years	80+	Standard
4	3	3	3	4	Transactor	3+ years	80+	All
5	4	4	4	4	All	All	All	All

FIGURE 7.16 INDEX COMBINATIONS AND DIMENSIONAL INTERPRETATION EXAMPLES

yellow for 4 to 6 percent, and red for greater than 6 percent). Credit portfolio segments viewed by the red, yellow, and green credit loss classifications appear in Figure 7.16.

To better visualize profitability as a function of these identical segments, suppose you colored them such that profitable accounts are found in green areas, marginal accounts occur in yellow areas, and unprofitable accounts reside in red areas. The result would be as that in Figure 7.17, which displays the identical credit portfolio segments as in the previous figure, only now having different color categories based on profitability.

This visualization of segments immediately surfaces the fact that a portion of the least-profitable accounts actually have an acceptable loss rate (lower left-hand segments is red in the profit view, but green in the credit loss view). This occurs because transactor accounts do not revolve balances and accrue interest charges and they have zero contractual losses, but do experience an occasional bankruptcy. Because the utilization on these segments is also very low, there are not sufficient interchange fees from merchants to turn a profit. A useful exercise is to rank segments by outstandings, losses, profits, attrition, and high delinquency to determine the best/worst performing segments and to devise appropriate segment-level account management strategies.

Now, suppose each segment housed its own behavioral simulation model, where each segment had its own transition matrix (as shown in Figure 7.18) and corresponding balances in each past-due category.

The result would be a separate loss forecast within each behavioral segment. This is important, because special attention may be focused on new segments where alternative data or other model assumptions were made to calculate default probabilities. Loss forecasts for these segments may be continuously updated and compared with their more mainstream segment counterparts.

The ability to view trends at the individual segment level is necessary because portfolio averaging and product-oriented aggregates typically mask underlying segment relationships and behavior. Said another way, many smooth trend lines are actually composed of a collection of nonlinear segment component time series which have differing *slopes* and *volatility*. Figure 7.19 displays four dollar-based time series, one each for attrition, contractual losses, bankruptcies, and outstandings. The topmost graph displays the trend on a total portfolio basis. The series of graphs in the figure show the corresponding time series for selected portfolio segments.

The reality is that line managers want to view financial results according to how the organization is structured (e.g., by lines of business, broad geographic region, acquisition channel, etc.). A credit portfolio manager will want to repartition the portfolio to focus on various performance measures across a different set of portfolio behavioral segments. The ability to model the portfolio in ways that most closely reflect the underlying processes at work will result in better predictive power. Fortunately, these views can both be accommodated by preserving the indicator fields at the

$ Attrition	-	42	50	-
$ Loss	63, 513	3,380	60,200	
$ O/S (M)	7,260	720	3,476	
O/S % Mix	64%	6%	30%	
Color	Green	Yellow	Red	

($000)		< 25% Std	< 25% Prem	25–79% Std	25–79% Prem	80% Std	80% Prem	TOTAL
Min Payer < 1 year	Cell#	1	2	3	4	5	6	
	$Attr	30	30	10	10	-	-	80
	$Loss	10	4	150	170	2,400	20,000	22,734
	$Outs	8,000	5,000	70,000	84,000	240,000	240,000	647,000
	%Mix	0.07%	0.05%	0.61%	0.74%	2.09%	2.12%	5.69%
	Color	Green	Green	Green	Green	Red	Red	Red
Min Payer 1–3 years	Cell#	7	8	9	10	11	12	
	$Attr	30	20	10	10	-	-	70
	$Loss	20	30	500	600	9,000	12,000	22,150
	$Outs	5,000	8,000	100,000	140,000	500,000	600,000	1,353,000
	%Mix	0.04%	0.07%	0.86%	1.22%	4.05%	5.29%	11.53%
	Color	Green	Yellow	Yellow	Yellow	Red	Red	Red
Min Payer 3+ years	Cell#	13	14	15	16	17	18	
	$Attr	170	50	10	10	-	-	240
	$Loss	80	30	1,700	1,400	7,400	9,000	19,610
	$Outs	20,000	10,000	500,000	250,000	1,200,000	666,000	2,646,000
	%Mix	0.19%	0.09%	4.22%	2.24%	10.51%	5.84%	23.09%
	Color	Green	Green	Green	Yellow	Red	Red	Red
Pay Down < 1 year	Cell#	19	20	21	22	23	24	
	$Attr	600	1,200	10	10	10	10	1,840
	$Loss	-	4	10	6	16	10	46
	$Outs	70,000	90,000	260,000	332,000	200,000	200,000	1,152,000
	%Mix	0.60%	0.75%	2.27%	2.92%	1.75%	1.80%	10.09%
	Color	Green	Green	Green	Green	Green	Green	Green
Pay Down 1–3 years	Cell#	25	26	27	28	29	30	
	$Attr	900	10	-	10	10	10	940
	$Loss	2	10	20	50	50	150	282
	$Outs	84,000	120,000	340,000	450,000	250,000	350,000	1,594,000
	%Mix	0.74%	1.05%	2.94%	3.98%	2.23%	3.06%	13.99%
	Color	Green	Green	Green	Green	Green	Green	Green
Pay Down 3+ years	Cell#	31	32	33	34	35	36	
	$Attr	2,400	1,000	10	10	10	10	3,440
	$Loss	10	4	100	400	100	140	754
	$Outs	230,000	180,000	900,000	630,000	500,000	420,000	2,860,000
	%Mix	2.05%	1.59%	7.79%	5.55%	4.48%	3.72%	25.17%
	Color	Green	Green	Green	Green	Green	Green	Green

FIGURE 7.17   ATTRITION, LOSS, OUTSTANDINGS, AND MIX BY LOW-, MODERATE-, AND HIGH-PROFIT SEGMENTS

		37	38	39	40	41	42	
Transactor < 1 year	Cell#	37	38	39	40	41	42	
	$Attr	140	140	10	10	10	10	320
	$Loss	2	8	2	20	16	4	52
	$Outs	80,000	50,000	80,000	40,000	10,000	10,000	
	%Mix	0.71%	0.39%	0.69%	0.39%	0.12%	0.08%	
	Color	Green	Green	Green	Green	Green	Green	Green
Transactor 1–3 years	Cell #	43	44	45	46	47	48	270,000
	$Attr	240	300	10	10	-	-	2.38%
	$Loss	4	20	40	50	100	160	374
	$Outs	90,000	80,000	80,000	70,000	10,000	10,000	340,000
	%Mix	0.74%	0.69%	0.71%	0.64%	0.09%	0.08%	2.95%
	Color	Green	Green	Green	Green	Red	Red	Red
Transactor 3+ years	Cell#	49	50	51	52	53	54	450
	$Attr	350	100	-	-	-	-	1,260
	$Loss	50	20	350	200	500	140	
	$Outs	140,000	132,000	90,000	90,000	132,000	10,000	594,000
	%Mix	1.24%	1.17%	0.78%	75%	1.09%	0.08%	5.11%
	Color	Green	Green	Yellow	Green	Yellow	Red	Red
TOTAL	$Attr	5	3	0	0	0	0	7.9
	$Loss	0	0	3	3	20	42	67.3
	$Outs	727	675	2,420	2,086	3,042	2,506	11,456
	%Mix	6.38%	5.83%	20.88%	18.42%	26.42%	22.07%	100.00%
	Color	Green	Green	Yellow	Yellow	Red	Red	Yellow

FIGURE 7.17 (continued)

Profit Per Acct. % of Accounts Total Profit Profit Mix	GREEN > $1,000 45% High > 90%	YELLOW < $50 20% Marg. < 10%	RED < $0 35% Unprof. 0 %			
		< 25% Std	< 25% Prem	25–79% Std	25–79% Prem	80% Std	80% Prem
Min Payer < 1 Year	Cell #	1	2	3	4	5	6
	Color	Green	Green	Green	Green	Yellow	Yellow
Min Payer 1–3 Years	Cell #	7	8	9	10	11	12
	Color	Yellow	Yellow	Green	Green	Red	Red
Min Payer 3+ Years	Cell #	13	14	15	16	17	18
	Color	Yellow	Yellow	Green	Green	Red	Red
Pay Down < 1 Year	Cell #	19	20	21	22	23	24
	Color	Yellow	Yellow	Green	Green	Green	Green
Pay Down 1–3 Years	Cell #	25	26	27	28	29	30
	Color	Yellow	Green	Green	Green	Green	Green
Pay Down 3+ Years	Cell #	31	32	33	34	35	36
	Color	Yellow	Green	Green	Green	Green	Green
Transactor < 1 Year	Cell #	37	38	39	40	41	42
	Color	Red	Yellow	Red	Green	Red	Red
Transactor 1–3 Years	Cell #	43	44	45	46	47	48
	Color	Red	Red	Green	Green	Red	Red
Transactor 3+ Years	Cell #	49	50	51	52	53	54
	Color	Red	Red	Green	Green	Red	Red

FIGURE 7.18 PROFIT COLORATION OF SEGMENTS (DATA SUPPRESSED)

For Segment 1231—Behavior: Min. Payer; Vintage: 1–3 Yr; Utilization: 80%+; Product: Standard

	1	2	3	4	5	6	7	8
1	0.6565	0.3419	0.0004	0.0002	0.0001	0.0001	0.0001	0.0000
2	0.3343	0.3639	0.2969	0.0005	0.0002	0.0001	0.0000	0.0000
3	0.1461	0.2091	0.1354	0.4921	0.0004	0.0002	0.0001	0.0000
4	0.1002	0.0579	0.0660	0.1390	0.6035	0.0027	0.0003	0.0000
5	0.0835	0.0098	0.0116	0.0517	0.1319	0.6803	0.0022	0.0003
6	0.0242	0.0106	0.0063	0.0164	0.0452	0.1290	0.7325	0.0003
7	0.0170	0.0045	0.0044	0.0045	0.0114	0.0354	0.0985	0.0321
8	0.0791	0.0287	0.0055	0.0039	0.0117	0.0615	0.2502	0.2137

For Segment 3232—Behavior: Transactor; Vintage: 1–3 Yr; Utilization: 80%+; Product: Prem

	1	2	3	4	5	6	7	8
1	0.9730	0.0270	0.0000	0.0000	0.0000	0.0000	0.0000	0.0000
2	0.1385	0.3891	0.4724	0.0000	0.0000	0.0000	0.0000	0.0000
3	0.1662	0.0656	0.0619	0.6985	0.0000	0.0000	0.0000	0.0000
4	0.0498	0.0063	0.0050	0.0261	0.9129	0.0000	0.0000	0.0000
5	0.1587	0.0000	0.0000	0.0371	0.1079	0.6963	0.0000	0.0000
6	0.0625	0.0133	0.0000	0.0175	0.0498	0.1938	0.6586	0.0000
7	0.0534	0.0217	0.0000	0.0000	0.0066	0.0401	0.1278	0.0166
8	0.0000	0.2296	0.0000	0.1266	0.0840	0.0000	0.1303	0.3056

For Segment 3332—Behavior: Transactor; Vintage: 3 + Yr; Utilization: 80%+; Product: Prem

	1	2	3	4	5	6	7	8
1	0.8864	0.1113	0.0000	0.0008	0.0000	0.0000	0.0000	0.0000
2	0.0910	0.4544	0.4496	0.0000	0.0000	0.0000	0.0000	0.0000
3	0.0335	0.1651	0.1659	0.6319	0.0000	0.0036	0.0000	0.0000
4	0.0517	0.0000	0.0000	0.0582	0.8761	0.0000	0.0140	0.0000
5	0.0703	0.0000	0.0000	0.0101	0.0933	0.8263	0.0000	0.0000
6	0.0313	0.0100	0.0000	0.0102	0.0101	0.1534	0.7850	0.0000
7	0.0049	0.0092	0.0017	0.0000	0.0147	0.0247	0.1855	0.0259
8	0.1463	0.0000	0.0000	0.0000	0.0000	0.0554	0.0000	0.0611

FIGURE 7.19 MONTHLY ACCOUNT TRANSITION RATES

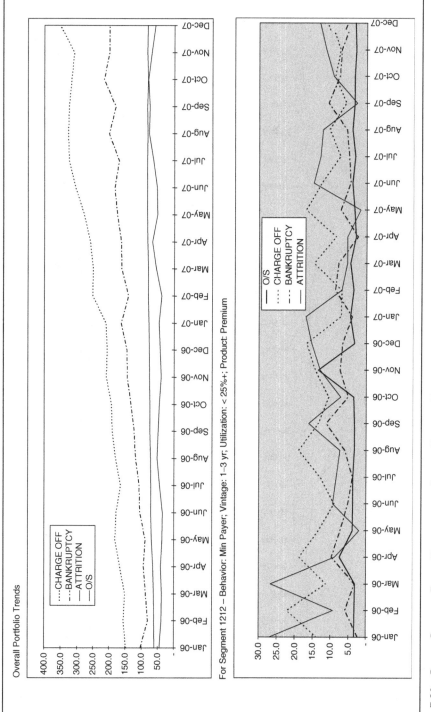

FIGURE 7.20 OVERALL PORTFOLIO TRENDS DECOMPOSE INTO SEGMENT TRENDS BY MONTH

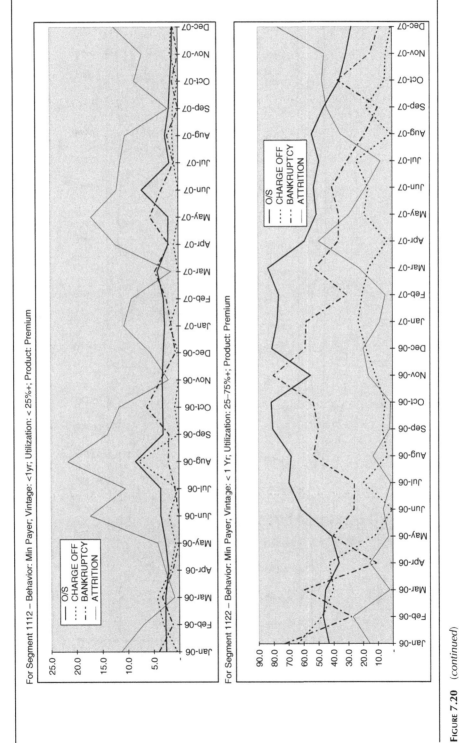

For Segment 1112 – Behavior: Min Payer; Vintage: <1yr; Utilization: < 25%+; Product: Premium

For Segment 1122 – Behavior: Min Payer; Vintage: < 1 Yr; Utilization: 25–75%+; Product: Premium

FIGURE 7.20 (continued)

296

individual account record level, so that any handle or segment scheme can be constructed from the detail, ensuring a single version of the truth.

SUMMARY

In Chapter 1 we discussed compliance program and corporate information evolution and we used the concept of maturity models in order to help determine appropriate strategies for the organization. Multilayered segmentation may be thought of in a similar way. For example, in the case of marketing financial products and services to consumers, lower levels of maturity use segmentation to improve operational outcomes, more specifically to: (1) reduce risk,[34] (2) improve product selling,[35] and (3) to profitably expand into new markets.[36] Higher levels of maturity use segmentation as a source of competitive advantage by creating organizational capabilities to build knowledge, creating new "insights" that are not available to competitors, and using the insights gained to build durable customer franchises. Customer knowledge can be used to build customer intimacy, whereby you better understand and respond to individual customer needs. It can also be used to better determine how to profitably enter new markets.

Even more broadly, this chapter outlined how multilayered segmentation may be used in community development and credit portfolio risk management. The tie-in to fair lending compliance is immediate through the concept of the handle, which we introduced in Chapter 5 and for which Chapter 6, together with its appendices, provides many examples on consumer and small business lending.

Successful segmentation schemes represent a synthesis of risk intelligence, compliance intelligence, and customer intelligence. Increasing emphasis on enterprise customer tiers and household relationships dictates an approach that takes into consideration the lifetime value of a relationship.[37] Constructing a solid and sustaining segmentation is the bedrock upon which much of the customer value initiatives must rest.

Challenger segmentation strategies, and new policies, require maintenance activities and ongoing validation to ensure key metrics associated with individual segments remain accurate. This is addressed in Chapter 8, where we demonstrate how multilayered segmentation, together with the methodologies described in the previous chapters, can be used to develop a modeling and process validation framework.

---

34. For example, fewer bad loans, lower "loan loss reserve requirements," better pricing on loan syndication, and so on.
35. For example, more efficiently selling loan products to customers that will use the products, thus enhancing revenue (and ultimately profitability) for the lender. The effect is a reduction in sales and marketing costs-per-profitable-loan dollar booked.
36. For example, the unbanked or nonmainstream consumer population.
37. Lifetime value relationship encompasses risk, revenue, potential future profit, product portfolio, propensity for acquiring additional products or increasing utilization of existing products, point in consumer life-cycle of needs, and so forth.

Appendix 7A
MATHEMATICAL UNDERPINNINGS OF BSM

For readers interested in some of the more technical details behind the forecasting method, the following is a sketch of the essential mathematical relationships used.

Model Inputs

The transition matrix shown in Figures 7.7 and 7.13 is a nonsingular square matrix of order 8: $Q_{8\times8}$. The absorbing state matrix in Figures 7.8 and 7.14 is a rectangular matrix: $R_{8\times3}$. The initial balance vector given in Figures 7.6 and 7.12 is termed $B_{1\times8}$.

Model Outputs

The inverse of the difference between the identity matrix and the $Q_{8\times8}$ matrix is called the fundamental matrix $N_{8\times8}$ of the Markov chain. Hence,

$$N_{8\times8} = (I_{8\times8} - Q_{8\times8})^{-1} \qquad (7A.1)$$

Fundamental Matrix for a Portfolio

59.563	3.514	1.243	0.870	0.679	0.475	0.390	0.049
48.846	4.341	1.535	1.075	0.838	0.587	0.481	0.061
35.248	2.236	1.890	1.323	1.032	0.722	0.592	0.075
38.172	2.252	0.796	1.558	1.215	0.851	0.698	0.088
32.323	1.907	0.674	0.472	1.368	0.958	0.786	0.100
20.869	1.231	0.435	0.305	0.238	1.166	0.957	0.121
12.560	0.741	0.262	0.183	0.143	0.100	1.082	0.137
5.387	0.318	0.112	0.079	0.061	0.043	0.035	1.303

To calculate the fundamental matrix, $N_{8\times8}$, it is necessary to solve a set of forward equations that characterize the stochastic movement of account dollars among the transient states.

In this example, the Portfolio Q-Matrix was:

	1	2	3	4	5	6	7	8
1	0.9500	0.0404	0.0000	0.0000	0.0000	0.0000	0.0000	0.0000
2	0.4000	0.2800	0.3218	0.0000	0.0000	0.0000	0.0000	0.0000
3	0.0097	0.0977	0.0900	0.7000	0.0000	0.0000	0.0000	0.0000
4	0.2175	0.0000	0.0000	0.0000	0.7800	0.0000	0.0000	0.0000
5	0.2974	0.0000	0.0000	0.0000	0.0000	0.7000	0.0000	0.0000
6	0.1774	0.0000	0.0000	0.0000	0.0000	0.0000	0.8200	0.0000
7	0.2020	0.0000	0.0000	0.0000	0.0000	0.0000	0.0000	0.0975
8	0.0696	0.0000	0.0000	0.0000	0.0000	0.0000	0.0000	0.2300

The portfolio R-Matrix was:

	1	2	3	4	5	6	7	8
1	0.0100	0.0000	0.0000	0.0000	0.0000	0.0000	0.0000	0.0000
2	0.0000	0.0000	0.0000	0.0000	0.0000	0.0000	0.7000	0.7000
3	0.0026	0.0026	0.0028	0.0028	0.0028	0.0028	0.0050	0.0050

The $(I_{8\times8} - Q_{8\times8})$- Matrix calculated was:

	1	2	3	4	5	6	7	8
1	0.0499	−0.0404	0.0000	0.0000	0.0000	0.0000	0.0000	0.0000
2	−0.4000	0.7199	−0.3218	0.0000	0.0000	0.0000	0.0000	0.0000
3	−0.0097	0.0977	0.9100	−0.7000	0.0000	0.0000	0.0000	0.0000
4	−0.2175	0.0000	0.0000	1.0000	−0.7800	0.0000	0.0000	0.0000
5	−0.2974	0.0000	0.0000	0.0000	1.0000	−0.7000	0.0000	0.0000
6	−0.1774	0.0000	0.0000	0.0000	0.0000	1.0000	−0.8200	0.0000
7	−0.2020	0.0000	0.0000	0.0000	0.0000	0.0000	1.0000	−0.0975

The previous matrix is then inverted to create the fundamental matrix. Recall from algebra that $1/(1 - x)$ can be approximated by the infinite series:

$$1/(1 - x) = 1 + x + x^2 + x^3 + x^4 + \cdots + x^{n-1} + x^n + \cdots \qquad (7A.2)$$

To calculate the first month's projections for payments and losses in Figure 7.10 the formula is:

$$B_{1\times8} \ Q_{8\times8} \ R_{8\times3} = D_{1\times3} \qquad (7A.3)$$

To calculate the second month's projections for payments and losses in Figure 7.10 the formula is:

$$B_{1\times8} \ [Q_{8\times8}]^2 R_{8\times3} = D_{1\times3} \qquad (7A.4)$$

To calculate the nth month's projections for payments and losses, the general formula is:

$$B \ Q^n \ R = D \qquad (7A.5)$$

In the *steady state*, we can:

- Determine the average number of months accounts will be on the books, given their current state, by summing the rows of the fundamental matrix
- Determine the absorption probabilities $A_{8\times3}$, shown in Figures 7.9 and **??**, using the matrix formula:

$$A_{8\times3} = N_{8\times8}R_{8\times3} \tag{7A.6}$$

- Determine the ultimate disposition of receivables using formula (1.2) and substituting N for the infinite series using formula (1.1) to obtain:

$$BNR = B\ [I + Q + Q^2 + Q^3 + \ldots + Q^{n-1} + Q^n + \ldots]\ R \tag{7A.7}$$

Calculations showing the error bounds on estimates, typically assume normality and are calculated at the 95 percent confidence level.[38]

---

38. Details can be found in Cyert, Davidson, and Thompson, p. 294.

Appendix 7B

DATA ELEMENT EXAMPLES FOR DYNAMIC RELATIONSHIP PRICING EXAMPLE

We share examples of some of the input data fields that are useful in developing a DRP segmentation model. The following list of data elements is by no means exhaustive:

- Age in months of highest bank card balance (if date open is unknown substitute status date to calculate age).
- Age of each internal account.
- Age of oldest trade.
- Ages of members of household.
- Aggregate balance of competitive bankcard trades (same as above).
- Aggregate balance of revolving competitive retail trades (same as above).
- Amount of liquid assets.
- Average utilization of competitive bankcard trades (same as above).
- Average utilization of revolving competitive retail trades (same as above).
- Behavior score.
- Bureau score differential.
- Credit bureau score six months ago.
- Credit card spending profile based upon aggregated transaction merchant codes.
- Credit limit of highest bank card balance.
- Current bureau score.
- Current lifetime value tier.
- Customer (household) profitability tier high threshold dollar amount and up; low threshold to high threshold dollar values; under low threshold dollar amount (may be set so as to break customer accounts into equal shares across the three profitability groups, e.g. 1/3 share each), where the thresholds are updated annually, and so that segmentation adjusts to profitability.
- Demand deposit account line of credit balance.
- Demand deposit account line of credit limit.
- Estimated relationship longevity in months.
- Life cycle category.
- Lifetime value category (current value to date + projected value).
- Likelihood of favorable response to cross-selling by product.
- Likelihood of favorable response to up-selling by product combination.
- Maximum credit limit on a bank card trade.
- Maximum delinquency for any trade on credit report in last 24 months.
- Maximum over-limit amount during past six months.
- Monthly income.

- Motivator category (price, convenience, brand, full spectrum of service, level of product customization desired).
- MSA where customer resides.
- Net worth.
- Number of bank card trades updated in last six months (for certain ranges of status codes a non-zero balance is required, for others not; certain industry or type code combinations require a balance date within the past 12 months. There may also be caps on line limits or balance amounts where limits are not available; exclude if date opened is unknown).
- Number of competitive bankcard trades (for certain ranges of status codes a nonzero balance is required, for others not unless a special comment code of a certain value is present; certain industry or type code combinations require a balance date within the past 12 months. There may also be caps on line limits or balance amounts where limits are not available).
- Number of dependents in household.
- Number of deposit products.
- Number of investment products.
- Number of loan products.
- Number of mortgage trades.
- Number of mortgage trades opened in the last six months.
- Number of nonrevolving trades.
- Number of nonrevolving trades opened in the last six months.
- Number of nonsufficient funds (NSF) checks in past three months.
- Number of promotional inquiries from certain industries reported in last six months.
- Number of revolving competitive retail trades (for certain ranges of status codes a nonzero balance is required, for others not; certain industry or type code combinations require a balance date within the past 12 months. There may also be caps on line limits or balance amounts where limits are not available).
- Number of times over-limit in past six months.
- Number of trades on credit report with a current satisfactory rating.
- Open date for newest bank card trade.
- Open date for oldest bank card trade.
- Open trades updated in last 12 months (driven off status codes and balance date fields).
- Overdraft protection (Y/N).
- Payment behavior on each open credit line (transactor, min payer, accelerated paydown, dormant) based on past four months.
- Potential lifetime value tier.
- Potential revenue discounted to present value.
- Potential revenue in dollars.
- Predicted bad debt by product and total.
- Predicted incremental costs of maintaining relationship (activity-based costing at customer level in place of averages by product).
- Predicted usage by product.
- Primary product category.
- Private banking customer indicator.
- Probability of response to a promotional offer, by type, based on past behavior.
- Product attrition.
- Propensity to attrite (by product).
- Propensity to attrite completely.

- Secondary product category.
- Similar information on products sold internally.
- Total balance of mortgage trades opened in the last six months.
- Total balance of non-revolving trades opened in the last six months.
- Total Trades 30 + DPD in past 12 months.
- Utilization of each revolving credit line, including overdraft.

8

MODEL VALIDATION

Risk and compliance models are widely used and relied on for business decision making. It is recognized that model development is a complex process and it is subject to a variety of errors. Business decisions that are based on misused or inaccurate models, can lead to serious consequences for a lending institution's reputation and profitability. This problem is termed *model risk*,[1] and it can arise from various sources including model assumptions, inputs, or development processing.[2] Model validation is a process used to reduce model risk by reviewing, monitoring, testing, and interpreting model inputs, processing, and outputs.[3] Validating models is a critical safeguard that ensures expectations for risk measurement and management are met.

This chapter discusses the implications of the previously discussed methodologies on model validation from both credit risk and compliance perspectives. We begin this chapter with a review of model validation components and related topics. We then present a model validation framework that incorporates methodologies including the multilayered segmentation (MLS), dynamic conditional process (DCP), the hybrid models, and universal performance indicator (UPI), as integral parts of a systematic approach. We explain how the integrated validation framework may be optimized so as to achieve both credit and compliance risk objectives. We also provide model monitoring and management strategies. In conclusion, we identify analytical process parallels between the hybrid modeling approach, compliance testing, and more traditional risk modeling (i.e., credit scoring).

MODEL VALIDATION FOR RISK AND COMPLIANCE INTELLIGENCE

Credit scoring models have been extensively used in consumer lending to assist a wide range of decision-making processes associated with both loan underwriting and pricing.[4] Automated

1. Model risk is in general classified into operational risk. See Jorion, Philippe. *Value at Risk: The New Benchmark for Managing Financial Risk*, McGraw-Hill, 2007, p. 26. Specific definitions of model risk may vary depending on the types of models. For pricing models, for example, model risk is defined as the risk arising from the use of an inadequate model (see Hull, John C., and Wulin Suo, "A methodology for assessing model risk and its application to the implied volatility function model," *Journal of Financial and Quantitative Analysis*, Vol. 37, No. 2, June 2002, p. 298). It is also defined as the risk arising from the use of a model which cannot accurately express market prices, or which is not a mainstream model in the market (see Kato, Toshiyasu, and Toshinao Yoshiba, "Model Risk And Its Control," *Monetary and Economic Studies*, December. 2000, p. 146).
2. Many factors can contribute to model risk. See Crouhy, Michel, Dan Galai, and Robert Mark, *Risk Management*, McGraw-Hill, 2001, pp. 585–594 for a comprehensive description of model risk typology.
3. According to OCC Bulletin 2000-16 (Model Validation, May 30, 2000), the OCC has observed several instances in which incorrect use of models created exposure to large losses.
4. For example, the Fair, Isaac and Company (FICO) score, which is primarily used in the consumer banking and credit industry, is calculated by using statistical methods. Other major credit reporting agencies, Equifax, Experian, and TransUnion all calculate their own credit scores. Credit scoring also can be used for corporate debt

consumer credit-scoring models have made it possible for lenders to process far more applications in a shorter period of time than was possible when manual loan underwriting processes were used. Furthermore, credit scoring has proven to be more efficient, objective, consistent, cost-effective, and transparent than the systems they have replaced.[5] As a result, this has significantly improved the efficiency, fairness, and accessibility of the mortgage market.

Credit models are necessarily complex because the business processes and policy rules that they embody, for both underwriting and pricing, are fairly intricate. Market competition among lenders ensures that loan decision model complexity will continue to increase as existing models are refined. Moreover, new, more dynamic, and more complex models are currently being developed to satisfy market needs in the most effective way. The application of increasingly more complex modeling techniques across a broader range of credit risk models will result in greater access to credit for a broader range of consumers. This will create additional new risk management challenges for lending institutions, lenders who must strive to maintain acceptable levels of loan delinquencies and defaults. To meet those challenges, lenders need to ensure their credit risk models are functioning as expected.[6] At the same time, they also have to ensure their credit risk models are in line with consumer protection regulations governing lending practices,[7] so as to minimize the risk of compliance violations.

Regulators and policymakers recognize the potential for misapplication, or misspecification, of credit models. Problems can occur at any point in the modeling process, including data gathering, data cleansing, observation selection, formulation of model assumptions, sourcing of business rules, actual model specification, model validation, model deployment, model execution, model monitoring, model maintenance, and model redevelopment. Even if the model is correct, care must be given to ensure that the proper model is used for the appropriate segment of business and that model performance is maintained at acceptable levels. Substandard performance in one or more of these areas can lead to regulatory actions that can affect the institution's credit ratings and capital requirements. Validation of credit risk models is a central component for supervisory examinations of banks' consumer lending businesses.[8] From credit and compliance perspectives, lenders face several model validation challenges, which we proceed to describe.

First, data quality issues and insufficient applicant information and loan performance history pose serious fundamental issues. Disparate treatment regression models focusing on race and ethnicity of the borrower cannot be reliably developed if a large segment of applicants are from a call center and the HMDA primary applicant race is coded as "7," indicating the information was not provided by the applicant for a significant number of applications. Development of credit scoring requires lenders to have access to a large amount of historical information on

---

based on certain statistical methods including classification/segmentation. See Altman, E. I., and A. Saunders. "Credit Risk Measurement: Developments over the Last Twenty Years," *Journal of Banking and Finance*, Vol. 21, 1998, pp. 1723–1724) for an overview of application of credit scoring systems in commercial lending. Also see Altman, Edward I., *Handbook of Corporate Finance*. John Wiley & Sons, 1986, pp. 44–50, and Falkenstein, Eris, "Credit Scoring for Corporate Debt," in Ong, Michael K. (ed.), *Credit Ratings: Methodologies, Rationale and Default Risk*. Risk Books, 2003, pp. 169–188.

5. See OCC Bulletin 2000-16, p. 2.
6. According to the Basel II framework, banks must have a robust system to validate model accuracy and consistency for all relevant risk components. See Basel Committee on Bank Supervision, "International Convergence of Capital Measurement and Capital Standards: A Revised Framework," June 2004, p. 125.
7. For example, Regulation B, Regulation AA, the Fair Housing Act, and so on. The new OCC procedures also address evaluation of credit scoring in the context of fair lending.
8. In 2005, the Basel II Accord Implementation Group (AIG) issued working paper 14 outlining model validation framework. The main principles include bank has primary responsibility for validation, validation is an iterative process and there is no single valuation method, model validation is to assess the predictive ability of risk estimates and use of ratings in risk processes, and validation should encompass both quantitative and qualitative elements. Although Basel II does not impose any standards on model validation process, systematic and enterprise-wide integrated approach should be developed to ensure effective and continuous model validation.

the performance of loans spanning all credit applicants. In reality, this kind of information is often unavailable for the unbanked, who have limited credit history or access to credit products. Therefore, loan-underwriting models that fail to consider cash payment performance as a suitable substitute for credit history may, for certain groups, amplify disparate impact. In these examples, the biggest challenge for model validation is to gather sufficient historical data, with enough defaults for credit models, or enough information on applicant race/ethnicity for compliance models, to ensure statistical validity. It can take two to three years to properly assess loan quality for loans granted at a point in time. Some aspects of model validation, such as loan defaults based on internal bank information, cannot be performed on new loan underwriting models that have not accumulated sufficient performance data.[9]

Second, validation metrics are needed that encompass qualitative factors, link to the multifaceted decision structure, and offer a range of actions (i.e., applicant segment distribution updating, or risk segment reweighting, as opposed to model abandonment). Developing a sound model validation framework that offers more comprehensive and consistent metrics is of increasing importance.[10] Basel II emphasizes the importance of qualitative, process-oriented component, in addition to quantitative statistical methods. Cohesive and consistent model performance metrics need to integrate both quantitative and qualitative measures. A simulation process can be used to address model sensitivity to policy threshold value ranges. This will facilitate a compliance assessment of a credit model by testing for potential disparate impact after a model has been constructed. As a result, compliance testing results may be incorporated into the credit model validation process to immediately forecast the fair lending compliance performance of the model relative to protected classes and consumer and/or geographic segments of interest.

Third, model validation needs to be enhanced by an efficient model monitoring and reporting process.[11] Typically, different models are required for different market segments, products, or programs. The modeling validation process can be costly and time consuming when the number of models increases significantly.[12] It is important to put a process in place to minimize required time and costs associated with monitoring, managing, and validating a large number of credit risk models. This process should also enable lenders to rank-order models to identify where the greatest risk exists, and determine if, or when, models require updating or redevelopment.

TYPICAL MODEL VALIDATION PROCESS, METHODS, METRICS, AND COMPONENTS

In this section, we provide a brief review of typical validation metrics and approaches, and their application areas. We also compare the most commonly used measures and methods, and their potential applications and limitations on model validation. Our goal here is to acquaint the reader with some basic concepts and also to highlight some areas that are addressed in later sections where the hybrid models are involved.

---

9. According to Jackson, P., and W. Perraudin "Regulatory Implications of Credit Risk Modeling," *Journal of Banking and Finance*, Vol. 24, 2000, pp. 1–14, there are three kinds of model validation: (1) standard model with public data, (2) standard model with bank specific data, and (3) nonstandard model with bank-specific data.

10. "The best defense against such 'model risk' is the implementation of a sound model validation framework that includes a robust validation policy and appropriate independent review." See OCC Bulletin 2000-16, p. 2.

11. Basel II emphasizes the importance of monitoring model performance and stability as part of model validation cycle. See Basel Committee on Bank Supervision, 2004, p. 86.

12. SAS Model Manager supports model validation process by tracking model performance degradation and monitoring input data distribution for a large number of models. See Chu, Robert, David Duling, and Wayne Thompson. "Best Practices for Managing Predictive Models in a Production Environment," SAS Institute Inc., 2007.

Typical Model Validation Areas and Main Components

Model validation is typically considered to be a continuous process and it should be performed throughout the entire model life cycle and all components.[13] In Figure 8.1, we present a summary of validation considerations by model inputs, processing, outputs, their main components, and related topics.

Validation is an ongoing, iterative process.[14] In practice, frequency of model validation varies for credit and compliance purposes. Model validation for compliance risk is performed periodically as part of the disparate treatment testing cycle within a corporate compliance program. Typical compliance testing cycles range from 12 to 24 months in duration. Model validation for credit risk is an exercise that occurs during the initial model development and then reoccurs when the model is first deployed and then periodically over time to ensure that a minimum performance level is maintained. Because it takes considerable time before account performance deteriorates for those accounts that do end up classified as bad, the validation of a new credit model's default predictions cannot really be assessed prior to 24 months from the time it is implemented. In practice, credit risk models are subject to second-guessing.

In the following subsections, we briefly discuss each of these validation areas and components in order to develop sufficient understanding for the next major section that presents a validation framework.

Validation Area	Validation Components	Related Topics
Inputs	1. Input assumptions 2. Input data 3. Lending policies and practices	• Appropriateness of assumptions • Sample size, selection method, and time frame • Data availability and quality • Differing business practices and inconsistent application of policies by lenders
Processing	1. Model development 2. Model selection 3. Model implementation	• Discretization • Model usage • Model estimate methods • Reject inference • Colinearity • Model selection criteria • Model algorithms and computation
Output	1. Model result interpretation 2. Holdout sample testing 3. Performance monitoring and reporting	• Model fit and estimates • Model risk ranking • Benchmarking • Regulatory constraints

FIGURE 8.1 MODEL VALIDATION AREAS, COMPONENTS, AND RELATED TOPICS

13. See OCC Bulletin 2000-16 for validation guidance. This guidance suggests that validation should be built into the development process and financial institutions should develop strategies to mitigate potential risks arising from reliance on computer-based financial models that are improperly validated or tested.

14. This is one of the validation principles as suggested by Basel Committee on Banking Supervision, "Update on Work of the Accord Implementation Group Related to Validation under the Basel II," Newsletter, No. 4, January 2005, p. 2.

Model Input Validation

In general, model inputs may contain the following main components:

- *Input assumptions.* This is typically related to the following issues:
  - *Assumptions about data and sampling.* For example, the prevailing and historical market and economic conditions at the time the model was originally developed implicitly lead to an assumption that the future will resemble those same conditions. How data were sampled poses other concerns, as noted in our earlier discussions about sampling. If there were some selection bias, or failure to capture certain information for a particular segment, the accuracy of model estimates could suffer substantially.
  - *Definition of credit risks.* This may vary by product and line of business. However, caution should be exercised to ensure that performance definitions are consistent. This is especially true when models span traditional banking business (prime lending) and consumer finance business (subprime lending). Subprime loans do not conform to prime underwriting standards primarily due to adverse information on the borrower's credit report.[15] We believe the subprime market has yet to establish a standard definition for each grade of subprime loan. A review of six major players in the subprime market revealed that, relative to the subprime factors cited, they had significant variations in business rules relative to these factors for assigning loans to the various grades.
  - *Definition of indeterminate performance behavior.*[16] Exclusion of observations falling into this group can have a significant impact on the credit model. As mentioned in Chapter 6, it can lead to overstatement of the default risk associated with relatively mild delinquency patterns.
- *Input data.* Since models are developed with historical data, they may not be able to generate consistent results in cases where loan policies and practices were in a state of flux, or if historical environmental factors introduced volatility, or if the applicant population was undergoing significant changes during the period. Specific examples include:
  - *Changes in loan underwriting or pricing policy.* Underwriting decision and pricing policy is affected by business and compliance requirements and subject to changes. Any significant changes in policy will have a direct impact on credit models, particularly when one or more primary factors are involved.
  - *Changes in economic state.* Macro or local economic factors such as the level of interest rates can affect defaults on variable priced loans. A rise in unemployment in an industry sector may disproportionately impact certain consumer or geographic segments. Credit policy tightens and loosens during economic cycles. Overall, if the model is based on data drawn during times of economic prosperity, it is entirely likely that the estimated probabilities of default would prove to be understated during times of recession.

---

15. The subprime market is composed of several risk layers that are denoted by Alt-A, B, C, and D grades. Additional factors that are used to assign loans to these subprime grades include credit score, past due history for housing payment separate from revolving and installment payments, presence or absence of any major adverse records together with explanations and whether or not the debts were brought current or cleared, any history of bankruptcy or foreclosure, qualifying debt ratio values, often specified in combination with loan-to-value ratio (LTV) ranges, residual income requirements, indication if fully documented income versus stated income, and maximum original LTV ratio which varies based on owner-occupancy of the property financed, product (fixed or variable and term) or loan type (purchase, refinance), documentation of income, cash out or debt consolidation condition, loan amount, property type (second homes, condos, primary single family dwelling), self-employment, and so on.

16. Indeterminate performance is loosely defined as performance that is not "good enough" to be classified as good and not "bad enough" to be classified as bad.

○ *Changes in competitive forces in various markets.* If a major lender enters the markets of a lender having an existing credit underwriting model developed for those markets, and this occurs after the time that the model was developed and implemented, then the performance of the model may suffer.[17]

○ *Data collection and sampling process.* It is important to validate data quality and eliminate or mitigate their impact before the data can be used for model development. For example, missing data and outliers should be examined and gauged for the potential impact on model variables and specifications, and appropriate remedies such as defaults setting or imputing should be implemented.[18] There are various software solutions available that are developed for those purposes.[19] In addition, sampling methods and process need to ensure representative samples of the current population characteristics in an efficient fashion.

○ *Population shift.* Credit-scoring model performance and effectiveness may diminish as a result of shifts in model inputs, which can include consumers' characteristics and economic conditions.[20] For a recent population shift, it is important to measure changes in borrowers' characteristics for current and recent applicants relative to applicants in the development sampling timeframe, particularly when one or more primary factors are involved. There are many statistics that can be used to evaluate the relevance of model input data and assumptions for credit risk models. Those include indices created to measure a shift or measure the agreement between the development sample and the holdout sample, such as stability indices.[21] Comparisons may be based on population proportion[22] or event proportion[23] across a given variable. The larger the index is, the greater the shift as it is assumed that a larger index exceeding a predefined threshold usually means the model performance is in question. These comparisons are usually performed quarterly.

• *Lending policies and practices.* Differences occur here for numerous reasons, such as:

○ *Lending policies and procedures.* They vary based on many factors, such a business lines, channels, and geographic markets. In addition, they may vary by loan purpose, lien status, or collateral type, to name a few. It is critical that modelers account for these differences by either developing or validating separate models for every variation, or by combining models where possible by taking into account any important differences within the model formulation.[24]

○ *Policy exceptions.* Examples may include employee loans or guaranteed loans which require special treatment and must be identified and tracked. As previously discussed,

---

17. Crouhy, Galai, and Mark, 2001, pp. 593–594 note that changes in market conditions are a source of model misapplication.
18. See also Chapter 5 for details about handling data quality issues.
19. Those include DataFlux and SAS Enterprise Miner.
20. See OCC Bulletin 97-24, Appendix: Safety and Soundness and Compliance Issues on Credit Scoring Models, May 20, 1997, p. 4.
21. Types of stability indices include variable stability index: measures the stability between the development sample and the actual sample based on population proportion (input variables), and event stability index: measure the stability between the development sample and the actual sample based on event proportion (target variable).
22. That is, the percentage of applicants falling into discrete groupings associated with a particular variable.
23. That is, the likelihood of a "bad performance" outcome relative to the groupings for a specific variable.
24. For example, in mortgage lending, a refinance application can take place with the same institution that holds the current mortgage (referred to as an *internal refinance*) or it can occur with a lender that does not hold the first mortgage (referred to an *external refinance*). The two types of refinances could be modeled separately, or they could be combined so long as the policy differences are accounted for in the definition of model variables and also provided an indicator variable is introduced in the model that identifies every observation as being either an internal, or external, refinance.

high/low side score overrides and mortgage fee waivers and pricing concessions all must be considered for their impact on input validation.

Model Processing Validation

Usually, model processing validation involves the following aspects:

- *Model development.* A primary distinction between more traditional approaches, such as credit scoring and the hybrid approach, is the hybrid approach use of the model consensus session (MCS). Some key areas in model development that bear consideration are:

  ○ *Variable discretization.* Model variable discretization presents a difficult problem for credit risk modelers that use the traditional approaches. For a scorecard, these are typically determined via data analysis (e.g., variable binning, covariance analysis, etc.). Scorecard development typically requires modelers to categorize variables by associating groups or ranges of values the variable can take on that possess similarly good/bad odds ratios. This categorization, or binning, of variables must be done with care because different schemes can have very different results due to their impact on interactions with other variables. Binning algorithms do exist to assist modelers, but they must be used with care.

  ○ *Variable selection.* Typically, the strength of a particular factor, and its correlation with other factors, governs to a large extent whether it will make its way into the final model. Predictor strength may be measured by the discrete analog of the divergence statistic, which is calculated by the formula $\sum_{i=1,n}[(PG_i - PB_i) * \ln(PG_i/PB_i)]$, where there are "n" subclassifications associated with the predictor variable in question. A simple example is described in Figure 8.2 with a housing variable that has three such subclassifications.

     We observe that the housing variable has predictive content in the fair range. A general scheme for assessing variable strength is provided in Figure 8.3, which summarizes possible divergence-based thresholds relative to candidate predictor variables in a model.

     The reader should bear in mind that these ranges apply to variables in isolation, and a variable that possesses only fair predictive content in isolation may afford greater information value in combination with another variable where a strong interaction exists. For scoring systems, variable selection is usually performed using a stepwise forward selection method where variables are added at every step and the weights are adjusted until maximum separation is achieved. In addition to separation, a penalty cost for misclassification can be added to the objective function, or profitability expression, and so on. Algorithms can also vary by method and include nonlinear optimization,

Housing	Pct Goods (A)	Pct Bads (B)	Difference (C = A − B)/100	G/B Ratio (D = A/B)	Log₂(Odds) (E = Log₂D)	Calculation (C*E)
Own	60	30	0.30	2/1	1	0.3
Rent	30	60	−0.30	1/2	−1	0.3
Other	10	10	0.0	1/1	0	0
Divergence						**0.60**

FIGURE 8.2 DIVERGENCE CALCULATION FOR A MODEL VARIABLE

Divergence Range	Interpretation
0.000–0.024	Worthless
0.025–0.890	Fair
0.900–0.299	Good
0.300–0.599	Strong
0.600–0.799	Very strong
0.800–2.000	Exceptionally strong

FIGURE 8.3   PREDICTIVE STRENGTH BASED ON DIVERGENCE

linear and mixed-integer programming, goal programming,[25] stochastic optimization,[26] and conjugate gradient methods.[27] The MCS associated with the hybrid modeling approach reduces the complexity introduced by advanced algorithms.

♦ *Model estimation methods.* This involves model theory and algorithms. There are many options available for deriving the weights for variables in a model. Among the many algorithms, none is best suited for all problems—picking an estimation method requires judgment and subject matter knowledge.[28] For the modeling approaches suggested in this book, there are common associated methods and will be discussed in detail in the later sections.[29]

♦ *Model specifications.* Typically, formulating model specifications can be a complicated process and involves various model selection methods such as stepwise, backward, or forward selections, particularly when there are a large number of variables to consider.[30] Chapter 5 was devoted to a more efficient formulation of this test that we refer to as the dynamic conditional process (DCP). If hybrid models are used, then the application of DCP is immediate, with little or no need for a MCS to gather specifications. An abbreviated MCS could be performed for the purpose of confirmation of the hybrid model. Impact on protected classes is addressed after the fact via independent compliance testing, most commonly using logistic regression analysis.

25. For details, see *SAS/OR 9.1 User's Guide: Mathematical Programming*, SAS Institute Inc., Cary, NC, USA, 2002.
26. For example, genetic algorithms and simulated annealing are two examples of methods that can help avoid local optima while iterating toward a global maximum separation of good and bad credit applicants. Problem formulations require careful design and considerable fine tuning.
27. The conjugate gradient method is a computationally efficient iterative method for solving sparse linear equation systems, and its algorithms are available in several SAS procedures such as the NLP procedure in SAS/OR software. For details on available algorithms and how to select an appropriate one, see *SAS/OR 9.1 User's Guide*, 2002, pp. 585–599.
28. See Henery, R., R. D. King, Feng, C., and A. Sutherland. "A Comparative Study of Classification Algorithms: Statistical Machine Learning and Neural Network," in *Machine Intelligence and Inductive Learning*, Oxford University Press, 1994, pp. 311–359.
29. In the simplest case, where the score is linear the weights are "best" that minimize the squared error. For logistic regression, the best weights are those that maximize the likelihood function associated with the Bernoulli probability law. The weights associated with the hybrid modeling approach described in Chapter 6 may be calculated using maximum likelihood estimation to fit a model to the handle using an iterative proportional fitting algorithm and then deriving weights for any conditionally associated secondary factors in a similar manner that restricts observations to the handle segment in question.
30. See Christensen, Ronald, *Log-Linear Methods and Logistic Regression*. Springer, 1997, pp. 211–239, on model selection for high dimensional tables.

◆ *Reject inference.* With traditional methods, this is normally addressed by a procedure that fractionally assigns declined applicants to good and bad groups based upon the observed correlation of their characteristics with default outcomes based upon observations of approved applicants. A problem occurs when the unknown group is dissimilar from the known group, or when there is additional information concerning the creditworthiness of the unknown group that is not taken into account. In those cases, it is likely that the riskiness of the declined applicants will be overstated.[31]

• *Model selection.* With traditional models, model choice can also include "palatability tests,"[32] but it is typically governed by predictive capability and misclassification error rate. So if the number of inquiries at the credit bureau is found to be predictive, then number of inquiries may become a model predictor variable. In this case, the fact that someone is shopping for a loan is considered a default risk factor and it lowers their credit score. In the case of logistic regression, the McFadden R^2 is often used to measure model strength and model fit is typically measured using the Hosmer-Lemeshow goodness-of-fit statistic. The Kullback divergence statistic[33] is often used to measure the predictive power of a scoring system, and values in the neighborhood of one or greater have been shown to separate creditworthy and noncreditworthy credit applicants at a statistically significant rate. One can also compare good and bad score distributions via a test of equality of means.

• *Model implementation.* Even when correct models are developed and selected, model implementation may still experience various problems. This is termed *model implementation risk*, which can be caused by many different factors including software programming, solution algorithms, computation efficiency, or hardware issues.[34] As complexity increases, there is greater probability and severity of model risk.[35] We note later on how MCS can help minimize model implementation risk.

Model Output Validation

Model output validation includes checking both model performance and compliance against expectations and requirements. Typically, model output validation involves several aspects. First, we need to select appropriate testing approaches. Data availability plays a critical role. Validating a credit risk model requires a large database with sufficient historical data and bad loans.[36] Some testing processes, such as back-testing, can be difficult because of insufficient history for time series data. As a result, the ability to back test credit risk models can be more limited than it is for market risk models. One suggested remedy to overcome the insufficient data issue for commercial

---

31. For typical methods of reject inference, see Leonard, K. J., "Credit Scoring and Quality Management," in Hand, D. J. and S. D. Jacka (eds.), *Statistics in Finance*, Hodder Arnold, 1998, pp. 112–113. For implementation of reject inference, see, for example, Thomas L. C., D. B. Edelman, and J. N. Crook, "Credit Scoring and Its Applications," SIAM Monographs on Mathematical Modeling and Computation, 2002, pp. 141–143.

32. Palatability may refer to nonintuitive risk categorization (e.g., reversals in risk assignment for intuitive monotone decreasing factors such as years in profession, years at address, etc.), or maintainability burdens (e.g., absolute income range definitions change due to inflation over time, etc.).

33. For formulas, please refer to Kullback, S., and R. A. Leibler. "On information and sufficiency," *Annals of Mathematical Statistics*, Vol. 22, 1951, pp. 79–86.

34. Other issues associated with incorrect model implementation can include approximation errors and insufficient simulation runs. See Crouhy, Galai, and Mark, 2001, p. 590.

35. See Jorion, 2007, pp. 550–551, for a description of model implementation risk and how it is related to model complexity.

36. For example, as a formal statistical approach commonly used for validating value at risk (VAR) models, back-testing requires sufficient data history to perform. For detailed discussion of backtesting VAR models, see Jorion, 2007, pp. 139–157.

credit risk models is cross-sectional simulation.[37] Resampling approaches, such as bootstrap and jackknife,[38] are also used to overcome data issues. However, changes in risk factors cannot be fully captured in the resampling process. This challenge leads to alternative evaluation methods such as scenario simulation, or stress testing.[39] Simulation analysis can be used to evaluate model performance and stability in various scenarios based on predictions regarding the vintage life cycle, changing credit quality, seasonality, management action, the macroeconomic environment, and the competitive environment.

Second, we need to test model outcomes. Validation on a holdout sample at development time is a standard and important practice. Holdout sample analysis can be in-time or out-of-time analysis. For holdout sample comparisons, one can compare the respective good and bad score distributions via a test of equality of means, or compare acceptance rates for good and bad performance groups between the development and holdout samples, respectively. A direct test of the difference in divergence for the two samples can also be performed.[40] Goodness-of-fit on a holdout sample tests to ensure a model will replicate and that it has avoided capturing noise in the data as predictive information value. Models that are strong predictors on the development sample, but fail to perform well on a holdout sample typically have been subjected to overfitting. Hybrid models have a distinct advantage in these instances, because a log-linear model can be fit to both the development and validation samples and individual terms can be isolated that account for any differences. This provides an explicit mechanism for dampening noise in the observed data. One complication that may arise is when a score cutoff or handle cell action is changed during an observation period. In this case, care must be taken to construct comparable development sample statistics to validate against the observed results.

Third, we need to interpret model outcomes. Model performance compliance validation requires examining and interpreting model results from regulatory perspective. For example, one can check model outputs against policy, rules, or regulatory requirements. As described in Chapter 5, analysis of model estimated coefficients can be used to identify possible disparate treatment. Override analysis results also can be used this purpose, and we describe this in a later section.

Typical Statistical Measures and Applications

Credit risk models can be developed with different qualitative or quantitative prediction tools and approaches. There are also numerous statistical metrics to measure their performance.[41] Deciding which model validation metrics are appropriate to use depends on the modeling approaches used, and the purposes and expected performance of models. For credit scoring models, discriminant

37. For example, Lopez and Saidenberg proposed evaluation methods for credit risk models based on cross-sectional simulation using a panel data approach. See Lopez, Jose A., and Marc R. Saidenberg, "Evaluating Credit Risk Models," *Journal of Banking and Finance*, Vol. 24, 2000, pp. 151–165.
38. For discussion of practical considerations for resampling methods see Good, Phillip I., *Resampling Methods: A Practical Guide to Data Analysis*. Birkhauser, 2001. See also Shau, J., and D. Tu, *The Jackknife and Bootstrap*. Springer, 1996, for more theoretical discussion.
39. Stress-testing examines a model's performance under extreme scenarios. Saunders and Allen suggested that it is possible to stress test credit risk models by using cross-sectional subportfolio sampling techniques. See Saunders, A. and L. Allen. *Credit Risk Measurement*, 2nd ed. John Wiley & Sons, 2002, pp. 192–195.
40. Sample statistics, in closed form, can be derived for the Kullback divergence statistic using maximum likelihood estimation, and the formula for the standard error and confidence interval at the 95 percent level can be specified based upon them.
41. In general, validation of model performance can be conducted from two aspects. One is to evaluate model discriminatory power or qualitative prediction, which is a model's classification ability to separate "bad" from "good." The other aspect is to measure model predictability, or quantitative prediction, that validates a model predicted results against the actual results.

Statistic Measure	Typical Applications	Pros & Cons
Kolmogrov-Smirnov (K-S) test	• Model performance comparison • Model input data analysis	• Test results may not depend on bucketing or binning. • Can measure absolute difference between two distributions for continuous distribution only • Cannot be used for predictive modeling
ROC curve	Model performance comparison	• Can incorporate misclassification costs • For rank ordering so it deals with relative classifications • May underestimate risk even a good ROC coefficient • Sensitive to class distribution. Not adequate for rare event class
Gini coefficient	Model performance comparison	• Convenient and easy for comparing shapes of distributions • Does not consider the class relative sizes • Cannot incorporate misclassification cost and does not differentiate error types • Limited to rank ordering
Cumulative gains charts and lift	• Population shift • Model performance comparison	• Good for making visual comparisons • Simple to use and easy to interpret • Test results depend on bucketing or binning
Chi-square statistic	Model performance comparison	• Test results depends on binning • Insensitive to class distribution • Assume independence of data • Considers all deviation the same weight • Can underestimate the true type I error given low frequency of default events • Compare actual with expected results

FIGURE 8.4 COMPARISONS OF TYPICAL STATISTICAL MEASURES

analysis (DA) is the classic modeling technique.[42] Currently, the most commonly used validation metrics are the ROC, the KS test, the chi-square test, and the Gini approach.[43] Figure 8.4 provides a summary of uses and pros and cons for some common statistical measures. This is by no means a complete list.

We now review the metrics in the order in which they appear in Figure 8.4:

- *The Kolmogrov-Smirnov (KS) test.* The KS test is used to measure model segmentation and classification capability.[44] It is widely used in credit scoring analysis to test if data has changed significantly since the model was built. It can be used to test if two groups of data (independent variables) differ significantly. The greatest discrepancy between the observed

---

42. Other available modeling techniques include decision trees, neural networks, linear/nonlinear programming, survival analysis, Markov chains, expert systems, and so forth. See Chapter 6's "Credit-Scoring Systems." See also Rosenberg, Eric, and Alan Gleit. "Quantitative Methods in Credit Management: A Survey," *Operations Research*, Vol. 42, No. 40, July–August 1994, pp. 589–613.

43. For a detailed comparison of these approaches, the users can refer to Hand, David, "Modeling Consumer Credit Risk," *IMA Journal of Management Mathematics*, Vol. 12, 2001, pp. 150–152; and Servigny A. D., and Renault Olivier, *Measuring and Managing Credit Risk*, McGraw-Hill, 2004, pp. 89–116.

44. Typically, K-S statistic is measured as the maximum absolute deviation between two cumulative distribution functions.

and expected cumulative frequencies is called the "D-statistic."[45] The KS test makes no assumption about the distribution of the data and the test statistic D is not affected by using different scales such as log. So it is generally more robust than the t-test. The KS test is limited only for testing data against a continuous distribution for a one-dimensional data sample.

- *Receiver operation characteristic curve (ROC).* A ROC curve is a graphical representation of the trade off between the false negative and false positive rates for every possible cut off. Equivalently, the ROC curve is the representation of the tradeoffs between sensitivity (Sn) and specificity (Sp). Here, sensitivity is the proportion of correctly classified defaults, or the true positive rate, and specificity is the proportion of correctly classified non-defaults. Therefore, 1—sensitivity is false negative rate (Type II error), and accordingly, 1—specificity is false positive rate (Type I error).[46] In general, the plot shows the false-positive rate on the X-axis and 1—the false negative rate—on the Y-axis. A model with a low Type II error rate, or a high probability of rejecting a default, is considered powerful.[47]

- *Gini coefficient.* The Gini curve, or Lorenz curve, is a graphical representation of the cumulative percent captured response curve.[48] The Gini coefficient is defined as a ratio of the areas on the Lorenz curve diagram.[49] The Gini coefficient does not differentiate false-positive errors from false-negative errors. This can be a significant disadvantage since, in practice, banks normally treat Type I errors differently from Type II errors.

- *Cumulative gains charts and lift.* This is a measure of the effectiveness of a predictive model calculated as the ratio between the results obtained with and without the predictive model.[50] Cumulative gains and lift charts are good visual aids for measuring model performance. Both charts consist of a lift curve and a baseline. The greater the area between the lift curve and the baseline, the better is the model. This measure is extensively used to evaluate model performance.

- *Chi-square test.* Chi-square is a widely used nonparametric test of statistical significance that can be applied to any univariate distribution. It measures how a random sample deviates from a given probability distribution function using $\sum (O - E)^2 / E$. The chi-square test is an alternative to KS goodness-of-fit tests and applied to binned data. So, the value of the chi-square test statistic can be affected by how the data is binned. The chi-square test can underestimate the true Type I error given low frequency of default events.[51] The chi-square test also requires a sufficient sample size to generate a valid chi-square approximation.

The above standard statistical methods face some challenges when applied to credit scoring model validation as shown in Figure 8.4. First, the KS statistic or Gini coefficient may

---

45. For detailed description of KS two-sample test, please see Boes, D. C., F. A. Graybill, and A. M. Mood. *Introduction to the Theory of Statistics*, 3rd ed. McGraw-Hill, 1974. See also, Knuth, D. E., § 3.3.1B in *The Art of Computer Programming, Vol. 2: Seminumerical Algorithms*, 3rd ed. Addison-Wesley, pp. 45–52, 1998.
46. The curve is measured by _1MSPEC_ = FALPOS / $(n - n_1)$, and _SENSIT_ = _POS/ n_1. Here, n is the sample size, n_1 individuals are observed to have a certain condition or event, _POS is the number of correctly predicted event responses, _FALPOS is the number of falsely predicted event responses. _SENSIT_(z) is the sensitivity of the test, and _1MSPEC_(z) is one minus the specificity of the test. See SAS/STAT, Chapter 39, Section 33, for details.
47. For a simple yet detailed description of ROC curve, see *Logistic Regression Examples Using the SAS System*, SAS Institute Inc., pp. 87–92, 1995.
48. See Sen, A. *On Economic Inequality*, Clarendon Press, 1997. For a recent review on Gini index, please see Xu, Kuan, "How Has the Literature on Gini's Index Evolved in the Past 80 Years?" Working Paper, Department of Economics, Dalhousie University. Retrieved on June 1, 2006.
49. Gini coefficient is usually measured as $G = 1 - 2\int L(x) dx$.
50. Here, lift is measured as the ratio of concentration rate with model to concentration rate without model.
51. Such as Hosmer-Lemeshow's chi-square test. See Hosmer and Lemeshow, 2000, pp. 147–156.

have some inherent limitations. According to Hand (2001), all of these suffer from one common weakness—they are based on a comparison of the predicted probability belonging to either good or bad, which represent a distorted sample of the total population. Thus, the developed models are likely to perform poorly on new applicants.[52] These methods measure the model's ability to rank risk throughout the entire sample without giving any special weight to performance near the accept/reject region.[53] The Gini coefficient, the KS statistic, and the information value do not take account of the class priors. It has been argued that using the KS test, ROC curve, or Gini coefficient as model validation measures can be misleading since they rely on a single threshold instead of the entire performance distribution.[54]

Another challenge is the group definition, which is one of the most severe problems associated with discriminant analysis.[55] To develop robust scoring models, data should be grouped by natural breaks to preserve the variable predictive information,[56] and this has been a persistent issue in practice.

We see another challenge; namely, the statistics described in Figure 8.4 are based on individual tests. Since credit model development and underwriting processes always involve multiple factors, it would be difficult to determine if those individual changes are significant enough to affect underwriting policy or model specifications. All those different metrics may measure credit risks from different perspectives, and no single metric is statistically powerful and robust enough to be sufficient. Often, multiple metrics are required to confirm validation results. However, multiple measures also can result in conflicting ranking and results.

We note that all of those methods are purely statistical and quantitative metrics. Model validation criteria can not be based on a single quantitative metric, and a quantitative metric should be complemented with qualitative elements. Therefore, judgmental factors such as business and regulatory requirements should be integrated into the process to validate models from both credit risk and compliance risk aspects.

AN INTEGRATED MODEL VALIDATION APPROACH

In this section, we propose an integrated framework that can be used to perform model validation from both regulatory compliance and model performance perspectives. Since credit scoring model validation has received widespread coverage, our discussion focuses primarily on the key differences associated with the validation of the hybrid model, which was introduced in Chapter 6. This framework is straightforward and easy to implement, and addresses the challenges described in the previous section.

Overall Validation Framework

The overall process for this integrated framework can be described in Figure 8.5. This framework involves the following four key processes:

---

52. See Hand, 2001, p. 151. See also Hand, 1998, p. 77.
53. See Burns, Peter, and Christopher Ody. Forum on Validation of Consumer Credit Risk Models, the Payment Cards Center of the Federal Reserve Bank of Philadelphia and the Wharton School's Financial Institutions Center, November, 2004, pp. 12–13. See also Hand, David, "Good Practice in Retail Credit Scorecard Assessment," Credit Research Centre, Credit Scoring and Credit Control Conference VIII, 2003.
54. Ibid.
55. See Eisenbeis, R. A. "Problems in Applying Discriminant Analysis in Credit Scoring Models," *Journal of Banking and Finance*, Vol. 2, No. 3, October 1978, pp. 205–219.
56. See Rosenberg and Gleit, 1994, pp. 593–596.

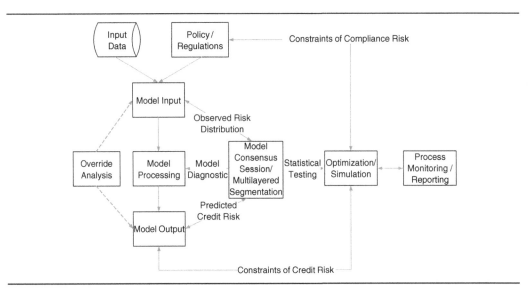

FIGURE 8.5   AN INTEGRATED MODEL VALIDATION FRAMEWORK

- *Integrate validation areas.* In this process, the three main validation areas (input, process, and output) are integrated through the handle concept. First, the population risk profile in model input data is represented and evaluated in terms of the handle cell distribution with multilayered segmentation (MLS). Population shifts and changes in risk profile are further examined across different protected groups and time points. Then models are evaluated through an efficient MCS to ensure appropriate model evaluation, specifications, and selection. Finally, the model predicted probability of default is associated with model input risk profile by the handle number. This allows a direct comparison between the observed risk in input data and the predicted risk in model outputs. The residual between the predicted risk score and the input risk distribution (or profile) is further analyzed for root causes.
- *Utilize override analysis results.* Depending on the degree of override incidence, override analysis results can be integrated into the process. On the one hand, the override process can be monitored by matching override incidence to handle cells. On the other hand, the override analysis results are used as feedback and integrated into the MLS process to facilitate handle creation and model performance evaluation.
- *Optimize validation results.* Validation optimization must consider two concurrent objectives. It needs to maximize the separation of creditworthy and noncreditworthy applications, while also minimizing the disparate impact to ensure comparable acceptance rate, pricing, and terms related to similarly situated protected- and nonprotected-class borrowers. This can be facilitated by adopting an initial feasible model specification through MCS.
- *Monitor validation process.* A model validation reporting system monitors, measures, and ranks models jointly by credit risk and compliance risk, and possibly other areas of concerns. This process integrates various model disparity indices derived from metrics within or outside of the validation framework. UPI methodology can be used to combine all forms of performance metrics into a single risk-ranking indicator.

Multilayered Segmentation for Model Input Validation

MLS, described in Chapter 7, can be used in model input validation. It enables the following four activities:

1. Creation of a risk distribution over discrete risk-homogeneous segments that are mutually exclusive and completely capture the essence of the input population of observations relative to the business purpose (e.g., loan underwriting, pricing, marketing, etc.).
2. Test for significance of a shift in the risk distribution across handle and action table cells using the KS statistic, the chi-square test, and so on.
3. Test for significance of shift in the frequency distribution across handle cells using the KS statistic, or the chi-square test. In addition, the form of the structured model can be tested using the G^2 likelihood ratio statistic to determine if any terms should be added or dropped.
4. Superimpose risk distributions for every protected class, or group of interest, with the corresponding control group to test to see if they are synchronized. Where significant differences exist, MLS points the way to the root cause(s).

Figure 8.6 describes the process of using the MLS process.

MLS-Based Risk Distribution Construction

MLS creates a *handle*, which represents all possible combinations of covariate patterns and describes the joint distribution of risk characteristics. Within each handle segment, applicants are considered more or less homogeneous in terms of default risk. A handle-based distribution offers several advantages. First, it allows specific treatment of data segments. Unlike a KS test, which does not take into consideration specific segments, a handle allows one to embed class priors by utilizing different thresholds and business policies. This, to a certain degree, overcomes the common weakness associated with the standard validation metrics as described earlier,[57] and allows more accurate, and explicit, testing of model discriminatory power. Second, a handle creates

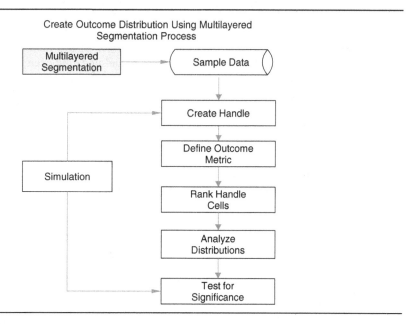

FIGURE 8.6 MLS PROCESS

57. See Hand, 2001, p. 151.

a natural grouping definition and its effectiveness does not depend on binning.[58] The number of classes depends on the number of handle cells. In the case of logistic regression, each handle cell represents a unique segment and a covariate pattern. The handle provides a natural binning,[59] which affords a more consistent measure of risk. This method can be used to overcome the inherent limitation of the chi-square test, which depends on number of binning classes. Third, it allows intuitive cross-sectional validation. A cohesive handle can be constructed using logical inferences to extrapolate values for segments that have sampling zeros or insufficient data. This helps overcome missing data and is especially powerful for reject inference. MLS provides the means to more effectively manage and validate a large number of models that are made possible with a cohesive handle.

Figure 8.7 is taken from Figure 6.67, Bank Card Primary Factor Handle Table. It illustrates that handle cell risk can be viewed and ranked by different metrics. As noted previously, this affords more comprehensive yet simple representation that jointly captures the attributes of all input variables simultaneously, versus other statistics such as KS, Gini coefficient, or t-test. It is also easier to interpret and audit because model performance validation results can be traced back to changes in data characteristics. More broadly, a handle associates input data attributes with variable selection, model specification, and model performance. In other words, it connects input data validation with model processing validation. As a result, the entire model validation process is more tightly woven and consistent. This approach is easy to implement with hybrid models. For nonhybrid models an MCS is recommended to construct the handle, as opposed to pure data-driven approaches, such as picking the variables possessing the highest predictive strength in the scorecard or other base model.

Constructing an MLS-based risk distribution involves the following steps:

- *Step 1. Define handle segments.* This is done using the MLS, which is based on MCS and selected quantitative methods as needed. For the hybrid models, this is done in Phase 2 of the hybrid system construction. Specifically, this process involves creating categories based on primary or secondary factors as described in Chapter 5. The DCP methodology can provide efficient use of input data by handling missing data and also by enabling the modeler to pool data from different segments. For hybrid models, "down the road" validation tests are actually transformed into a model updating exercise that can be performed on as frequent a basis as performance data becomes available. This is due to the adaptive nature of the hybrid model, whereby shifts in risk distributions can be captured and viewed at the segment level and segment risk estimates can be refreshed. This is in contrast to traditional models where one must redevelop the system when significant shifts occur in risk distributions.

- *Step 2. Rank-order handle cells.* Since each handle represents a unique data attribute and within each group all applications are homogenous and have the same degree of default risk, with past default history,[60] we can use a cumulative gains chart to rank-order the risk of handle cells. Within each handle segment, we observe the incidence of goods, bads, rejects, and override outcomes. This information is used to calculate the observed default rate. The risk ranking, or distribution, of the handle cells forms a basis for assessing the overall risk profile of the validation sample. Figure 8.8 shows an example of how handle

---

58. Binning refers to the process of mapping ranges of values for the predictor variable into discrete groups, for example, the variable years-at-address which takes on values of 0,1,2,3,4,5,6,7,8,9,10, … may be grouped into the intervals, or bins, of: under two years, two to four years, and 5 or more years. The bins are usually formed by associating values that have similar risk.

59. This group definition reflects business reality and is intuitively more robust. See Rosenberg and Gleit, 1994, pp. 593–594 for the importance of group definition for discriminant analysis in credit scoring.

60. If there is no past default history then we need to apply business judgment based on the user's previous experience.

Handle	Risk	Actual Default Rate	Estimated Default Rate
1	0	0.0001	0.0001
2	1	0.001	0.001
4	1	n/a	0.0026
10	1	0.008	0.008
3	2	n/a	0.01
5	2	0.02	0.013
7	2	n/a	0.0165
11	2	0.03	0.03
13	2	0.035	0.035
14	2	0.04	0.04
16	2	n/a	0.045
19	2	0.05	0.05
20	2	0.06	0.06
22	2	0.08	0.08
6	3	0.1	0.1
8	3	0.2	0.2
12	3	0.25	0.25
15	3	n/a	0.3
17	3	0.35	0.35
23	3	0.4	0.4
9	4	0.5	0.5
18	4	0.6	0.6
21	4	n/a	0.65
24	4	0.7	0.7
25	4	n/a	0.75
26	4	0.8	0.8
27	5	0.9999	0.9999

FIGURE 8.7   COHESIVE HANDLE WITH INFERRED RISK ESTIMATES

cells are ranked by the observed default risk. In addition to default, the handle distribution also can be created based on measures such as profitability, return on investment, and so on.

- *Step 3. Compare risk distributions.* For credit risk validation, compare validation sample against model development sample. Here, the shift in overall risk profile can be captured with a handle distribution explicitly. We perform a simple chi-square test with appropriate degrees of freedom, to determine the significance of sample difference. If it is significant, further analysis is required to determine the factors, or their combinations, which contribute to the shift. For compliance validation, we examine for the same sample, the handle distribution by individual protected classes versus the nonprotected class (the control group).

Risk Rank	Handle Number	Credit History	Loan to Value Ratio	Debt to Income Ratio	Income	Beauru Score	Loans	Total Number Loans	% Cumulative Loans	%Default	Number of Defaults
1	8	Fair/Poor	Low	High	Low	Low	402	402	5.03	80%	256
2	0	Fair/Poor	High	High	Low	Low	656	1058	13.23	77%	403
3	12	Fair/Poor	Low	High	Low	High	328	1386	17.33	72%	187
4	4	Fair/Poor	High	High	Low	High	628	2014	25.18	70%	367
5	16	Fair/Poor	High	Low	Low	Low	221	2235	27.94	68%	123
6	24	Fair/Poor	Low	Low	Low	Low	134	2369	29.61	67%	73
7	20	Fair/Poor	High	Low	Low	High	178	2547	31.84	66%	95
8	5	Fair/Poor	High	High	High	High	327	2874	35.93	56%	149
9	28	Fair/Poor	Low	Low	Low	High	200	3074	38.43	55%	90
10	9	Fair/Poor	Low	High	High	Low	172	3246	40.58	53%	73
11	1	Fair/Poor	High	High	High	Low	375	3621	45.26	51%	162
12	2	Good	High	High	Low	Low	281	3902	48.78	48%	111
13	3	Good	High	High	High	Low	214	4116	51.45	47%	81
14	17	Fair/Poor	High	Low	High	Low	130	4246	53.08	46%	50
15	13	Fair/Poor	Low	High	High	High	286	4532	56.65	44%	103
16	18	Good	High	Low	Low	Low	164	4696	58.7	44%	57
17	25	Fair/Poor	Low	Low	High	Low	82	4778	59.73	43%	26
18	21	Fair/Poor	High	Low	High	High	108	4886	61.08	39%	34
19	10	Good	Low	High	Low	Low	179	5065	63.31	38%	56
20	11	Good	Low	High	High	Low	92	5157	64.46	37%	28
21	19	Good	High	Low	High	Low	94	5251	65.64	33%	26
22	26	Good	Low	Low	Low	Low	93	5344	66.8	32%	25
23	29	Fair/Poor	Low	Low	High	High	443	5787	72.34	31%	109
24	27	Good	Low	Low	High	Low	103	5890	73.62	27%	21
25	14	Good	Low	High	Low	High	184	6074	75.93	25%	37
26	22	Good	High	Low	Low	High	159	6233	77.91	22%	30
27	30	Good	Low	Low	Low	High	266	6499	81.24	22%	47
28	23	Good	High	Low	High	High	83	6582	82.28	19%	13
29	31	Good	Low	Low	High	High	717	7299	91.24	18%	102
30	6	Good	High	High	Low	High	325	7624	95.3	18%	48
31	15	Good	Low	High	High	High	204	7828	97.85	15%	25
32	7	Good	High	High	High	High	172	8000	100	14%	18

FIGURE 8.8 RANKING HANDLE CELLS

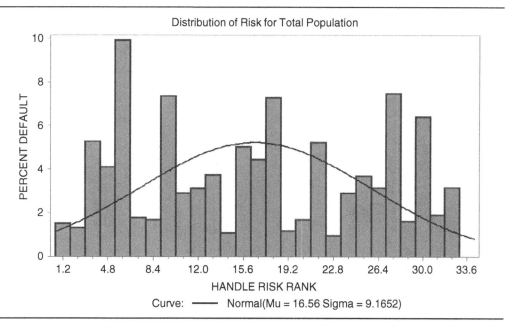

FIGURE 8.9 OVERALL RISK DISTRIBUTION

Here, the difference between the protected and nonprotected distribution can be captured.[61] A significant difference in risk distribution across protected groups may indicate disparate impact or treatment.

- *Step 4. Simulate and compare distributions.* For each handle cell, calculate the percentage of default: C_{ti} = total number of defaults/total number of loans. This can be calculated for the overall population as shown in Figure 8.9. This also can be done over time for development sample and validation sample, respectively. Figure 8.10 shows an example of comparison of risk simulated distribution over time that corresponds to all credit applicants for an arbitrary loan product. We have collapsed the 32 handle cells shown in Figure 8.8 into 9 homogenous groups. The trend is, on the surface, unsettling at best, because the frequencies associated with the higher risk groups have increased.

- *Step 5. Test for compliance.* Statistical tests such as KS can be used for testing the significance in risk ranking across different groups, such as race or ethnicity, as shown in Figure 8.11. When there is a significant difference between those two distributions, there is disparate impact, and possibly disparate treatment.[62] The KS test can be used to test for this, as shown in Figure 8.12.

- *Step 6. Threshold simulation.* By considering a range of possible thresholds, consistency of the handle risk ranking can be examined across different protected groups versus the control group. A range of thresholds for primary factors can be used to calculate possible outcomes

61. Again, we can perform a simple chi-square test with appropriate degrees of freedom, to determine the significance of the difference. If it is significant, further analysis is required to determine the factors, or their combinations, which contribute to the difference.
62. See Chapter 6's Hybrid System Construction.

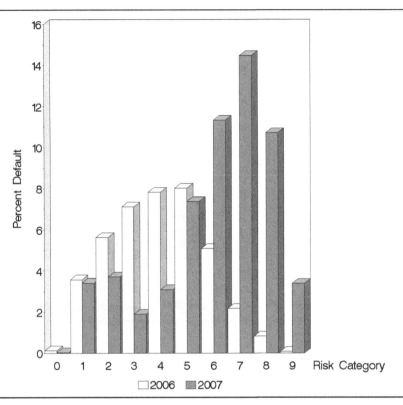

FIGURE 8.10   COMPARISON OF RISK DISTRIBUTION OVER TIME

of the handle distribution.[63] The thresholds that generate the best model performance, at varying levels of disparate impact, can be compared and validated against existing policy thresholds. In this way, model sensitivity to the threshold values can be determined relative to both credit risk and compliance risk. Threshold simulation may also be performed on alternative models to assess impact on borrowers falling in, or outside of, the credit mainstream.

Implications for Model Compliance

MLS-based model input validation can be readily interpreted from compliance perspective. For example, from Figure 8.8, the implications are immediate relative to the corresponding loan default rate trend year to year. The real question is: "What is driving the shift in risk distribution in the applicant population?" Possible scenarios include that there has been a new significant marketing emphasis, or that the primary risk measurement tool is the credit bureau score, which has been, on average, migrating downward over the period. Another important question is: "Has riskiness of the applicant population truly increased, or is that conclusion based more upon the way risk is measured?" If there had been a large influx of "thin-file" applicants who possess excellent noncredit payment histories for rent, utilities, car payments, and the like, then the "trend" could be misleading and there may be profitable business that is not being captured. In order to determine

---

63. See Chapter 5, note 27, for an example of a policy threshold for a handle variable that varies by mortgage product/program.

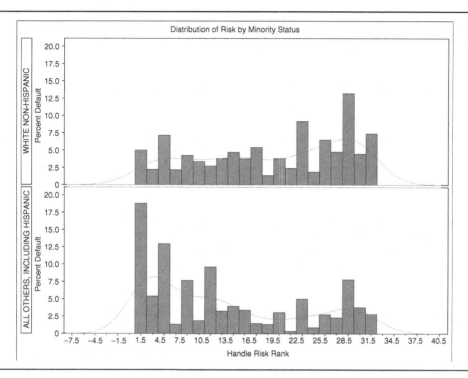

FIGURE 8.11   RISK PROFILE CURVES BY MINORITY STATUS

Kolmogorov-Smirnov Test for Variable Risk Rank			
Classified by Variable Race/Ethnicity			
Race/Ethnicity Values	N	EDF at Maximum	Deviation from Mean at Maximum
White non-Hispanic	3,242	0.306909	−10.63844
All others, including Hispanic	4,758	0.621059	8.781572
Total	8,000	0.49375	
Maximum deviation occurred at observation	4,051		
Value of risk rank at maximum	13.0		

Kolmogorov-Smirnov Two-Sample Test			
(Asymptotic)			
KS	0.154229	D	0.31415
KSa	13.79465	Pr > KSa	< .0001

FIGURE 8.12   K-S TEST FOR STATISTICAL SIGNIFICANCE OF DIFFERENCE IN RISK DISTRIBUTIONS ACROSS MINORITY STATUS

the key drivers of the perceived trend, more analysis is required. Of fundamental concern is that the models used to underwrite loans are valid and that they also afford fair access to credit.

Using the Multilayered Segmentation Approach to Validate Model Performance

Model performance in this section is considered from both a credit and compliance perspective. MLS provides a dual perspective that empowers modelers with a more complete and accurate validation process for assessing model performance. This process is depicted in Figure 8.13.

In this process, model performance validation results are directly associated with model input validation via handle cells. This allows for the comparison of the observed risk distribution with the predicted risk distribution and easy interpretation of any possible inconsistency. In the case of the hybrid model, the probability of default is identical for all observations within a handle cell and a distribution comparison can be readily made. Figure 8.14 shows how model output is associated with the model input using hybrid model handle numbers. For a nonhybrid model, each observation may have a unique probability of default within a cell and the within-group variance needs to be taken into consideration. In this example, there are 5 decision variables and 32 handle cells, which represent 32 unique combinations of covariate patterns.

To compare the risk distributions between the input and the output, we need to conduct a statistical test to determine if the inconsistency or difference is statistically significant. A test can be performed based on either the changes in rank ordering of the risk distributions, or the residuals between the observed and predicted probabilities. Various methods, such as the KS test, analysis of variance (ANOVA) test, chi-square test, and so on, can be easily performed for this purpose.[64] In case of the chi-square test statistic, we substitute the development sample estimates for the expected counts, and the validation sample estimates for the observed counts. Both model outputs represent "through-the-door" populations, where rejects have been assigned to good and bad performance groups.

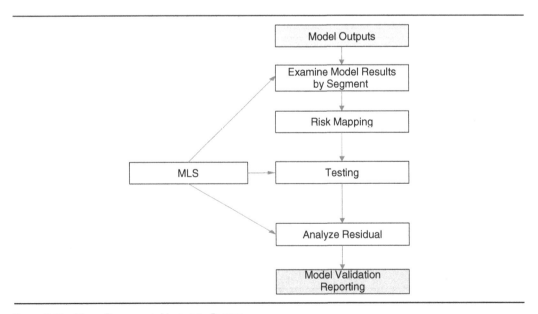

FIGURE 8.13   MODEL PERFORMANCE VALIDATION PROCESS

---

64. For example, one can use SAS procedures NPAR1WAY, GLM, or ANOVA. See *SAS/STAT User's Guide*, SAS Institute Inc., 2003.

Handle Number	Observed Probability Default	Predicted Probability Default	Risk Rank / Observed	Risk Rank / Predicted	Residual
0	0.772	0.772	2	1	0
1	0.511	0.62	11	7	−0.109
2	0.485	0.469	12	14	0.016
3	0.466	0.299	13	23	0.167
4	0.704	0.662	4	5	0.042
5	0.564	0.486	8	13	0.079
6	0.179	0.338	30	21	−0.159
7	0.135	0.198	32	29	−0.062
8	0.803	0.752	1	2	0.05
9	0.525	0.594	10	8	−0.069
10	0.384	0.442	19	16	−0.058
11	0.373	0.276	20	24	0.097
12	0.722	0.637	3	6	0.085
13	0.442	0.458	15	15	−0.016
14	0.253	0.314	25	22	−0.061
15	0.152	0.181	31	30	−0.028
16	0.68	0.707	5	3	−0.027
17	0.463	0.537	14	11	−0.074
18	0.442	0.386	16	18	0.056
19	0.333	0.233	21	27	0.101
20	0.664	0.582	7	9	0.082
21	0.391	0.402	18	17	−0.011
22	0.224	0.267	26	25	−0.043
23	0.191	0.149	28	31	0.042
24	0.67	0.683	6	4	−0.014
25	0.426	0.51	17	12	−0.084
26	0.321	0.36	22	20	−0.04
27	0.266	0.214	24	28	0.052
28	0.545	0.555	9	10	−0.01
29	0.311	0.376	23	19	−0.065
30	0.219	0.246	27	26	−0.027
31	0.182	0.136	29	32	0.046

FIGURE 8.14 COMPARISON OF RISK DISTRIBUTION BETWEEN MODEL INPUT AND MODEL OUTPUT

Validation of Model Results from Credit Risk Perspective

Model performance needs to be regularly validated against actual risk distributions to ascertain if there are any differences in ranking of the MLS cells over time based on loan performance. The Hosmer-Lemeshow chi-square test can be used to test how well the predicted probability of default (PD) matches the actual PD. The *predicted* PD determines a handle cell relative rank in terms of default risk, while the *actual* PD can be represented with cell rank in terms of default frequency for that cell. The difference between the predicted rank and the actual rank of a handle cell represents the *residual* that can be used to measure the model performance. Sensitivity of handle cell ranking to different thresholds can be assessed for impact on model performance. For example, mean square error (MSE) can be calculated to measure potential model performance based on the difference between the observed risk and the predicted risk for each set of thresholds. In this way, proposed changes to credit policy can be evaluated to identify specific borrower segments impacted and gauge the resulting effect on portfolio risk.

Model performance also needs to be validated against the actual frequency distributions for good, bad, and rejected credit applicants to determine whether or not the three individual structural models and the combined total applicant (known plus unknown) model still each apply. This is because models may rank order risk the same, but the magnitude of the estimated loan approvals, or loan losses, may shift over time. One scheme to accomplish this would be to use the development sample for specification of the low order interactions and fit a saturated model based on actual cumulative distributions acquired since model deployment. These cumulative distributions may be gathered at periodic intervals, to identify and measure any differences in the higher order effects. You may use the log-likelihood test statistic $G^2 = -2 * \sum_i x_i * \ln (m_i/x_i)$, where the validation sample counts are the x_i and the model estimated counts are the m_i. By expanding the expression $G^2 = 2 * \sum_i x_i * \ln (x_i) - 2 * \sum_i x_i * \ln (m_i)$, you find that the first quantity is purely a function of the validation counts, while the second is the kernel of the log-likelihood based on the development sample. G^2 measures the goodness of fit between the model and the actual (post-model deployment) observed frequency distributions of good, bad, and rejected applicants relative to the MLS. Furthermore, the likelihood ratio statistic has the nice property that it can be broken down conditionally to test for each individual effect in the model. In symbolic form, this partitioning of the statistic takes the form $G^2(2) = G^2[(2)|(1)] + G^2(1)$, where model (2) contains a subset of the u-terms in model (1) (i.e., they are nested), and $G^2[(2)|(1)]$ represents the conditional log-likelihood ratio statistic for model (2) given model (1). Further, if $G^2(2)$ and $G^2(1)$ are asymptotically distributed as χ^2 with ν_1 and ν_2 degrees of freedom, respectively, then $G^2[(2)|(1)]$ is asymptotically distributed as χ^2 with $(\nu_2 - \nu_1)$ degrees of freedom.

Another aspect of validation is to compare system performance for different consumer segments. For example, the internal cells could be based upon nonmainstream borrowers, while the margins may reflect mainstream borrowers. If alternative data variables are used for nonmainstream borrowers and there is insufficient performance data on the nontraditional applicants, then this type of scheme can be useful to assess the relative performance of alternative scorecards. To deal with missing data (typically there are insufficient nonmainstream bads to sample), then a combination of using "similarly situated mainstream bad observations" (e.g., with respect to the MLS structure), we can use the following procedure for removing sampling zeros:

- Fit a model "loosely" to the nontraditional data, augmenting with mainstream observations as needed.
- Use the fitted values obtained in Step 1 i.e., $\{y_{ijklm}\}$ (e.g., in a five-dimensional case) to estimate the prior probabilities $\{\lambda_{ijklm}\}$ via the equation $\lambda_{ijklm} = (y_{ijklm} / n)$ where n = sample size. (In order to make the discussion more general, let "θ" denote a subscript set of arbitrary size—in this example so far $\theta = \{i,j,k,l,m\}$).

- Compute the weighting factor:

$$\hat{w} = \frac{n^2 - \sum_\theta x_\theta^2}{\sum_\theta (x_\theta - n\lambda_\theta)^2} \tag{8.1}$$

Where the x_θ's are the observed cell counts.
- Compute the cell estimates:

$$m_\theta^* = np_\theta^* = \frac{n}{n + \hat{w}}(X_\theta + \hat{w}\lambda_\theta) \tag{8.2}$$

- Calculate G^2 to compare performance of the model on the non-mainstream borrower group[65] using the estimated frequencies as well as cell counts, that is, both p_θ^*, and m_θ^* .

Validation of Model Results from Compliance Risk Perspective

Protected class status in the MLS cells is known for HMDA reportable loans. The entire handle distribution can be compared between protected class and their nonprotected class counterparts via a log-likelihood test statistic $G^2 = -2 * \sum_i x_i * \ln(m_i/x_i)$.[66] Significant differences point to factors that can explain disparate impact patterns. It is a straightforward exercise to examine acceptee population mix or acceptance rates for each individual protected group, with respect to the MLS, and any subset, or cross combination of dimensions, that make it up. For example, a significant result may lead to the identification of two three-way patterns and three two-way patterns of interaction that account for a difference in loan originations for a particular group, such as African-American credit applicants, relative to their white non-Hispanic counterparts (control group). Finally, one can measure the impact of proposed policy threshold changes on fair lending performance. This is accomplished by varying the threshold amounts within pre-specified ranges and then measuring how the handle distribution changes for individual groups using a chi-square statistic. Outcomes can be decisioned with the updated action tables and the corresponding multidimensional acceptance rate tables can be generated and compared to find specific multiway interaction differences relative to the control group.

Model Processing Validation

As described in Chapter 6, hybrid models utilize an efficient model consensus session (MCS) method to control and manage model specifications. MCS determines which primary and secondary factors to include in the model, the conditions when to include secondary factors, and the interactions between or among them. The MCS process can be used to validate model processing. Figure 8.15 describes how this process is accomplished.

Model Development

In the model development process, variable selection is governed by business reality. Credit experts possessing deep knowledge of industry and secondary market models, and also specific experience with the lending institution in question, form a consensus view in an MCS on primary and secondary model variables. Hence, variables that do not affect underwriting, or pricing, decisions are not included in the models. In contrast to a pure data-driven approach as described in an earlier section, this is the application of MCS to developing the hybrid models.[67]

---

65. See Bishop, Fienberg, and Holland, 1975, pp. 401–402.
66. As described in Chapter 6, this statistic has advantages over other common statistics such as chi-square test.
67. In theory, the hybrid approach could be used without a model consensus session (MCS), but that is not the approach the book advocates. In the absence of a complete MCS, there are numerous procedures that can be

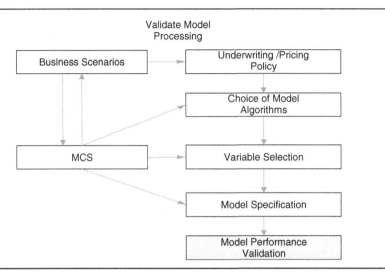

Validate Model Processing

Business Scenarios → Underwriting /Pricing Policy → Choice of Model Algorithms → Variable Selection → Model Specification → Model Performance Validation

MCS

FIGURE 8.15 MODEL DEVELOPMENT VALIDATION PROCESS

- *Model usage.* Credit risk models are developed based on certain assumptions, such as assumptions about the model usage and possible adaptability for other purposes. For example, the model is developed for credit underwriting based on data from a particular region and then is applied to a different region with a different approval threshold, or perhaps is used to estimate probability of default at the account, rather than segment, level for portfolio loss forecasting.
- *Variable categorization.* For a hybrid model, this categorization process is largely determined by credit policy guidelines and the MCS described in Chapter 6. Hybrid models can also be tested for the significance of individual interactions by successively fitting nested models that differ only in one term, namely the interaction of interest. The statistical significance of the individual interaction term can be determined. Variable interactions and thresholds are determined differently based on the type of model.
- *Primary variables.* Key variables are classified as primary variables, and they are selected so that each of them measures the unique characteristics of the credit data. For example, credit history (captures past willingness and ability to pay obligations as agreed), loan-to-value ratio (LTV) (provides borrower capital and collateral value considerations), debt-to-income ratio (DTI) (provides borrower capacity and indebtedness information), and so on.
- *Secondary variables.* Other variables are classified into secondary factors. Some of the secondary variables (e.g., payment shock[68] in mortgage lending) may potentially measure the similar things as some of the primary variables (e.g., debt ratio or payment-to-income ratio) and therefore may be correlated with them. However, a secondary variable only

---

used as mentioned previously for scorecard development. In addition, there is a procedure based upon a Kullback Divergence Statistic (Goldstein and Dillion, 1978) that determines the incremental contribution of newly entering variables in light of variables already included in the model. And another procedure by Lachin and Schachter (1974), which performs stepwise selection and requires minimum probabilities to be specified for the addition of a variable or deletion of a variable already selected. Both of these procedures were used to produce the examples of hybrid models appearing in this chapter and in Chapter 6. See Lachin, John M., and J. Schachter. "On Stepwise Discriminant Analysis to Credit Scoring," *Psychophysiology*, Vol. 11, No. 6, 1974, pp. 703–709, and Goldstein, Matthew, and William R. Dillion. *Discrete Discriminant Analysis*. John Wiley & Sons, 1978, pp. 83–86.

68. Payment shock is defined as the ratio of the new housing payment to the current housing payment, expressed as a percent. Typically, a high payment shock is any percentage greater than 125 percent.

comes into play when the primary variables are weak or missing. This further reduces the effects of collinearity.

- *Model specifications.* The variable selection process, governed by business reality, makes validation of model specifications straightforward. As discussed in Chapter 5, in regression analysis, model misspecifications are often related to collinearity, which occurs when two or more input variables are strongly correlated. Collinearity can inflate the variances of the parameter estimates when the analysis involves small and moderate sample sizes. Collinearity may also result in wrong signs and magnitudes of regression coefficient estimates, and consequently in incorrect conclusions about relationships between independent and dependent variables. To deal with collinearity, one needs to identify the causes and remove the effects.[69] There are many remedial methods available for this process, such as Bayesian techniques, robust estimation, and principal component analysis. The MCS approach minimizes model misspecifications and reduces the impact of collinearity by incorporating judgmental elements to create and use new variables. In some circumstances, new variables are created to capture the interaction and conditions between/among input variables. In some instances, neither of the variables in question appears in the model. For example, a new interaction variable can be created to capture the degree of risk that is jointly determined by a primary factor and secondary factor. For example, in our direct auto loan example in Figure 6.60, we could define a variable that has a value of one if the term of the loan is grater than 60 months and the vehicle is used, and zero otherwise. That interaction variable could be included in the handle without including either loan term or age of vehicle.

- *Reject inference.* In cases where the prevailing system is not a hybrid system, an MCS is very beneficial. It enables the development of a handle, or segmentation. Using the handle, reject inference can be more effectively addressed via application of the DCP approach to capture the approve/decline mechanism, coupled with the use of the handle to view homogeneous risk groups to assign rejected applicants to good and bad performance groups. If the prevailing system is a hybrid system, there is no data to base reject inference on, with the possible exception of overrides. It is suggested that customer segments that are close in proximity to the minimum acceptable credit risk be selected on a random basis for controlled experimentation to determine if there is opportunity to open up additional segments for credit under possibly different terms and pricing to compensate for additional risk.

Model Selection

This involves selection process and appropriate selection criteria as discussed below:

- *Selection process.* Once the model is constructed and tested, there may be opportunities for refinement where data provide some more detailed insight into the strength and interplay of model variables. With the hybrid approach, model selection is largely performed in the MCS, while with a nonhybrid model, the MCS needs to be performed prior to model selection. Any changes to specification relating to the choice of primary and secondary factors would need to be validated via a follow-up with MCS participants. This is true for modeling the current approve/decline decision, as well as for improving good/bad performance

---

69. For a detailed discussion of collinearity diagnostics and remedial methods, see Belsley, David A. Edwin Kuh, and Roy E. Welsch, *Regression Diagnostics: Identifying Influential Data and Sources of Collinearity*. John Wiley & Sons, 1980, pp. 192–242. Also, statistical regression procedures are available in widely used statistical program packages such as SAS procedures REG, ROBUSTREG, or ENTROPY *SAS/STAT User's Guide*, SAS Institute Inc., 2003 Cary, NC, USA.

prediction. For example, even if the color of a car were available and predictive of performance (say owners of red cars tended to default at greater rates than owners of cars painted other colors), a model having the color of the auto as a predictor variable would not be used, because it does not bear any linkage to a borrower's ability or willingness to repay the loan.

- *Selection criteria.* There are various criteria that are used in practice. For hybrid models, the MCS determines the primary and secondary model variables, their conditional structure, and how they interact within various segments. The remaining work is one of quantification of the MCS specified model. Naturally, a typical measure of predictive validity is the misclassification error rate for goods and bads. An aspect of the quantification of the MCS model is the detail around how to assess and quantify the specified interactions among the MCS primary and secondary variables. In the case of the primary variables, one must fit models to the sampled data to construct structural models for good, bad, and reject applicant populations. This entails the use of a statistic that is asymptotically distributed as a central chi-square (χ^2).

For illustration purpose, we provide an example for hybrid models. The appropriate measure of goodness of fit of the model here is the likelihood-ratio statistic $G^2 = -2 * \sum_i x_i * \ln (m_i/x_i)$[70] with the number of degrees of freedom appropriate to the set of m_i, where x_i are the observed values in the ith cell, and the m_i are the maximum likelihood estimates, or the fitted values in the ith cell. We draw upon the example appearing in Chapter 6 for the selection of a structural model for the bad risk population. Results from a high-dimensional parameterization of the sampled data indicated the following model would be appropriate for an initial hypothesis as to the structure of the bad risks:

$$\ln(m^B_{ijklmn}) = U + U_{2356}(jkmn) + U_{123}(ijk) + U_4(l) \tag{8.3}$$

The value of the likelihood ratio statistic was 20.3295. Next, three other models were tested with the following results:

Effects Present	Net Gain	Alpha Level
235, 236, 256, 356, 123, 4	7.0999	0.3720
235, 256, 123, 4	2.9457	0.4303
236, 123, 35, 4	3.6236	0.0112

The simplest model that does not exclude terms found to be significant was found to be:

$$\ln(m^B_{ijklmn}) = U + U_{236}(jkn) + U_{256}(jmn) + U_{123}(ijk) + U_4(l) \tag{8.4}$$

This example shows that the MCS can reveal what variables are of primary importance. The fitting of a structural model is an exercise to capture important interactions between those predictor variables so that the most powerful and reliable risk estimates for loan performance can be derived.[71] This process was discussed in detail in Chapter 6's Hybrid System Construction.

---

70. Log-ratio statistic approximately follows a chi-square distribution and is widely used to determine if the difference in likelihood scores among the two models is statistically significant.
71. As mentioned in Chapter 5, resampling methods such as jackknife and bootstrap can be used to select the model with more consistent and reliable model estimation.

Model Validation and Override Analysis

There are various situations where legitimate credit exceptions are made based upon additional information outside of the model's credit risk boundaries. It is generally acknowledged that some system overrides are unavoidable. We previously examined the impact of overrides, which, like validation, need to be considered from both credit risk and compliance perspectives. In Chapter 6 we introduced loan override analysis process and how the hybrid system construction can be used to improve that process. In this section we describe how the results of override analysis can be incorporated into the model validation process. In particular, we discuss the implications of override analysis results on both model performance and compliance risk.

Override analysis is performed in conjunction with credit-scored loans. We note that the identical concerns relative to potential discriminatory aspects of particular scorecards characteristics also apply to override criteria. For example, overriding a credit scoring decision based upon whether or not someone had a phone in their name would be a violation of Equal Credit Opportunity Act (ECOA).[72] Finance company reference is another characteristic that may have greater correlation with inner city populations that, because of where they live, they have less access to bank branches than they do to subprime lenders. Those areas are most likely low-income areas and often have a high percentage of minority households. Hence, override factors that appear to have a significant negative impact on a protected class of credit applicants should be fully assessed, and alternative factors should be sought that have predictive power, but are nondiscriminatory in nature.

In theory, disparate treatment risk cannot be eliminated by using a credit scoring system. The risk is twofold. First is the risk that the scoring system itself is discriminatory, that is, similarly qualified borrowers who fall into protected versus nonprotected classes may score lower because one or more scoring factors has a biased estimate of their creditworthiness. Under the effects test of the ECOA, a plaintiff can win the case for discrimination if it can be demonstrated that another scoring system exists which is equally predictive of creditworthiness and treats the protected classes more favorably than the system in question.[73] The second type of risk associated with credit scoring systems is when individual subjective judgment occurs, as in the case of system overrides. As long as human judgment is a factor, the possibility for discrimination against a protected class of applicants exists. The focus of fair lending compliance testing in this chapter is on the second potential source of risk, namely the scoring system override process.

As is the case for overage/underage analysis for mortgage loans, rigorous monitoring requires the ability to perform statistical tests to determine if the incidence of overrides differs significantly for various protected classes of borrowers when compared with the control group. Consider the following home improvement loan underwriting, where the treatment group is comprised of African-American applicants and white non-Hispanic applicants make up the control group. Suppose that the lender's credit policy requires that low-side overrides be held to 5 percent or less, while high-side overrides must be maintained below a ten percent threshold. The example in Figure 8.16 appears to be within compliance guidelines for the home improvement scorecard when reviewed by credit policy risk management. However, from a fair lending compliance view, the situation is clearly in need of further analysis.

In this example, the mix of high- and low-side overrides is skewed in both instances in favor of the control group. These data are sufficient to assert that the override process has a disparate impact on African-American applicants for home improvement loans, for the period in question.

---

72. See Hsia, David, "Credit Scoring and the Equal Credit Opportunity Act," *Hastings Law Journal*, Vol. 30, No. 2, September 1978, pp. 418–422.
73. Ibid., p. 418.

Override Type/Group	Number	Percent
Low-side		
• Control group	390	6
• Treatment group	105	3
Total LSOs	495	5
High-side		
• Control group	520	8
• Treatment group	420	12
Total HSOs	940	9
Nonoverrides		
• Control group	5,590	86
• Treatment group	2,975	85
Total nonoverrides	8,565	86
Total applications	10,000	100
• Control group	6,500	65
• Treatment group	3,500	35

FIGURE 8.16 HOME IMPROVEMENT SCORECARD OVERRIDE MONITORING SUMMARY FOR 3Q2006

In order to further assert that the override process had a disparate treatment effect, one needs to show that the credit applicants in the control and treatment groups possessed similar qualifications relative to the lender's prevailing underwriting standards. Certainly, the fact that both groups have been credit scored means that the applicants in question in each group have been put in the same bucket relative to the score cutoff, but we do not know how they may differ relative to policy override factors.

In the case where a hybrid model is constructed, overrides fall into handle cells, and they can be analyzed in relation to their segment counterparts. Within that context, one can compare the distribution differences between protected classes and control group using the likelihood ratio statistic (G^2). For groups having a significant difference, the individual handle cells can be examined to determine why protected and non-protected class credit applicants would have different override rates. In the case where a hybrid model does not exist, traditional predictive modeling[74] is used to identify possible contributing factors.

Credit and Compliance Optimization Process

This section discusses how an optimization process might be integrated into validation process to balance credit and compliance risk objectives. This process is depicted in Figure 8.17. The formulation of the mathematical programming problem is important, and care must be taken to specify the objective(s) and all applicable constraints. In general we can start with a simple linear programming formulation that can yield acceptable results. Using a champion/challenger approach, different problem formulations and solution algorithms are tested and the one with the most useful solutions is adopted as a champion that is later subjected to challenges from an

---

74. This includes classification trees (chi-square automatic interaction detection, classification and regression trees, etc.), logistic regression, or neural network.

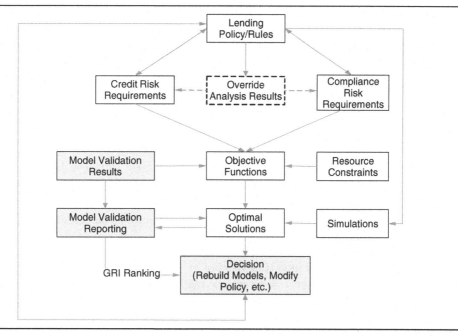

FIGURE 8.17 CREDIT AND COMPLIANCE OPTIMIZATION PROCESS (CCOP)

evolution of competing methods and more sophisticated problem formulations. The standard form of a linear programming (LP) problem is:

$$\text{Maximize } d + c^T x \tag{8.5}$$
$$\text{Such that } Ax \leq b, \ x \geq 0,$$

where

 d = a constant term

 x = an n-column vector corresponding to n decision variables, c = an n-row vector of objective function coefficients corresponding to the decision variables,

 A = an m-by-n matrix whose rows correspond to problem constraints and that specifies coefficients for every decision variable within every constraint row,

 b = an m-column vector corresponding to bounds associated with the individual row constraints.[75]

We proceed to describe some problem formulation aspects for the optimization of credit risk and fair lending compliance.

One can leverage the connection between risk management and compliance by integrating and optimizing their respective models. The dual objective is to maximize model predictability for "good versus bad" performance and to minimize disparate impact on all protected classes, subject to a set of constraints that encompass line of business, regulatory, credit risk, portfolio and resource limitations.[76] The outputs from this optimization process can be used to balance the trade-offs between compliance risk and credit risk and make decision on model rebuilding

75. Sakarovitch, M. *Notes on Linear Programming*. Van Nostrand Reinhold Company, 1971, p. 18.

76. With careful selection of relevant constraints, this optimization process can be easily implemented with linear programming methods. See *SAS/OR 9.1 User's Guide: Mathematical Programming*, 2002, SAS Institute Inc., Cary, NC, USA. pp. 207–328.

according to available resources.[77] In practice, a single objective function may be adopted, with the second objective expressed as a series of constraints.[78] An example of a specific instance of validation optimization for loan approval would be to maximize separation of good and bad default risk distributions subject to restricting the difference between protected class i and the corresponding nonprotected class, denial rates, for similarly situated credit applicants in handle cell j, to be less than ε_{ij} percent and constraints that encompass line of business, regulatory, and portfolio limitations. (e.g., not exceed certain thresholds).

Establish Decision Variables: $X_{ijklmnopqr}$

The first step, which is nontrivial, is to define the set of decision variables, denoted as "x." Their interpretation is based on the values of subscript patterns, where the subscripts are defined to denote key business parameters for the optimization problem, for example:

i. Protected class membership indicator: separate range of numbers for treatment groups and control groups

j. Handle cell number (identifies the segment)

k. Portfolio strategy/action table number

l. Variable type, where $1 =$ acceptance rate, $2 =$ default rate, $3 =$ acceptee population mix, $4 =$ total population frequency, $5 =$ expected total population frequency, $6 =$ observed counts, $7 =$ expected counts, $8 =$ market penetration, ...

m. Market identifier (e.g., MSA, state, etc.)

n. Channel identifier

o. Legal entity/line of business

p. Loan purpose/product/program identifier

q. Scenario identifier—where scenarios may be probability weighted

r. Time (e.g., quarter/year identification, etc.)

This example is an illustration of more of a "general case" along with the types of decision variable dimensions that may be desired or required. How many subscripts are needed, and which among them, or possibly others, should be used, depends on the problem definition. This will vary by lending institution.

It is suggested that before embarking on the development of a comprehensive model, an initial simplified model be developed that can be incrementally enhanced in an orderly and systematic fashion. As subscripts are added to the decision variables, the values they are allowed to take on should be restricted to just two or three for initial experimentation. A very important consideration is when to add a subscript, versus segmenting the data and building separate models for each segment. There is no general rule that applies, and this is where controlled experimentation can be used to determine the most advantageous approach.

Establish Objective Functions

For each individual candidate model, we compute optimal thresholds, which, in turn, determine the total number of conditional or interaction variables as covariate patterns that minimize X^2, the Pearson chi-square statistic. The objective function is to identify the optimal policy thresholds

---

77. The trade-offs and relationship between model risk and compliance risk can be described in a quadrant plot similar to Figure 3.15, and an example will be provided at a later section of the chapter.

78. There are techniques, such as goal programming, that allow for optimization of multiple objective functions. See Schniederjans, Marc J., *Goal Programming: Methodology and Applications*, Springer, 1995, pp. 21–42 for goal programming model formulation details. For the sake of illustration, we have opted to maintain a more simplified approach and methodology.

that maximize credit access, subject to credit default, and other constraints.[79] A formulation of the problem may express the objective function as minimizing deviance of strategy from expected outcome, relative to all parameters described above. Here we may use the chi-square form to minimize the deviance between the observed and expected handle cell frequencies:

$$\text{Minimize } X^2 = \Sigma\{(x_{ijk4mnopqr} - X_{ijk5mnopqr})^2/(X_{ijk5mnopqr})\}, \tag{8.6}$$

where the subscripts *ijklmnopqr* are defined as previously indicated. This formulation can be modified to allow for an LP approach. One option would be to use an alternative risk measure as an objective function, or to reformulate the problem with appropriate risk constraints, where X^2 is replaced with an alternative measure, such as mean absolute deviation (MAD). MAD is defined as the sum of the absolute deviations of the observed and fitted values over all handle cells. This translates to the following general form of the objective function[80]:

$$\text{Minimize MAD}(x_{ijklmnopqr}) = \sum_{i} \cdots \sum_{r} |x_{ijklmnopqr} - x_{ijklmnopqr}| \tag{8.7}$$

The objective function can be expanded to consider additional model performance factors. For example, you could maximize the predictive ability as measured by the development sample results, plus the ability to satisfactorily replicate as measured by the validation sample, plus the stability of the models as measured by the variation of policy thresholds and other model givens. As was the case with the dual objective associated with compliance (credit access) these additional objectives can be addressed as model constraints or as post-optimality exercises to check the sensitivity of an optimal solution to these additional considerations.[81] Another alternative would be to address these aspects as part of the model reporting and ranging process using UPI that is described at the beginning of the next section.

Identify Constraints

There are various constraints[82] that need to be considered when maximizing model performance (or, equivalently, minimize error rate), and some examples are:

- *Compliance constraints.* Recall from Chapter 6 that there is a range of possible action tables associated with a hybrid model. In this example, there is a separate overall acceptance rate, and an associated set of acceptance rates for subgroups of credit applicants, for each choice of a risk index cutoff point. In evaluating a particular model validation, a range of "c" alternative hybrid model action tables is included, with associated values, as input to the optimization model. A primary focus of the optimization model relates to matched-pair logic, since the constraints on similarly situated applicants are directly impacted. For example, there is some guidance on a maximum absolute difference in incomes or loan amounts to be eight percent, in addition to other matching criteria, such as

79. Alternatively, one can minimize the summary of the Pearson residuals between the observed and fitted values, error rate, Gini coefficient, model lift, KS statistic can also be used in setting objective functions.
80. In practice, the modeler must remove the absolute value signs to create a problem formulation that the optimization routine can effectively solve. There are different options on how to accomplish this that have varying impacts on the number of rows and columns in the model.
81. For details on how to conduct sensitivity analysis of changing inputs on the optimal solutions, see, for example, Fang, Shu-Cherng, and Sarat Puthenpura, *Linear Optimization and Extentions—Theory and Algorithms*, Prentice-Hall, Inc., 1993, pp. 78–86. See also *SAS/OR ® 9.1 User's Guide: Mathematical Programming*, 2002, SAS Institute Inc., Cary, NC, USA, pp. 258–261.
82. We provide several categories of examples but some other categories may be included, such as model testing-related constraints. These relate to model stability and fit and we omit the details here due to our primary focus on validation linkage to the credit and compliance risk aspects of model formulation.

similar product, same market, similar time of application, and so on.[83] The mathematical representation of these constraints would resemble the following set of inequalities:

$$x_{Tjkl} - x_{Cjkl} \leq \varepsilon_{ijkl},$$

where $i = T$ denotes treatment group and $i = C$ denotes the control group and i ranges over the number of treatment groups, say 1 to n_T and control groups, say 1 to n_C; $j = 1, \ldots m$; $k = 1, \ldots, c$; $l = 1$ signifies variable type is acceptance rate where $n = n_T + n_C$ is the number of identifiable protected classes and control groups (relative to race, ethnicity, gender for HMDA data), m is the number of distinct handle cells in the hybrid model, c is the number of alternative risk index cut-off strategies, x_{ijkl} and x_{ijkl} represent the ith protected class, and nonprotected class, acceptance rates for the jth handle cell in the kth action table associated with the hybrid model, and ε_{ijk} represents the upper bound on the difference between acceptance rates for protected class i falling within the handle cell j, associated with action table k. In the event more granularity is desired for the definition of similarly situated borrowers than is afforded by the handle, then the subscript "j" can be defined to denote the "similarly situated group j."

- *Credit risk constraints.* Consider a range of possible action tables associated with a hybrid model. There is a separate overall default rate, and an associated set of default rates for subgroups of credit applicants, independent of the choice of a risk index cutoff point. In evaluating a particular model validation, a range of "c" alternative hybrid model action tables is included, with associated values, as input to the optimization model. A primary focus of the optimization model relates to achieving a desired overall risk/return target, which translates to selection of handle cells having default rates in an acceptable range. Furthermore, in this case we want to ignore protected class status as we compare default rates for alternative action table-based strategies. The mathematical representation of these constraints would resemble the following set of inequalities:

$$x_{+jk2} \leq \delta_{jk2}, \quad j = 1, \ldots m, k = 1, \ldots, c;$$

$l = 2$ signifies variable type is default rate

where m is the number of distinct handle cells in the hybrid model, c is the number of alternative risk index cutoff strategies, $x + jk2$ represents the default rate for the jth handle cell in the kth action table associated with the hybrid model, and δjk represents the upper bound on the default rate for handle cell j associated with action table k. There may be other credit constraints that relate to the dimensions making up the handle cell index (e.g., LTV). In that case, the number of high LTV loans could be constrained by number, or frequency, by collapsing the handle on all but the LTV dimension (i.e., by summing the $x_{ijklmnopqr}$'s over the appropriate values of the handle cell subscript "j" and specifying the bound for the right-hand side of the constraint inequality).

- *Business constraints.* Different lines of business have different loan policies and restrictions. Successive optimizations may be run on alternative models that can be created by varying the predetermined policy thresholds for each of the credit model predictors. Results can be examined to gauge the sensitivity of validation optimization to how the credit risk model variables are categorized or the sensitivity to policy thresholds for various loan products and programs. In the event models are evaluated for deployment across lines of businesses, then there may be an additional set of conditions and an additional line of business subscript to allow for any restrictions that may apply.

---

83. See Avery, Robert B., Patricia E. Beeson, and Paul S. Calem. "Using HMDA Data as a Regulatory Screen for Fair Lending Compliance," *Journal of Financial Services Research*, Vol. 11, February/April 1997, pp. 19–37.

- *Portfolio constraints.* The most common example of a portfolio constraint would relate to concentrations. For example, if there was a geographic concentration restriction on particular market areas and one or more of the validation models was superior because of higher potential acceptance rates that included those areas, then higher achievable acceptance rates for a protected class relative to similarly situated borrowers may not be possible because it would trigger a portfolio concentration exception to policy. Constraints could be added to avoid selecting models that will exceed concentration limits for the portfolio. The same example would hold for small business lending, where we might be considering industry concentrations. Most lenders restrict the dollar ratio of loans in a particular industry that are outstanding to Tier 1 capital (plus allowance for loan and lease losses). For example, a bank may not want more than a 15 percent ratio for convenience store loans, church loans, start-up companies (independent of sector), and so on. In small business lending the modeler could substitute low/moderate income borrowers or business locations for protected class designations, and the corresponding middle-/high-income bracket for nonprotected-class designations.

Optimal Solutions

A linear programming (or other mathematical programming) formulation of this dual objective problem may not yield an optimal solution that sufficiently addresses all of the various aspects relative to credit and compliance concerns. This case may prove to be the rule, rather than the exception. In these circumstances, an improved solution may be developed using alternative approaches. One such example might be scenario simulations that are created based on business objectives and constraints, as described above, where certain problem parameters are allowed to vary within proscribed ranges. In any event, compliance regulations, examination guidance, corporate credit and compliance policies, and sound business judgment should be used to select the best models that balance the trade-offs between compliance risk and credit risk.

Model Validation Reporting Using UPI Methodology

Model management is an extension of model validation process. It provides an environment to effectively validate and update models. As the number of models increase, model management plays a significant role in monitoring, interpreting, maintaining, and reporting model validation results.

When validating a model, it is critical to determine what the model is validated against. Many different metrics can be used for this purpose. The main idea here is to show how model performance is measured against expectations and benchmarks, which can be defined with a set of disparity indices as described in Chapter 5. The entire process is depicted in Figure 8.18.

Previously we have described validation input data and performance metrics. The first step is to create performance indices that involve defining disparity indices. Recall from Chapter 3 that a disparity index is defined as the actual performance measure relative to its expected performance measure. The actual model performance measure will appear in either the numerator, or denominator, of the index depending upon the nature of the index. Indices that measure positive aspects of model performance, such as stability, have the actual model performance measure positioned in the numerator. Indices that measure negative aspects of model performance, such as model lift decay,[84] have the actual model performance measure positioned in the denominator. Examples of those indices include:

---

84. There are various indices that can be used to track model performance degradation. For example, SAS Model Manager includes model decay lift as one of the indicators for the purpose of validating production models.

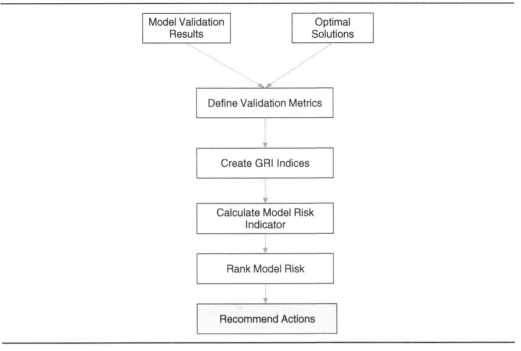

FIGURE 8.18   UPI METHODOLOGY FOR MODEL VALIDATION REPORTING

- Model performance residual index (MRI) is the difference between the actual risk profile and predicted risk distribution of the champion, or benchmark, model relative to the difference between the actual risk profile and predicted risk distribution for the challenger model. Values in excess of one indicate the challenger model is a closer fit to the actual data.

$$\text{MRI} = \chi^2_{\text{champion}} / \chi^2_{\text{challenger}}$$

- Model lift decay index (MLI) measures the change in model lift for the champion model relative to the champion model.[85] Values in excess of one indicate the challenger model possesses superior predictive strength.

$$\text{MLI} = G_{\text{challenger}} / G_{\text{champion}},$$

where G denotes the Gini coefficient defined in Figure 8.4.

- Model stability index (MSI) measures the ability of the challenger model to rank order segments over time relative to that for the champion, or benchmark, model. Instability in ordering would suggest that the model is not capturing the underlying and relatively constant information about the risk of different credits. Values in excess of one indicate the challenger model possesses superior stability.

$$\text{MSI} = T_{\text{champion}} / T_{\text{challenger}},$$

---

85. Model decay is a serious challenge faced by organizations and can be measured with changes in model lift overtime. See Chu, Dulling, and Thompson, 2007.

where T denotes the Wilcoxon signed rank test statistic[86] calculated for every handle cell based on the corresponding risk index value that is measured at the same two points in time for both challenger and champion models. In the case where multiple points in time are to be considered, the Friedman rank test[87] can be substituted for the Wilcoxon signed rank test.

- Model usage index (MUI) is the ratio of the utilization rates for the challenger and champion models, respectively. Values in excess of one indicate the challenger model is more highly utilized than the benchmark champion model.

$$\text{Usage Rate}_{\text{challenger}} = \text{number of usage instances for challenger model/} \\ \text{number of usage instances for all models}$$

$$\text{Usage Rate}_{\text{champion}} = \text{number of usage instances for champion model/} \\ \text{number of usage instances for all models}$$

$$\text{MUI} = \text{Usage Rate}_{\text{challenger}}/\text{Usage Rate}_{\text{champion}}$$

- Model aging index (MAI) is the ratio of the utilization rates for the champion and challenger models, respectively. Values in excess of one indicate the challenger model is newer than the benchmark champion model.

$$\text{Aging Rate}_{\text{challenger}} = \text{time since last rebuild for challenger model/} \\ \text{average time since last rebuild for all models}$$

$$\text{Aging Rate}_{\text{champion}} = \text{time since last rebuild for champion model/} \\ \text{average time since last rebuild for all models}$$

$$\text{MAI} = \text{Aging Rate}_{\text{champion}}/\text{Aging Rate}_{\text{challenger}}$$

- Model profitability index (MPRI) is the ratio of the difference in expected profit and actual profit over all segments in the hybrid model for the champion and challenger models, respectively. Values in excess of one indicate the challenger model is tracking closer to profitability targets than the benchmark champion model. The chi-square statistic is computed on the actual versus expected profit in each handle cell. This measure should not be confused with assessing which model is more profitable. Positive and negative variations have the same weight in the calculation.

$$\text{MPRI} = \chi^2_{\text{champion}}/\chi^2_{\text{challenger}}$$

The next step is to calculate risk indicator values for each individual model. Each model has values for both credit risk and compliance risk. This process was outlined in Chapter 3, where the set of performance disparity indices, based on our model evaluation criteria, are applied. We can further categorize these model risk indicator values into quadrants, using the reference lines based on predefined index values as shown in Figure 8.19.[88] The four quadrants are:

---

86. Wilcoxon signed rank test is a nonparametric alternative to the t test when the normal distribution assumption is not satisfied, and this test is available in the SAS UNIVARIATE procedure. For more details, see Conover W. J., *Practical Nonparametric Statistics*, 3rd ed. John Wiley & Sons, 1999, pp. 352–360. See also Hollander, M., and D. A. Wolfe. *Nonparametric Statistical Methods*, 2nd ed., John Wiley & Sons, 1973, pp. 26–33.
87. The Friedman rank test can have more test power when there are six or more points in time (or treatments). See Conover, 1999, pp. 367–368.
88. This can be determined by institution specific compliance or performance requirements. The validation optimization described in the previous section can be used to enhance the outcome.

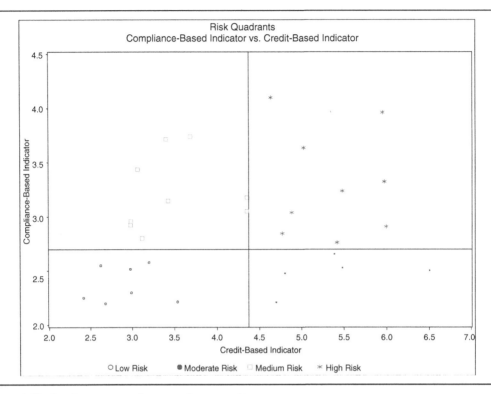

FIGURE 8.19   RISK QUADRANTS FOR CREDIT AND COMPLIANCE MODELS

1. *High-risk quadrant.* High credit disparity and high compliance disparity. Models in this quadrant are underperformers compared with the norm in sustainable credit risk predictive power and also exhibit relatively high disparate impact for similarly situated credit applicants (i.e., applicants in the same handle in a hybrid model).
2. *Medium-risk quadrant.* High credit disparity and low compliance disparity. Models in this quadrant are under-performers compared with the norm in sustainable credit risk predictive power, but are average or have relatively low disparate impact for similarly situated credit applicants.
3. *Moderate- or low-risk quadrant.* Low credit disparity and high compliance disparity. Models in this quadrant are average or better compared with the norm in sustainable credit risk predictive power and also exhibit relatively high disparate impact for similarly situated credit applicants (i.e., applicants in the same handle in a hybrid model).
4. *Low- or no-risk quadrant.* Low credit disparity and low compliance disparity. Models in this quadrant are average or better compared with the norm in sustainable credit risk predictive power and are average, or have relatively low, disparate impact for similarly situated credit applicants.

The final step is to calculate the total model risk indicators. The total risk indicator is used to measure and rank order model total risk. Figure 8.20 is an example of using several typical indices to create model risk indicator across different models.

Model Number	Model Lift Decay Index	Model Performance Index	Model Profitability Index	Model Stability Index	Risk Indicator
97	3	9	1	0.15	5.8012
99	2	6	3	0.08	5.1576
70	1	10	0	0.32	4.9298
46	1	9	3	0.83	4.9196
48	1	10	1	0.4	4.637
86	3	0.2	3	0.87	4.5554
96	2	2.5	3	0.32	4.3998
100	3	1	0	0.11	4.3578
91	3	0.33	2	0.52	4.2439
93	3	1.67	1	0.83	4.1068

FIGURE 8.20 EXAMPLE OF MODEL RISK INDICATOR RANKING

Interpreting Validation Results and the Model Update/Rebuild Decision

A proper interpretation of model validation results must consider sample size and sample selection method, which we previously covered in Chapter 2. Certainly, the output of model validation includes the final recommendation to do nothing, or adjust the model (if possible), rebuild the existing models, or implement an alternative model. This will depend on not only objective statistical criteria but also business needs, constraints, and regulatory requirements. This is due to the fact that a model's performance depends on multiple factors. For example, a model's performance is likely to be better in a stable economic environment than one that is more volatile or, worst case, chaotic. Therefore, it is important to balance evidence from a variety of metrics when building and evaluating models. It is also important to base a model re-build decision on an observation window of sufficient duration. In other words, a three-month window for assessing performance, rather than a one-month window, may prove to be desirable.

One of the central issues facing a lending institution is to ensure their loan underwriting process is sound and compliant with all applicable laws and regulations. The model optimization process can be used to achieve this objective and help make decisions around the necessity and timing of model retirement and redevelopment. The model optimization process we have described can be used to minimize model-related risk. There are many changes that occur over time that can impact model performance. Some of those changes occur due to the macro-economic cycle. As interest rates have risen, option priced and adjustable rate mortgage defaults have been repricing. This will cause the related application-time risk profiles of defaulted borrowers who may have acceptable risk profiles at the time of the mortgage application, to be associated with bad performance the next time a model is developed. At the same time, a new marketing push to penetrate into new markets, coupled with heightened competitive pressures, could cause a lender to penetrate deeper into the risk pool of applicants. As a result, the risk distribution of credit applicants coming through the door will experience significant shifts. The optimization process described responds to these circumstances by identifying when a model needs to be rebuilt, deciding the optimal time to rebuild the model, and determining the optimal number of models to rebuild.

We anticipate new generations of consumer credit models that will incorporate alternative data and a practical consideration is managing a persistent and increasing operational burden of model development, verification, testing, performance benchmarking, deployment, and retirement of traditional and alternative models. Model life cycle management will become even more of a focal point, with the imperative to ensure that models are constantly reevaluated and either updated, if possible, or replaced as soon as performance drops below a predetermined threshold.

SUMMARY

This chapter described an integrated model validation framework based on the methodologies described in the previous chapters. Those methodologies include the multilayered segmentation (MLS), dynamic conditional process (DCP), the hybrid models risk evaluation/policy formulation system (REPFS), and universal performance indicator (UPI). This validation framework integrates compliance validation components into the credit risk validation process to ensure that credit models appropriately balance risk and return while meeting compliance requirements. This balancing process can be formulized using the credit and compliance optimization process (CCOP). We defined model performance metrics that capture various aspects of model validation and dual objectives of credit and compliance risk management. We further used risk quadrants to examine the relation between credit risk and compliance risk to achieve the optimal balance relative to benchmark, or other, reference points. This framework also connects different model validation areas with a unified metric *handle* to simplify validation processing and enhance efficiency and interpretability. The framework supports Basel II model validation principles through effective integration of both quantitative and qualitative components, and by providing results that are highly actionable across different model areas and components.

While the framework and examples used for illustration have been mainly for consumer lending default risk models, the methodology can be applied in many other situations, such as creating risk tiers for loss forecasting and estimating default probabilities for risk rating categories used in commercial credit.

CLOSING OBSERVATIONS

A lot of ground has been covered in this book. During the course of our research, we have encountered many parallels between the worlds of compliance and credit risk management. Figure 8.21 provides a summary of elements of hybrid credit models, fair lending testing, and credit scoring, relative to analytical frameworks, but it is by no means exhaustive.

In general, hybrid models (leftmost column) provide an additional layer of transparency and connectedness between credit risk management (rightmost column) and compliance risk management (middle column).

The natural question may arise: "Why use a hybrid model for the under banked, when you could simply segment data and develop a scoring model using alternative data?" The answer is that for certain loan products, in certain geographies, there may not be sufficient data to develop a purely quantitative model. The hybrid model allows for an expert to determine primary factors and, when warranted, assign weights to variables in order to render a model capable of decisioning loans with limited available data. Because of the adaptive nature of the hybrid model, loans associated with risk profiles that lack sufficient data can be closely monitored and information updated so that any segment-level deterioration can be identified swiftly and corrective action taken. Also, as data accumulates, judgmental weights can be modified, or replaced, by new weights based on measured performance. The validation optimization framework, including UPI-driven model ranking, plays an important role in early warning, model enhancement, and in mitigating model risk.

Credit Integrated With Compliance	Compliance Assessment	Credit Risk Management
Hybrid Credit Models	**Fair Lending Testing**	**Credit Scoring**
Generic loan product model	Identify largest exposures with the universal performance indicator (UPI)	Generic or industry-option bureau score
Institution–specific, loan product–specific, channel-specific hybrid model[a]	Refine description of exposure and identify the population of interest[b]	Institution-specific, loan product-specific, channel-specific credit score[c]
Define multistage process (including MLS/handles)	Sampling & significance testing	Scorecard adaptability test
REPFS: construct strategy-specific action tables	Control for policy and known causes and retest using DCP	Scorecard development
Overall, and handle cell, model validation	Model validation & assessment	Model validation
Multidimensional segment analysis including disparate impact analysis via UPI	Matched-pair comparisons (optimization)	Override business rules updating
Applicant profile analysis	Identify members of injured class	Population stability analysis
Handle cell risk index updating and DCP-based disparate treatment testing	Quantify financial injury	Validation: G/B separation and rank ordering
Quantify overall lift from REPFS update	Quantify the magnitude of expected loss	Decision to keep or retire scorecard
Impact of a change in policy, including thresholds, and CCOP-based sensitivity analysis	Risk mitigation strategy	Impact of a change in cutoff score

FIGURE 8.21 CREDIT AND COMPLIANCE RISK ANALYTICAL PARALLELS

[a]Entails determining how many systems or stages per systems will be required.
[b]Exposure is characterized by UPI component factors relating to observed outcomes. The population of interest is defined by protected class and other classification variables.
[c]Entails determining the required number of scorecards and the basis for selecting which scorecard to use during application processing.

Even for traditional credit scoring model validation, hybrid models may still play an important role. This is because they make conditional structures and interactions between predictor variables explicit and they allow predictive performance to be examined in detail within homogenous risk segments that comprise the handle, rather than just score bands alone. As a result, variances in risk can be traced to primary factors and closely related risk profiles (neighboring handle cells and "neighborhoods of handle cells") can be viewed for similarities and any outlier segments noted for deeper analysis.

This book introduced five new methodologies that deal with credit and compliance risk management, namely:

- *Universal performance indicator (UPI).* For creating a comprehensive view of compliance and credit risks at different levels, for example geographic, organizational and so forth
- *Dynamic conditional process (DCP).* For effective compliance testing and credit risk modeling by better utilizing data and emulating business reality

- *Hybrid credit models (REPFS).* An alternative credit risk modeling using either traditional or nontraditional credit information by taking the advantages of both statistical scoring models and judgmental and business criteria.
- *Multilayered segmentation (MLS).* For developing integrated segmentation schemes to perform assessment for various segments including neighborhood and underbanked lending/investment.
- *Credit and compliance optimization process (CCOP).* For integrating credit and compliance objectives within the model validation process to achieve optimal business decisions and strategies.

The integration of these approaches in lenders' credit risk management and fair lending compliance programs will prove beneficial to all stakeholders, including lenders, borrowers, secondary market conduits, investors, and regulators. There are few endeavors more important than the quest to provide safer, fairer, and profitable access to capital for individuals and businesses in order to improve the quality of lives and to foster sustainable economic growth and greater prosperity for all. We believe we have only scratched the surface of possibilities in this constantly evolving field.

INDEX

Printed in the United States
By Bookmasters